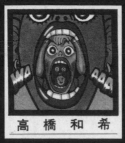

高橋 和希

MAN, IT REALLY IS HARD WORKING ON A WEEKLY DEAD-
LINE! I'M SO BUSY, I CAN'T PLAY THE GAMES I LIKE. I
WANNA SIT BACK AND GET SOME GAMING TIME IN, AND
THE GAME I WANT TO PLAY MOST RIGHT NOW
IS...TABLETOP ROLEPLAYING GAMES (RPGS)! IN THE
PAST, ME AND MY FRIENDS WOULD GET TOGETHER AND
HAVE A GOOD OL' TIME DOING THIS. WE'D STAY UP ALL
NIGHT AND HAVE TONS OF FUN. I DEFINITELY RECOM-
MEND TABLETOP RPGS TO ANYONE. RECENTLY, I
HAVEN'T BEEN ABLE TO HOOK UP WITH MY FRIENDS, BUT
SOON WE GOTTA GET TOGETHER AND FIRE IT UP AGAIN!
    —KAZUKI TAKAHASHI, 1997

Artist/author Kazuki Takahashi first tried to
break into the manga business in 1982, but
success eluded him until **Yu-Gi-Oh!** debuted
in the Japanese **Weekly Shonen Jump** magazine in
1996. **Yu-Gi-Oh!**'s themes of friendship and fighting,
together with Takahashi's weird and wonderful art,
soon became enormously successful, spawning a
real-world card game, video games, and two anime
series. A lifelong gamer, Takahashi enjoys Shogi
(Japanese chess), Mahjong, card games, and tabletop RPGs, among other games.

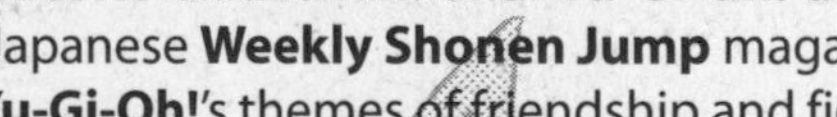

**YU-GI-OH! VOL. 3**
**The SHONEN JUMP Graphic Novel Edition**

This graphic novel contains material that was originally published in English in the second two-thirds of **SHONEN JUMP** #7, all of **SHONEN JUMP** #8 and #9, and the first one-third of #10.

STORY AND ART BY
KAZUKI TAKAHASHI

Translation & English Adaptation/Anita Sengupta
Touch-Up Art & Lettering/Kelle Han
Cover, Graphics & Layout Design/Sean Lee
Senior Editor/Jason Thompson

Managing Editor/Elizabeth Kawasaki
Director of Production/Noboru Watanabe
Executive V.P./Editor-in-Chief/Hyoe Narita
Senior Director of Licensing & Acquisitions/Rika Inouye
V.P. of Sales & Marketing/Liza Coppola
V.P. of Strategic Development/Yumi Hoashi
Publisher/Seiji Horibuchi

PARENTAL ADVISORY
Yu-Gi-Oh! is rated "T" for teens. It may contain violence, language, alcohol or tobacco usage, or suggestive situations. It is recommended for ages 13 and up.



Printed in Canada.

Published by VIZ, LLC
P.O. Box 77010 • San Francisco, CA 94107

SHONEN JUMP Graphic Novel Edition
10 9 8 7 6 5 4 3 2
First printing, November 2003
Second printing, October 2004

www.viz.com

THE WORLD'S MOST POPULAR MANGA
SHONEN JUMP GRAPHIC NOVEL
www.shonenjump.com

SHONEN JUMP GRAPHIC NOVEL

# Yu-Gi-Oh!™

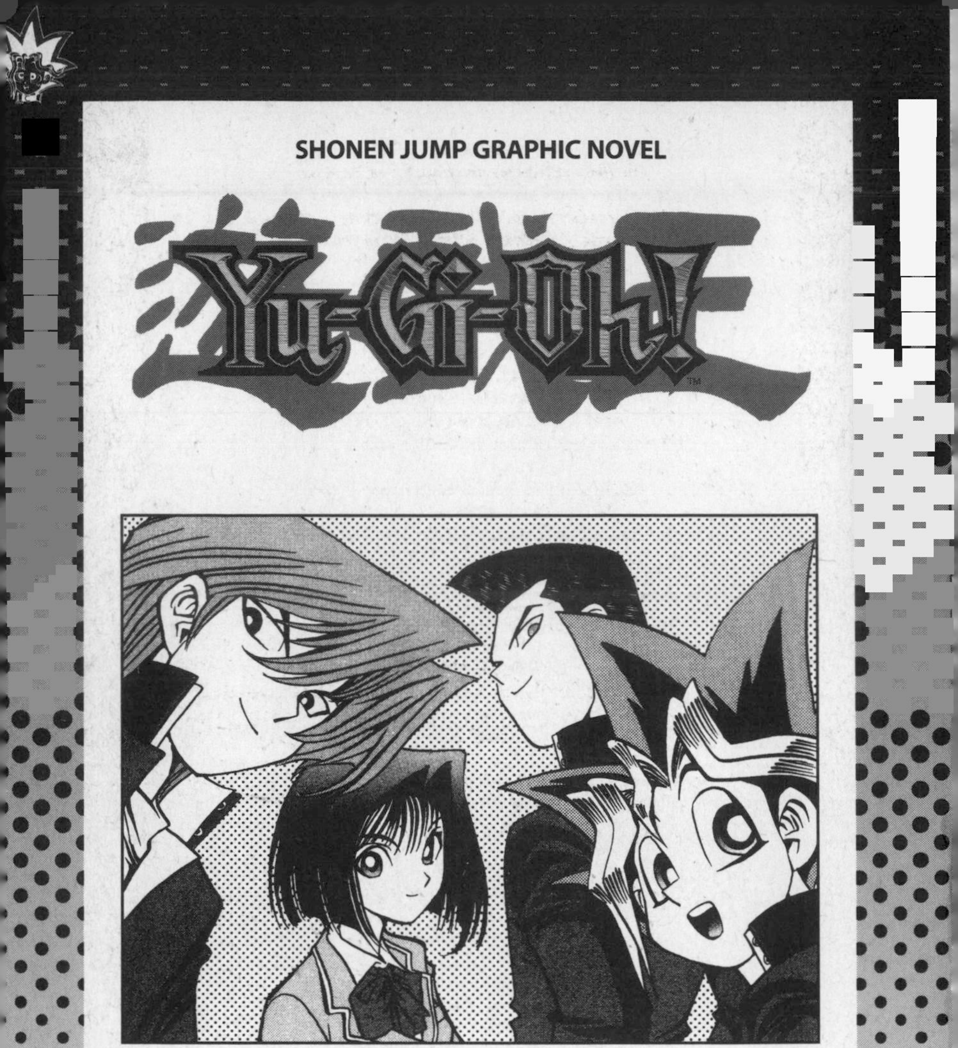

## Vol. 3
## CAPSULE MONSTER CHESS

STORY AND ART BY
**KAZUKI TAKAHASHI**

## THE STORY SO FAR...

When an Egyptian museum exhibit came to Tokyo, an unwelcome visitor came along with it: Shadi, the keeper of the Millennium Items, who sought to kill the archaeologist and museum owner who had desecrated the tomb. But Shadi was startled to discover that the Millennium Puzzle had been solved for the first time in 3,000 years—by Yugi Mutou! Using the Millennium Key to go inside Yugi's soul, Shadi fought the "other" Yugi—and was defeated. Determined to have a rematch, Shadi turned the archaeologist into a mindless zombie, to terrorize Yugi's "other self" into coming out!

**DARK YUGI**

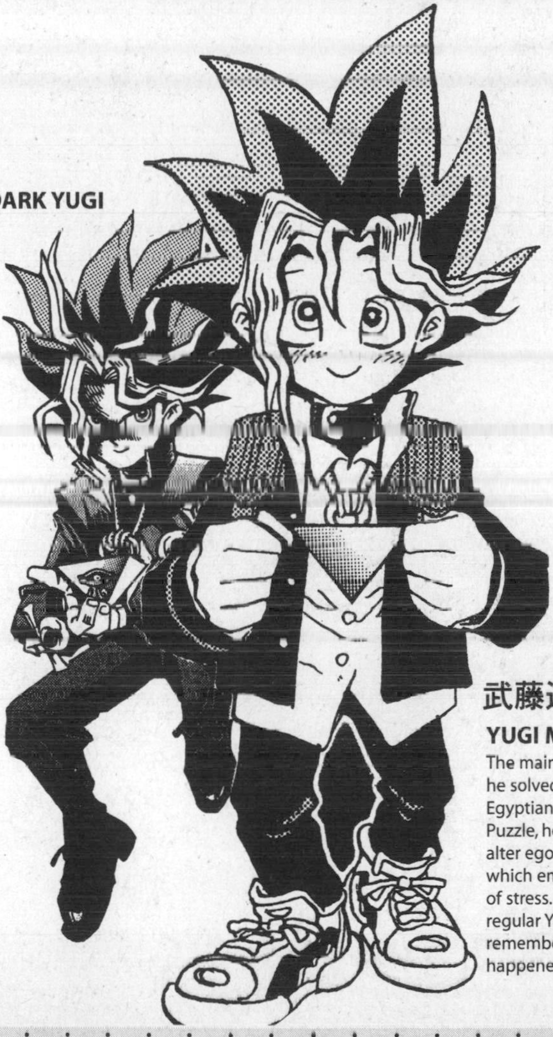

**武藤遊戯**

**YUGI MUTOU**

The main character. When he solved the ancient Egyptian Millennium Puzzle, he developed an alter ego, "Dark Yugi," which emerges in times of stress. Afterwards, the regular Yugi doesn't remember what happened.

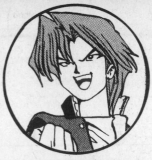

## 城之内克也
### KATSUYA JONOUCHI

Yugi's classmate, a tough guy who gets in lots of fights. He used to think Yugi was a wimp, but now they are good friends. In the English anime he's known as "Joey Wheeler."

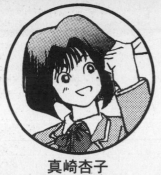

## 真崎杏子
### ANZU MAZAKI

Yugi's classmate and childhood friend. She fell in love with the charismatic voice of Yugi's alter ego, but doesn't know that they're the same person. Her first name means "Apricot." In the English anime she's known as "Téa Gardner."

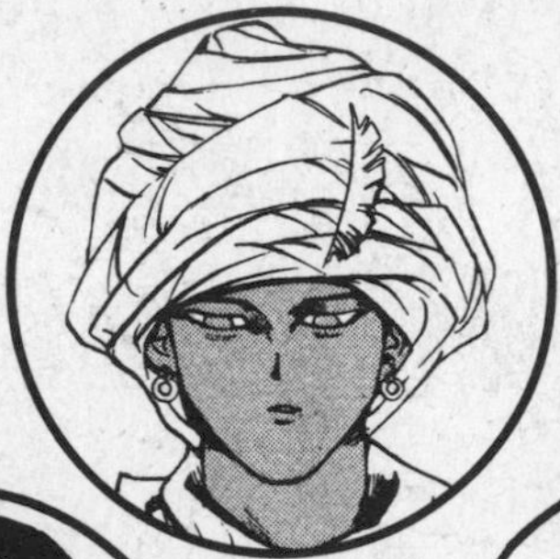

### SHADI

A mysterious mystic whose bloodline has guarded the tombs of Egypt for 3000 years. He owns the Millennium Scales, which can weigh a person's sins, and the Millennium Key, which he can use to look inside people's souls and control them.

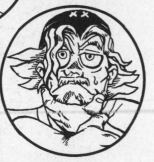

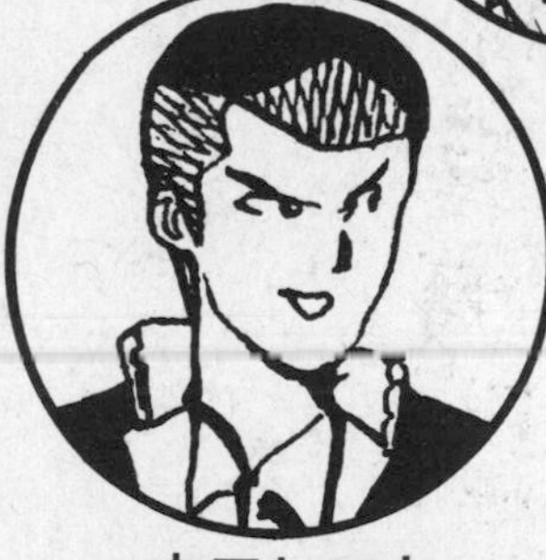

## 本田ヒロト
### HIROTO HONDA

Yugi's classmate, a friend of Jonouchi. In the English anime he's known as "Tristan Taylor."

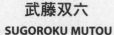

## 武藤双六
### SUGOROKU MUTOU

Yugi's grandfather, the owner of the Kame ("Turtle") game store, and a friend of the archaeologist Professor Yoshimori.

# Yu-Gi-Oh!

## Vol. 3

## CONTENTS

| | | |
|---|---|---|
| Duel 16 | Shadi's Challenge | 7 |
| Duel 17 | Game Start! | 33 |
| Duel 18 | Second Stage | 57 |
| Duel 19 | Final Stage | 79 |
| Duel 20 | Game Over | 99 |
| Duel 21 | Digital Pet Duel | 121 |
| Duel 22 | American Hero (Part 1) | 141 |
| Duel 23 | American Hero (Part 2) | 161 |
| Duel 24 | Capsule Monster Chess | 182 |
| Previews | | 208 |

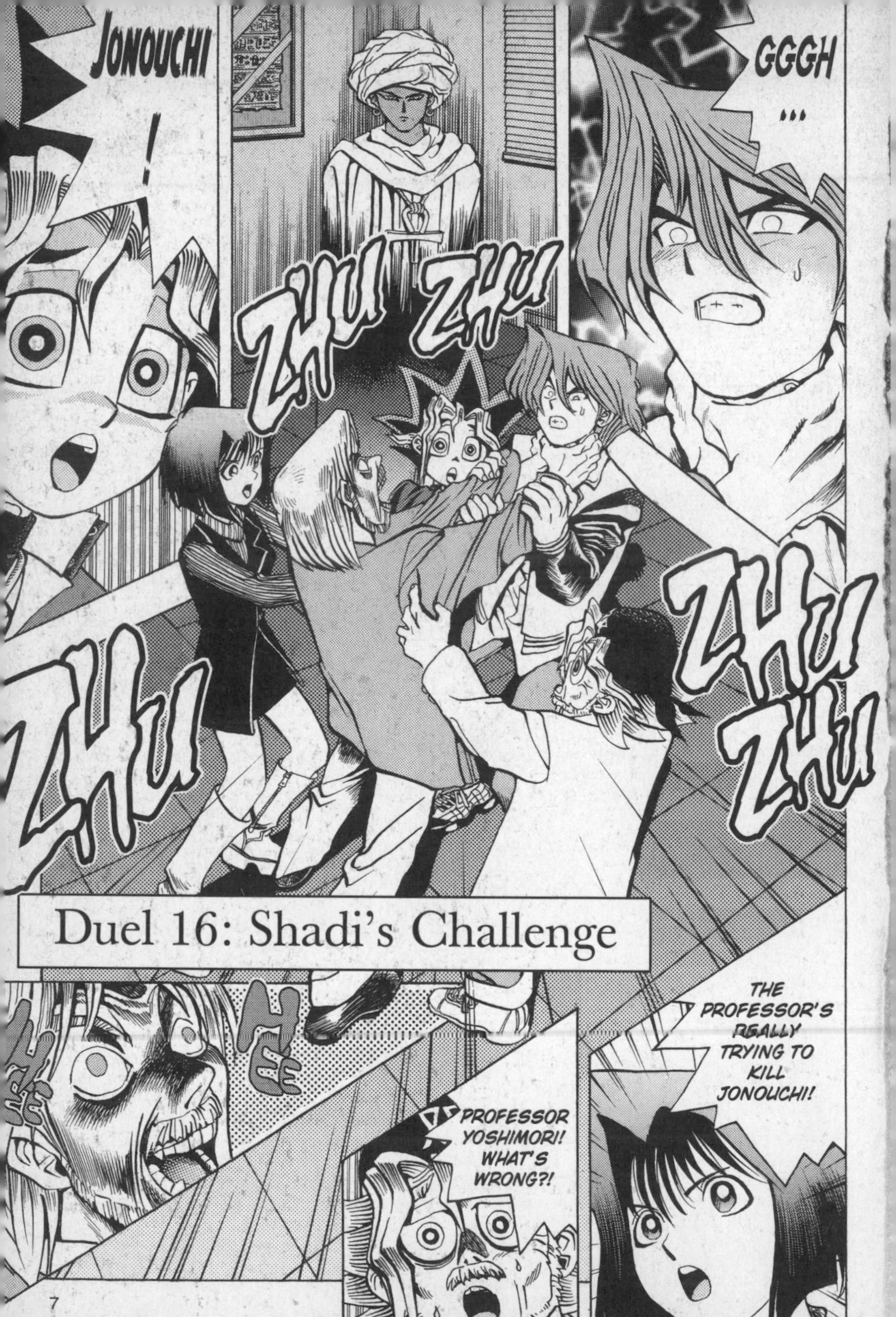
GGGH...
JONOUCHI!
ZHU ZHU
ZHU
ZHU ZHU
ZHU ZHU
Duel 16: Shadi's Challenge
THE PROFESSOR'S REALLY TRYING TO KILL JONOUCHI!
PROFESSOR YOSHIMORI! WHAT'S WRONG?!
HE HE HE

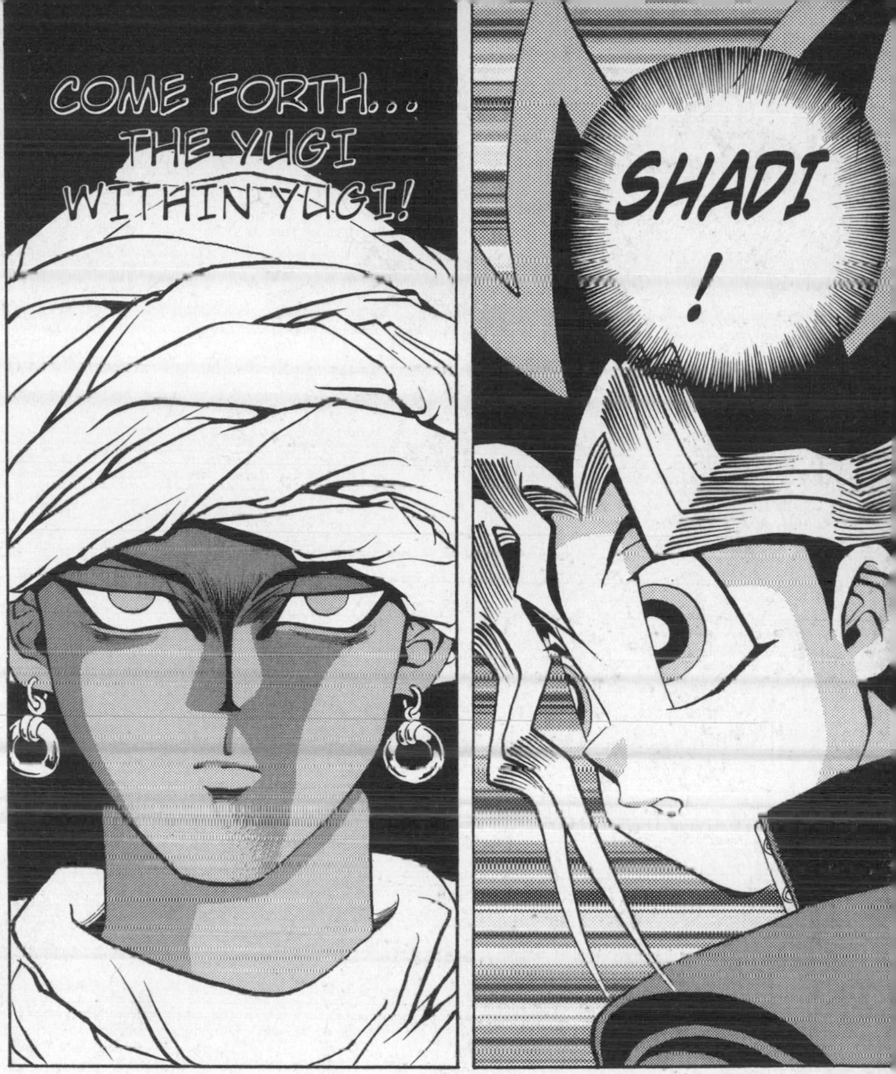
SHADI!
COME FORTH... THE YUGI WITHIN YUGI!

# Duel 16: Shadi's Challenge

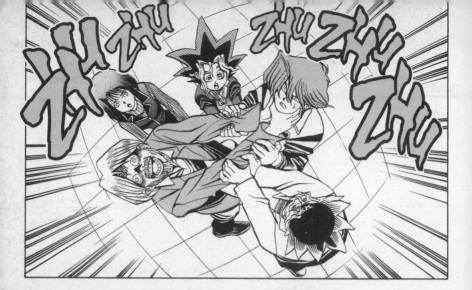

ZHU ZHU ZHU ZHU ZHU

JONOUCHI
!

HIS STRENGTH IS INSANE! I CAN'T BUDGE HIS ARMS!

URRRGH
...!

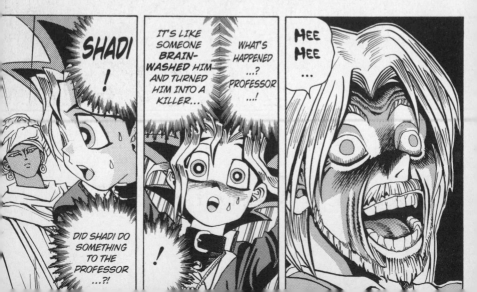

SHADI
!

IT'S LIKE SOMEONE BRAIN- WASHED HIM AND TURNED HIM INTO A KILLER...

WHAT'S HAPPENED ...? PROFESSOR ...!

HEE HEE
...

DID SHADI DO SOMETHING TO THE PROFESSOR ...?!

!

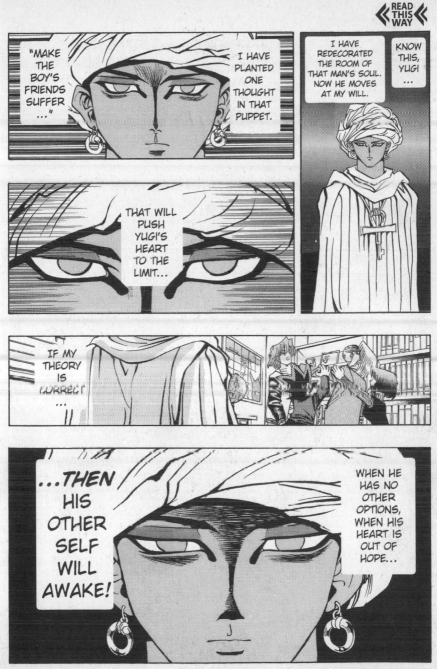

"MAKE THE BOY'S FRIENDS SUFFER..."

I HAVE PLANTED ONE THOUGHT IN THAT PUPPET.

I HAVE REDECORATED THE ROOM OF THAT MAN'S SOUL. NOW HE MOVES AT MY WILL.

KNOW THIS, YUGI...

THAT WILL PUSH YUGI'S HEART TO THE LIMIT...

IF MY THEORY IS CORRECT...

...THEN HIS OTHER SELF WILL AWAKE!

WHEN HE HAS NO OTHER OPTIONS, WHEN HIS HEART IS OUT OF HOPE...

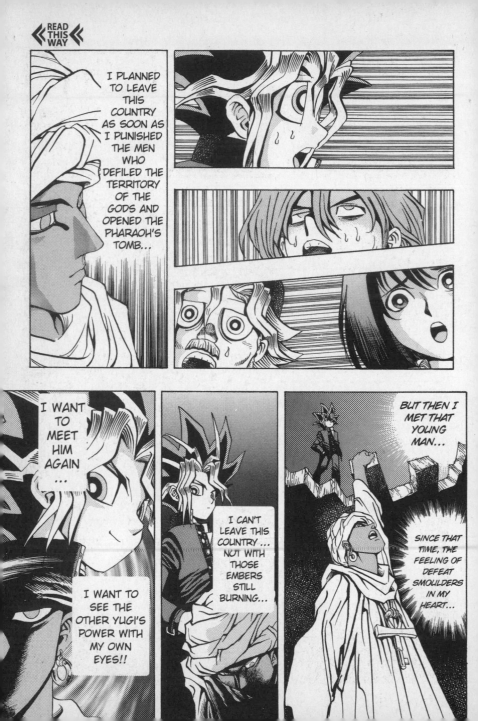

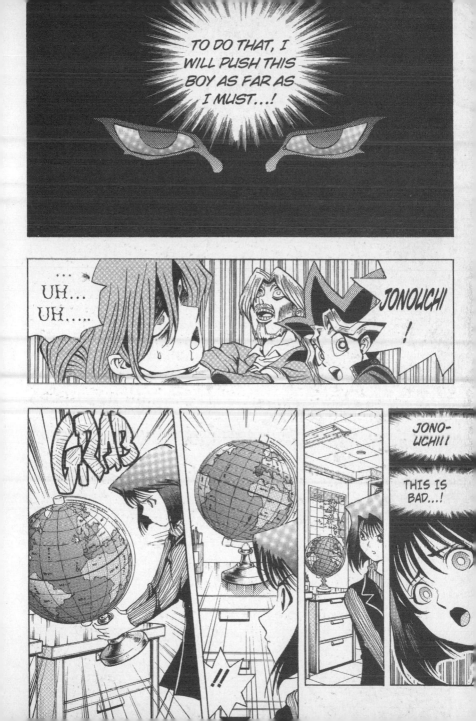

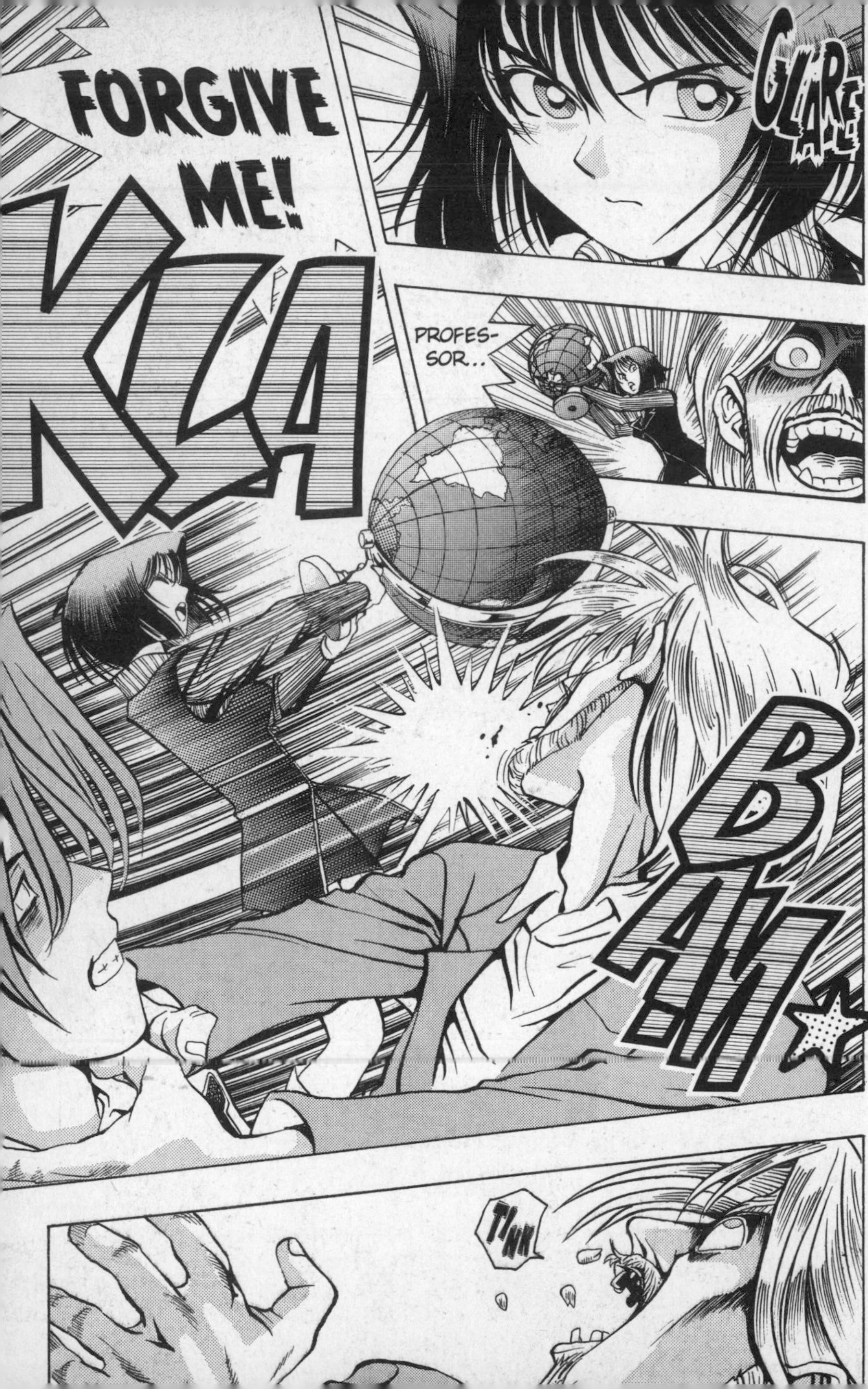
GLARE
PROFES-
SOR...
FORGIVE ME!
KLA
BAM
TINK

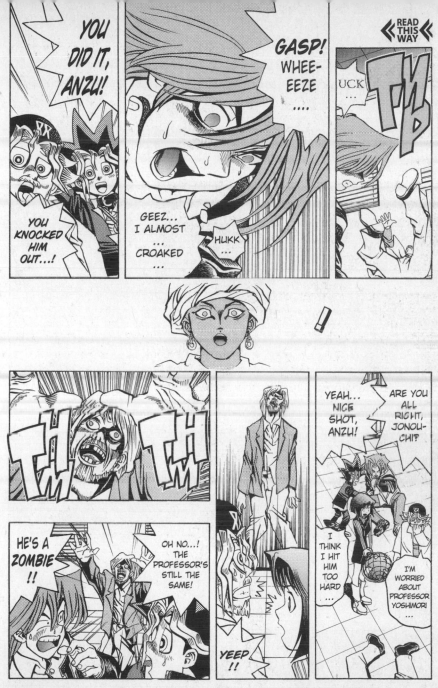

14

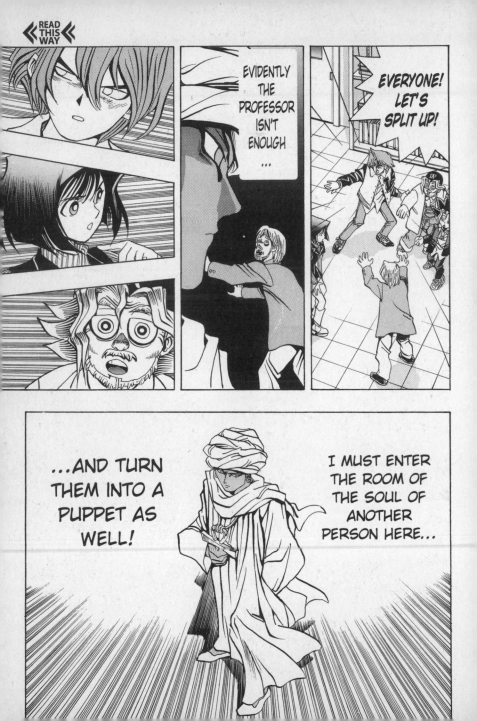

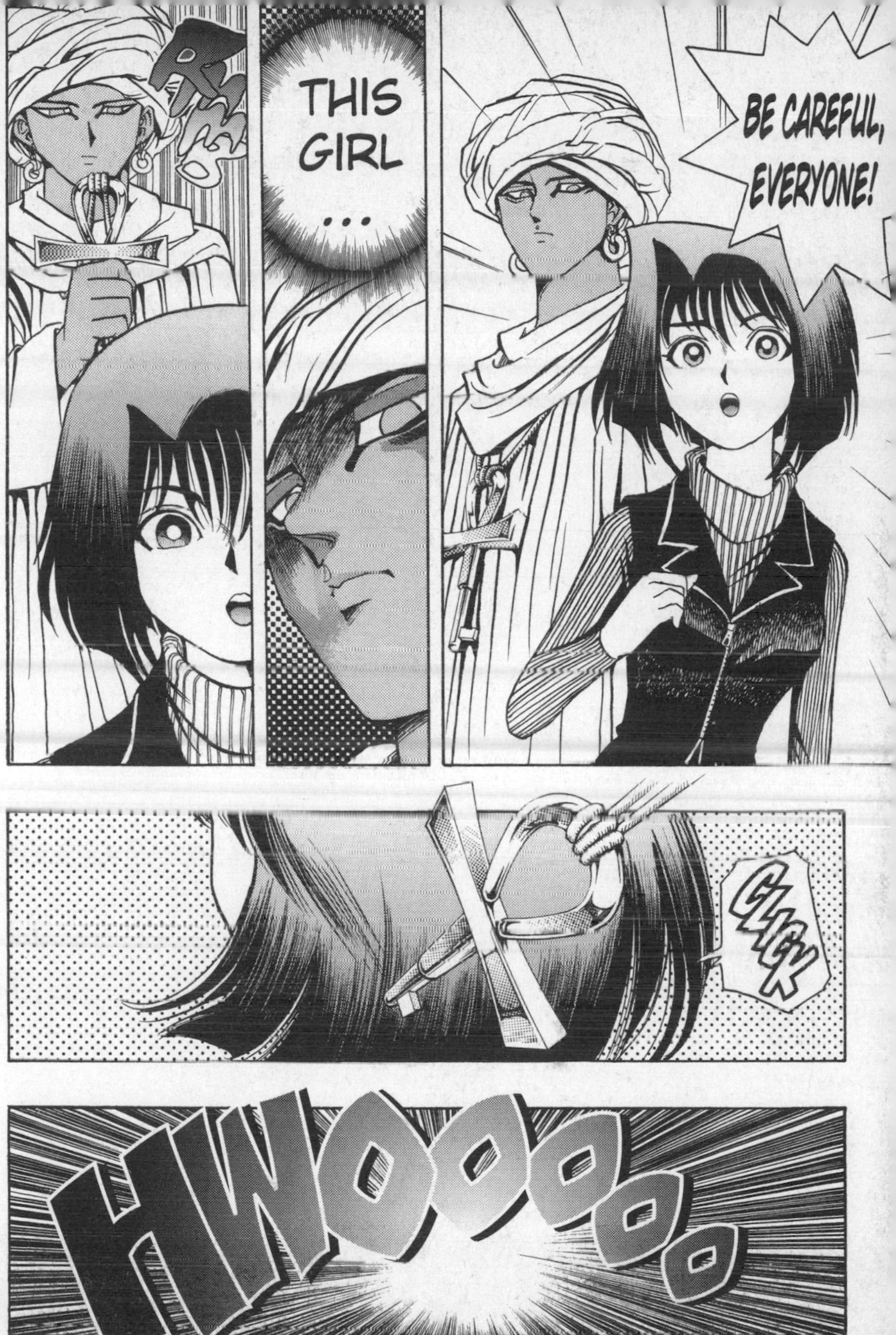
BE CAREFUL, EVERYONE!
THIS GIRL ...
CLICK
HWOOOOO

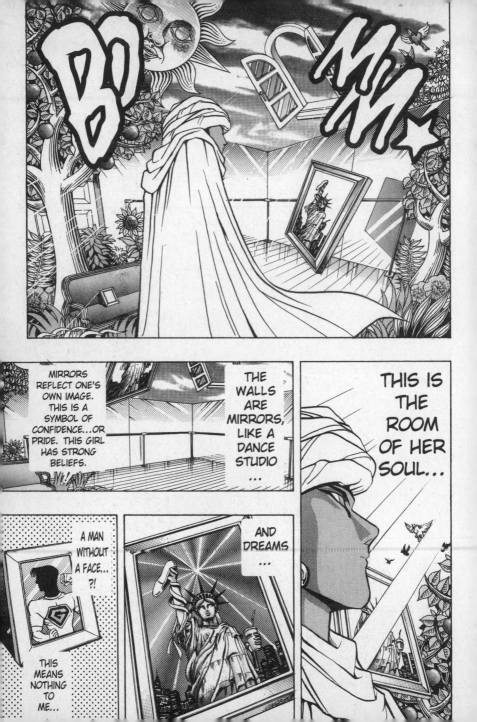

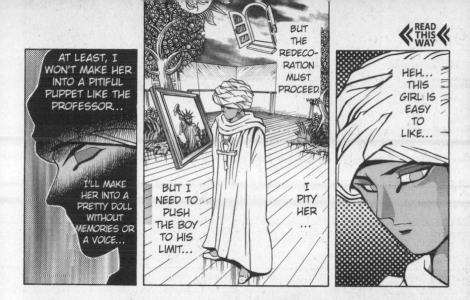

AT LEAST, I WON'T MAKE HER INTO A PITIFUL PUPPET LIKE THE PROFESSOR...

I'LL MAKE HER INTO A PRETTY DOLL WITHOUT MEMORIES OR A VOICE...

BUT THE REDECO-RATION MUST PROCEED.

BUT I NEED TO PUSH THE BOY TO HIS LIMIT...

I PITY HER ...

HEH... THIS GIRL IS EASY TO LIKE...

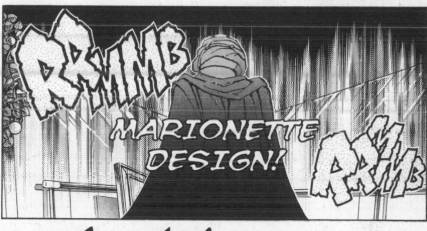

RRMMB

MARIONETTE DESIGN!

RRMB

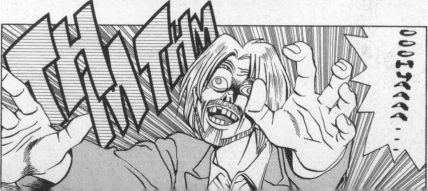

OOOHYAAAA...!

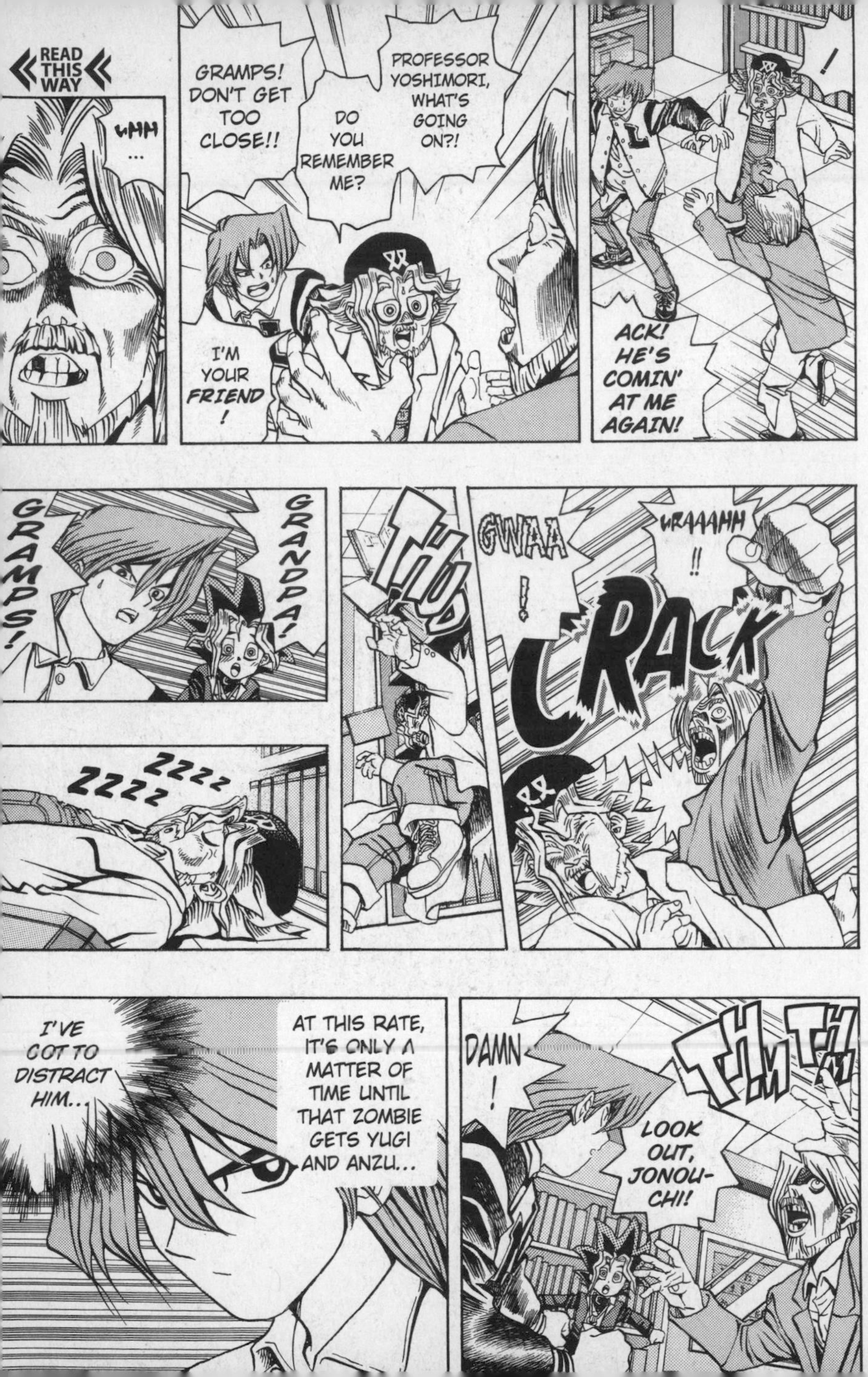
READ THIS WAY
!
ACK! HE'S COMIN' AT ME AGAIN!
PROFESSOR YOSHIMORI, WHAT'S GOING ON?!
DO YOU REMEMBER ME?
GRAMPS! DON'T GET TOO CLOSE!!
I'M YOUR FRIEND!
UHH ...
URAAAHH!!
CRACK
GWAA!
THUD
GRANDPA!
GRAMPS!
ZZZZ
ZZZZ
DAMN!
LOOK OUT, JONOUCHI!
AT THIS RATE, IT'S ONLY A MATTER OF TIME UNTIL THAT ZOMBIE GETS YUGI AND ANZU...
I'VE GOT TO DISTRACT HIM...

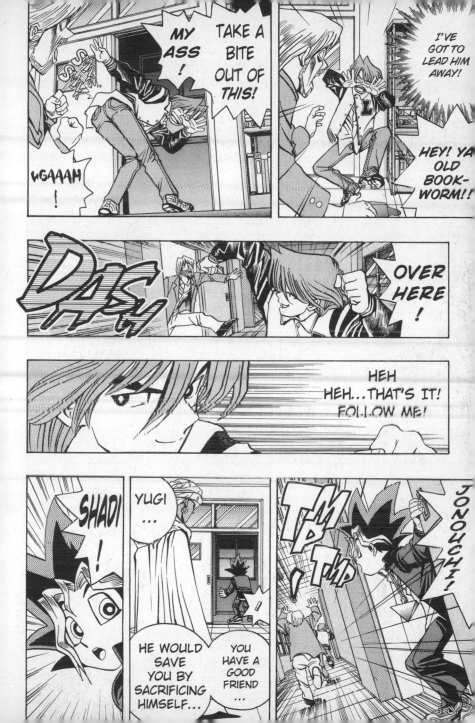

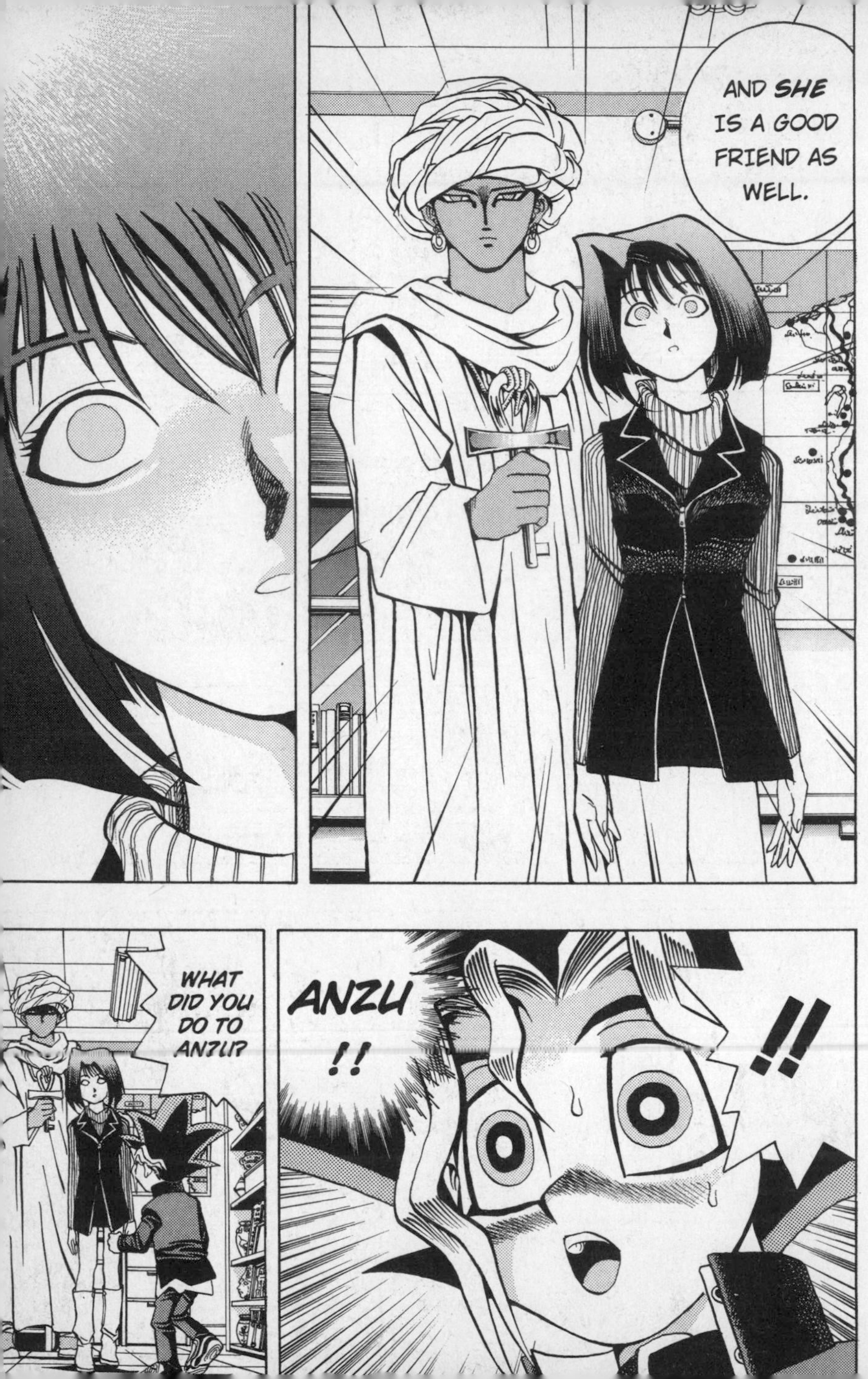
AND SHE IS A GOOD FRIEND AS WELL.
ANZU !!
!!
WHAT DID YOU DO TO ANZU?

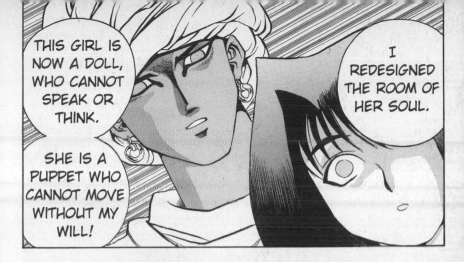

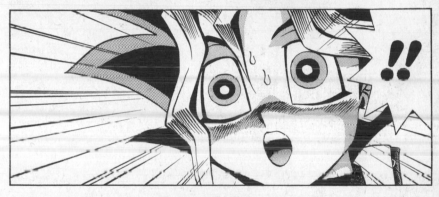

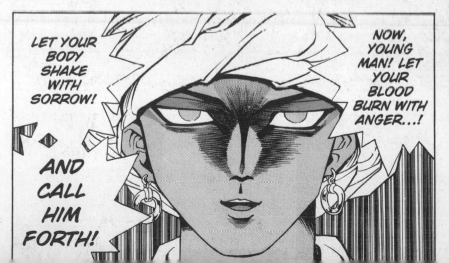

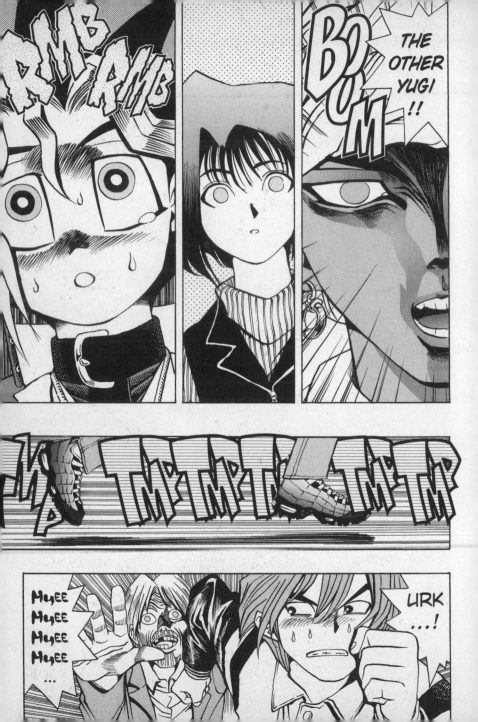

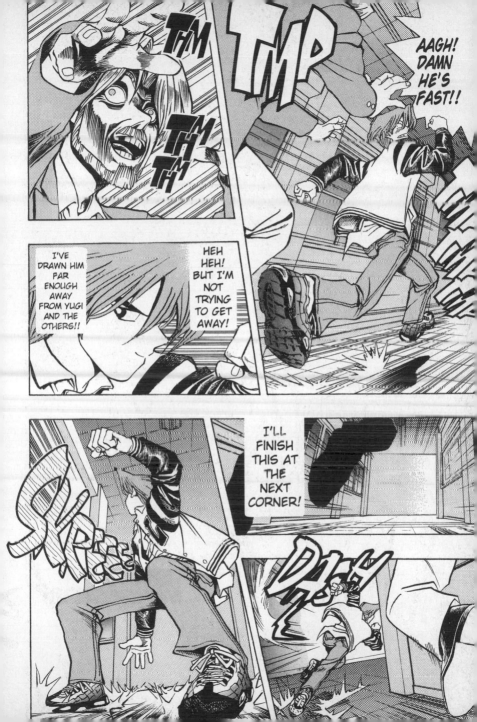

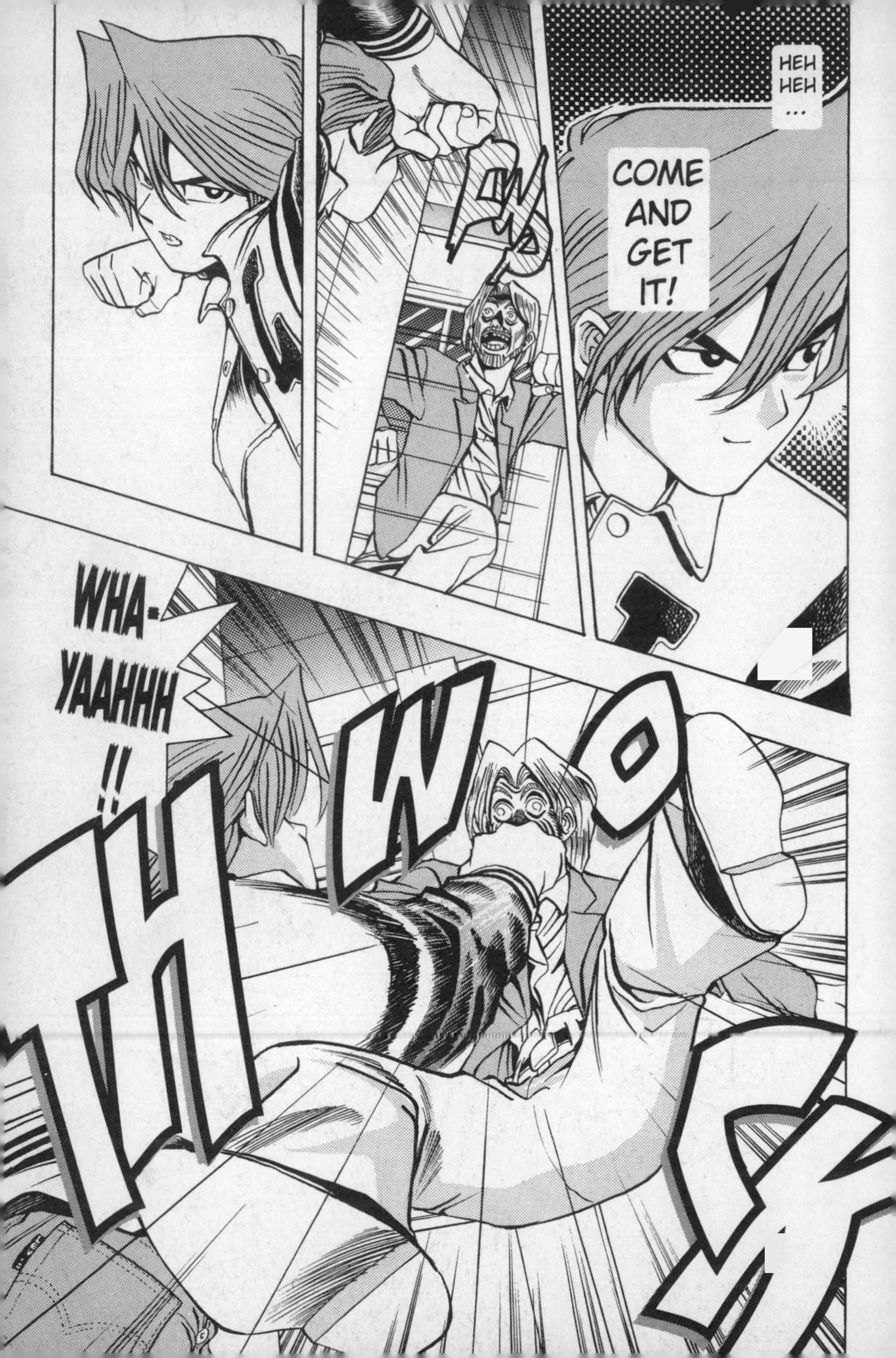
HEH HEH ...
COME AND GET IT!
WHA-YAAHHH!!

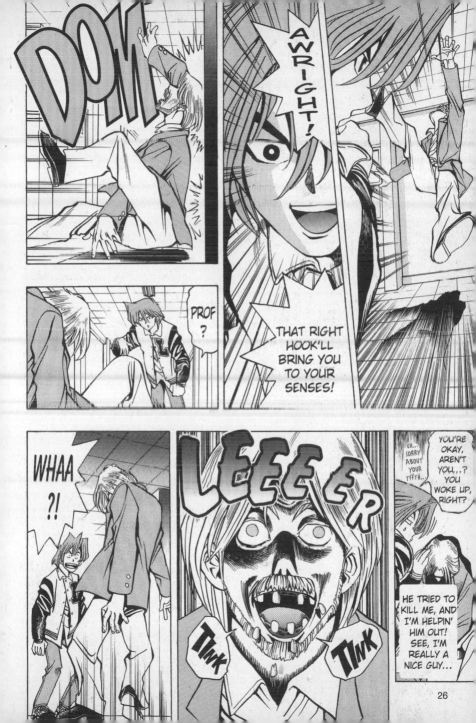

26

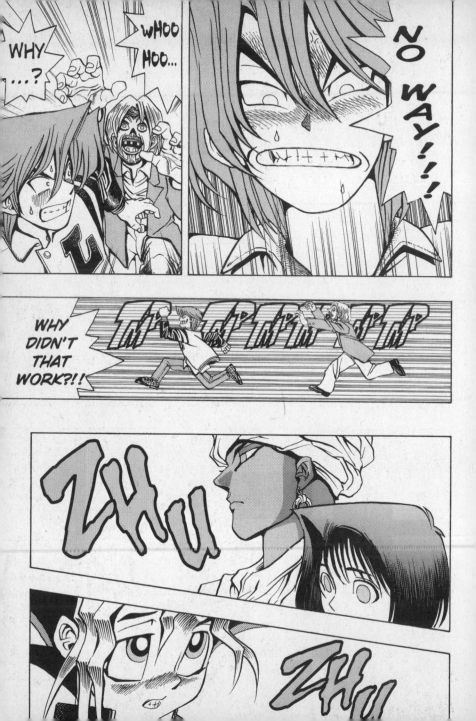

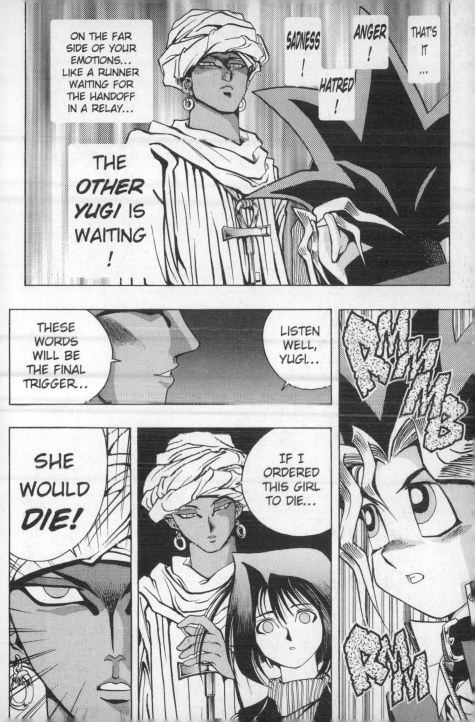

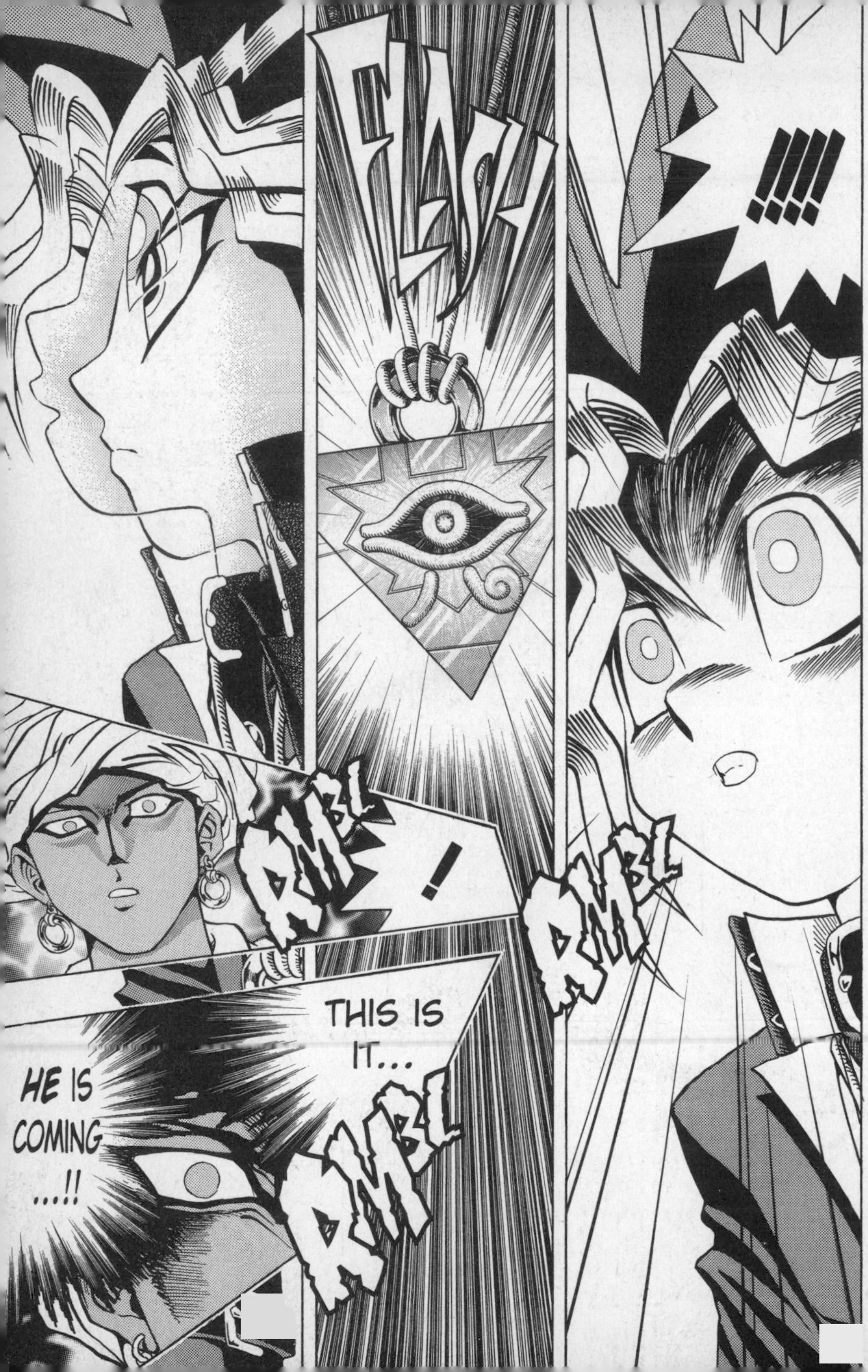
!!!!!
RMBL
FLASH
RMBL
!
THIS IS IT...
RMBL
HE IS COMING ...!!

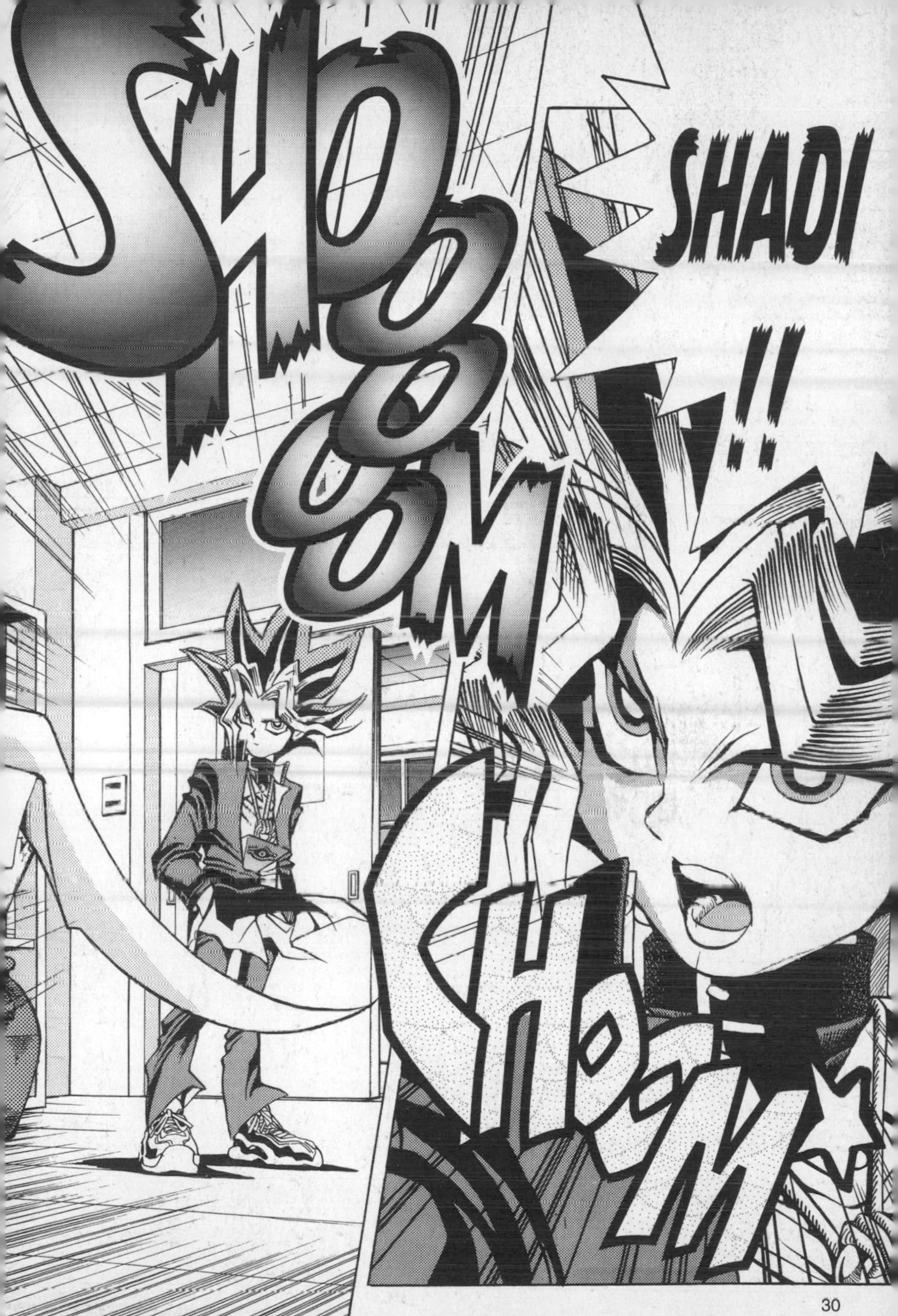
SHADI!!
SHOOM
SHOOOOOM

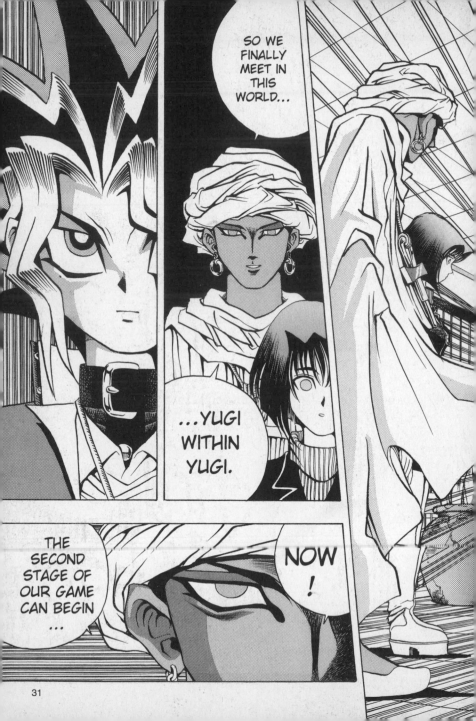

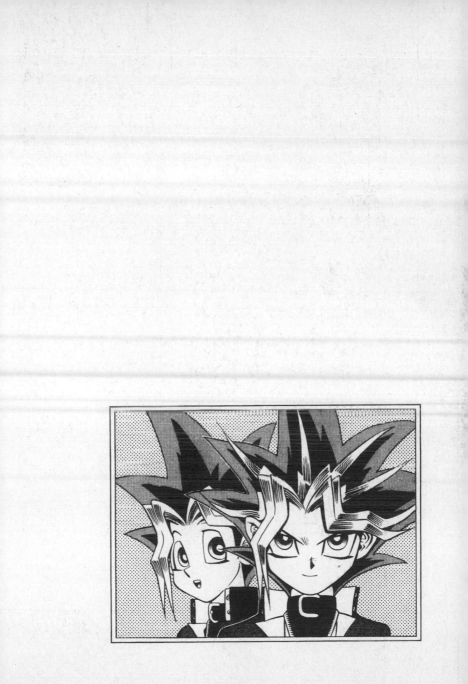

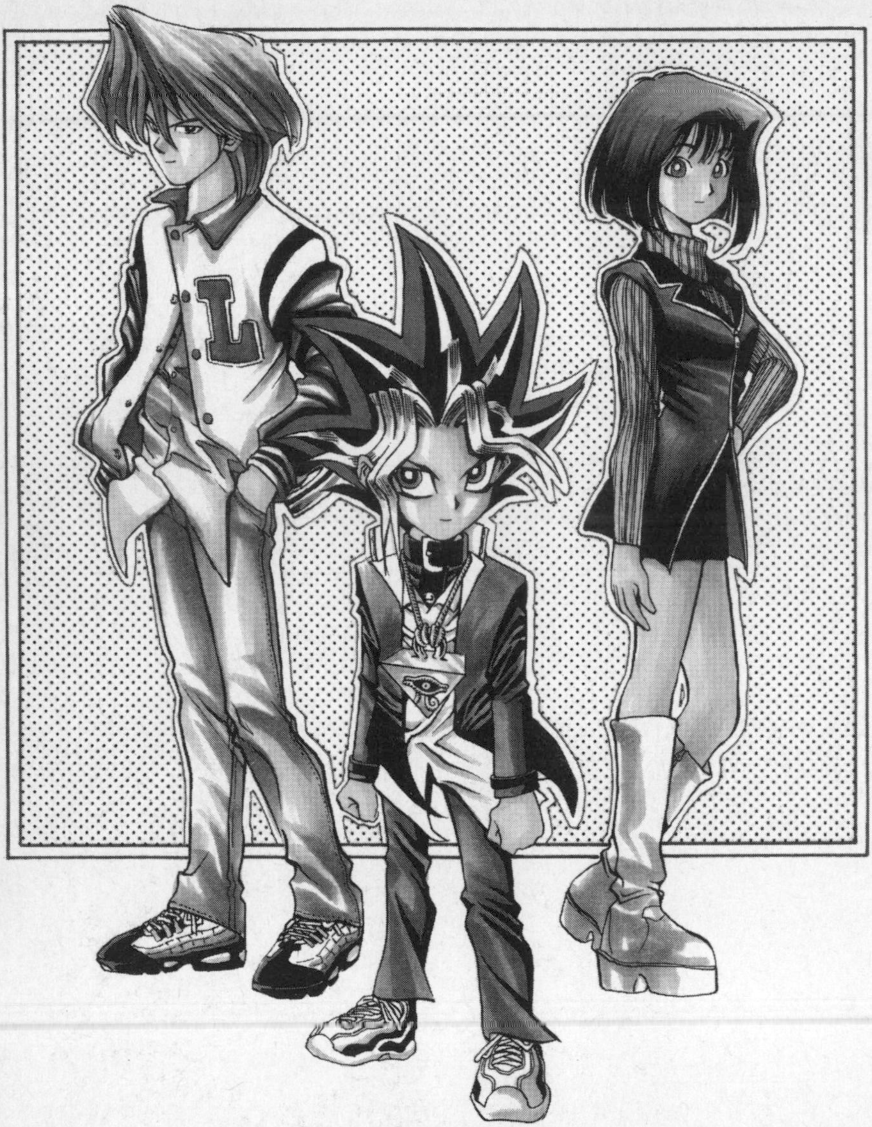

# Duel 17: Game Start!

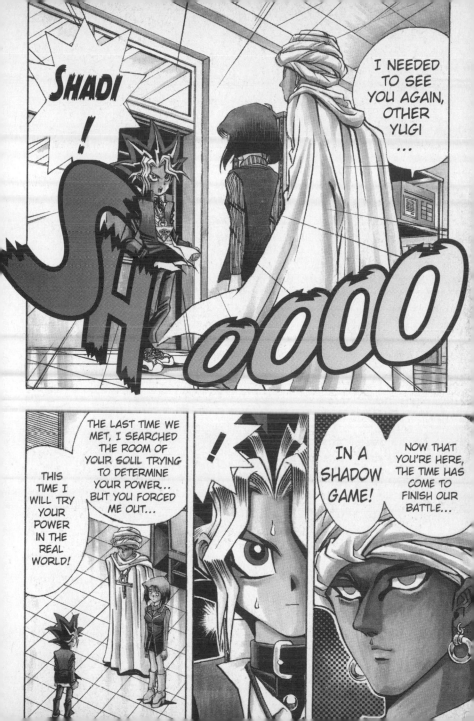

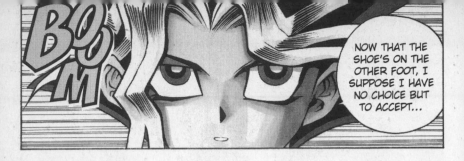

NOW THAT THE SHOE'S ON THE OTHER FOOT, I SUPPOSE I HAVE NO CHOICE BUT TO ACCEPT...

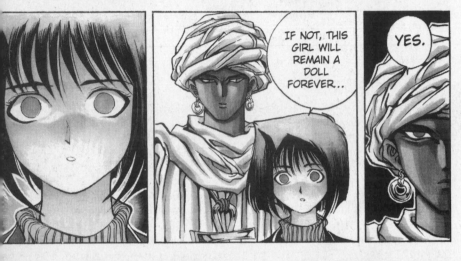

IF NOT, THIS GIRL WILL REMAIN A DOLL FOREVER...

YES.

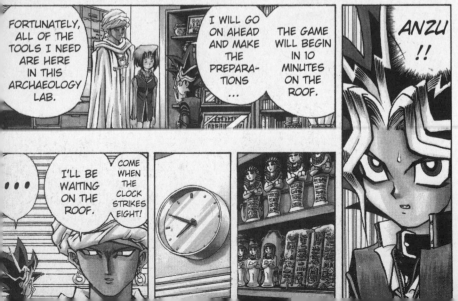

FORTUNATELY, ALL OF THE TOOLS I NEED ARE HERE IN THIS ARCHAEOLOGY LAB.

I WILL GO ON AHEAD AND MAKE THE PREPARATIONS...

THE GAME WILL BEGIN IN 10 MINUTES ON THE ROOF.

ANZU!!

...

I'LL BE WAITING ON THE ROOF.

COME WHEN THE CLOCK STRIKES EIGHT!

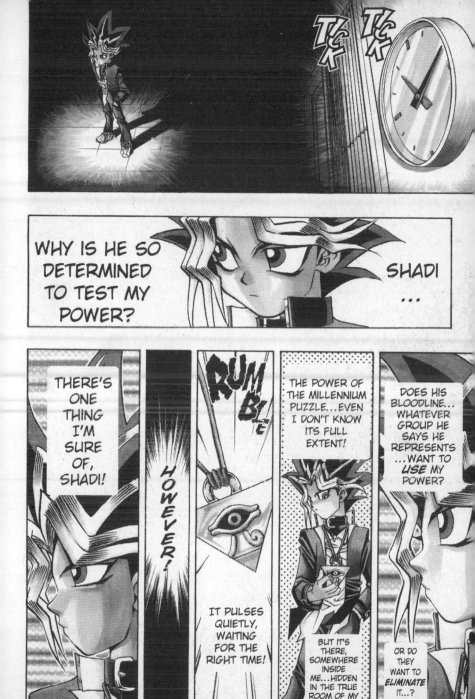

TCK TCK

WHY IS HE SO DETERMINED TO TEST MY POWER?

SHADI...

THERE'S ONE THING I'M SURE OF, SHADI!

HOWEVER!

RUMBLE

IT PULSES QUIETLY, WAITING FOR THE RIGHT TIME!

THE POWER OF THE MILLENNIUM PUZZLE...EVEN I DON'T KNOW ITS FULL EXTENT!

BUT IT'S THERE, SOMEWHERE INSIDE ME...HIDDEN IN THE TRUE ROOM OF MY SOUL...

DOES HIS BLOODLINE... WHATEVER GROUP HE SAYS HE REPRESENTS ...WANT TO *USE* MY POWER?

OR DO THEY WANT TO *ELIMINATE* IT...?

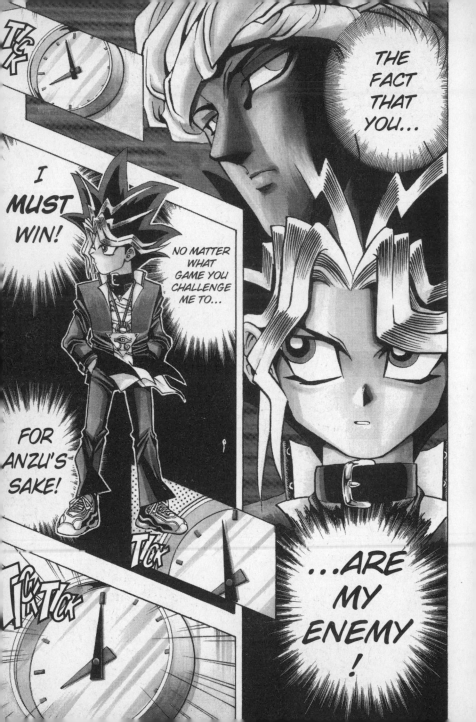

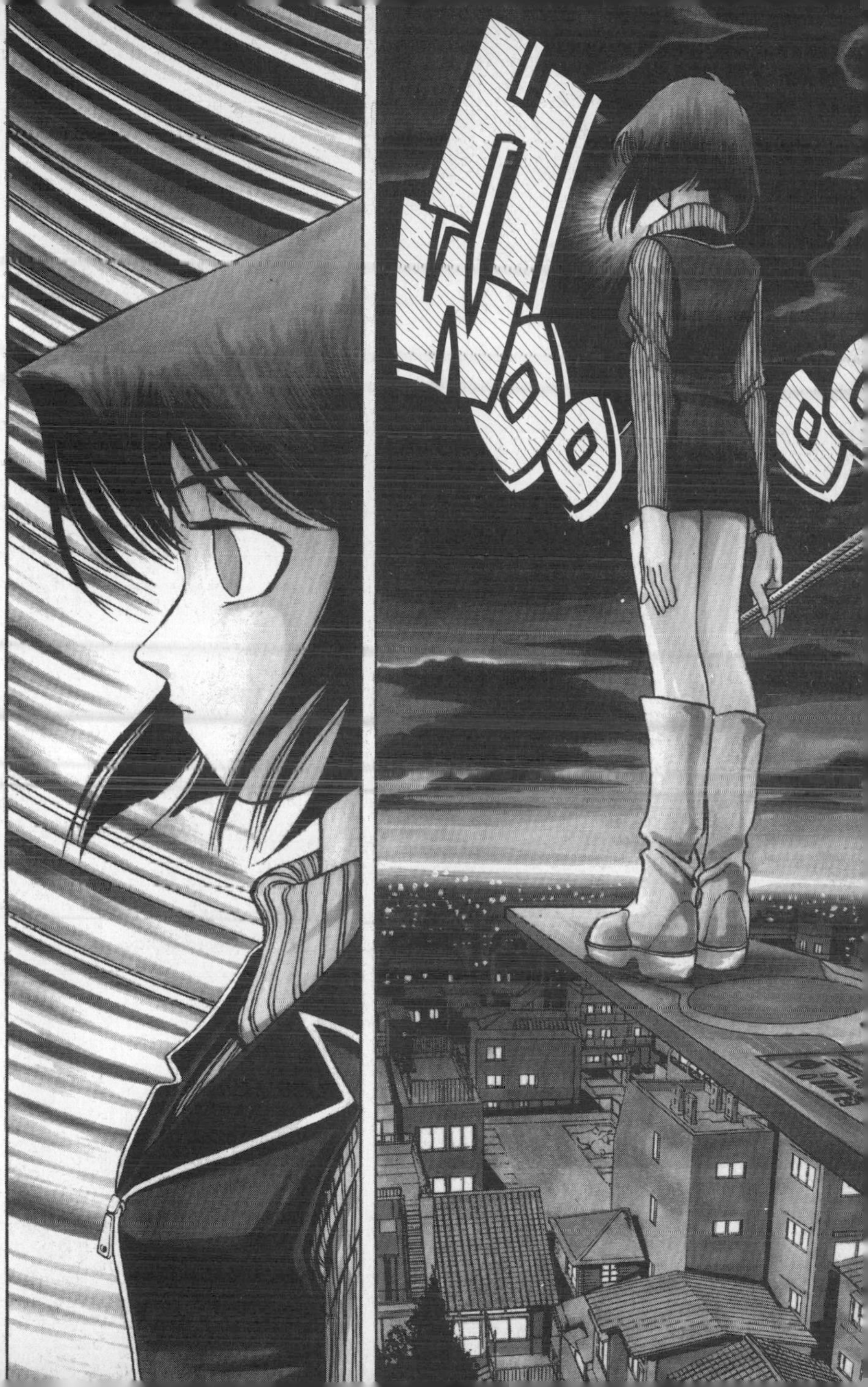
WHOOOO

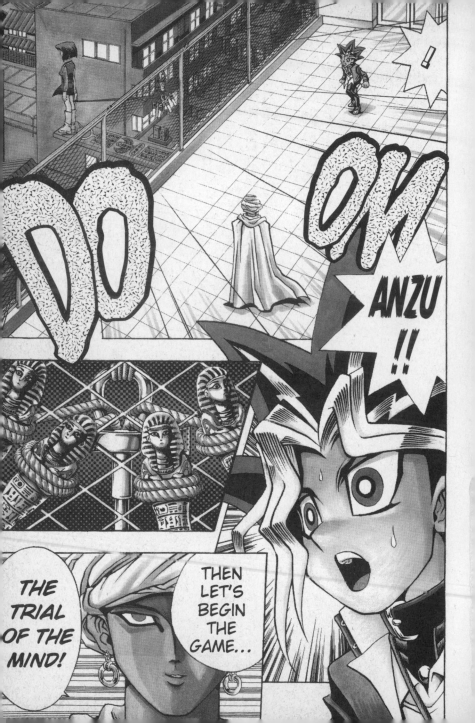

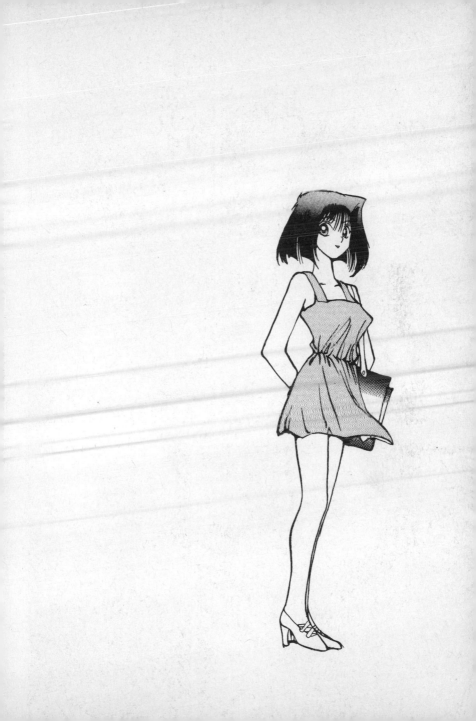

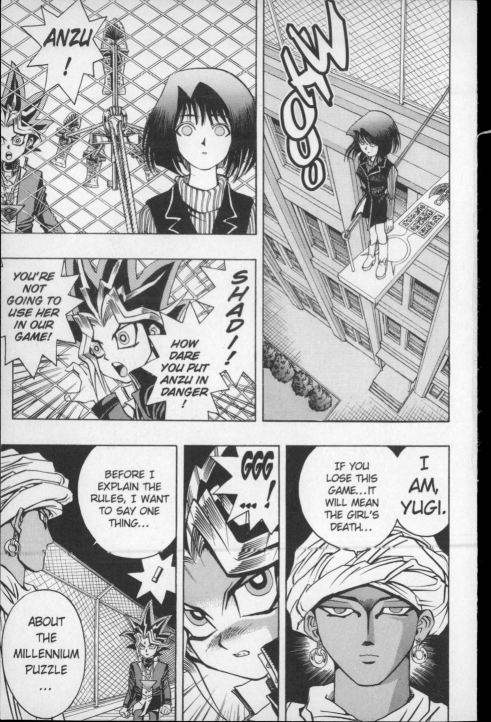

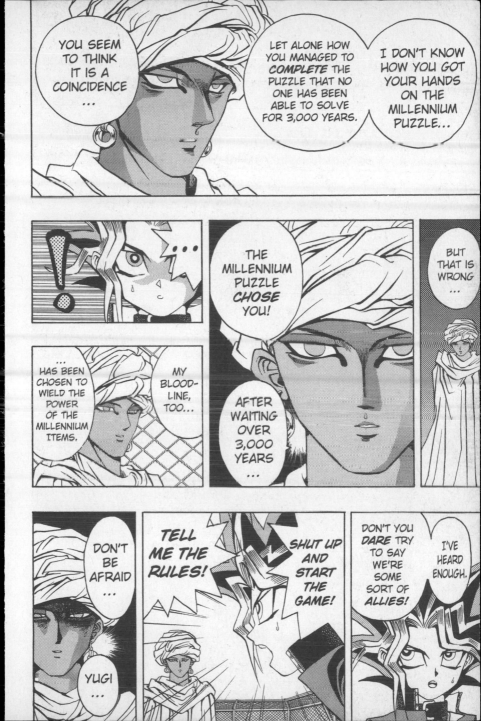

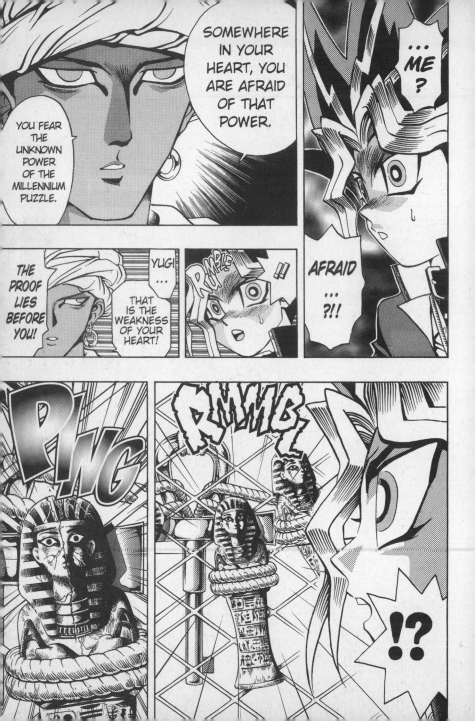

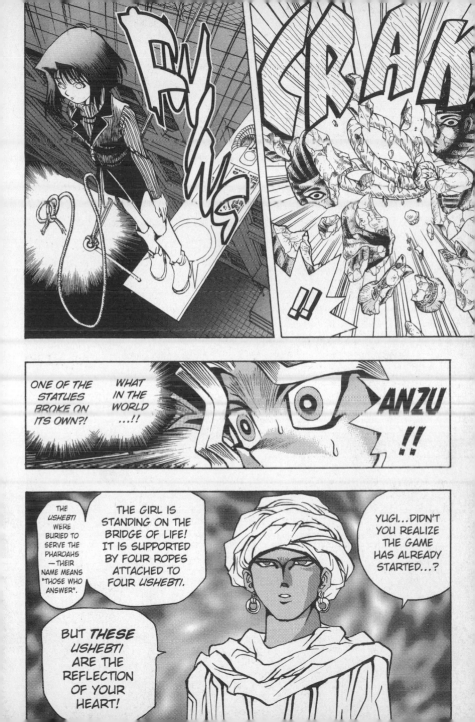

ONE OF THE STATUES BROKE ON ITS OWN?!

WHAT IN THE WORLD ...!!

ANZU!!

THE *USHEBTI* WERE BURIED TO SERVE THE PHAROAHS —THEIR NAME MEANS "THOSE WHO ANSWER".

THE GIRL IS STANDING ON THE BRIDGE OF LIFE! IT IS SUPPORTED BY FOUR ROPES ATTACHED TO FOUR *USHEBTI*.

YUGI...DIDN'T YOU REALIZE THE GAME HAS ALREADY STARTED...?

BUT *THESE* *USHEBTI* ARE THE REFLECTION OF YOUR HEART!

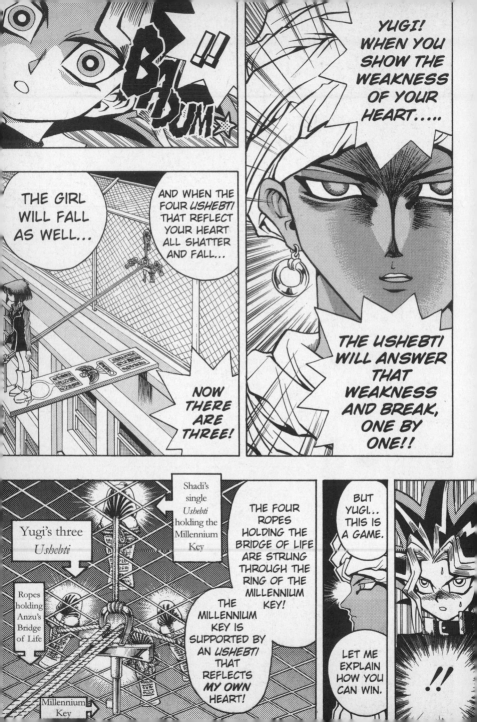

**BA-DUMP !!**

YUGI! WHEN YOU SHOW THE WEAKNESS OF YOUR HEART.....

THE GIRL WILL FALL AS WELL...

AND WHEN THE FOUR *USHEBTI* THAT REFLECT YOUR HEART ALL SHATTER AND FALL...

NOW THERE ARE THREE!

THE USHEBTI WILL ANSWER THAT WEAKNESS AND BREAK, ONE BY ONE!!

Yugi's three *Ushebti*

Shadi's single *Ushebti* holding the Millennium Key

Ropes holding Anzu's Bridge of Life

Millennium Key

THE FOUR ROPES HOLDING THE BRIDGE OF LIFE ARE STRUNG THROUGH THE RING OF THE MILLENNIUM KEY! THE MILLENNIUM KEY IS SUPPORTED BY AN *USHEBTI* THAT REFLECTS *MY OWN* HEART!

BUT YUGI... THIS IS A GAME.

LET ME EXPLAIN HOW YOU CAN WIN.

!!

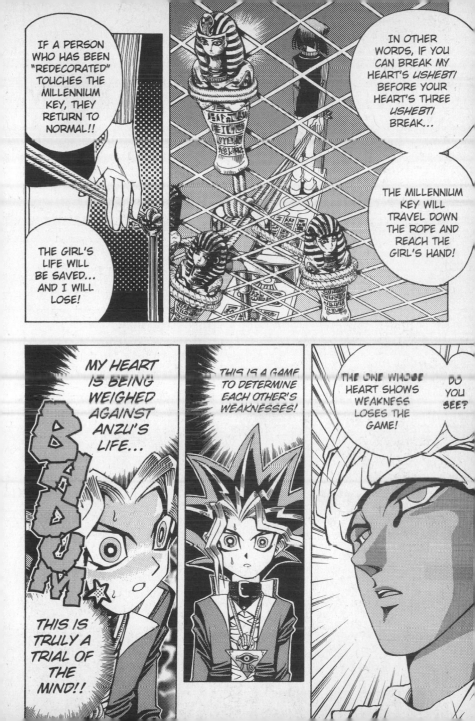

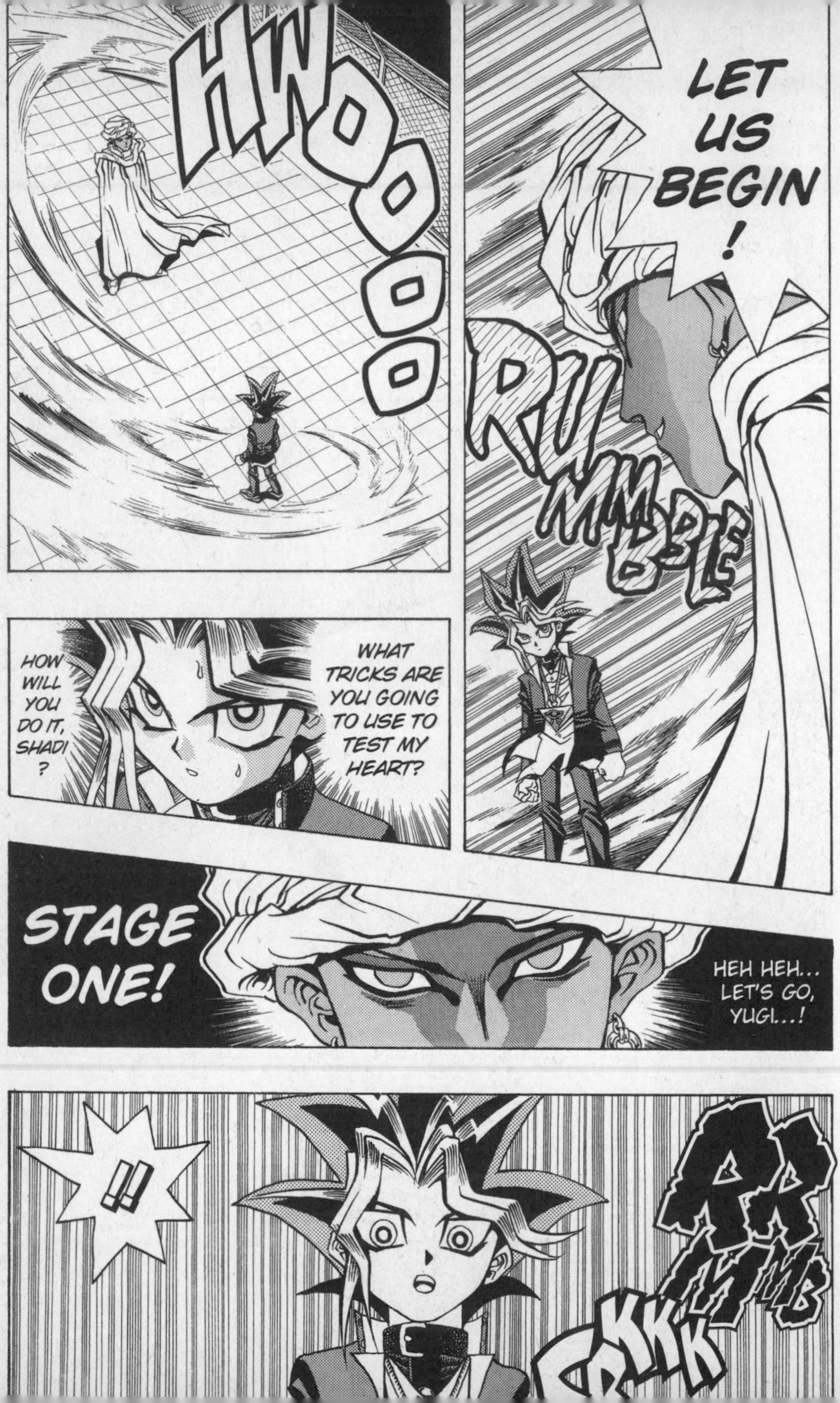

LET US BEGIN!
RUMMBBLE
HWOOOOO
WHAT TRICKS ARE YOU GOING TO USE TO TEST MY HEART?
HOW WILL YOU DO IT, SHADI?
HEH HEH... LET'S GO, YUGI...!
STAGE ONE!
!!

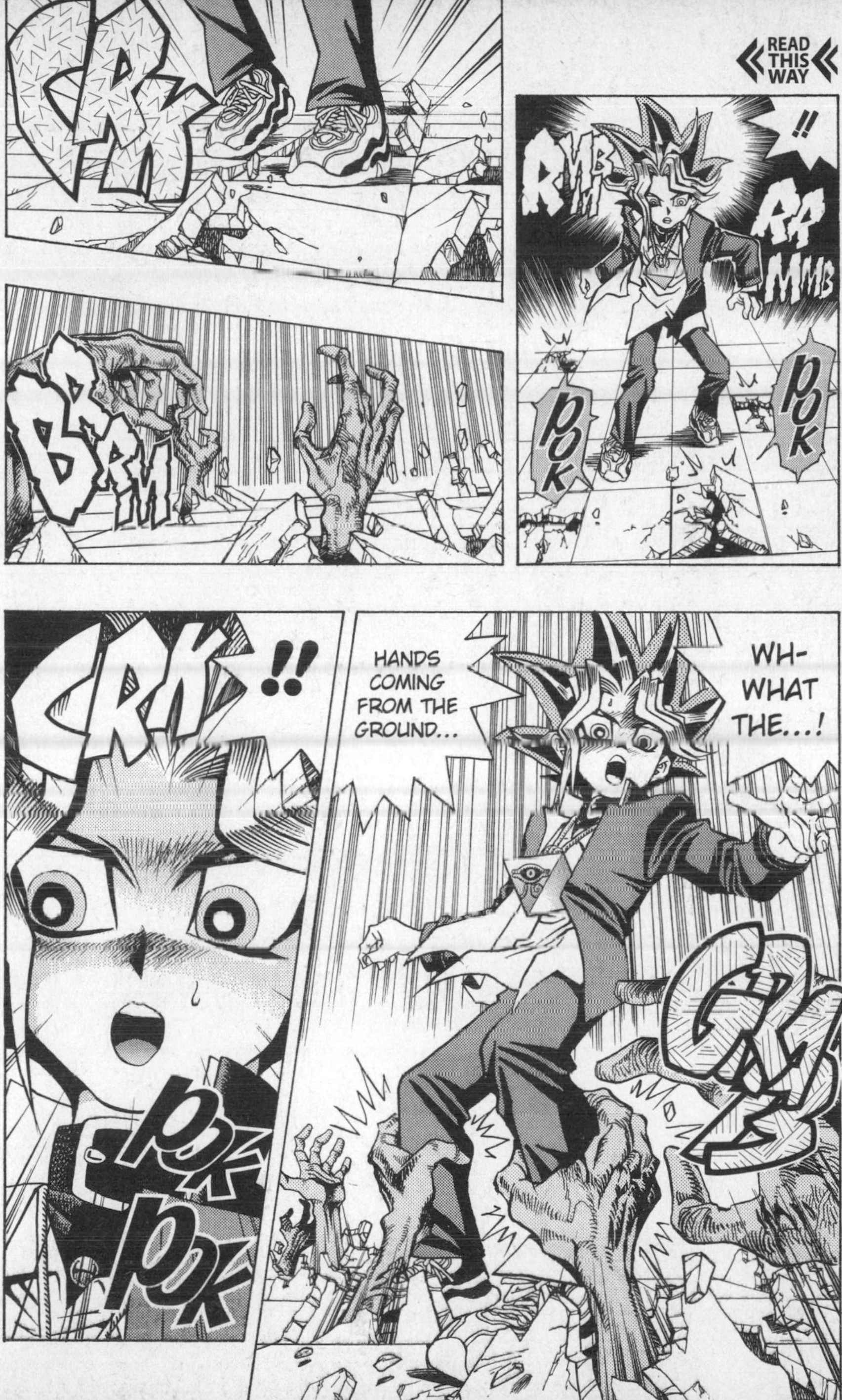
READ THIS WAY
RMB
!!
RA MMB
POK
POK
CRAK
BRAM
WH- WHAT THE...!
HANDS COMING FROM THE GROUND...
CRAK!!
POK POK POK

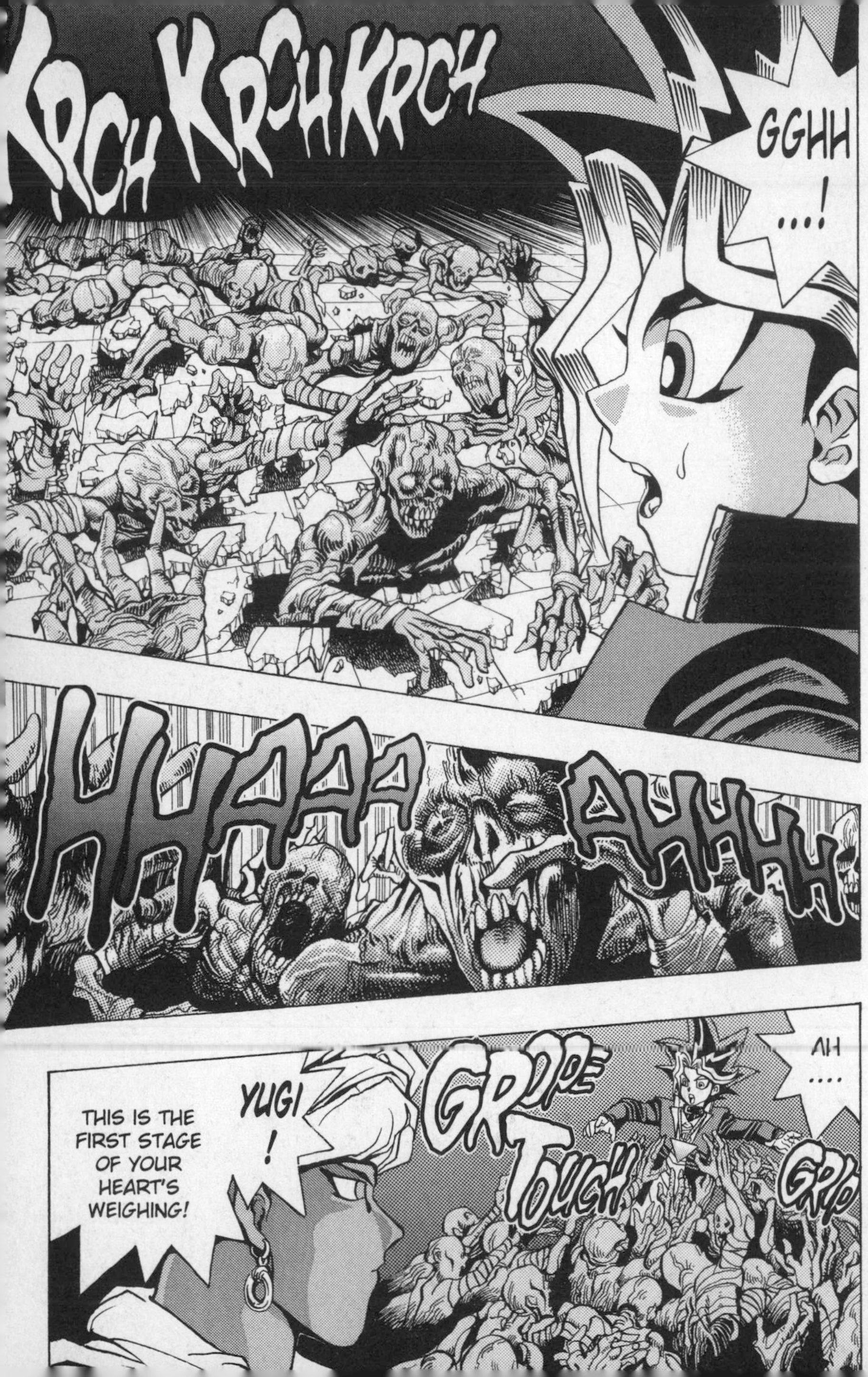
GGHH ! ...!
KRCH KRCH KRCH
HHAAA AHHHH
AH ....
GR PE
TOUCH
GRIP
YUGI !
THIS IS THE FIRST STAGE OF YOUR HEART'S WEIGHING!

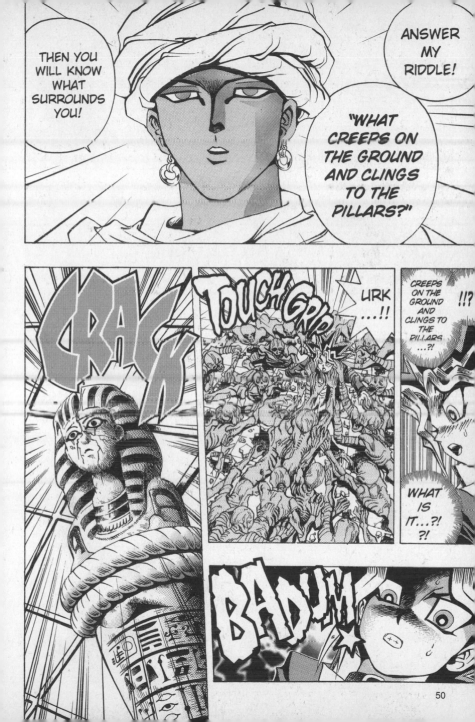

50

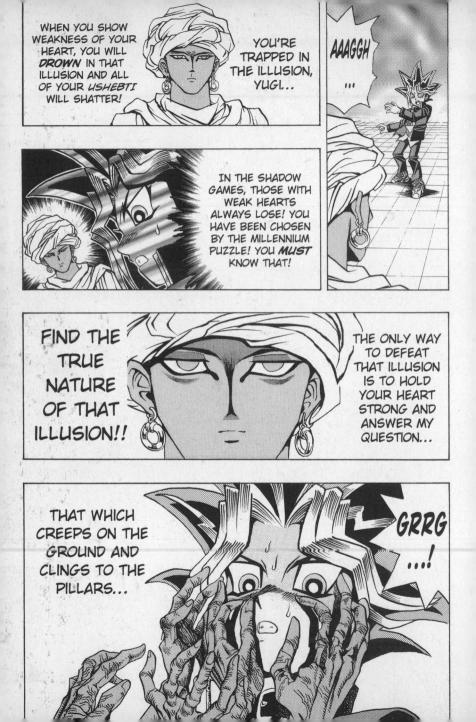

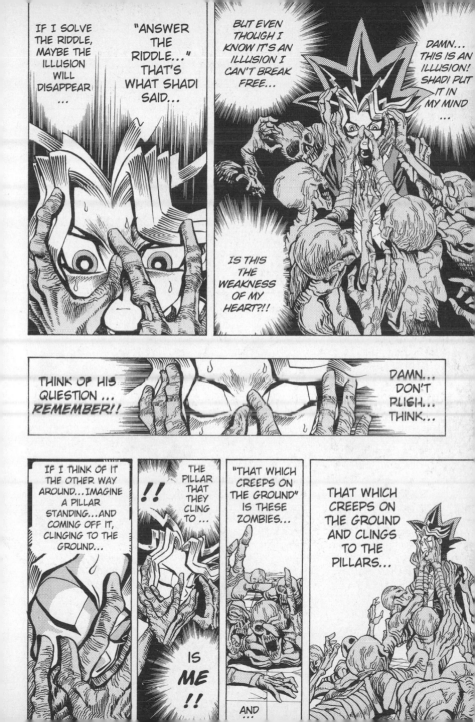

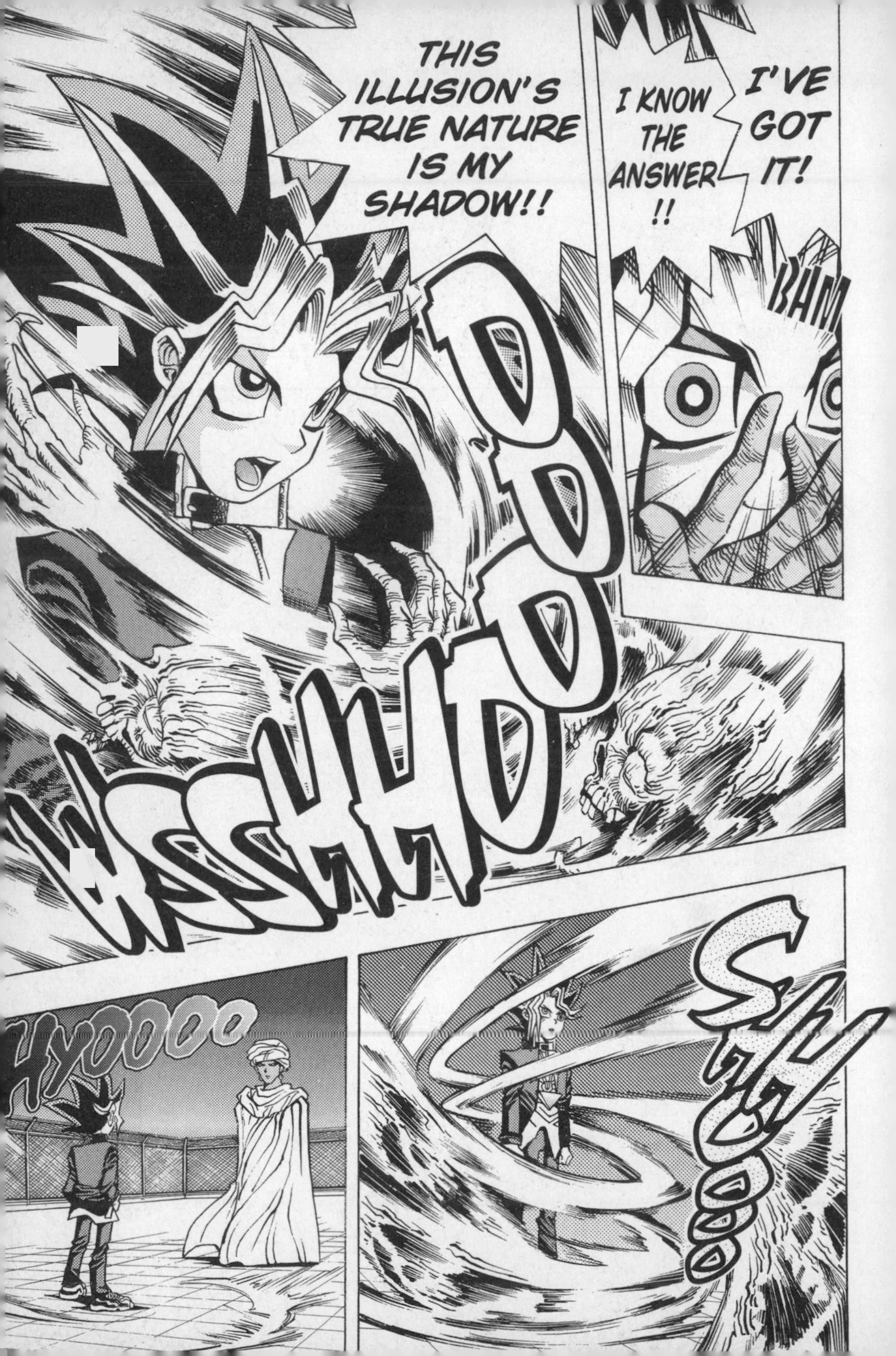
I'VE GOT IT!
I KNOW THE ANSWER!!
BAM
THIS ILLUSION'S TRUE NATURE IS MY SHADOW!!
HYOOOO

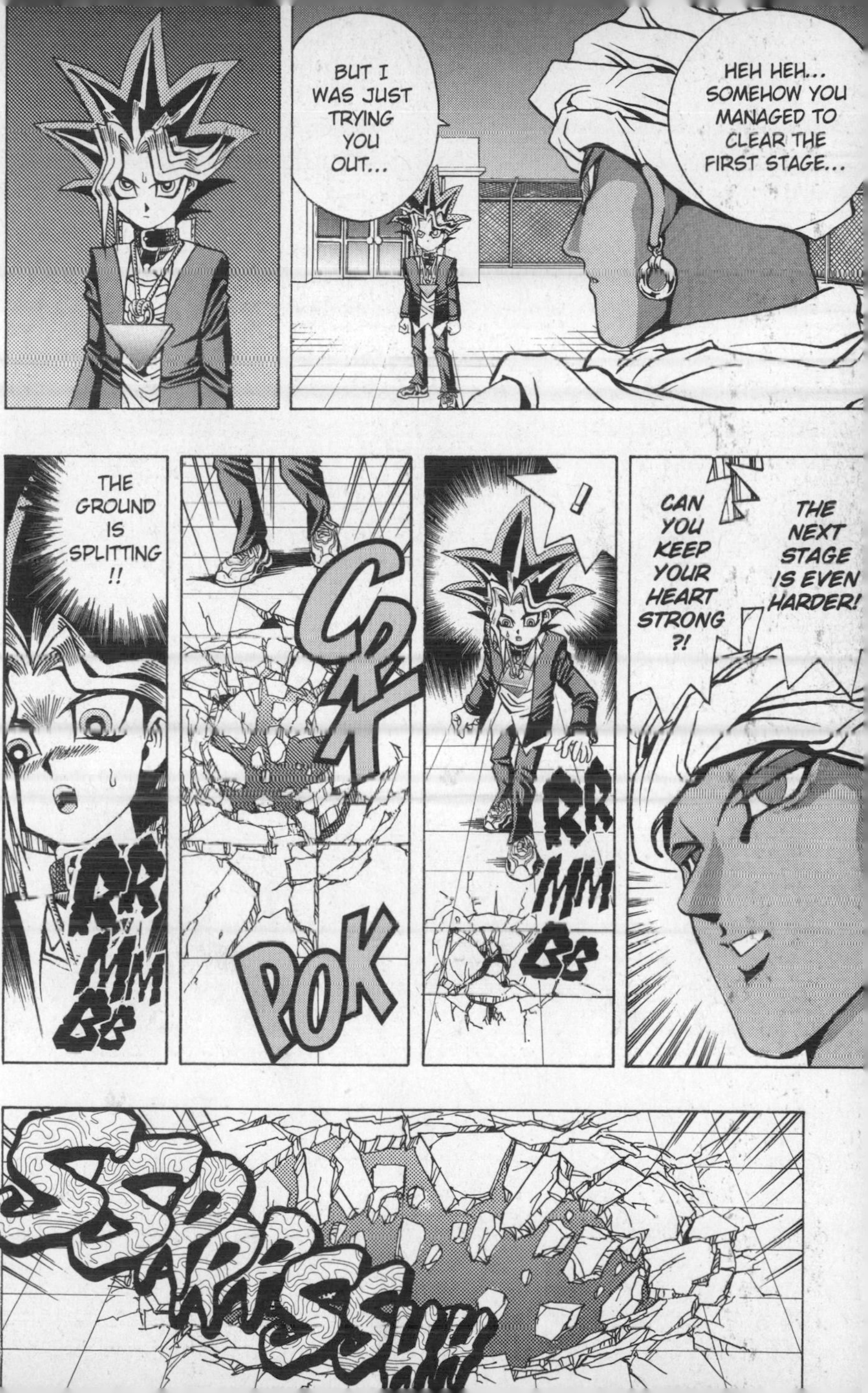

HEH HEH... SOMEHOW YOU MANAGED TO CLEAR THE FIRST STAGE...
BUT I WAS JUST TRYING YOU OUT...
THE NEXT STAGE IS EVEN HARDER!
CAN YOU KEEP YOUR HEART STRONG ?!
!
RRMMBB
CRK
POK
THE GROUND IS SPLITTING !!
RRMMBB

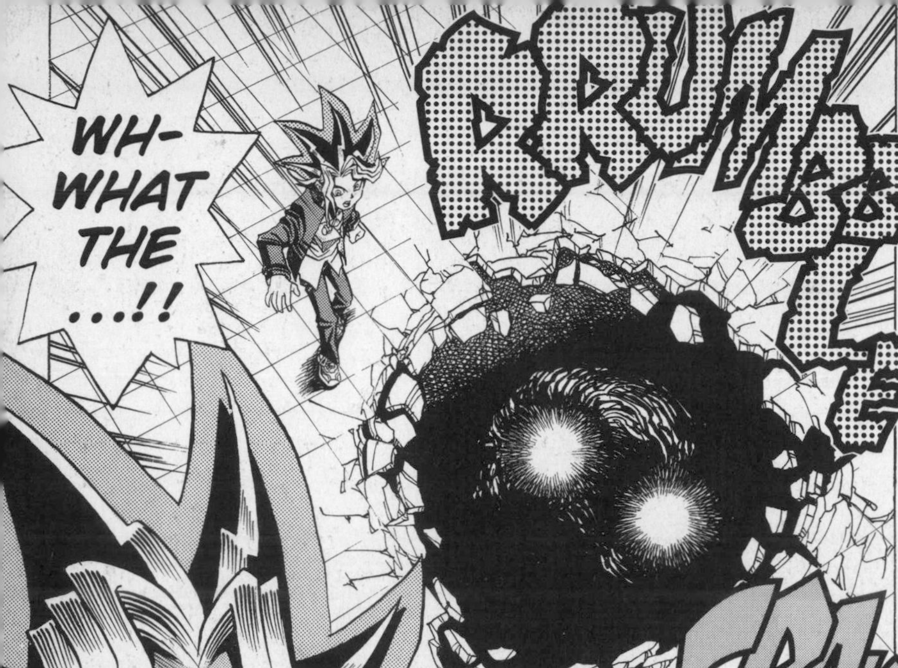
CRUMBLE
WH-WHAT THE ...!!
CRAK
CRUNCH

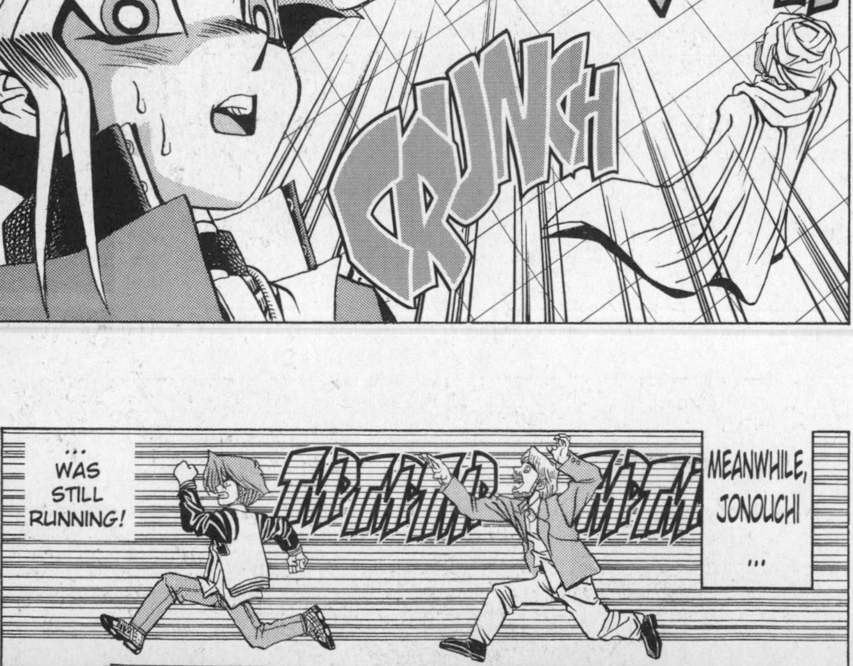
MEANWHILE, JONOUCHI ...
... WAS STILL RUNNING!

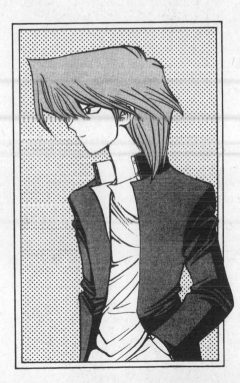

# Duel 18: Second Stage

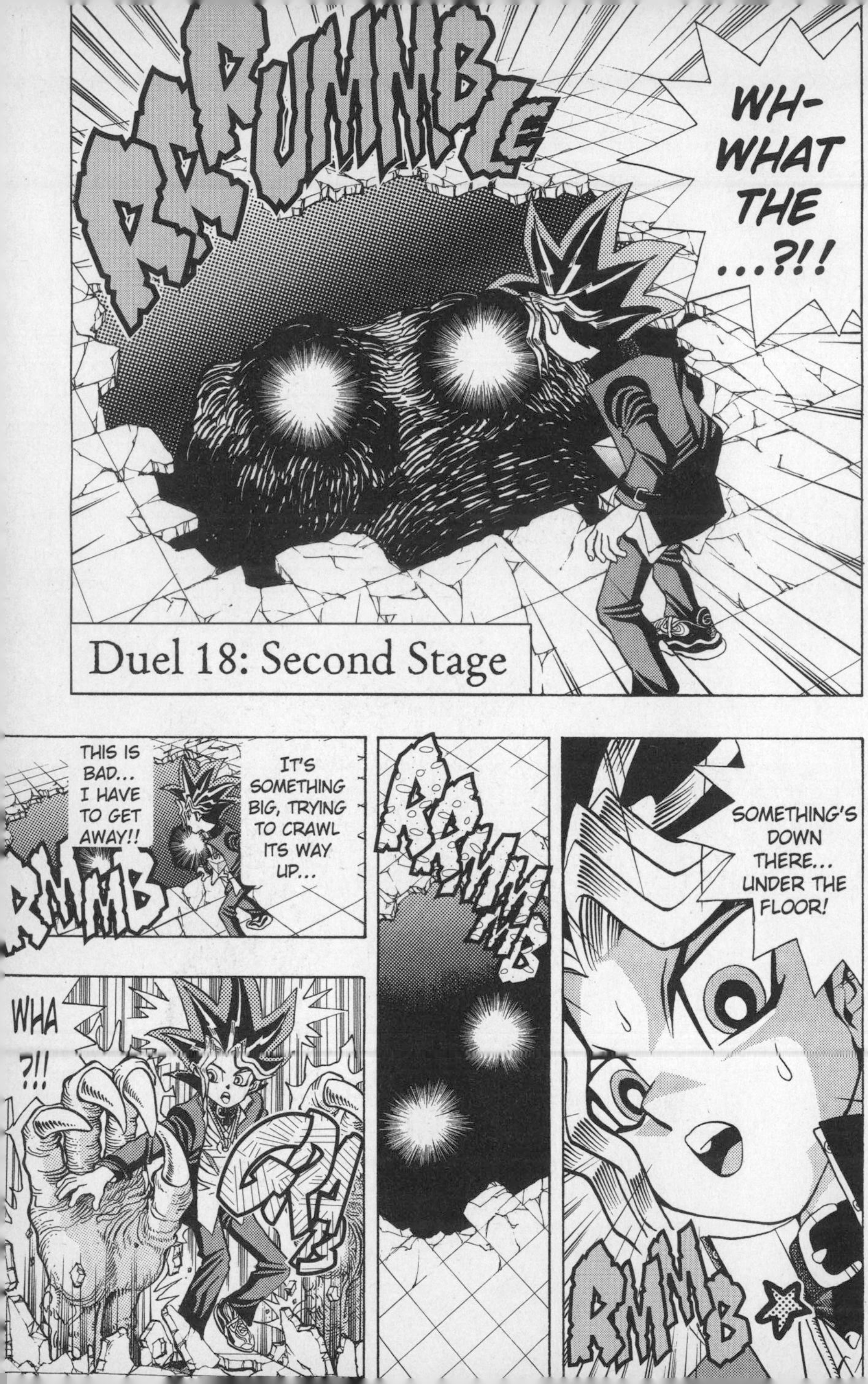
WH-
WHAT THE ...?!!
SOMETHING'S DOWN THERE... UNDER THE FLOOR!
RMMB
IT'S SOMETHING BIG, TRYING TO CRAWL ITS WAY UP...
THIS IS BAD... I HAVE TO GET AWAY!!
RMMB
WHA ?!!

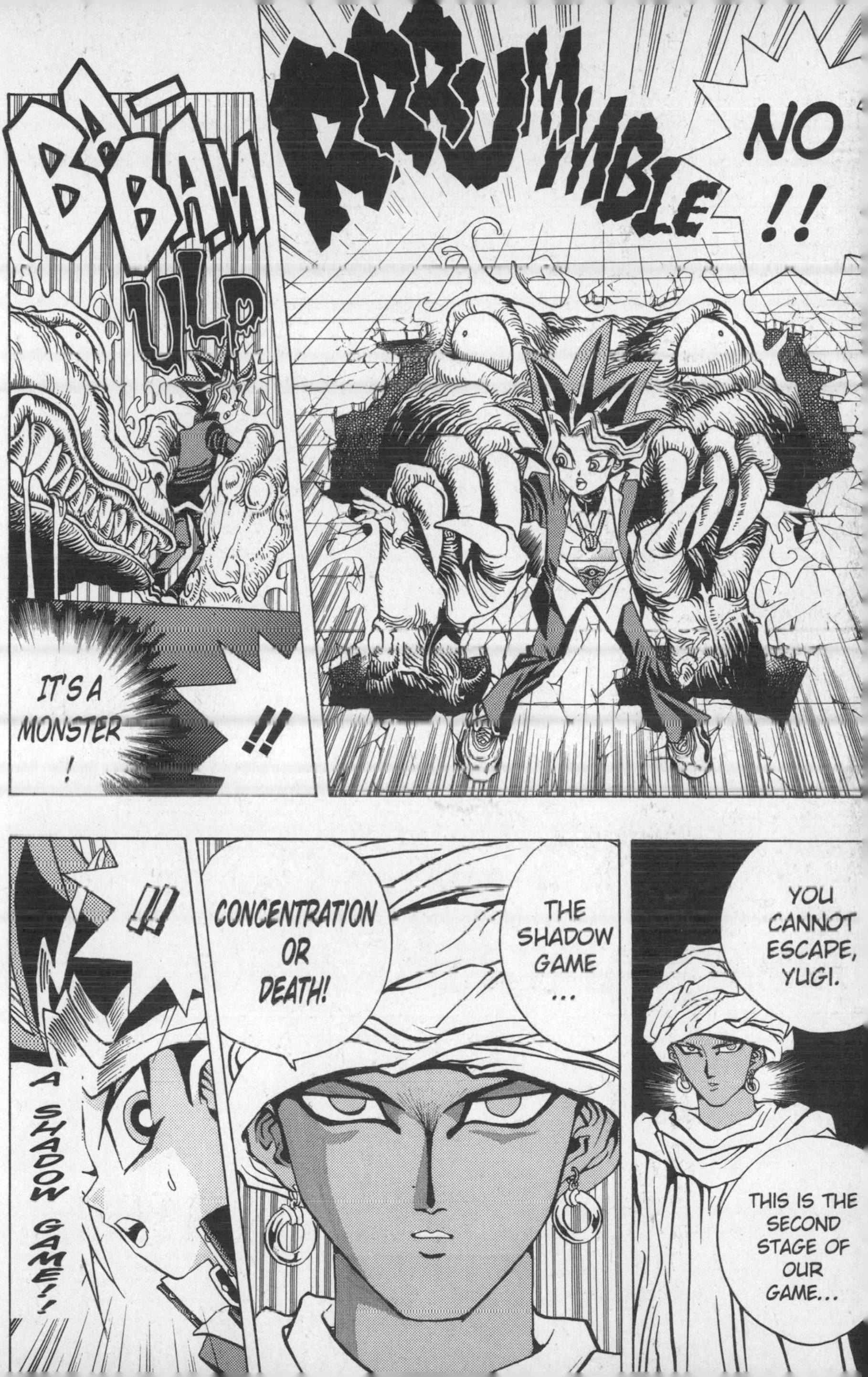
NO!!
RRRUMMBLE
BABAM
ULP
IT'S A MONSTER!!!
YOU CANNOT ESCAPE, YUGI.
THIS IS THE SECOND STAGE OF OUR GAME...
THE SHADOW GAME...
CONCENTRATION OR DEATH!
!!
A SHADOW GAME!!

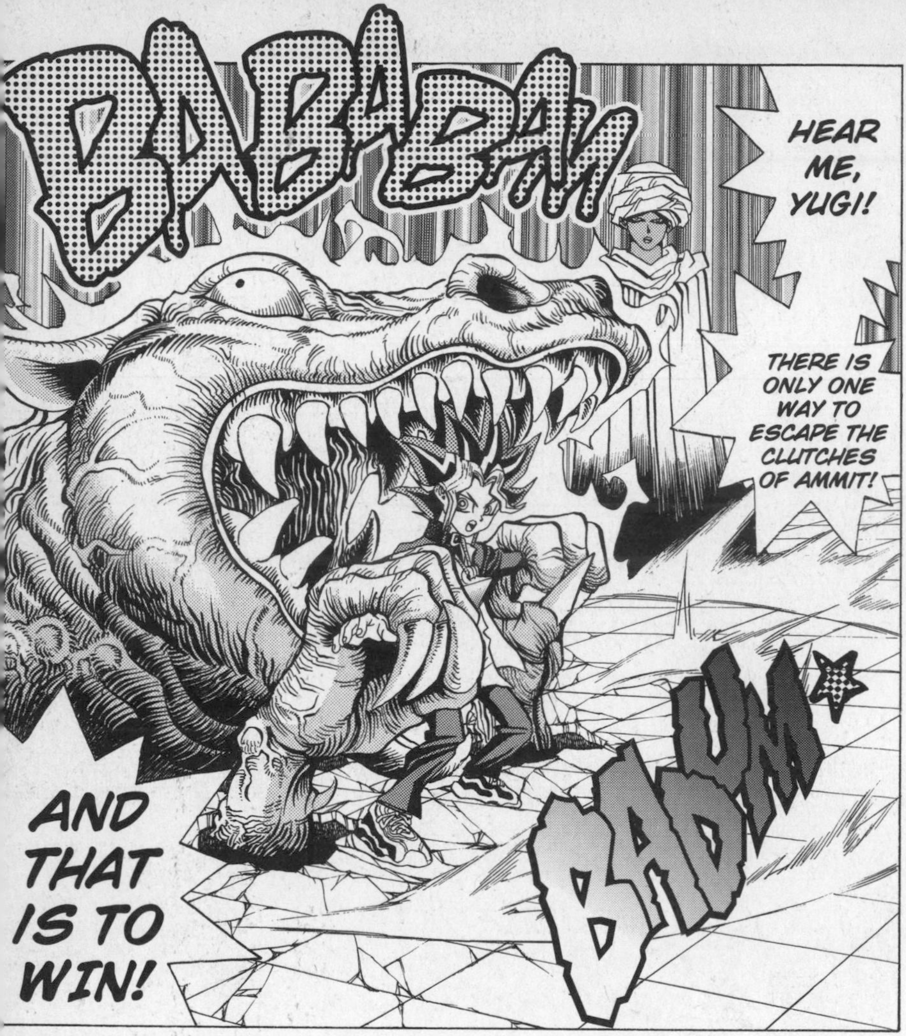
HEAR ME, YUGI!
BABABAM
THERE IS ONLY ONE WAY TO ESCAPE THE CLUTCHES OF AMMIT!
BADUM
AND THAT IS TO WIN!

# Duel 18: Second Stage

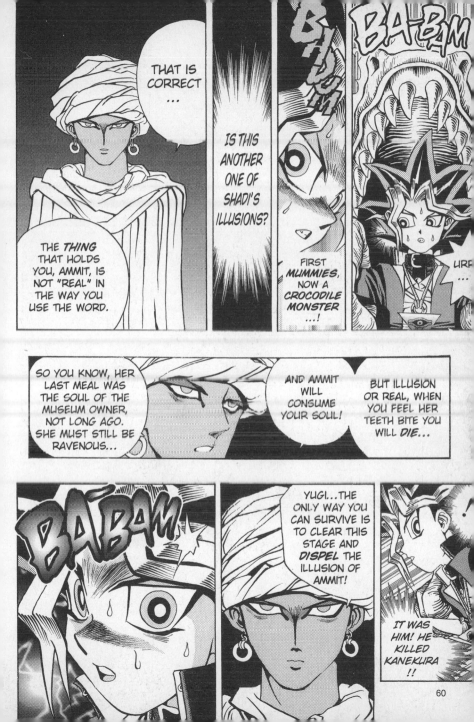

THAT IS CORRECT...

THE *THING* THAT HOLDS YOU, AMMIT, IS NOT "REAL" IN THE WAY YOU USE THE WORD.

IS THIS ANOTHER ONE OF SHADI'S ILLUSIONS?

FIRST *MUMMIES*, NOW A *CROCODILE MONSTER*...!

URP...

SO YOU KNOW, HER LAST MEAL WAS THE SOUL OF THE MUSEUM OWNER, NOT LONG AGO. SHE MUST STILL BE RAVENOUS...

AND AMMIT WILL CONSUME YOUR SOUL!

BUT ILLUSION OR REAL, WHEN YOU FEEL HER TEETH BITE YOU WILL *DIE*...

YUGI...THE ONLY WAY YOU CAN SURVIVE IS TO CLEAR THIS STAGE AND *DISPEL* THE ILLUSION OF AMMIT!

IT WAS HIM! HE KILLED KANEKURA!!

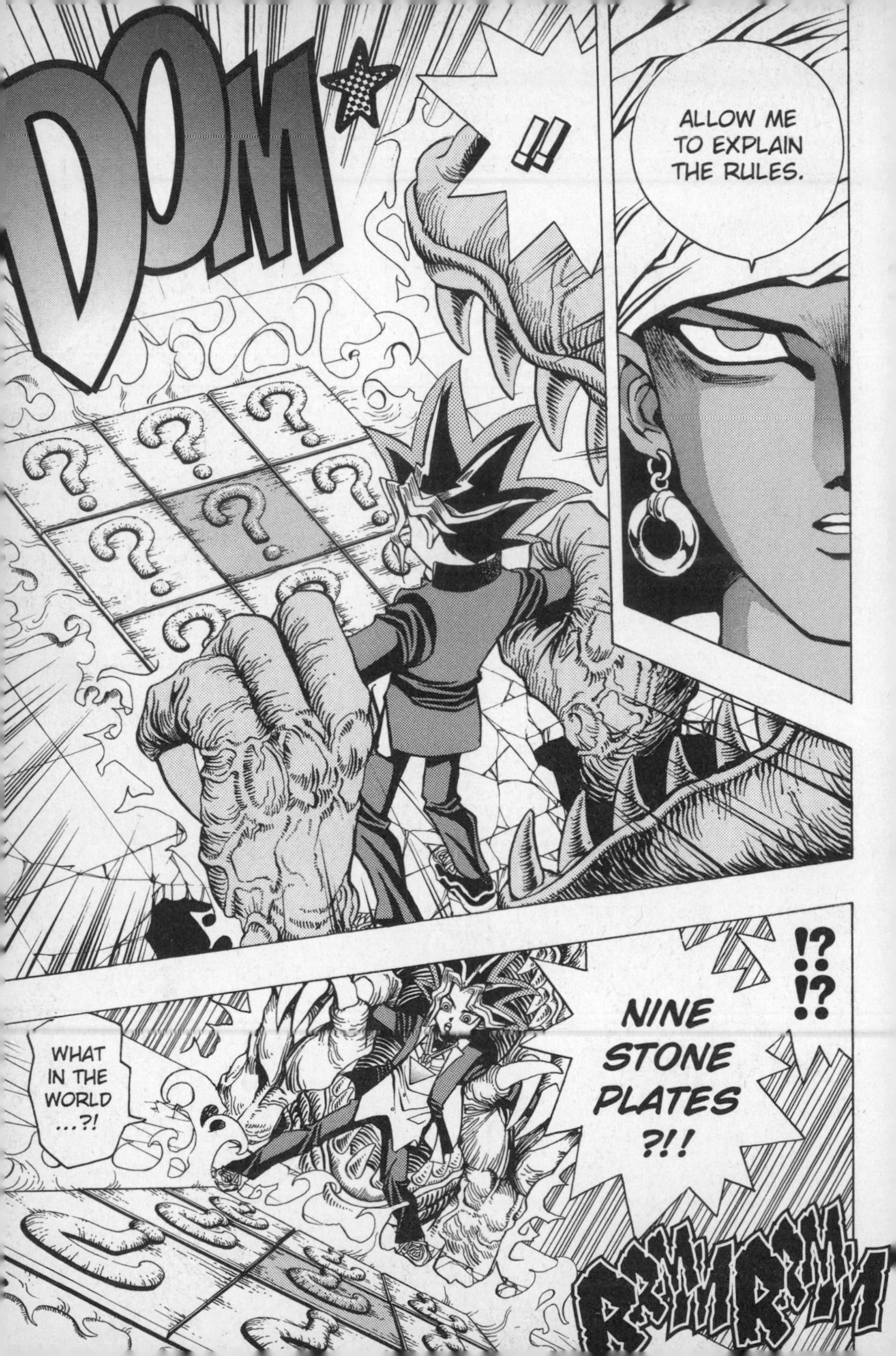
ALLOW ME TO EXPLAIN THE RULES.
!!
DOOM
!? !?
NINE STONE PLATES ?!!
WHAT IN THE WORLD ...?!

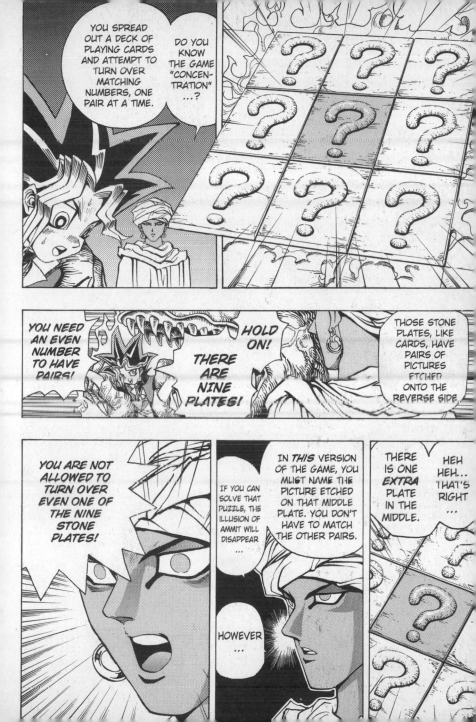

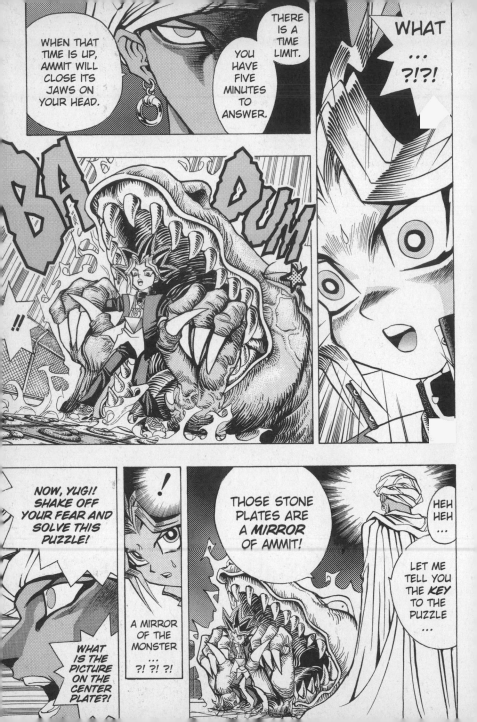

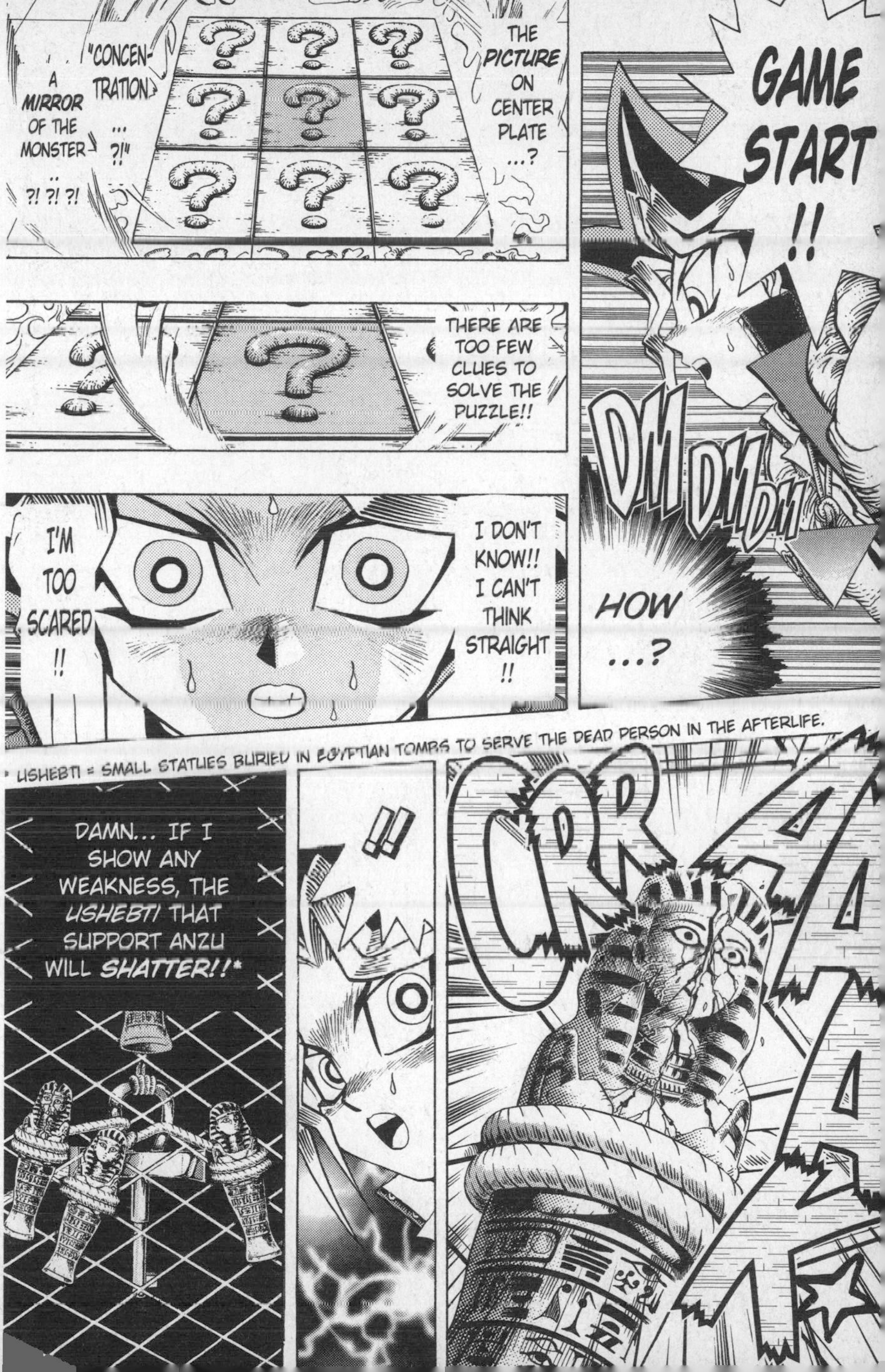
GAME START!!
DM DM DM DM
HOW ...?
THE PICTURE ON CENTER PLATE ...?
"CONCEN-TRATION" ... ?!"
A MIRROR OF THE MONSTER .. ?! ?! ?!
THERE ARE TOO FEW CLUES TO SOLVE THE PUZZLE!!
I DON'T KNOW!! I CAN'T THINK STRAIGHT!!
I'M TOO SCARED!!
CRR
!!
DAMN... IF I SHOW ANY WEAKNESS, THE USHEBTI THAT SUPPORT ANZU WILL SHATTER!!*

* USHEBTI = SMALL STATUES BURIED IN EGYPTIAN TOMBS TO SERVE THE DEAD PERSON IN THE AFTERLIFE.

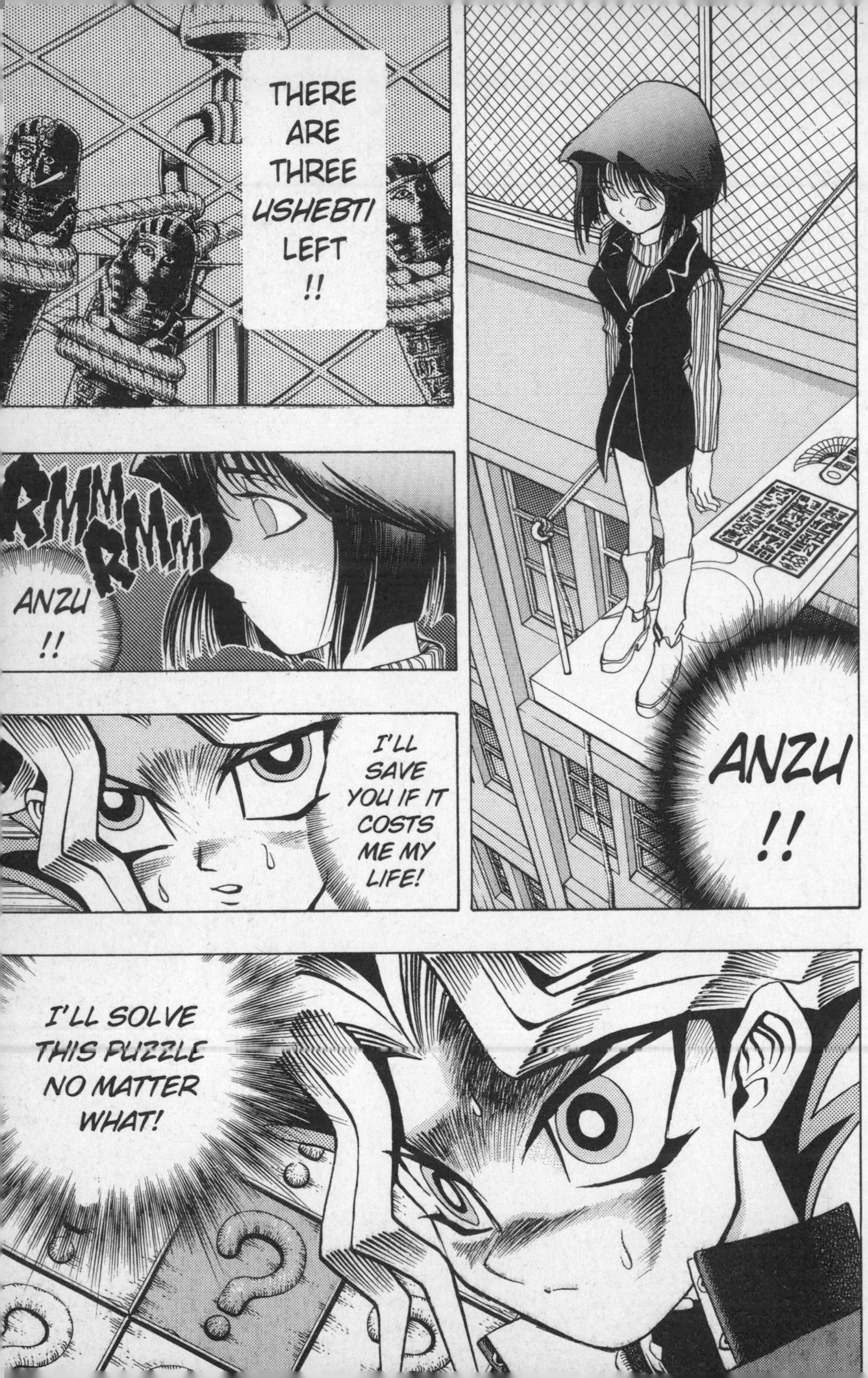
ANZU !!
THERE ARE THREE USHEBTI LEFT !!
RMM RMM RMM
ANZU !!
I'LL SAVE YOU IF IT COSTS ME MY LIFE!
I'LL SOLVE THIS PUZZLE NO MATTER WHAT!

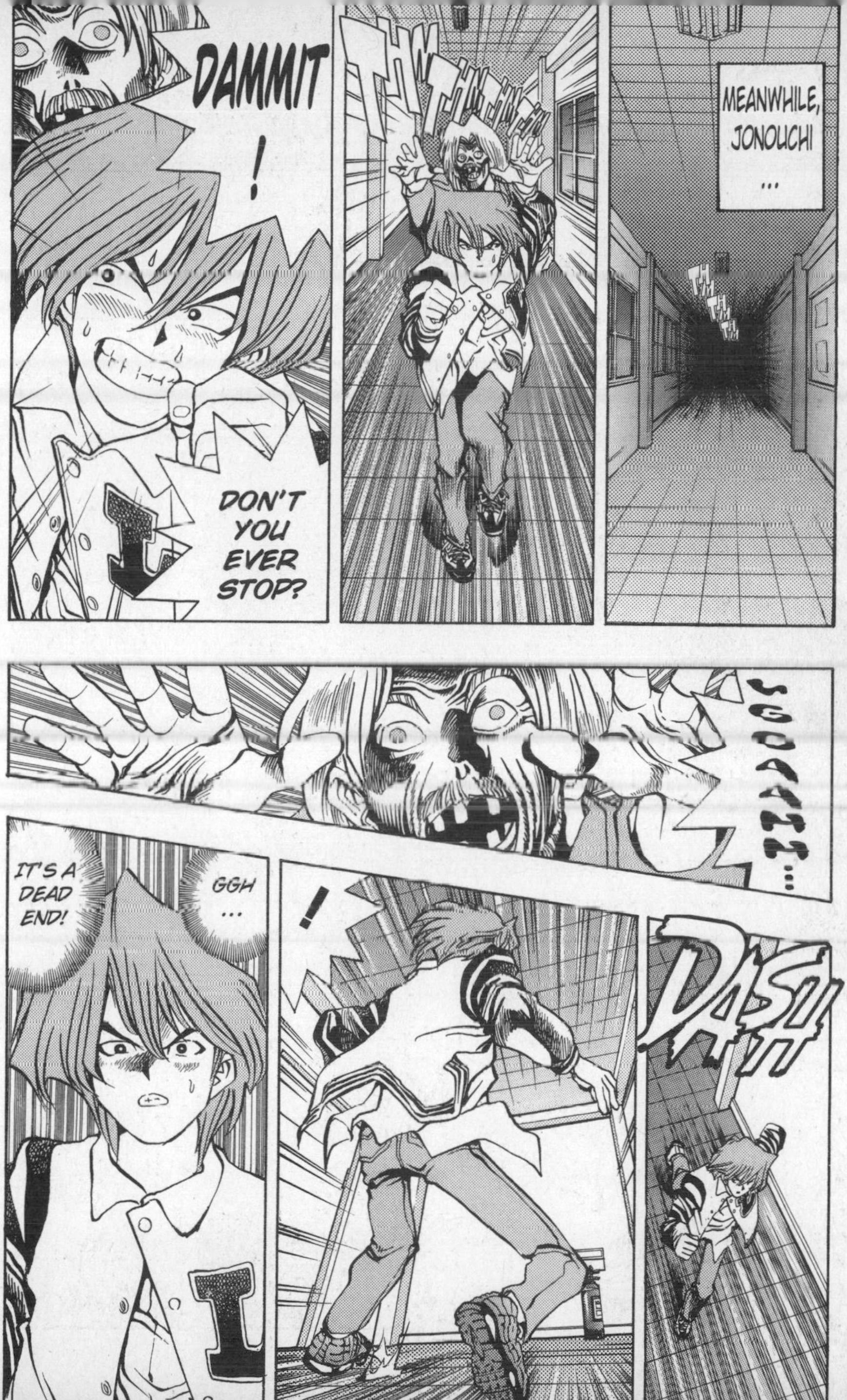
MEANWHILE, JONOUCHI ...
THM THM THM
THM THM THM THM
DAMMIT
!
DON'T YOU EVER STOP?
UGOAAHH...
DASH
!
GGH ...
IT'S A DEAD END!

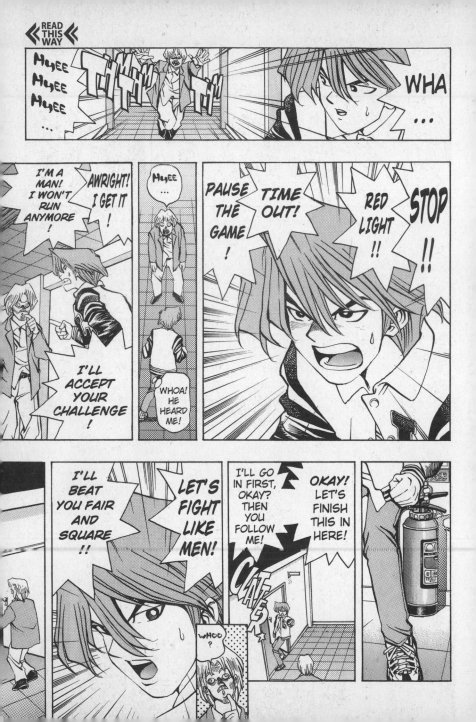

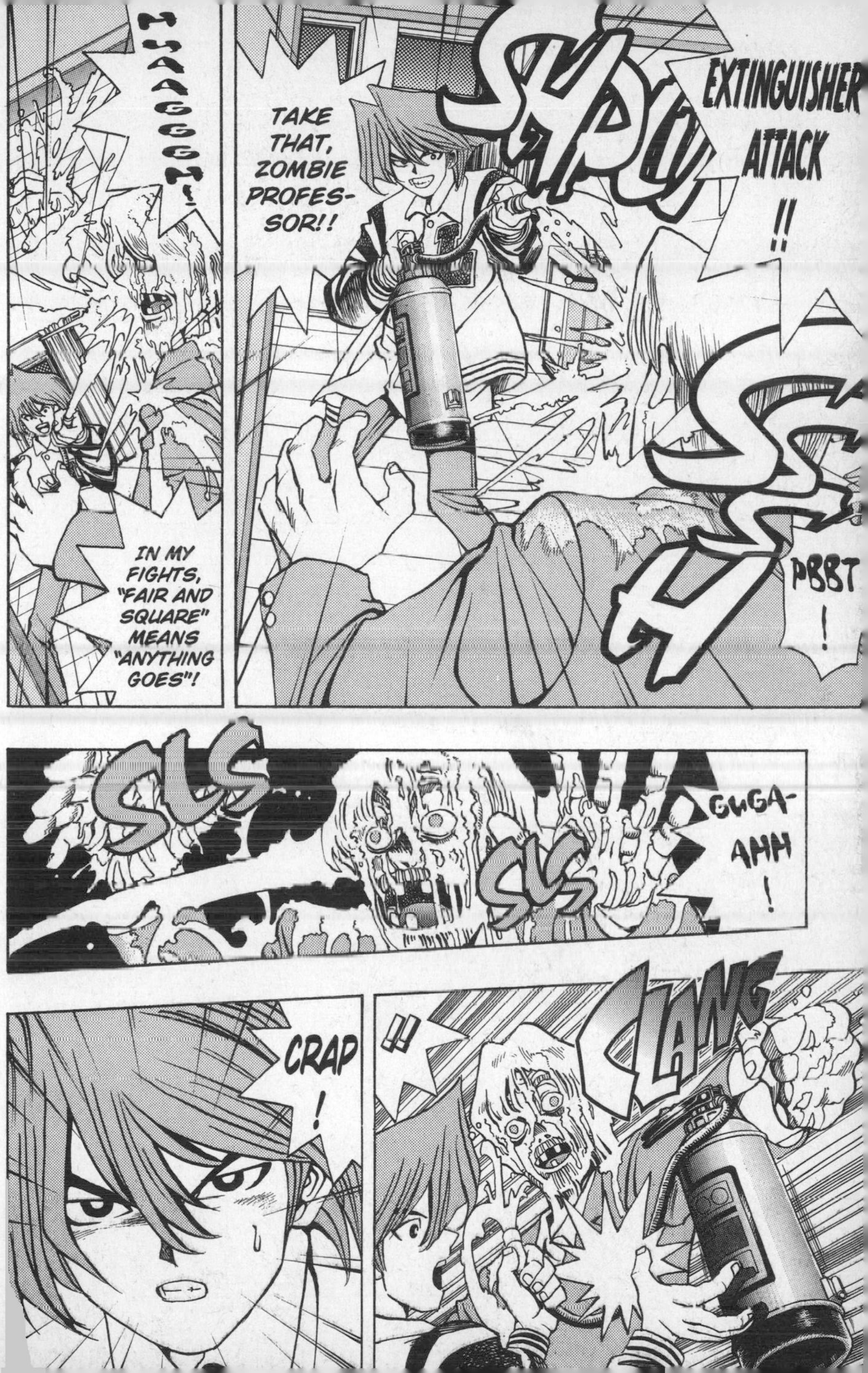
EXTINGUISHER ATTACK !!
TAKE THAT, ZOMBIE PROFESSOR!!
PBBT !
HUAAGGGH!
IN MY FIGHTS, "FAIR AND SQUARE" MEANS "ANYTHING GOES"!
GUGA-AHH !
!!
CLANG
CRAP !

READ THIS WAY

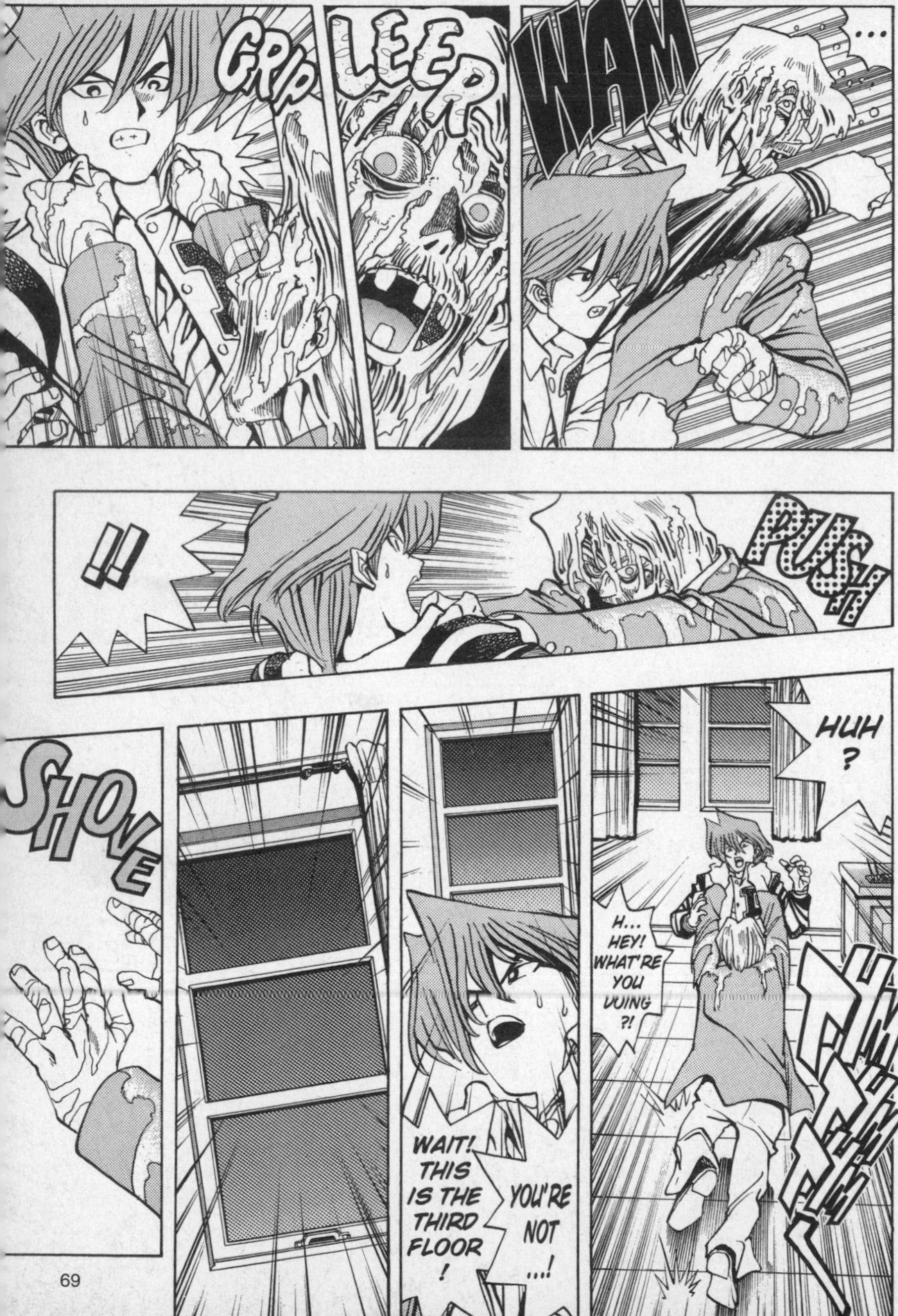

WAM
...
LEEP
GRIP
PUSH
!!
HUH ?
H... HEY! WHAT'RE YOU DOING ?!
WAIT! THIS IS THE THIRD FLOOR !
YOU'RE NOT ...!
SHOVE

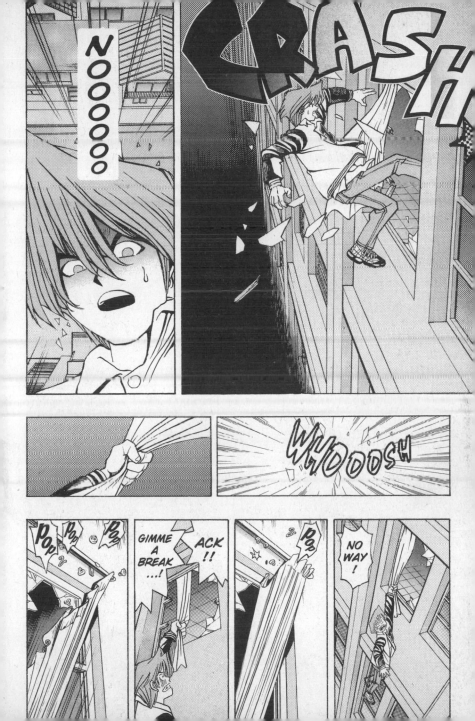

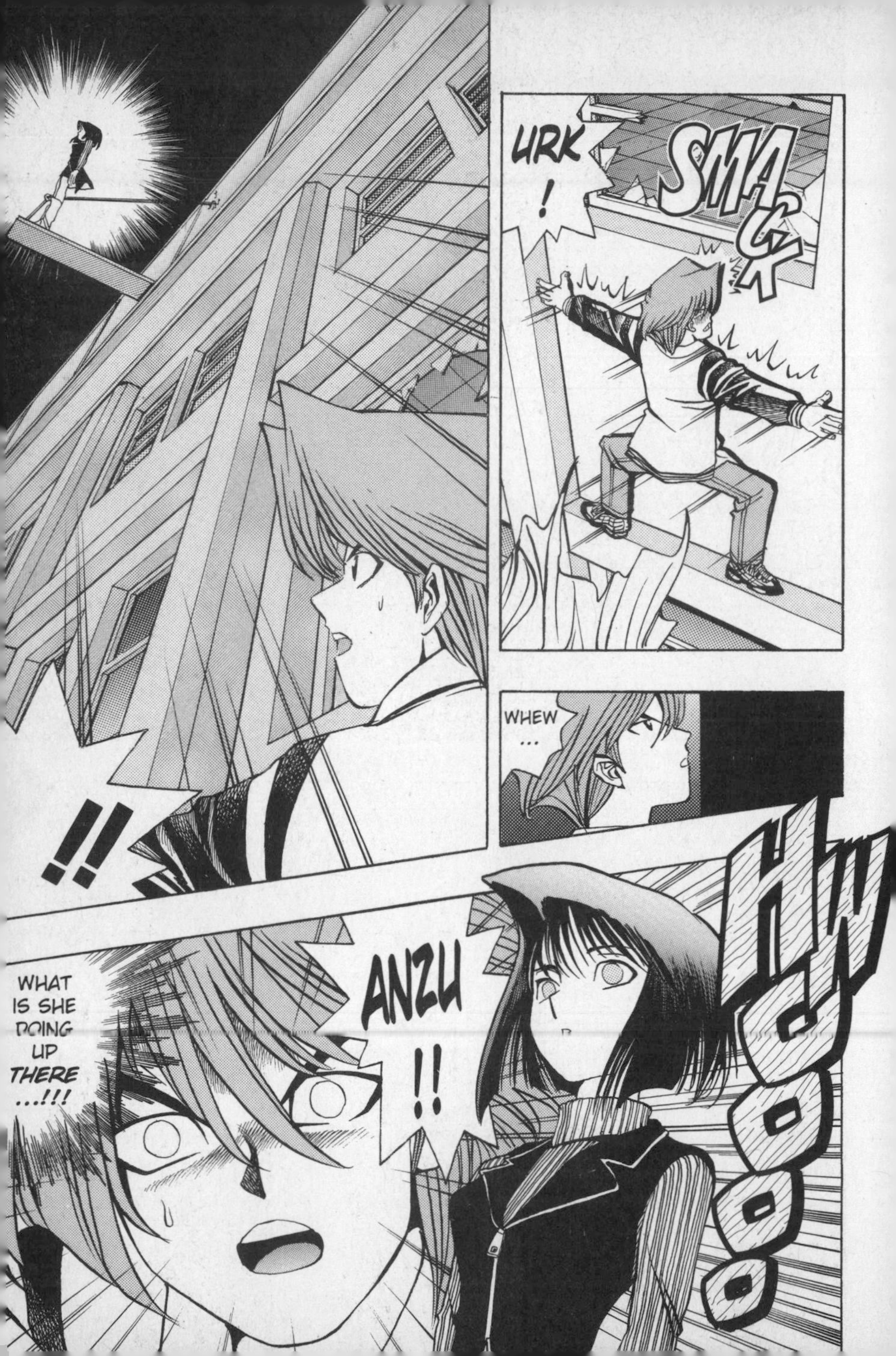
SMACK
URK
!
WHEW
...
!!
HWOOOO
ANZU
!!
WHAT IS SHE DOING UP THERE ...!!!

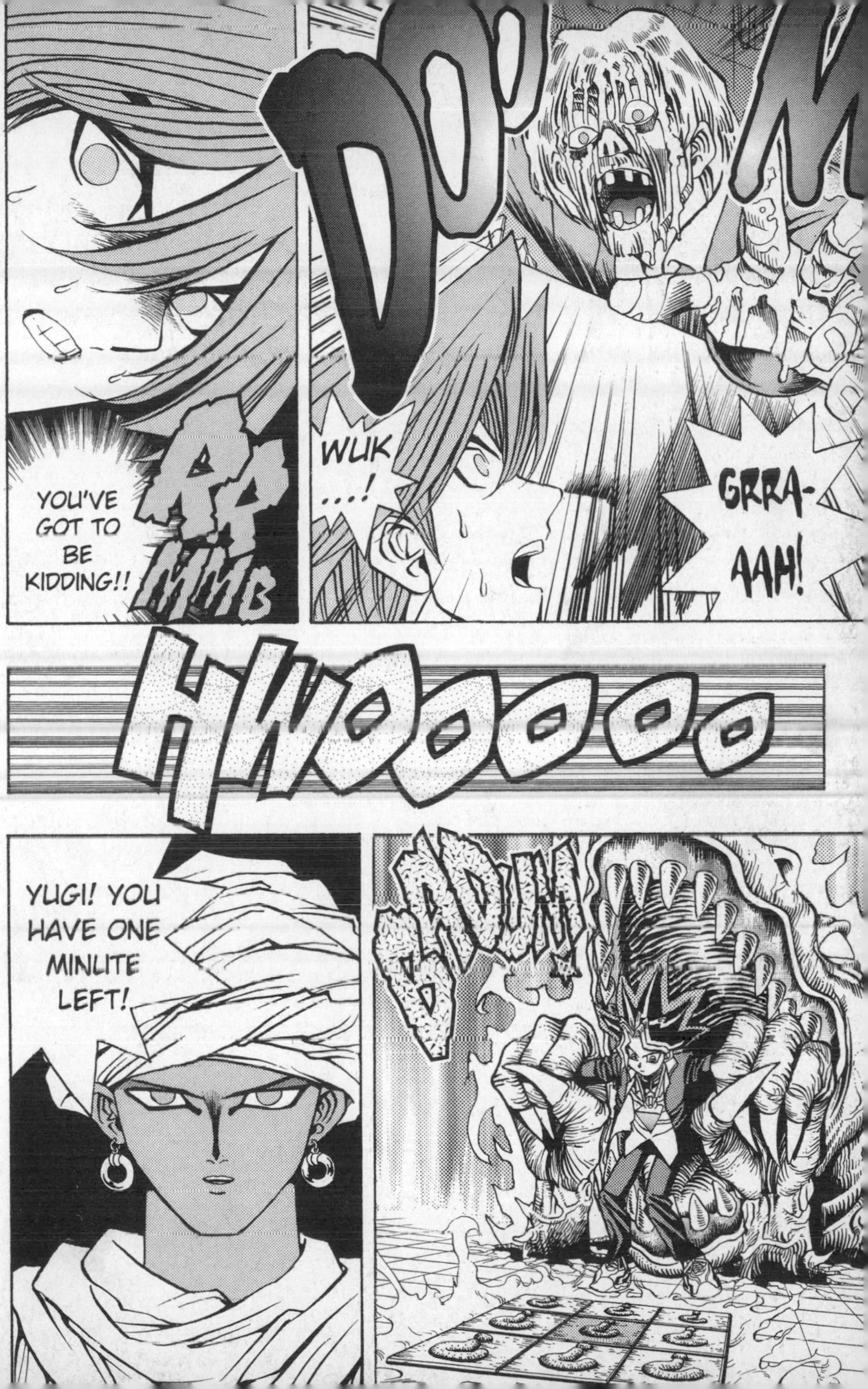

WUK ...!
GRRA-AAH!
YOU'VE GOT TO BE KIDDING!!
HWOOOOO
YUGI! YOU HAVE ONE MINUTE LEFT!

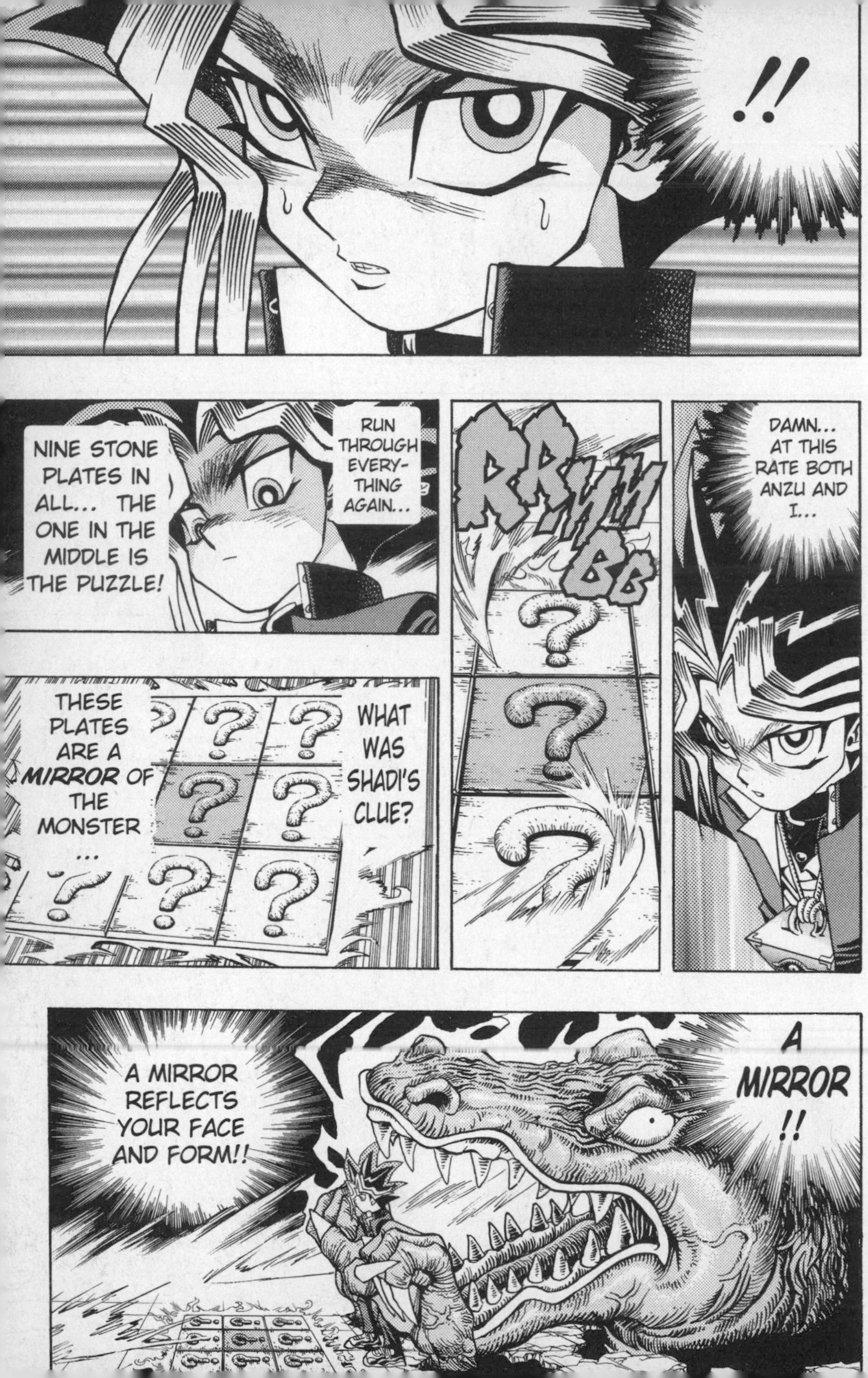
!!
DAMN... AT THIS RATE BOTH ANZU AND I...
RRMMBB
RUN THROUGH EVERY-THING AGAIN...
NINE STONE PLATES IN ALL... THE ONE IN THE MIDDLE IS THE PUZZLE!
WHAT WAS SHADI'S CLUE?
THESE PLATES ARE A *MIRROR* OF THE MONSTER ...
A MIRROR!!
A MIRROR REFLECTS YOUR FACE AND FORM!!

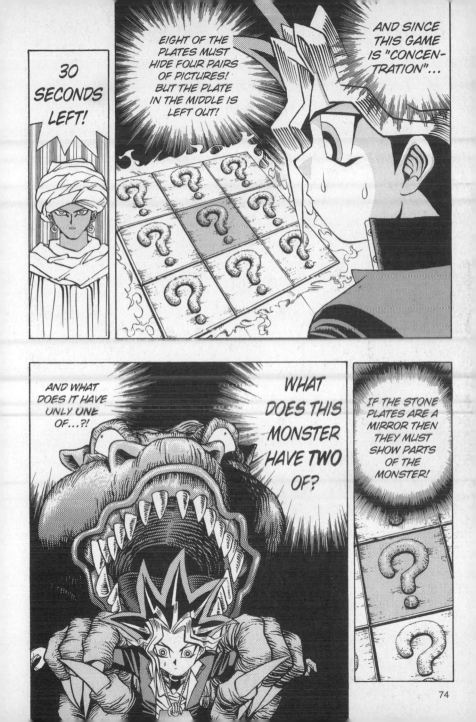

READ THIS WAY

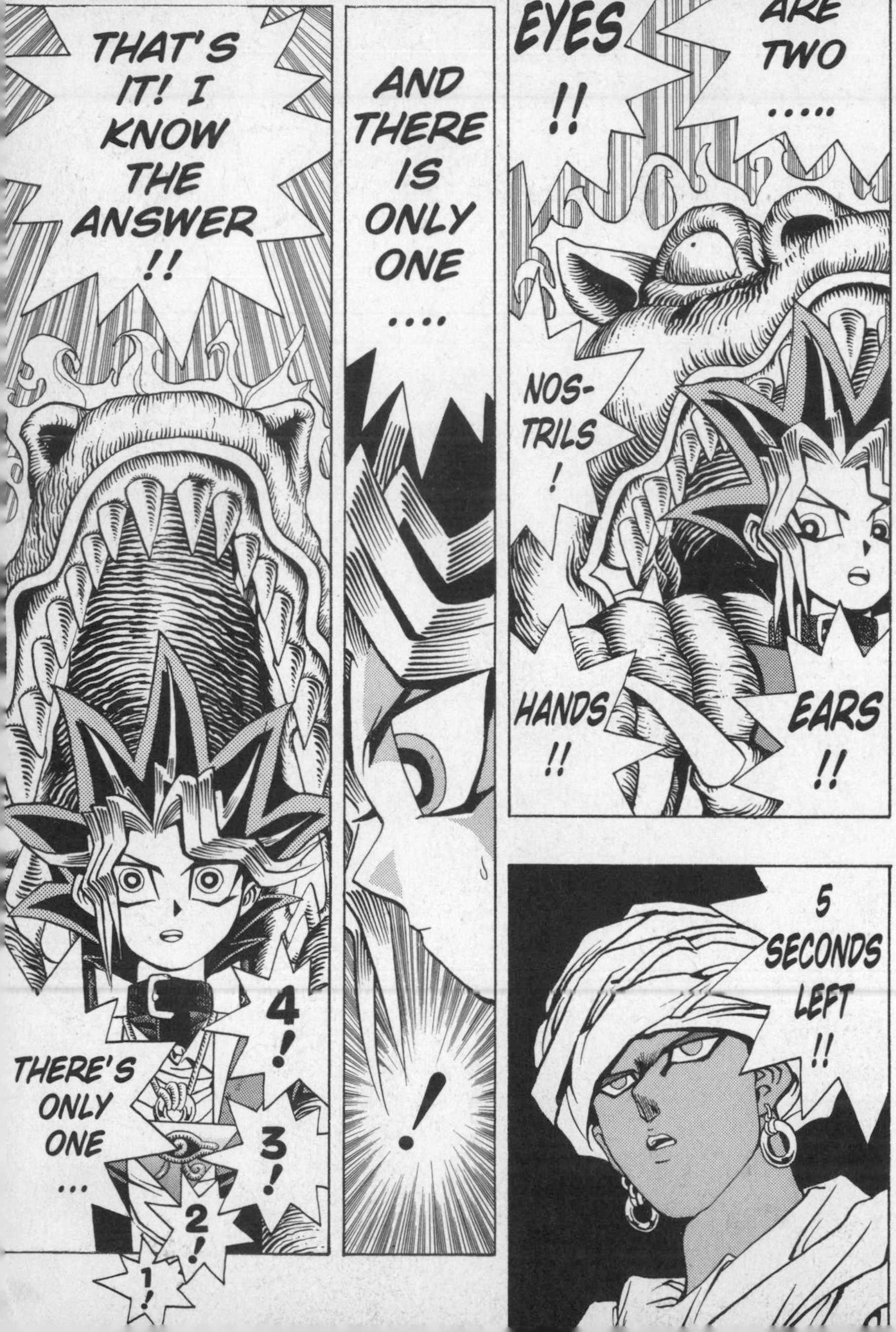

THERE ARE TWO .....
EYES !!
NOS-TRILS !
EARS !!
HANDS !!
5 SECONDS LEFT !!
AND THERE IS ONLY ONE ....
!
THAT'S IT! I KNOW THE ANSWER !!
4 !
3 !
THERE'S ONLY ONE ...
2 !
1 !

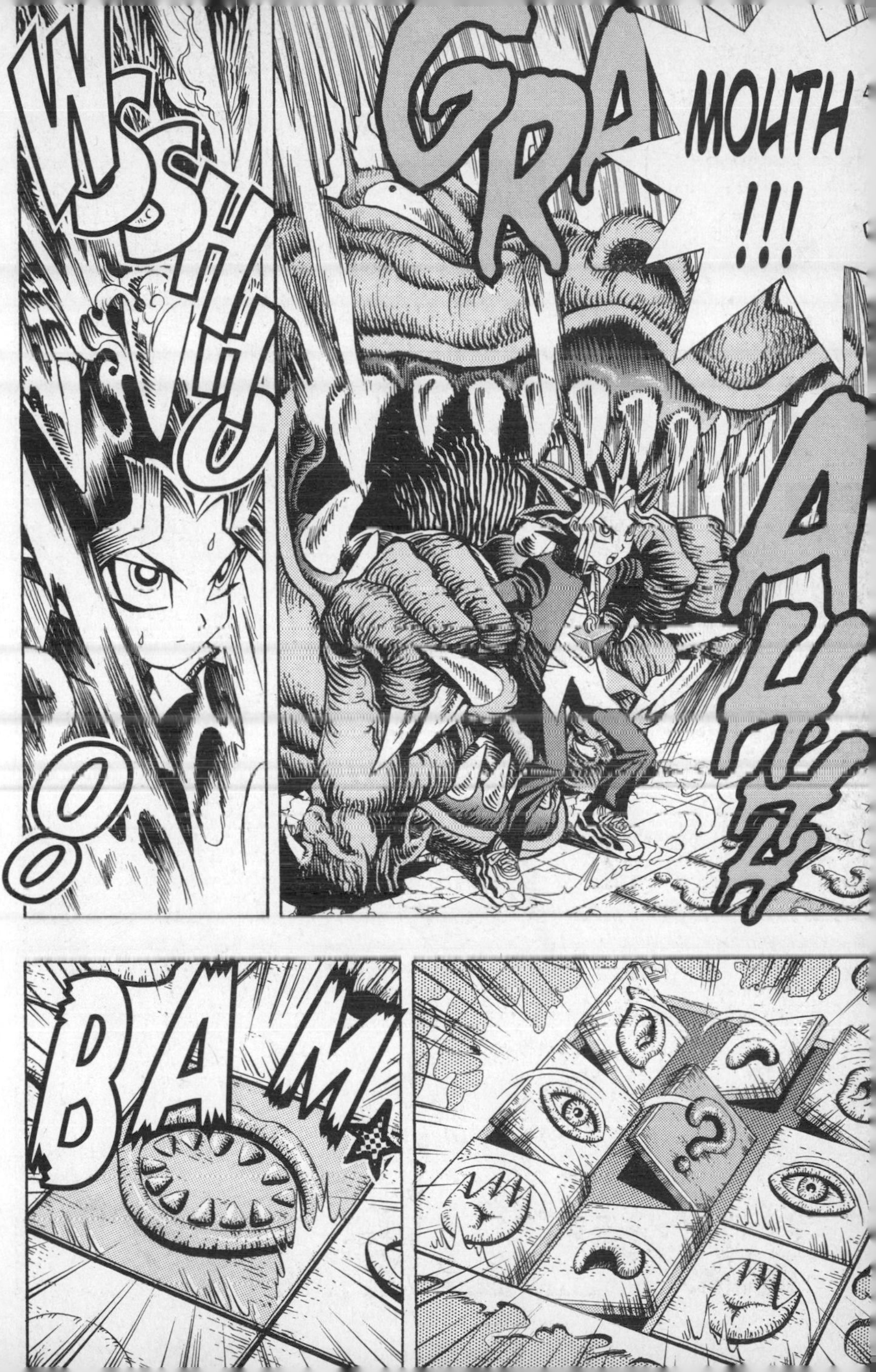
GRA
MOUTH !!!
BAM

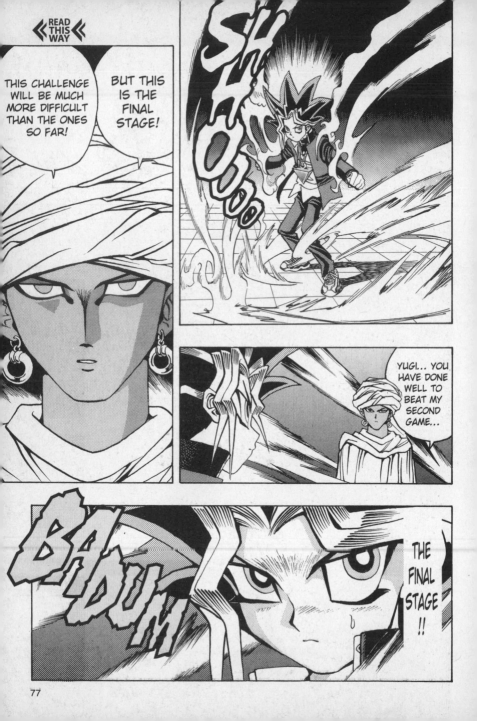

THIS CHALLENGE WILL BE MUCH MORE DIFFICULT THAN THE ONES SO FAR!

BUT THIS IS THE FINAL STAGE!

SHHOUUU

YUGI... YOU HAVE DONE WELL TO BEAT MY SECOND GAME...

BA DUM

THE FINAL STAGE!!

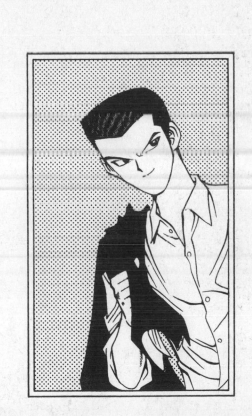

# Duel 19: Final Stage

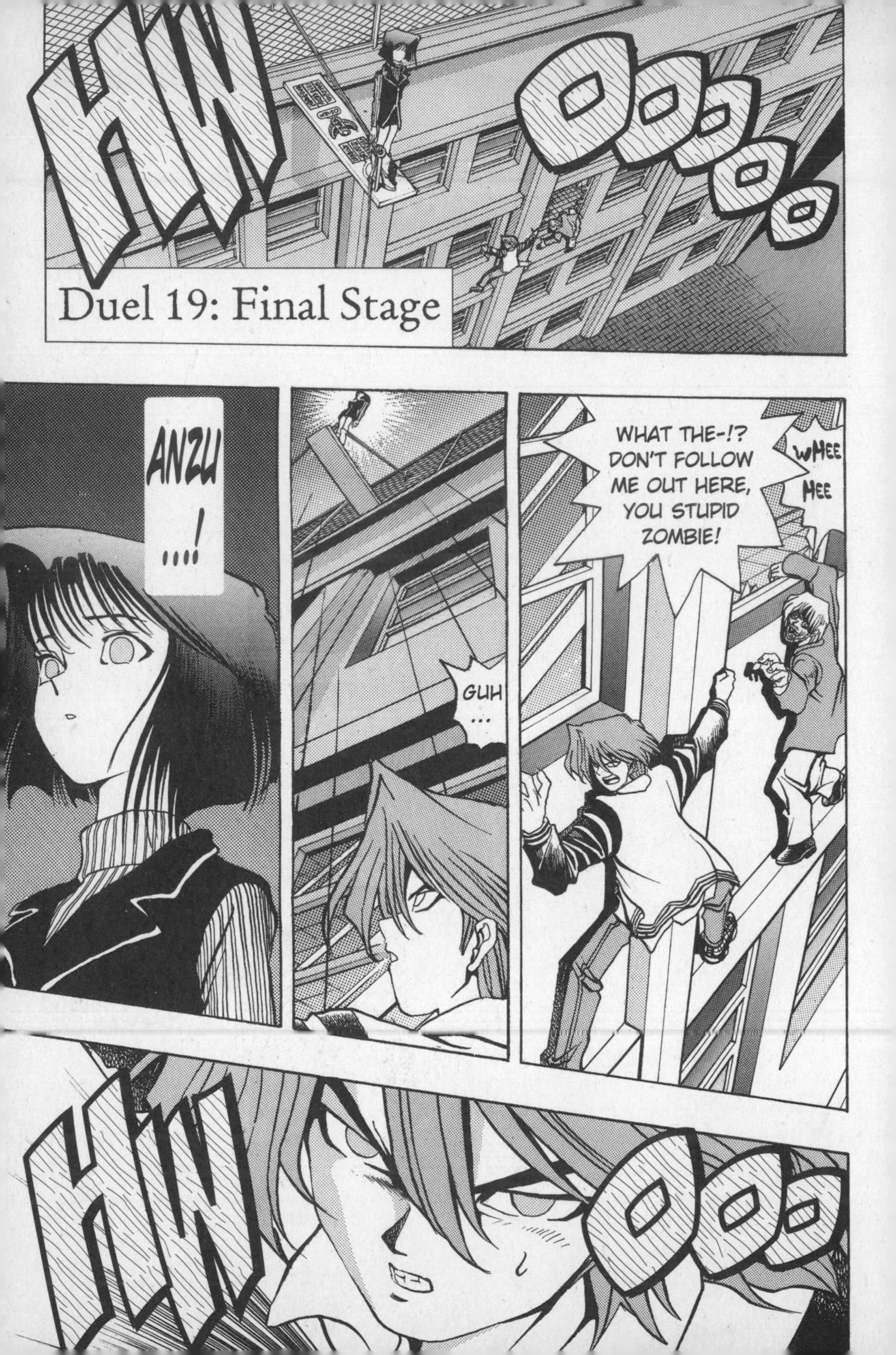
HIN
OOOOO
WHEE HEE
WHAT THE-!? DON'T FOLLOW ME OUT HERE, YOU STUPID ZOMBIE!
GUH ...
ANZU ...!
HIN
OOOO

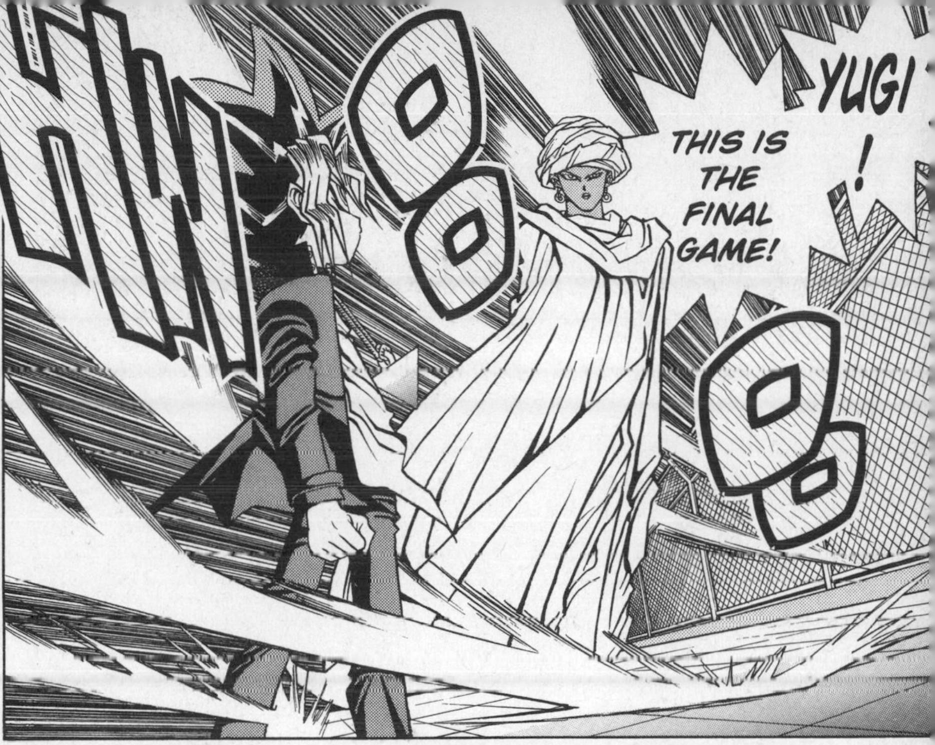
YUGI!
THIS IS THE FINAL GAME!

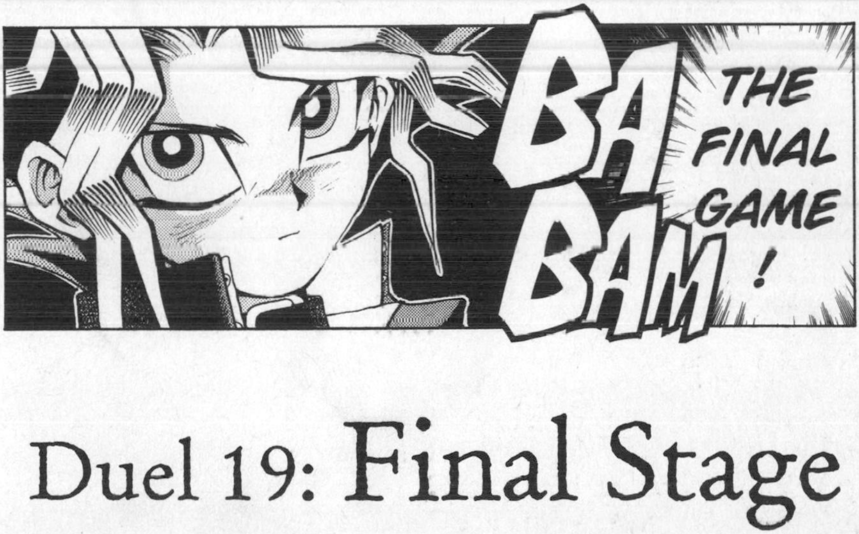
THE FINAL GAME!
BA BAM

# Duel 19: Final Stage

READ THIS WAY

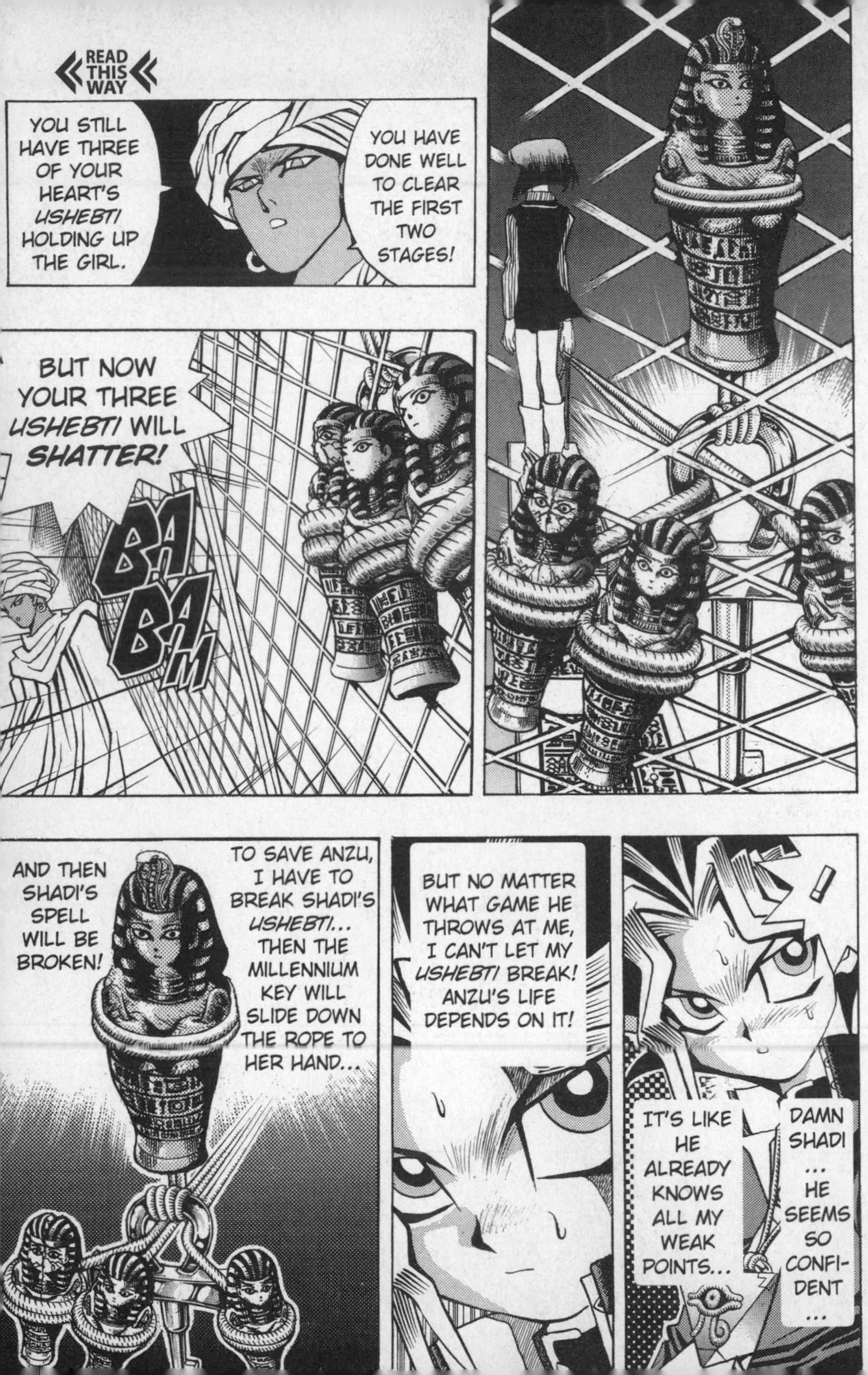
YOU HAVE DONE WELL TO CLEAR THE FIRST TWO STAGES!
YOU STILL HAVE THREE OF YOUR HEART'S *USHEBTI* HOLDING UP THE GIRL.
BUT NOW YOUR THREE *USHEBTI* WILL ***SHATTER!***
BA BA BAM
DAMN SHADI ... HE SEEMS SO CONFIDENT ...
IT'S LIKE HE ALREADY KNOWS ALL MY WEAK POINTS...
BUT NO MATTER WHAT GAME HE THROWS AT ME, I CAN'T LET MY *USHEBTI* BREAK! ANZU'S LIFE DEPENDS ON IT!
TO SAVE ANZU, I HAVE TO BREAK SHADI'S *USHEBTI*... THEN THE MILLENNIUM KEY WILL SLIDE DOWN THE ROPE TO HER HAND...
AND THEN SHADI'S SPELL WILL BE BROKEN!

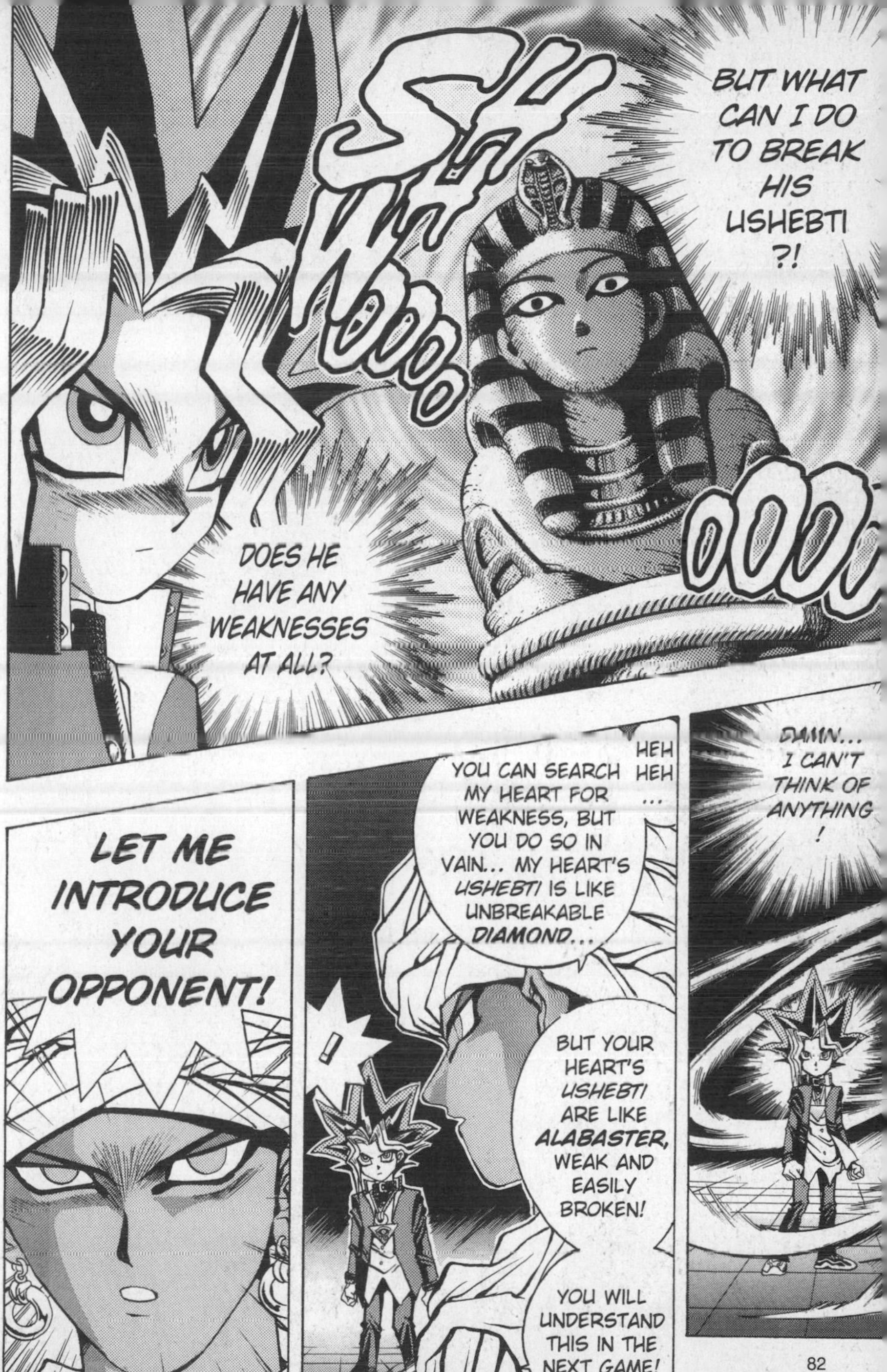
BUT WHAT CAN I DO TO BREAK HIS USHEBTI ?!
DOES HE HAVE ANY WEAKNESSES AT ALL?
DAMN... I CAN'T THINK OF ANYTHING!
HEH HEH ...
YOU CAN SEARCH MY HEART FOR WEAKNESS, BUT YOU DO SO IN VAIN... MY HEART'S USHEBTI IS LIKE UNBREAKABLE DIAMOND...
!
BUT YOUR HEART'S USHEBTI ARE LIKE ALABASTER, WEAK AND EASILY BROKEN!
YOU WILL UNDERSTAND THIS IN THE NEXT GAME!
LET ME INTRODUCE YOUR OPPONENT!

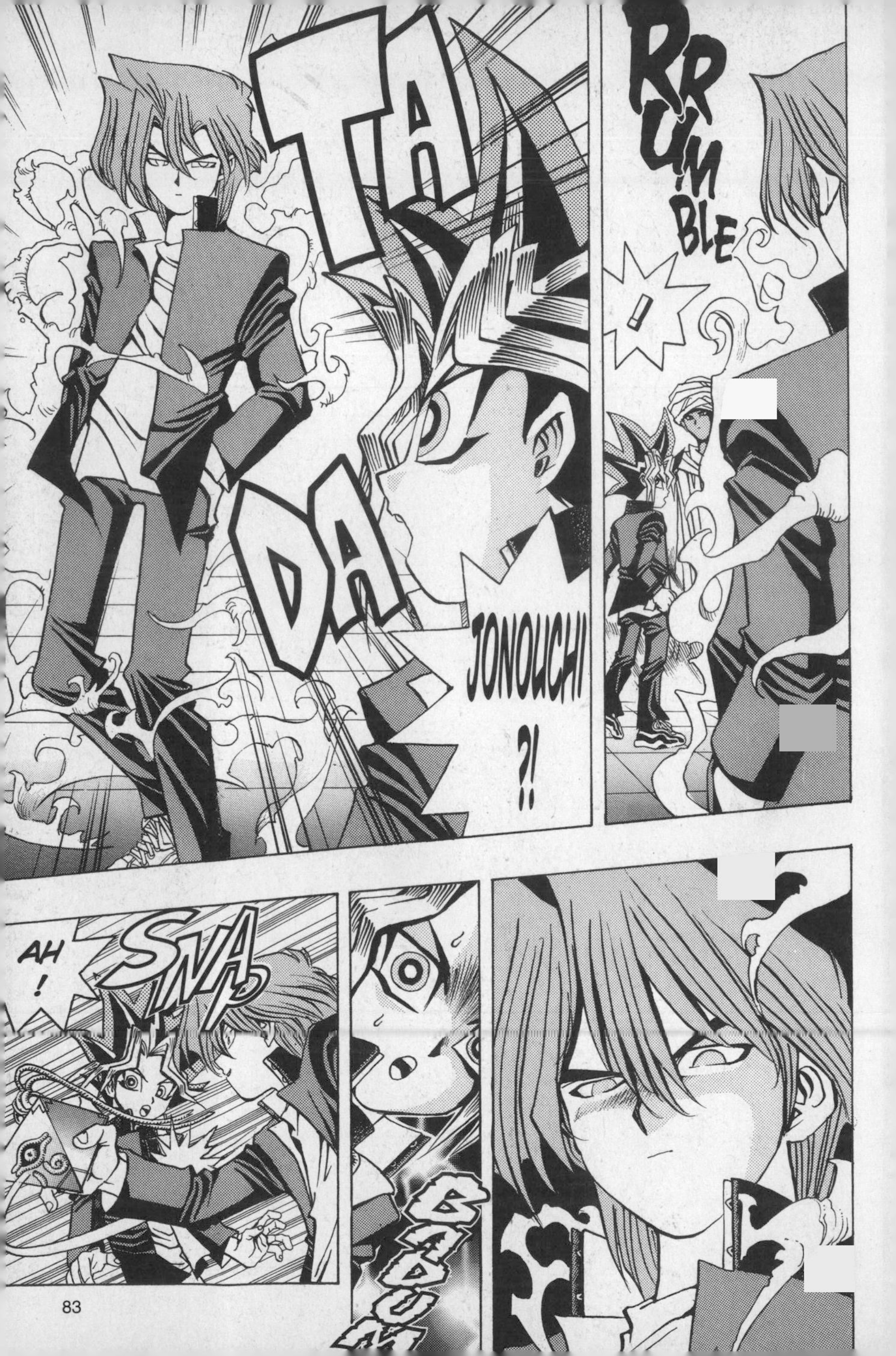
RRUMBLE
!
TA
DA
JONOUCHI ?!
BADU
SNA
AH !

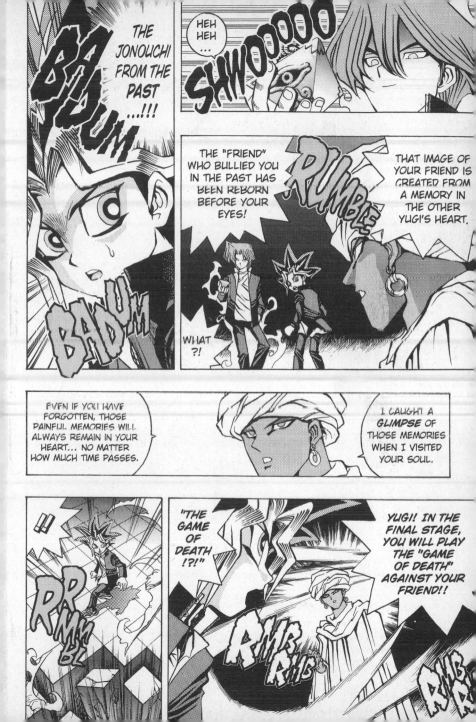

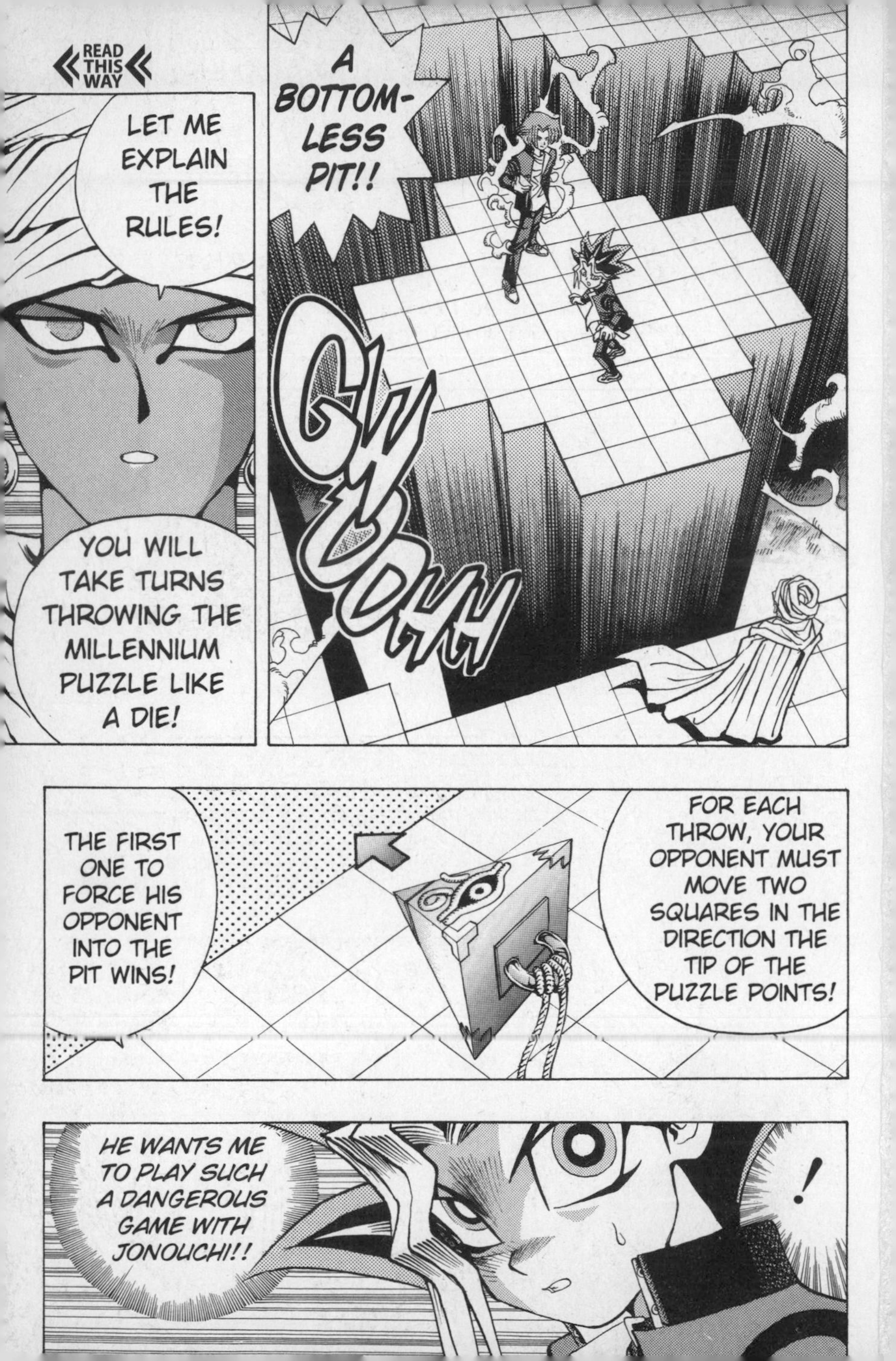
READ THIS WAY
A BOTTOMLESS PIT!!
LET ME EXPLAIN THE RULES!
YOU WILL TAKE TURNS THROWING THE MILLENNIUM PUZZLE LIKE A DIE!
FOR EACH THROW, YOUR OPPONENT MUST MOVE TWO SQUARES IN THE DIRECTION THE TIP OF THE PUZZLE POINTS!
THE FIRST ONE TO FORCE HIS OPPONENT INTO THE PIT WINS!
!
HE WANTS ME TO PLAY SUCH A DANGEROUS GAME WITH JONOUCHI!!

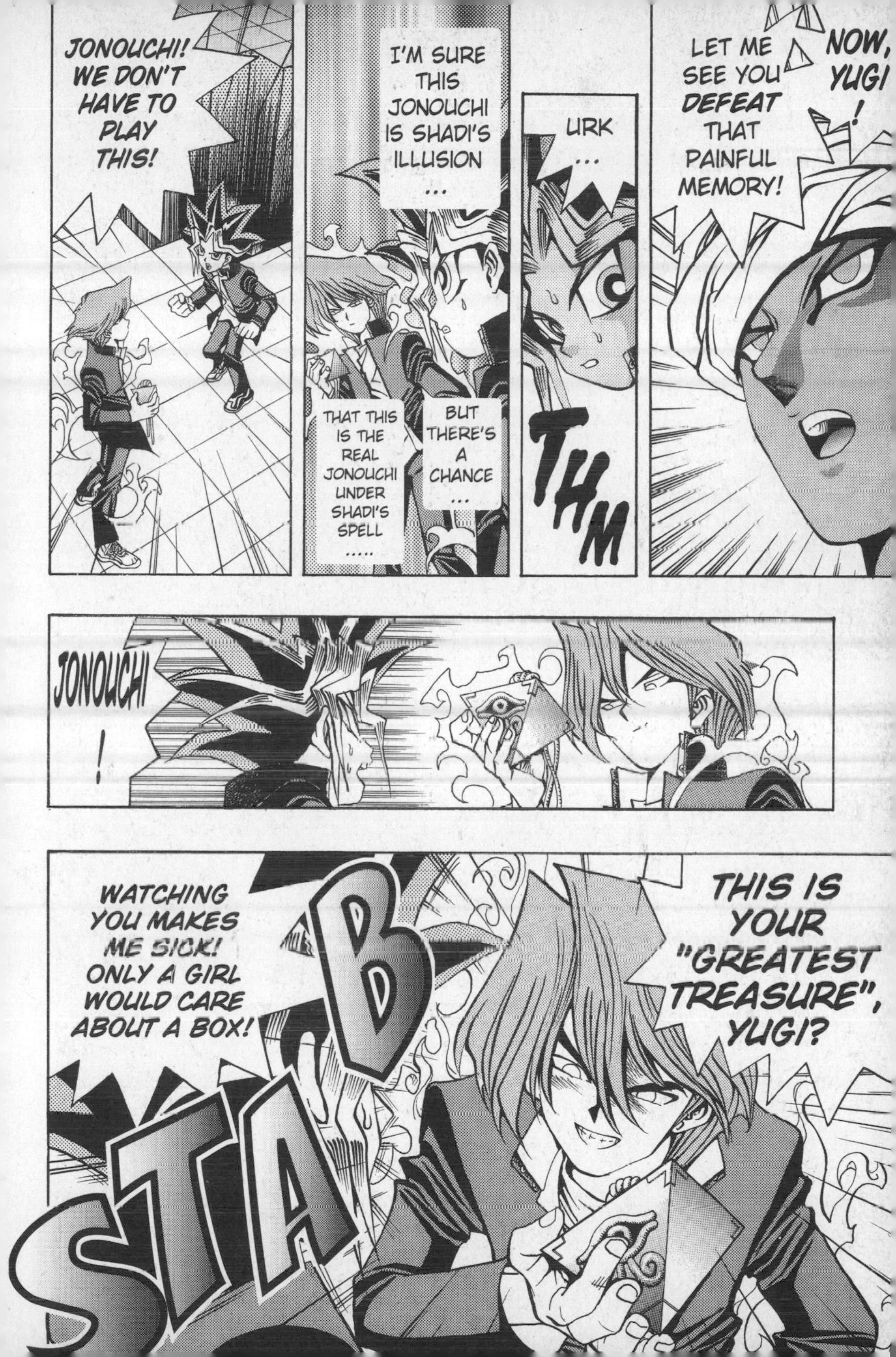
NOW, YUGI!
LET ME SEE YOU DEFEAT THAT PAINFUL MEMORY!
URK ...
THM
I'M SURE THIS JONOUCHI IS SHADI'S ILLUSION ...
BUT THERE'S A CHANCE ...
THAT THIS IS THE REAL JONOUCHI UNDER SHADI'S SPELL .....
JONOUCHI! WE DON'T HAVE TO PLAY THIS!
JONOUCHI !
THIS IS YOUR "GREATEST TREASURE", YUGI?
WATCHING YOU MAKES ME SICK! ONLY A GIRL WOULD CARE ABOUT A BOX!
STAB

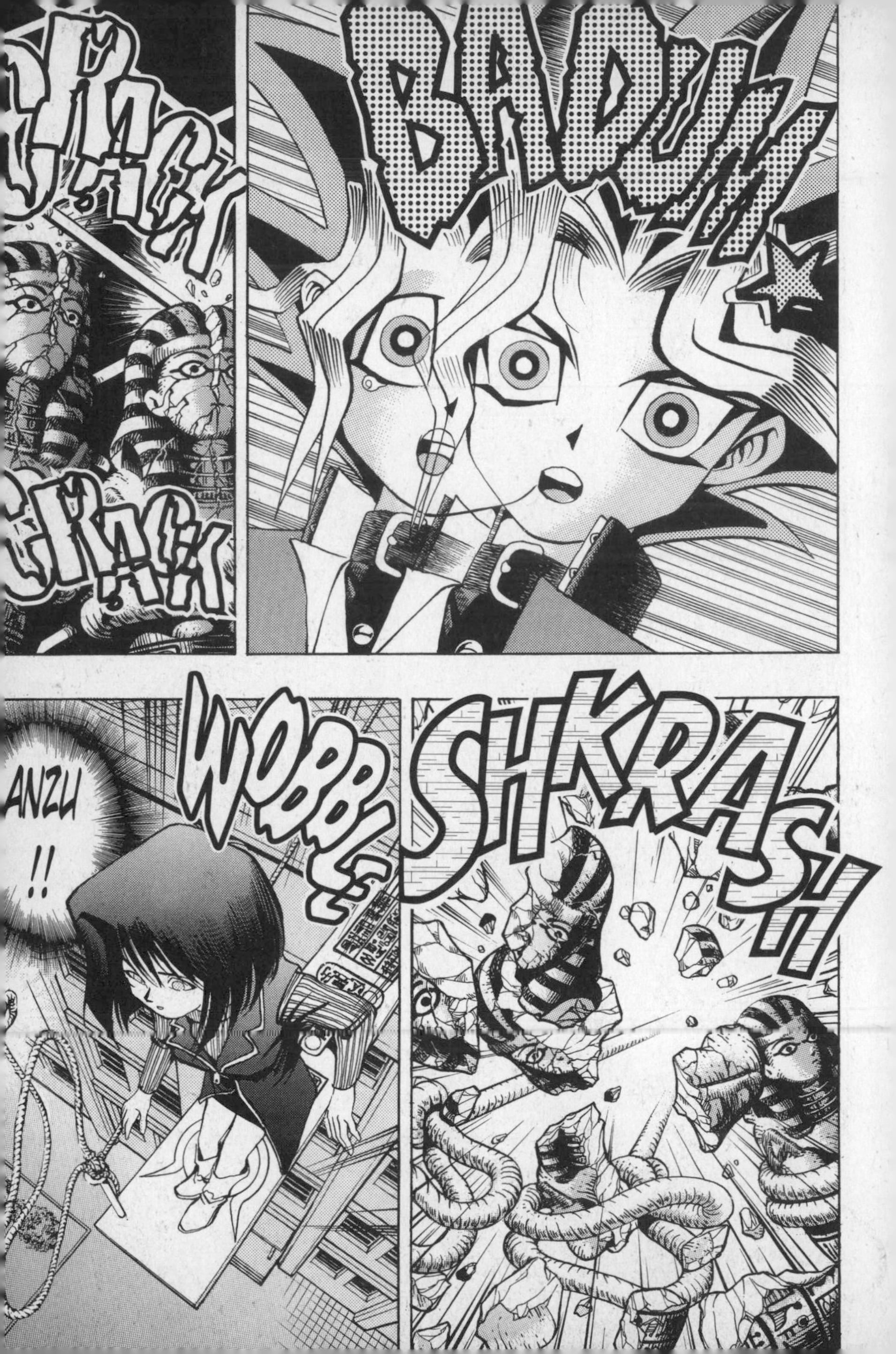
BADUM
CRACK
CRACK
SHKRASH
WOBBLE
ANZU !!

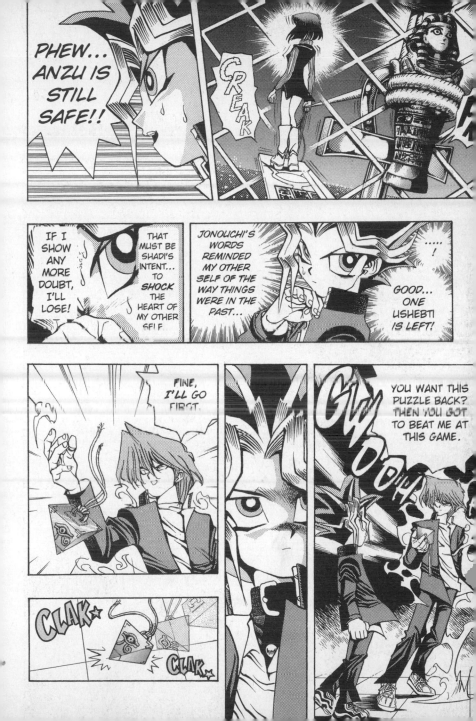

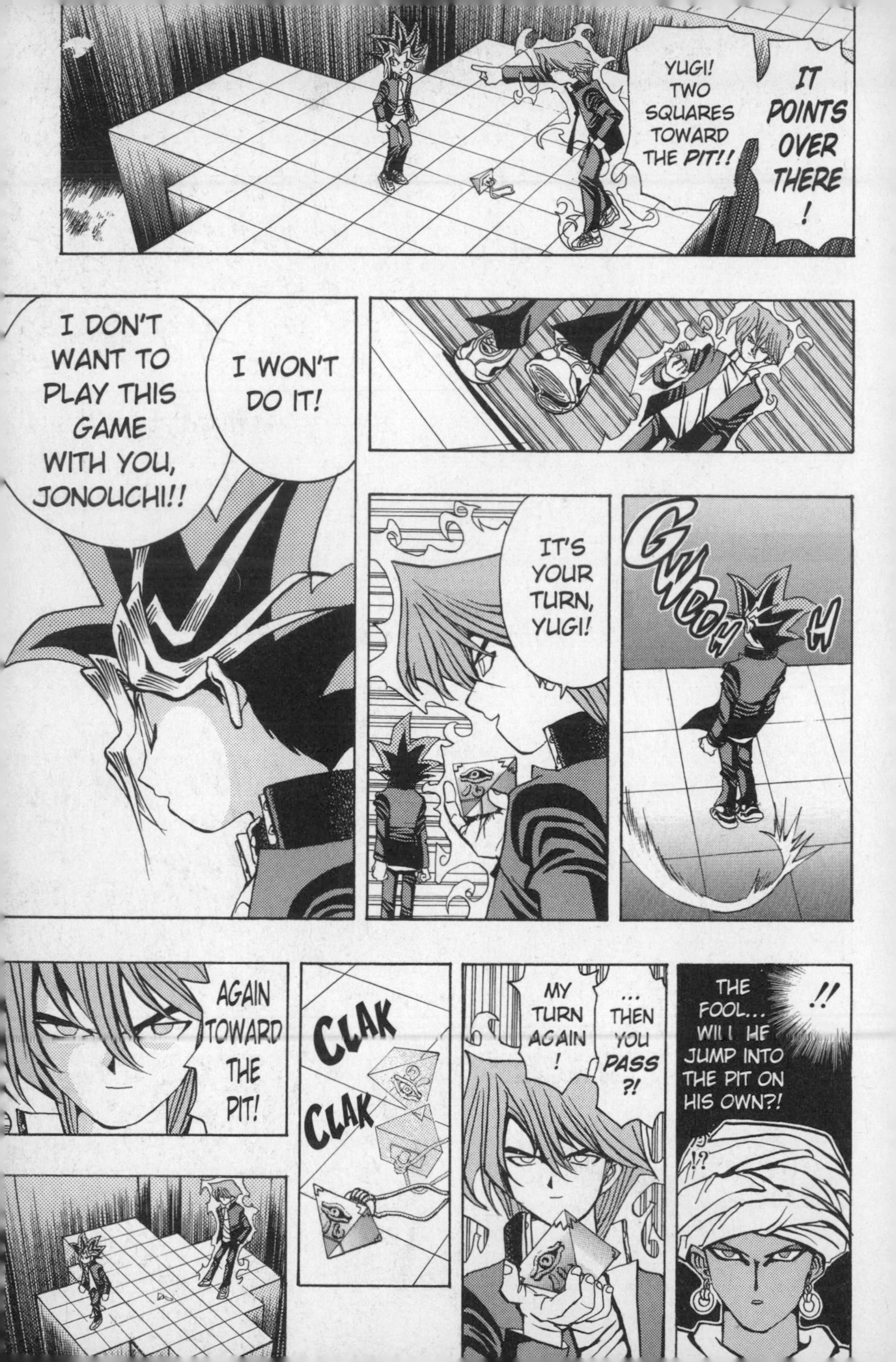
IT POINTS OVER THERE !
YUGI! TWO SQUARES TOWARD THE PIT!!
GWOOOHH
IT'S YOUR TURN, YUGI!
I WON'T DO IT!
I DON'T WANT TO PLAY THIS GAME WITH YOU, JONOUCHI!!
!!
THE FOOL... WILL HE JUMP INTO THE PIT ON HIS OWN?!
!?
... THEN YOU PASS ?!
MY TURN AGAIN !
CLAK
CLAK
AGAIN TOWARD THE PIT!

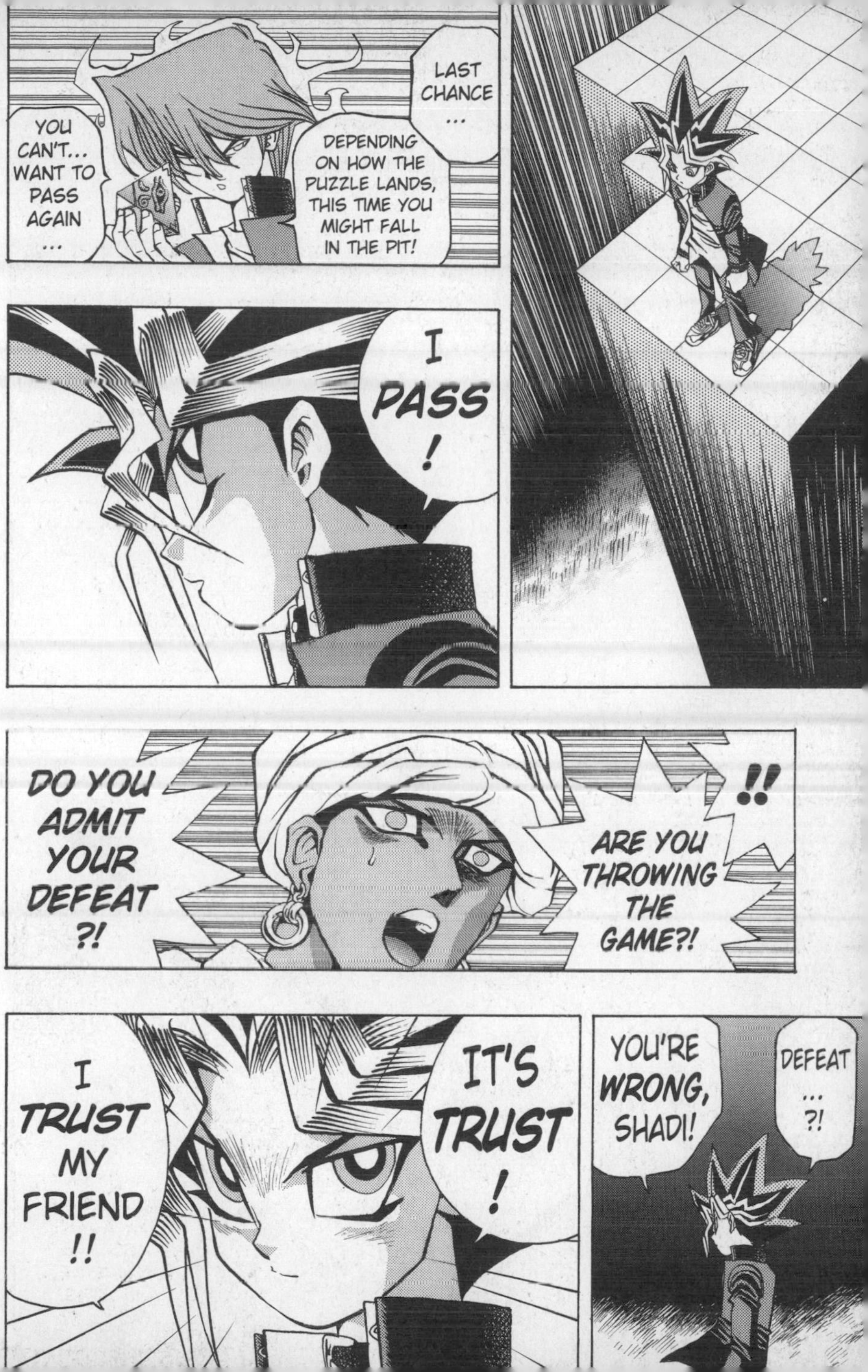
LAST CHANCE ...
DEPENDING ON HOW THE PUZZLE LANDS, THIS TIME YOU MIGHT FALL IN THE PIT!
YOU CAN'T... WANT TO PASS AGAIN ...
I PASS!
!!
ARE YOU THROWING THE GAME?!
DO YOU ADMIT YOUR DEFEAT ?!
DEFEAT ... ?!
YOU'RE WRONG, SHADI!
IT'S TRUST!
I TRUST MY FRIEND!!

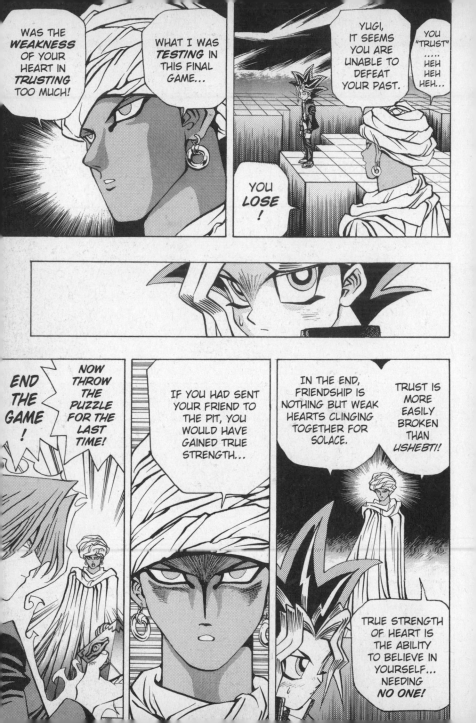

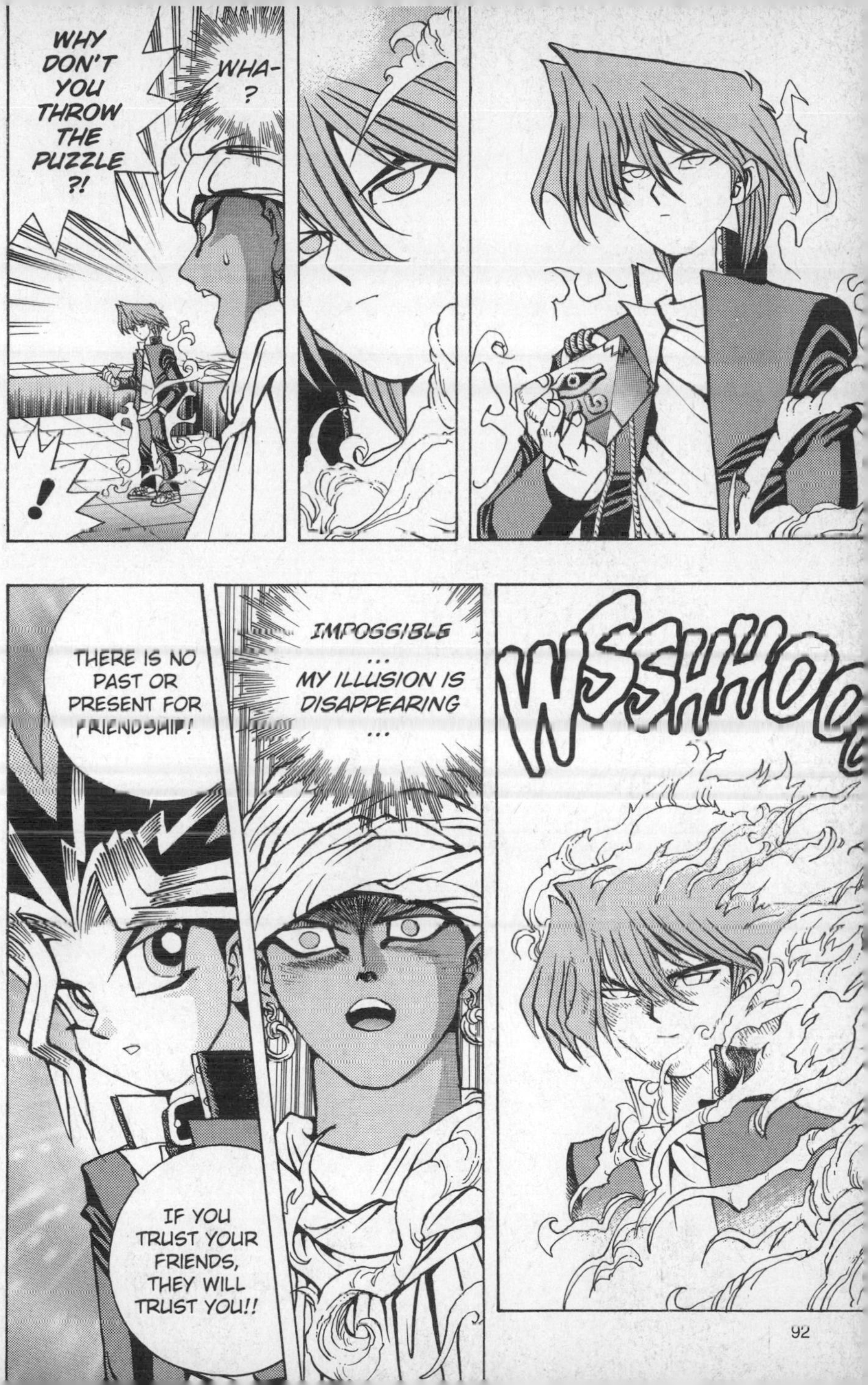
WHY DON'T YOU THROW THE PUZZLE ?!
WHA- ?
WSSHHOOO
IMPOSSIBLE ... MY ILLUSION IS DISAPPEARING ...
THERE IS NO PAST OR PRESENT FOR FRIENDSHIP!
IF YOU TRUST YOUR FRIENDS, THEY WILL TRUST YOU!!

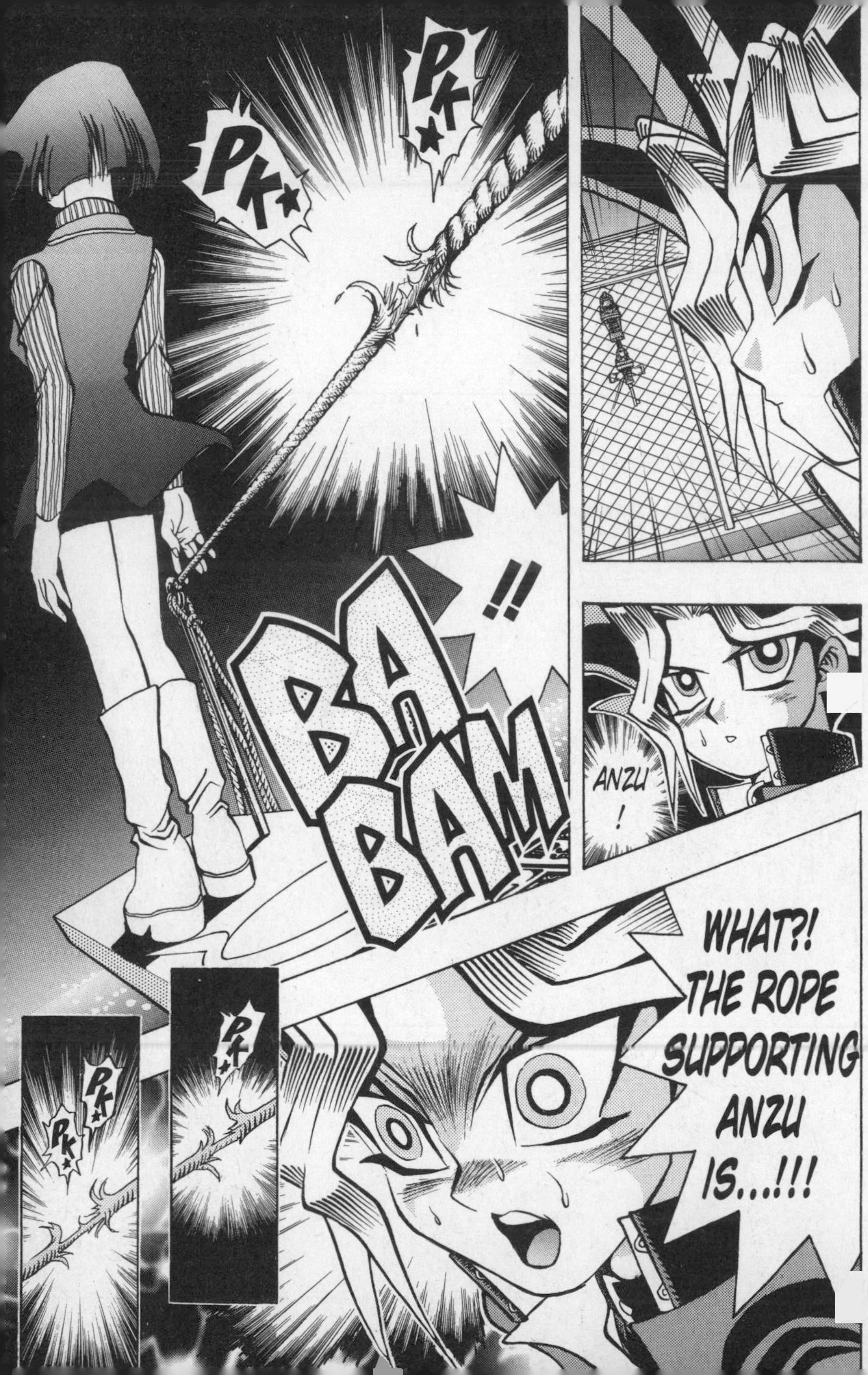
ANZU!
PK
PK
BA BAM
!!
WHAT?! THE ROPE SUPPORTING ANZU IS...!!!
PK
PK
PK

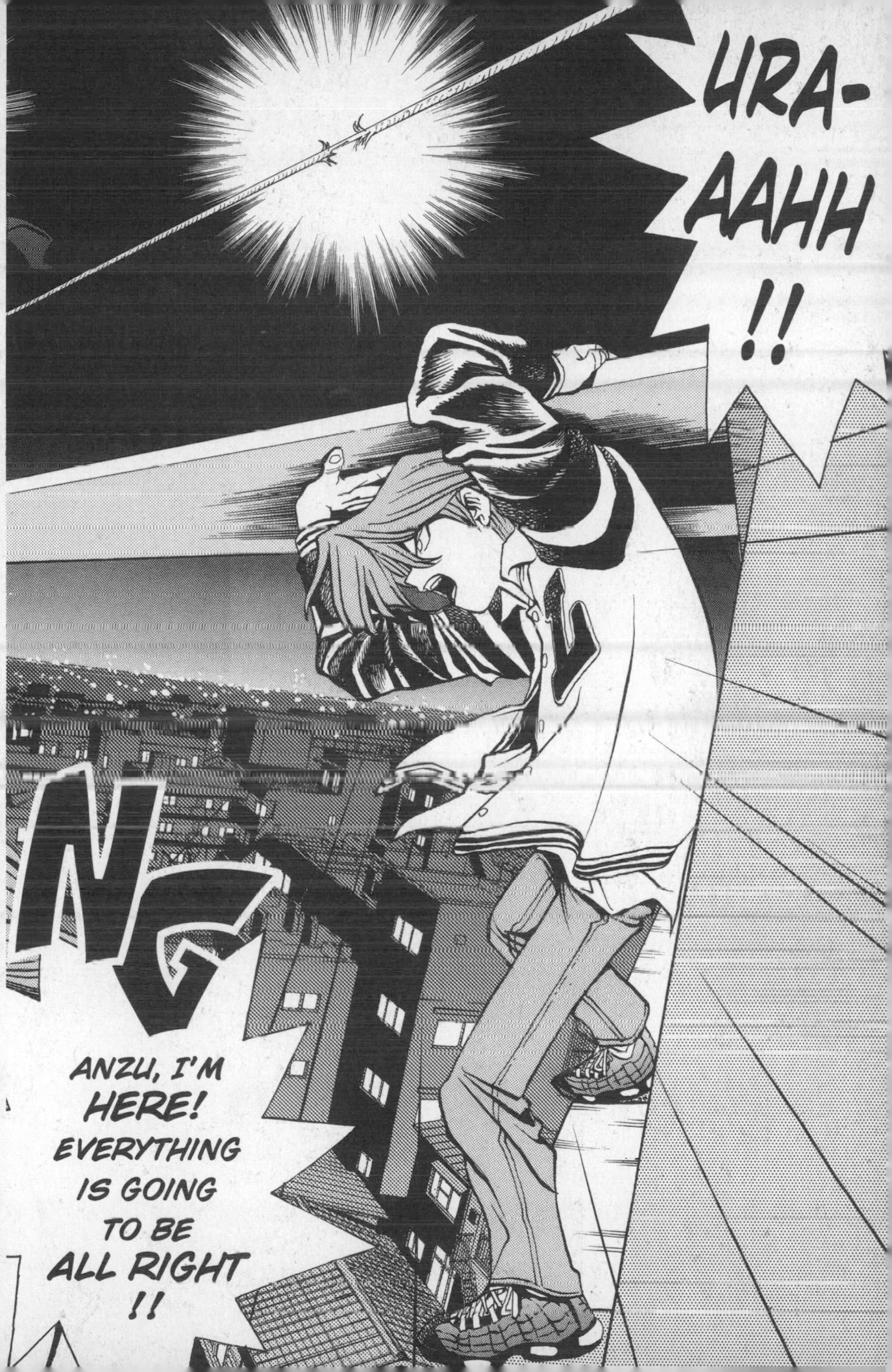
URA-AAHH !!
NG
ANZU, I'M HERE! EVERYTHING IS GOING TO BE ALL RIGHT !!

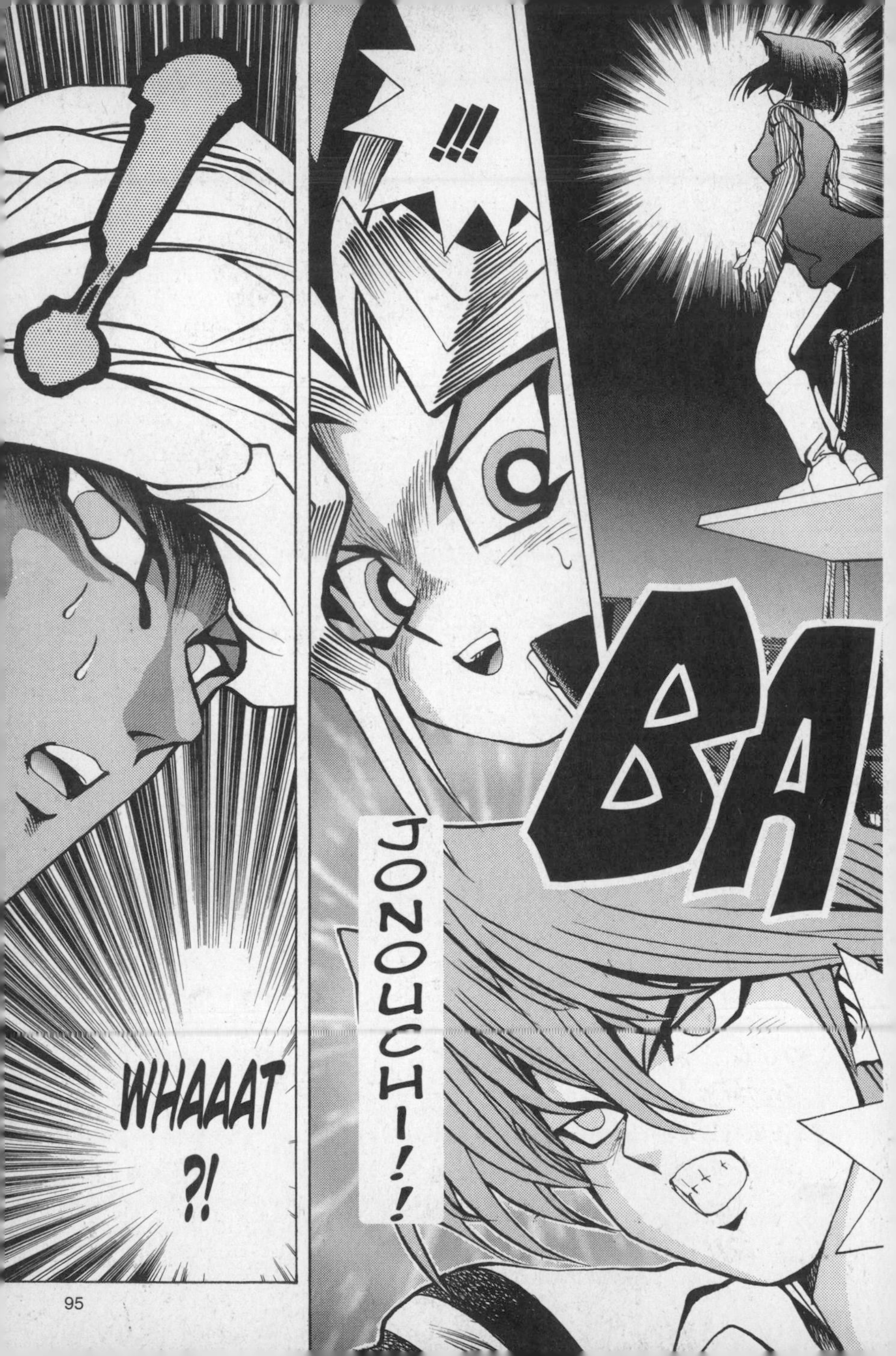
!!!!
BA
JONOUCHI!!!
!
WHAAAT ?!

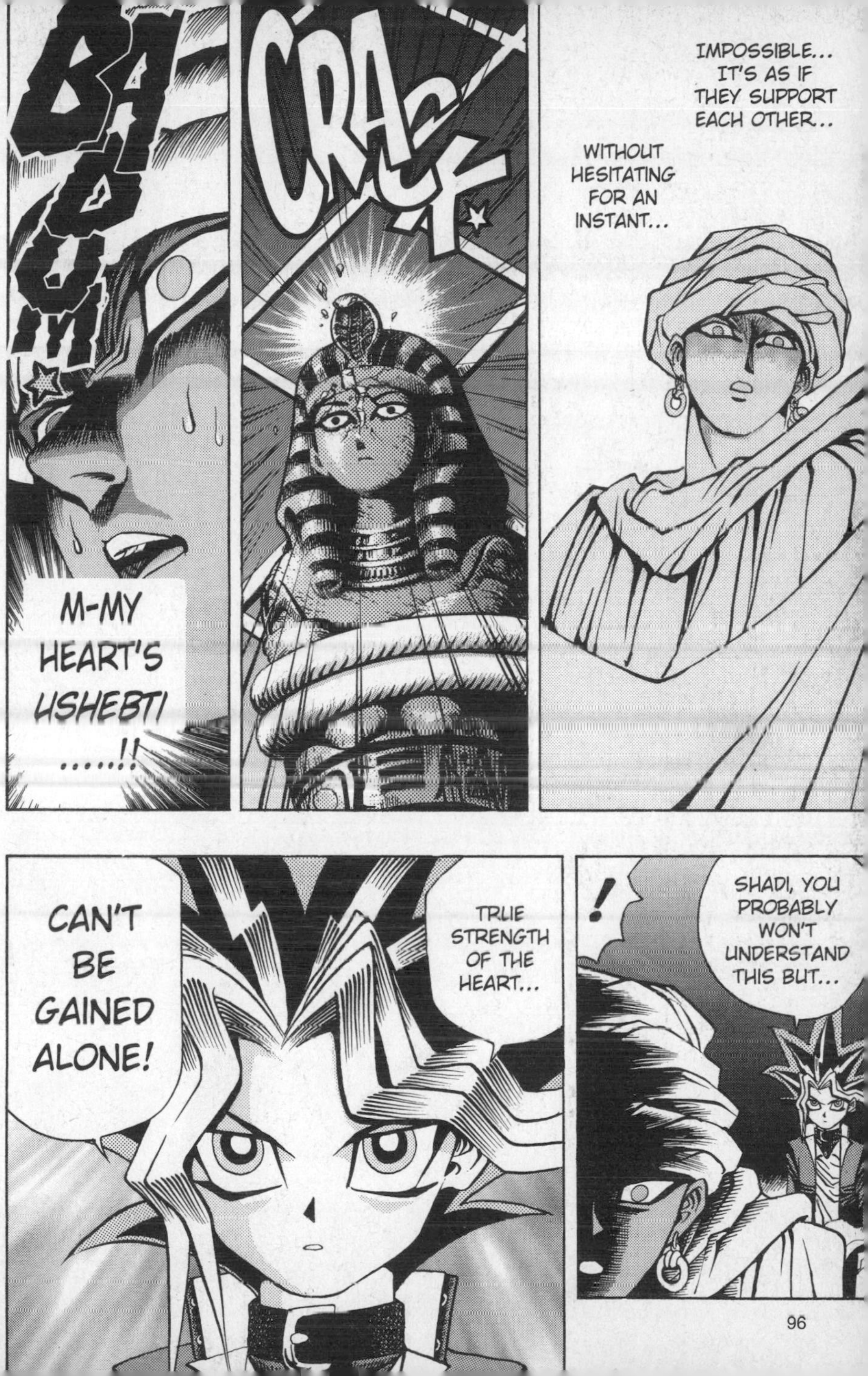
IMPOSSIBLE... IT'S AS IF THEY SUPPORT EACH OTHER...
WITHOUT HESITATING FOR AN INSTANT...
CRACK
M-MY HEART'S USHEBTI ......!!
!
SHADI, YOU PROBABLY WON'T UNDERSTAND THIS BUT...
TRUE STRENGTH OF THE HEART...
CAN'T BE GAINED ALONE!

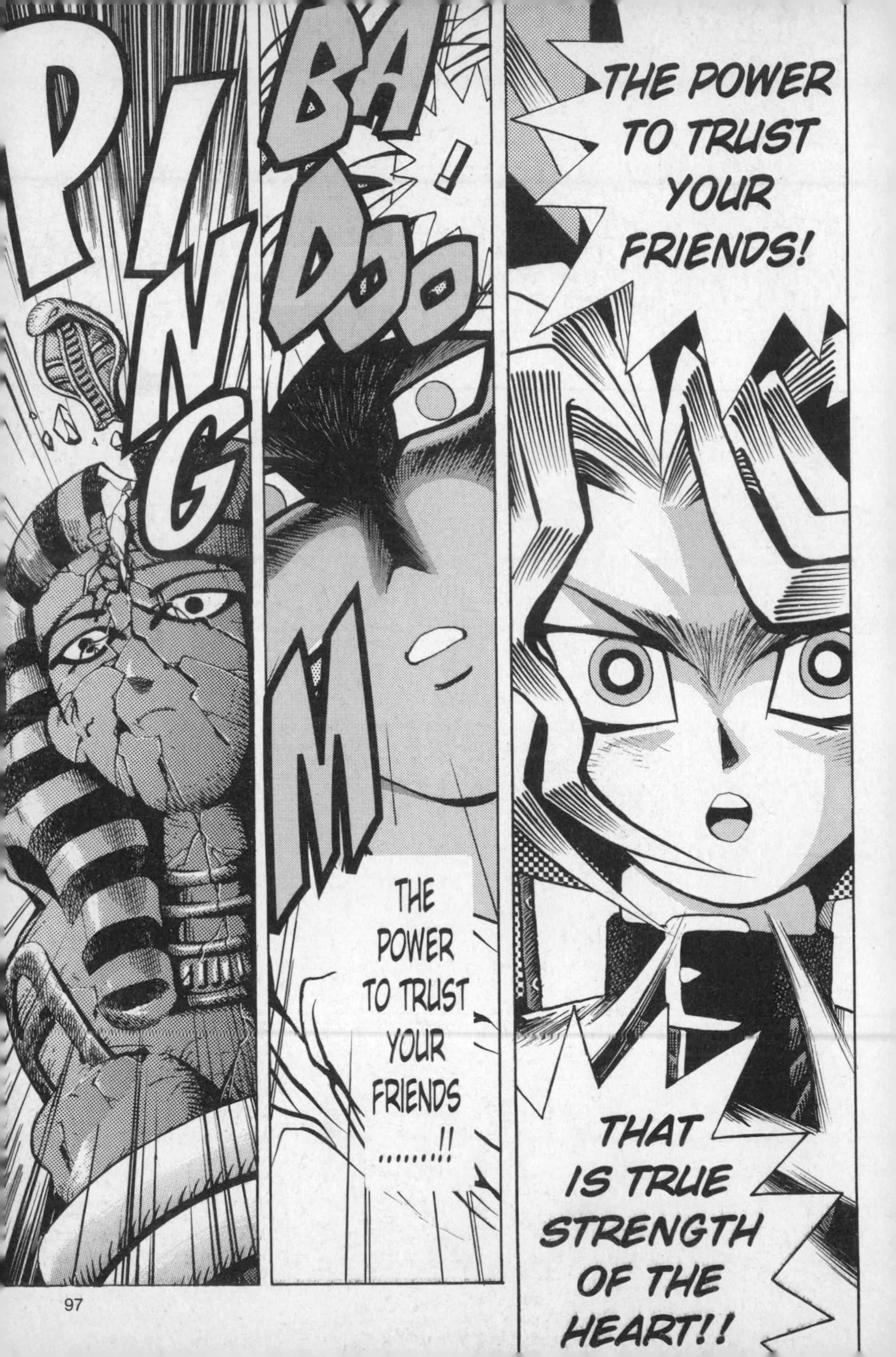
THE POWER TO TRUST YOUR FRIENDS!
THAT IS TRUE STRENGTH OF THE HEART!!
BA! DOOM
THE POWER TO TRUST YOUR FRIENDS ........!!
PING

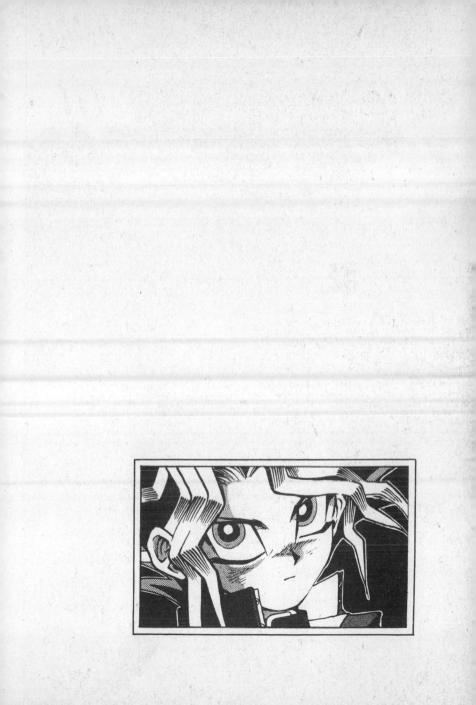

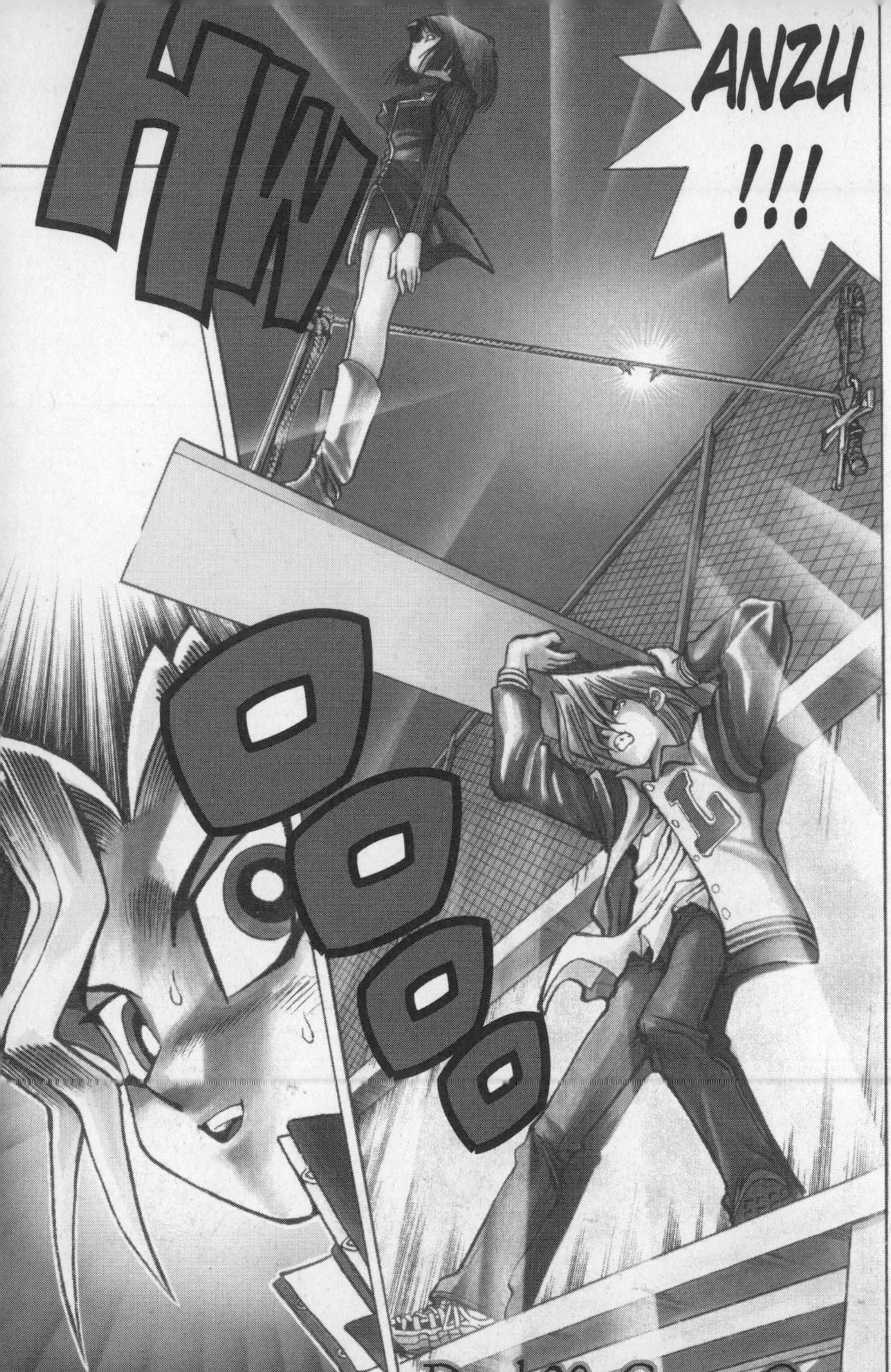
ANZU !!!
HWOOOO

Duel 20: Game Over

# Duel 20: Game Over

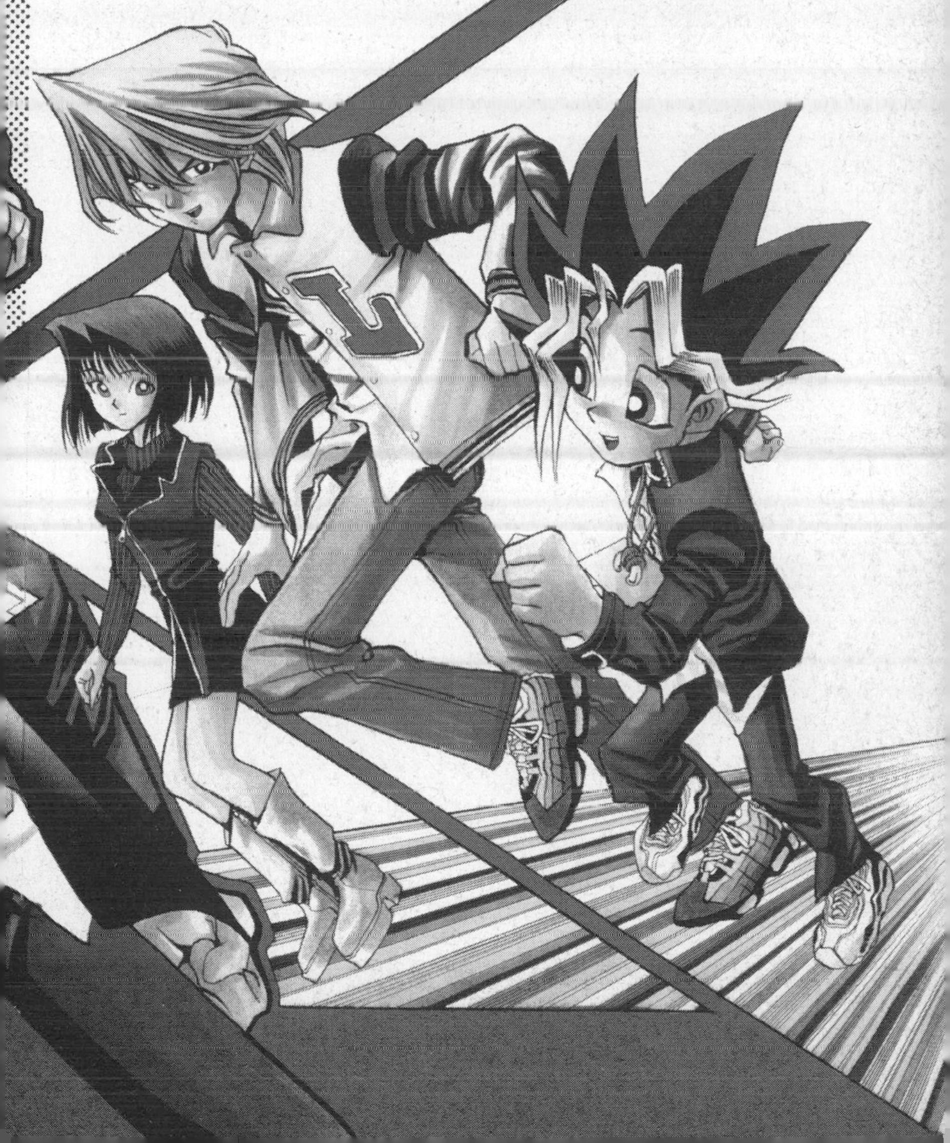

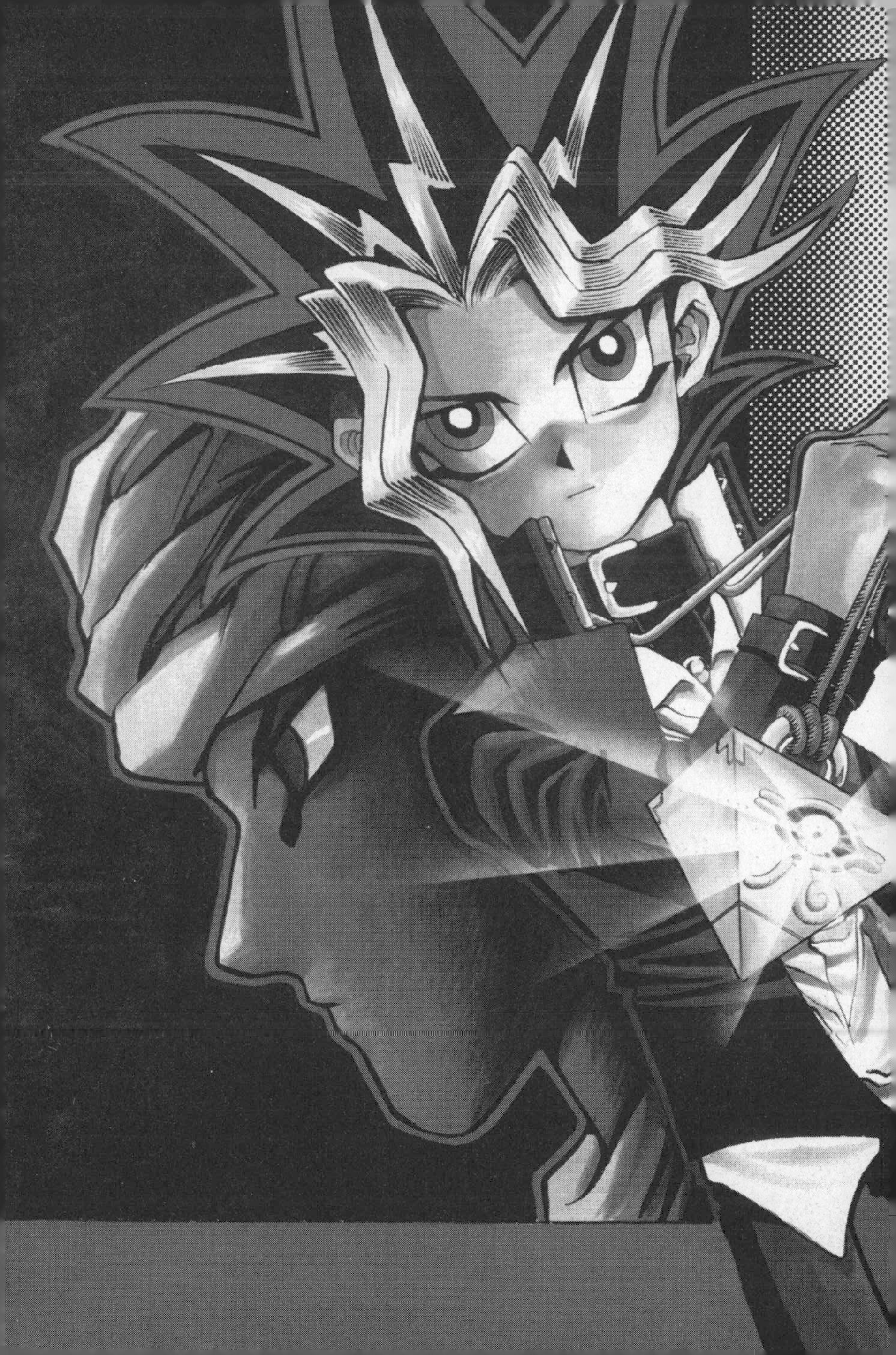

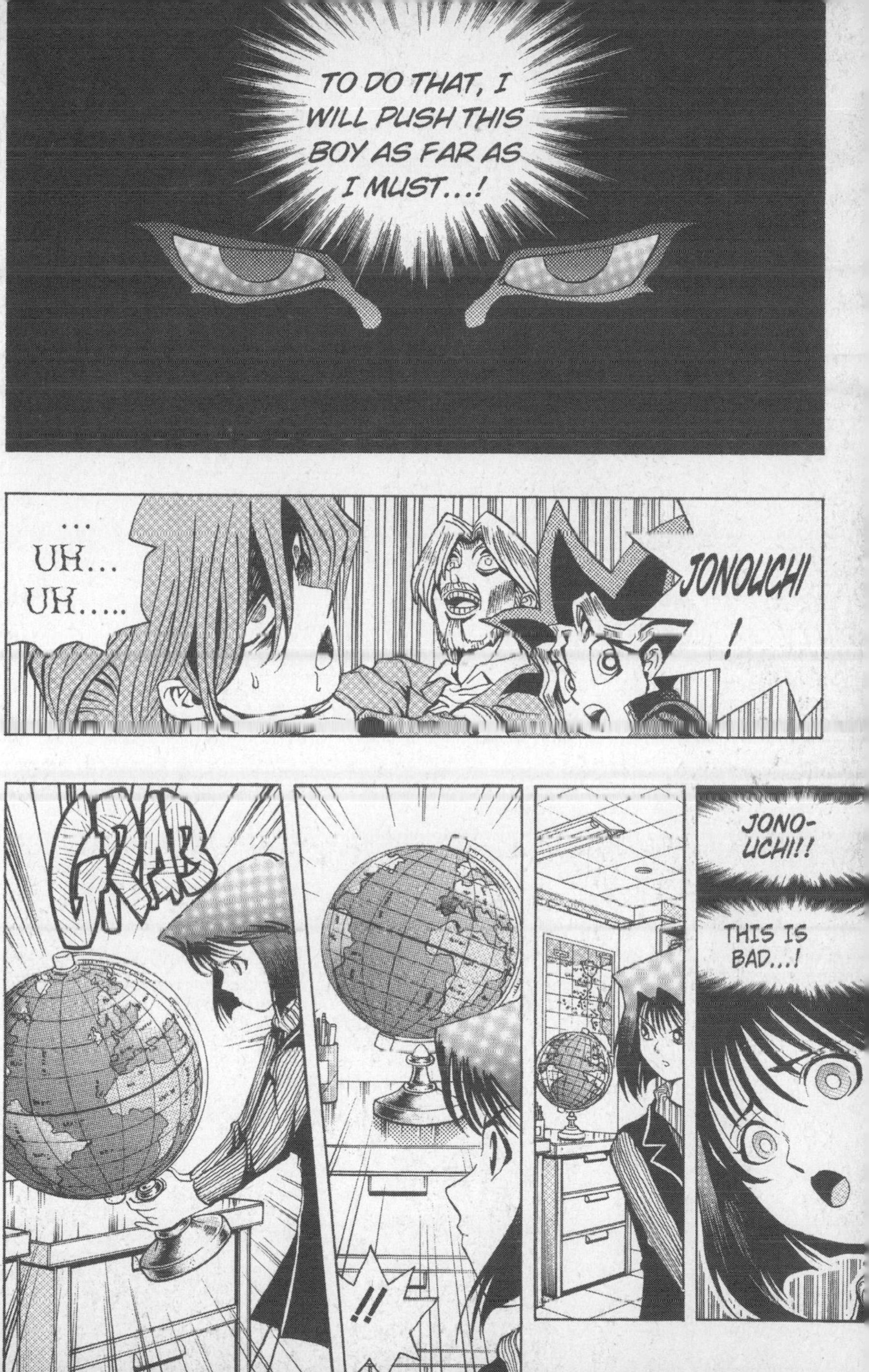
TO DO THAT, I WILL PUSH THIS BOY AS FAR AS I MUST...!
JONOUCHI!
... UH... UH.....
JONO-UCHI!!
THIS IS BAD...!
!!
GRAB

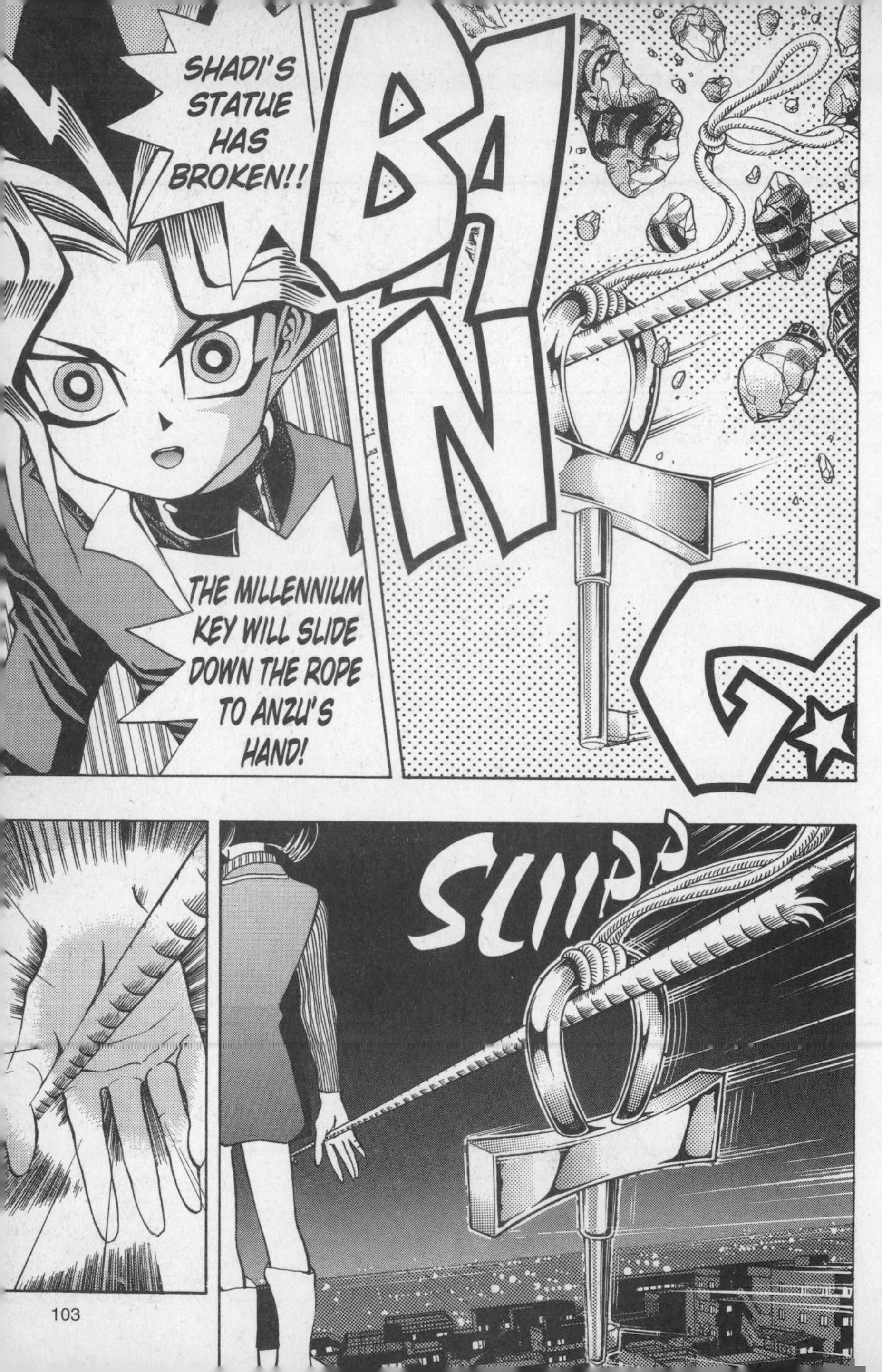
BANG
SHADI'S STATUE HAS BROKEN!!
THE MILLENNIUM KEY WILL SLIDE DOWN THE ROPE TO ANZU'S HAND!
SLIPP

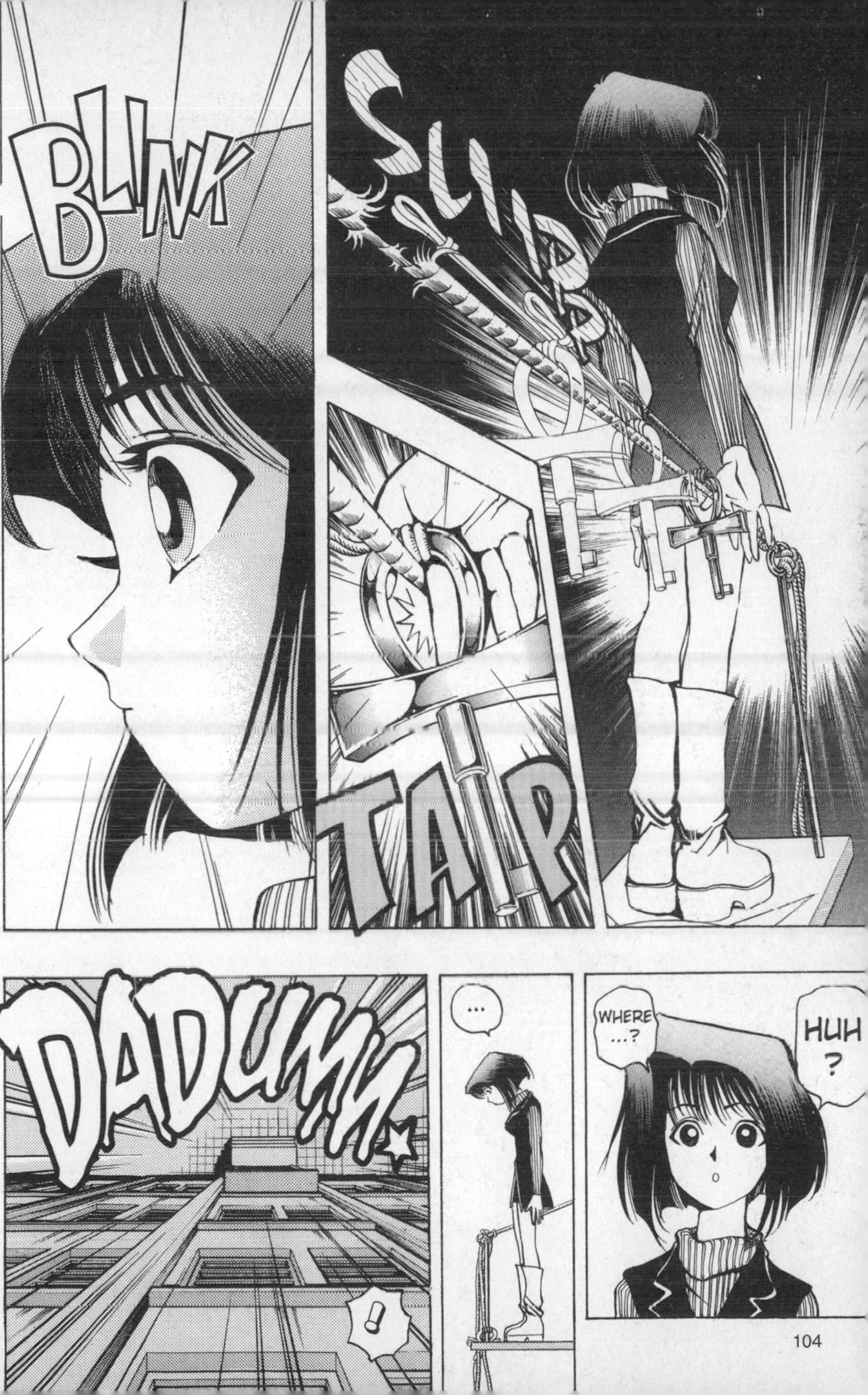
SLIIIP
TAP
BLINK
HUH ?
WHERE ...?
...
DADUMM
!

READ THIS WAY

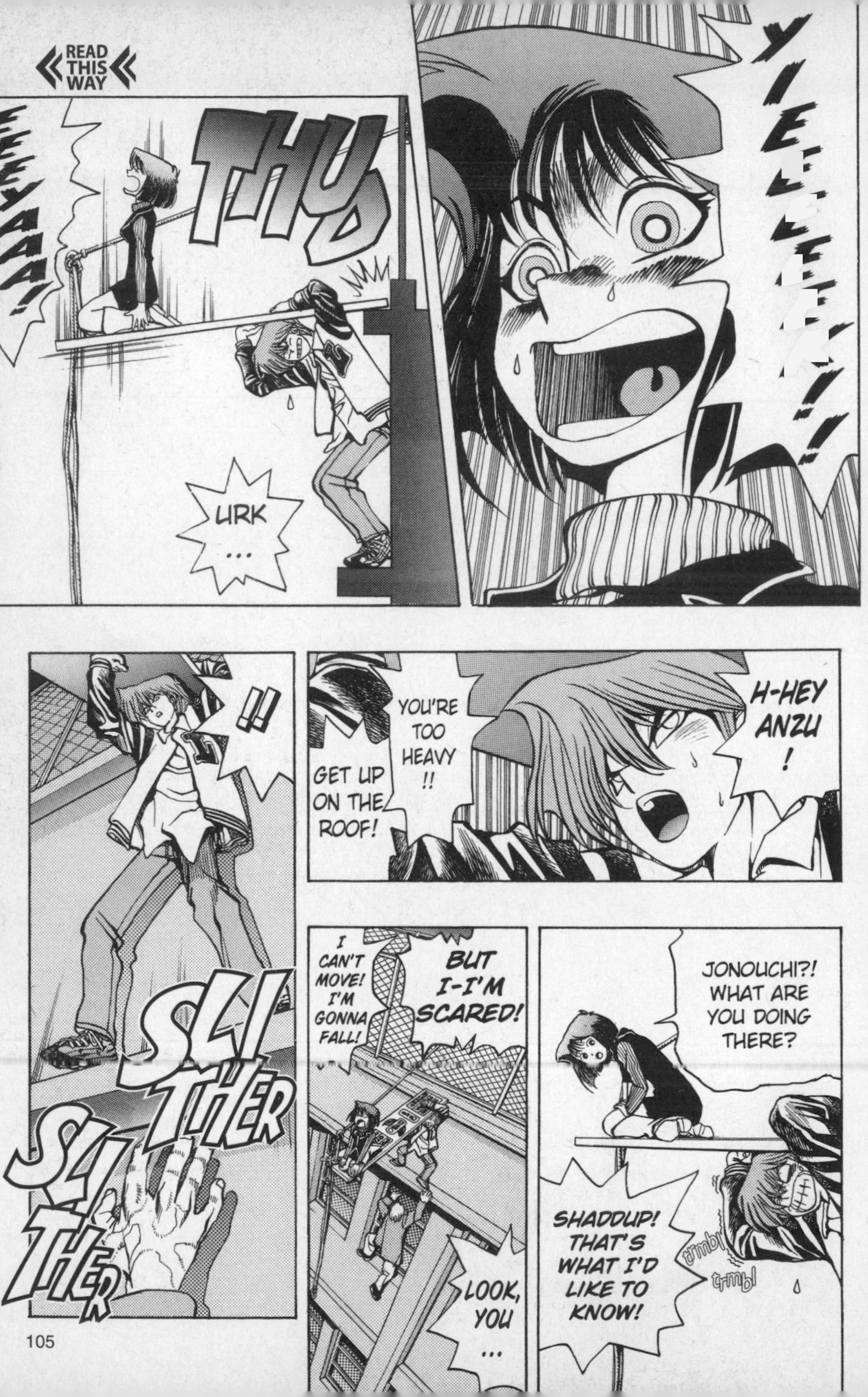

YIEEEEEK!!!
EEEEYAAAA!
THUD
URK ...
H-HEY ANZU!
YOU'RE TOO HEAVY!!
GET UP ON THE ROOF!
JONOUCHI?! WHAT ARE YOU DOING THERE?
SHADDUP! THAT'S WHAT I'D LIKE TO KNOW!
trmbl
trmbl
BUT I-I'M SCARED!
I CAN'T MOVE! I'M GONNA FALL!
LOOK, YOU ...
!!
SLITHER
SLITHER

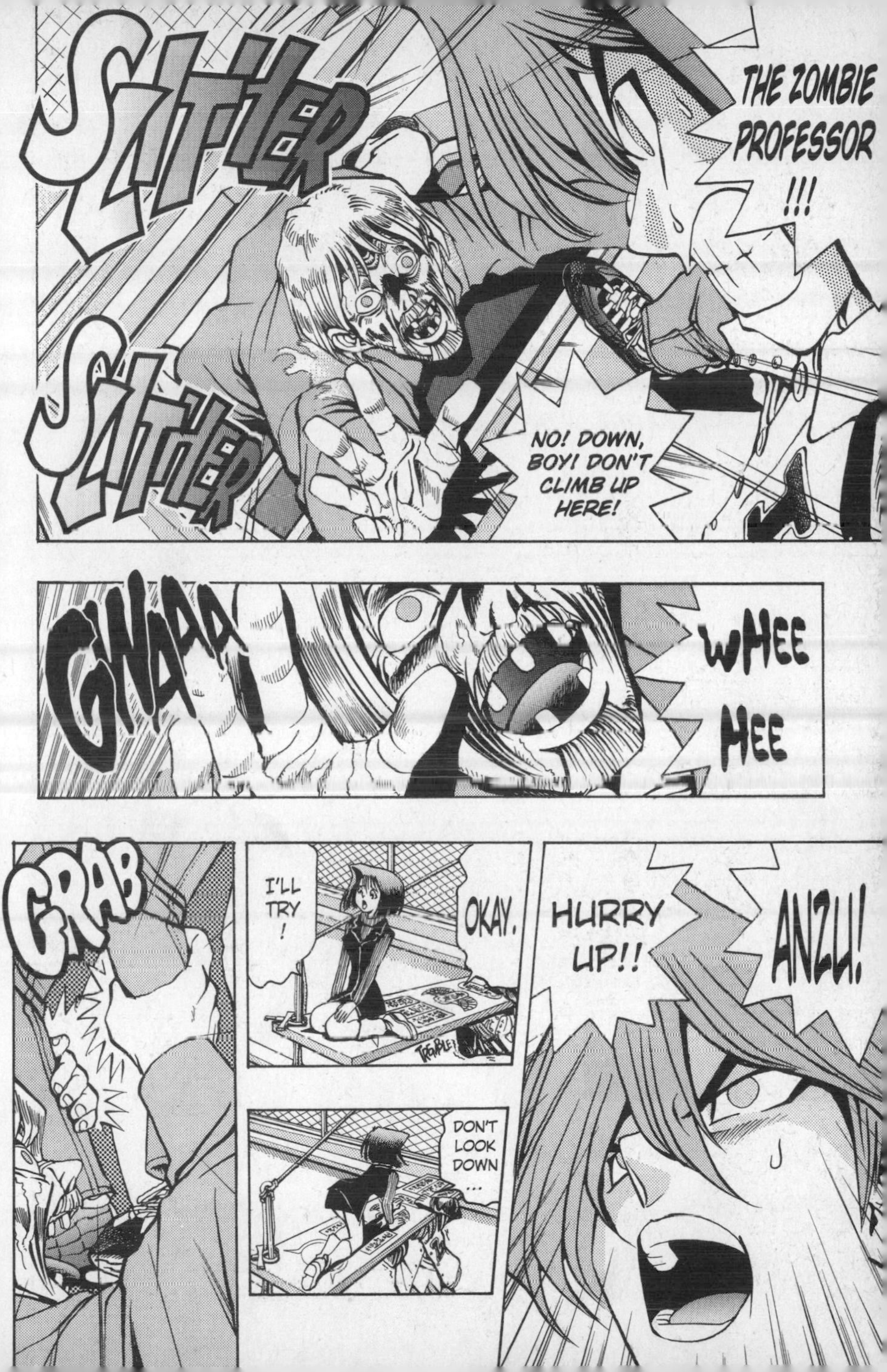
THE ZOMBIE PROFESSOR !!!
SLITHER
NO! DOWN, BOY! DON'T CLIMB UP HERE!
SLITHER
WHEE HEE
GNAA
ANZU!
HURRY UP!!
OKAY.
I'LL TRY !
DON'T LOOK DOWN ...
GRAB

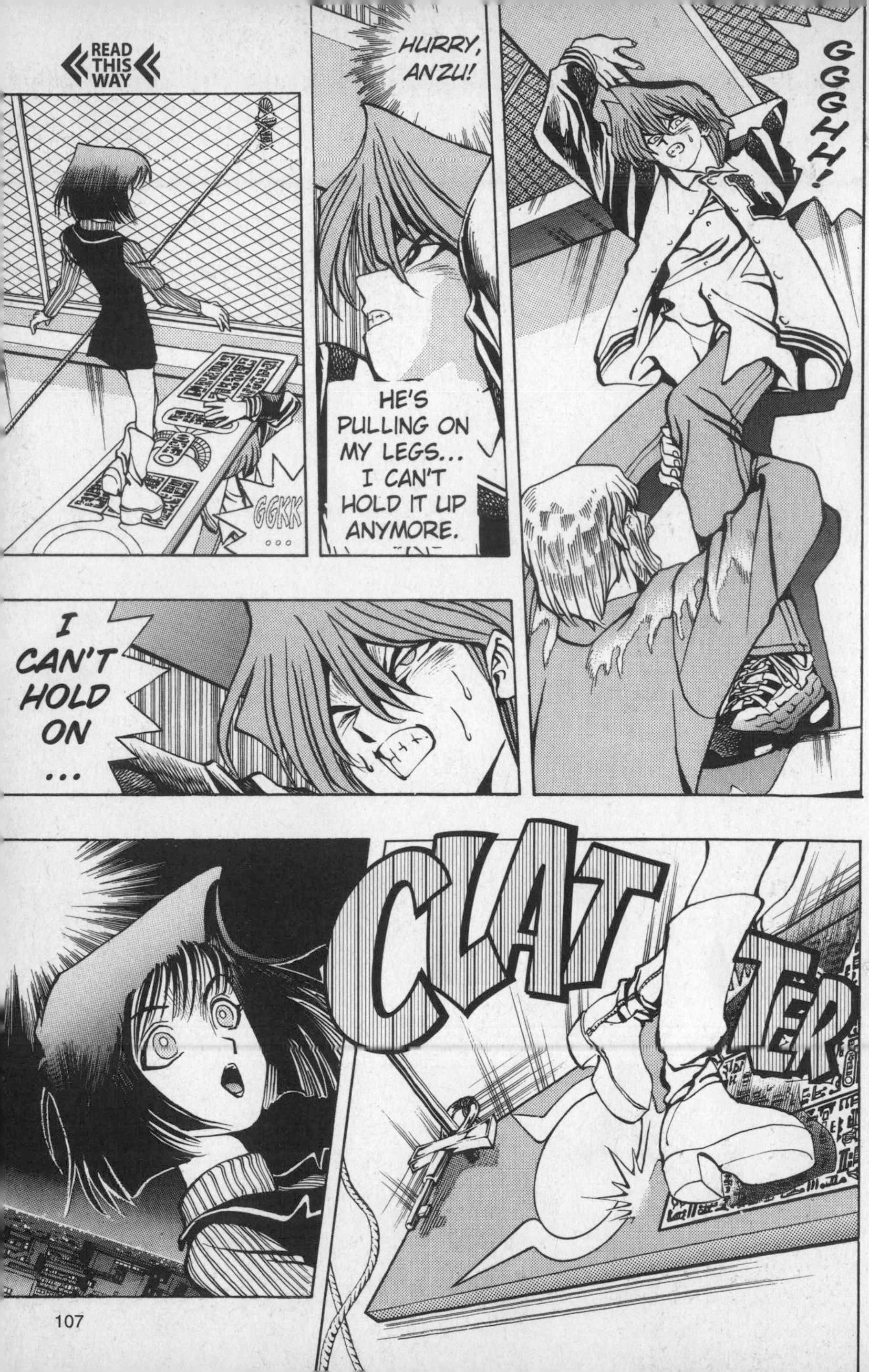
READ THIS WAY
GGGHH!
HURRY, ANZU!
HE'S PULLING ON MY LEGS... I CAN'T HOLD IT UP ANYMORE.
GGKK...
I CAN'T HOLD ON...
CLATTER

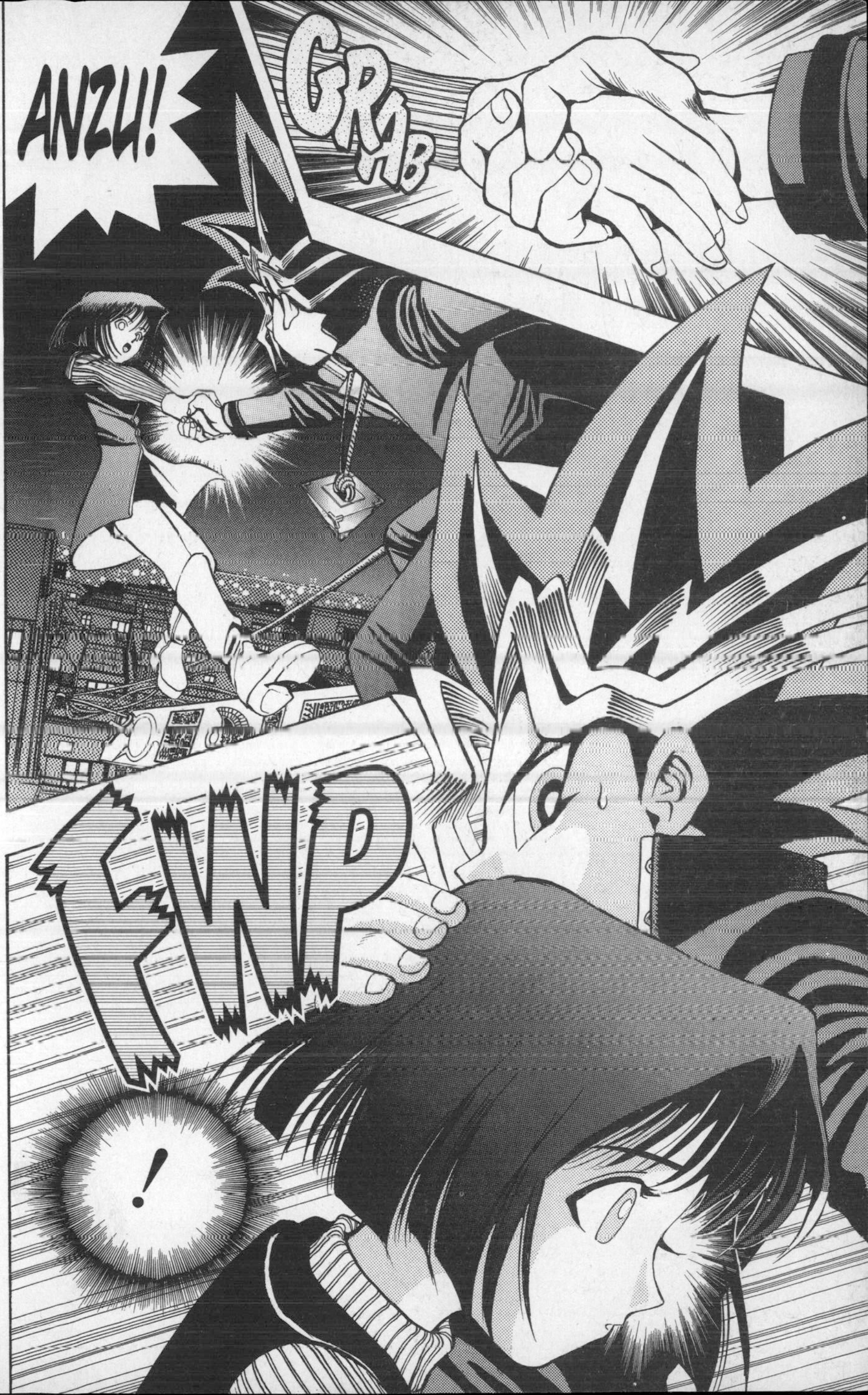
GRAB
ANZU!
FWP
!

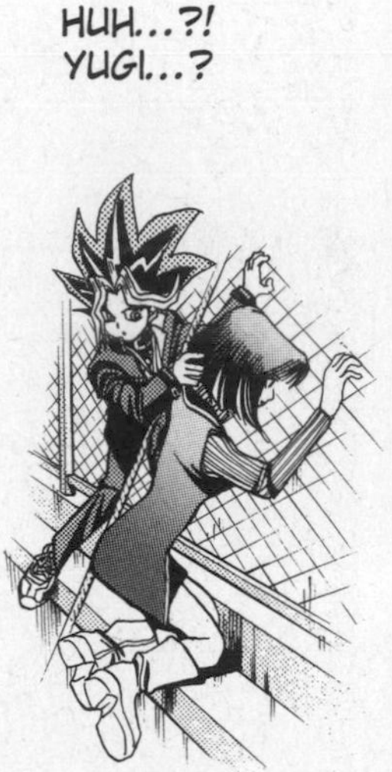
HUH...?!
YUGI...?

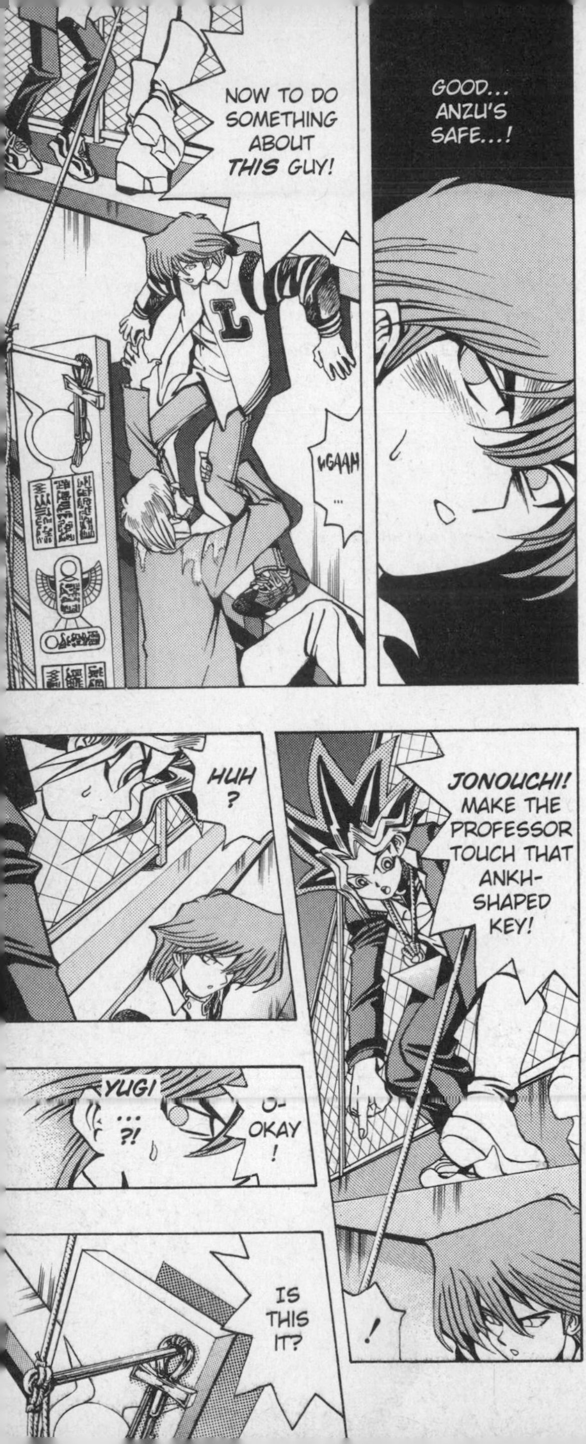
GOOD... ANZU'S SAFE...!
NOW TO DO SOMETHING ABOUT THIS GUY!
UGAAH ...
JONOUCHI! MAKE THE PROFESSOR TOUCH THAT ANKH-SHAPED KEY!
HUH ?
YUGI ... ?!
O-OKAY !
IS THIS IT?
!

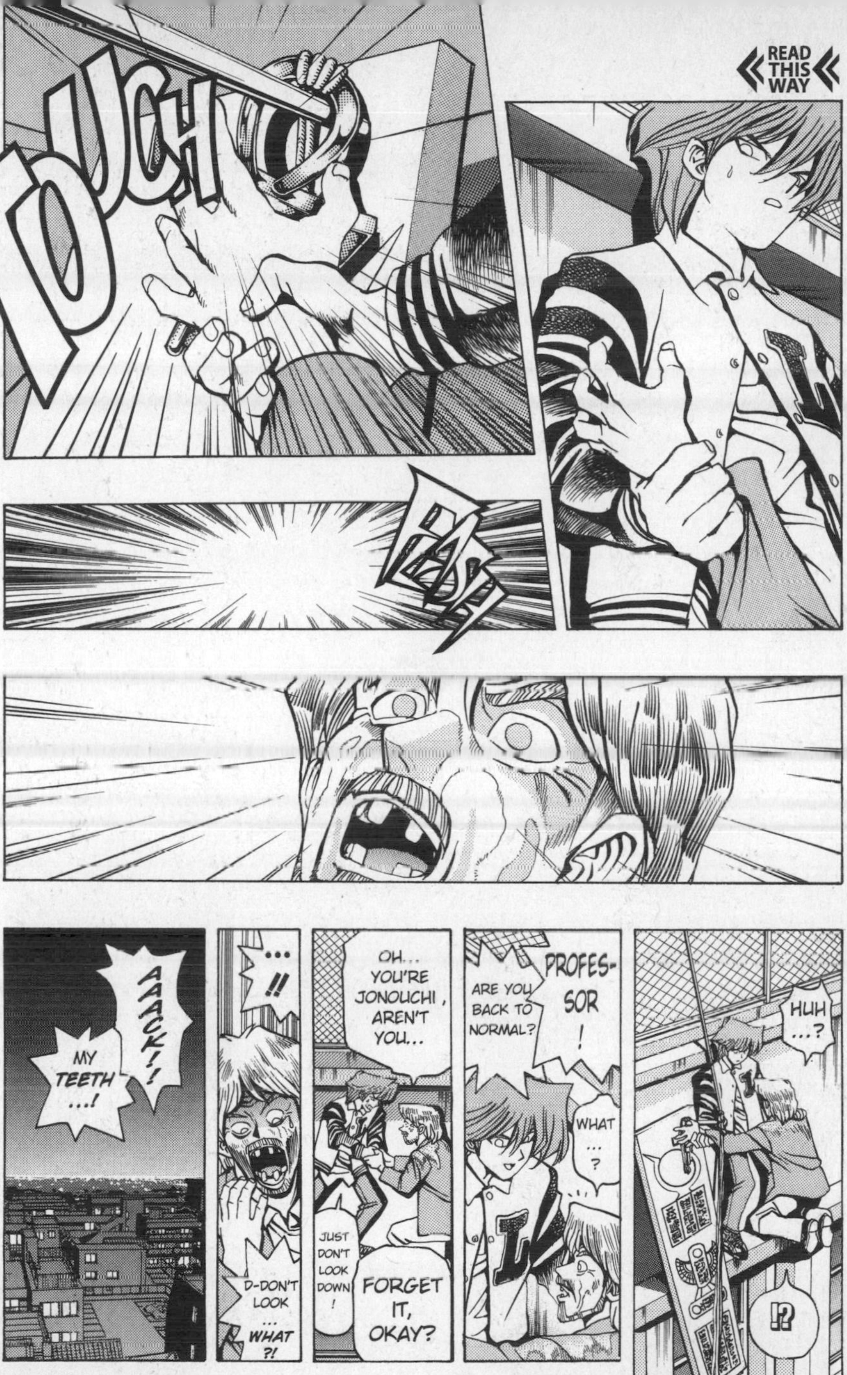
READ THIS WAY
TOUCH
HUH ...?
!?
PROFES- SOR !
ARE YOU BACK TO NORMAL?
WHAT ...?
OH... YOU'RE JONOUCHI, AREN'T YOU...
JUST DON'T LOOK DOWN!
FORGET IT, OKAY?
...!!
D-DON'T LOOK ... WHAT ?!
AAAACK!!
MY TEETH ...!

READ THIS WAY

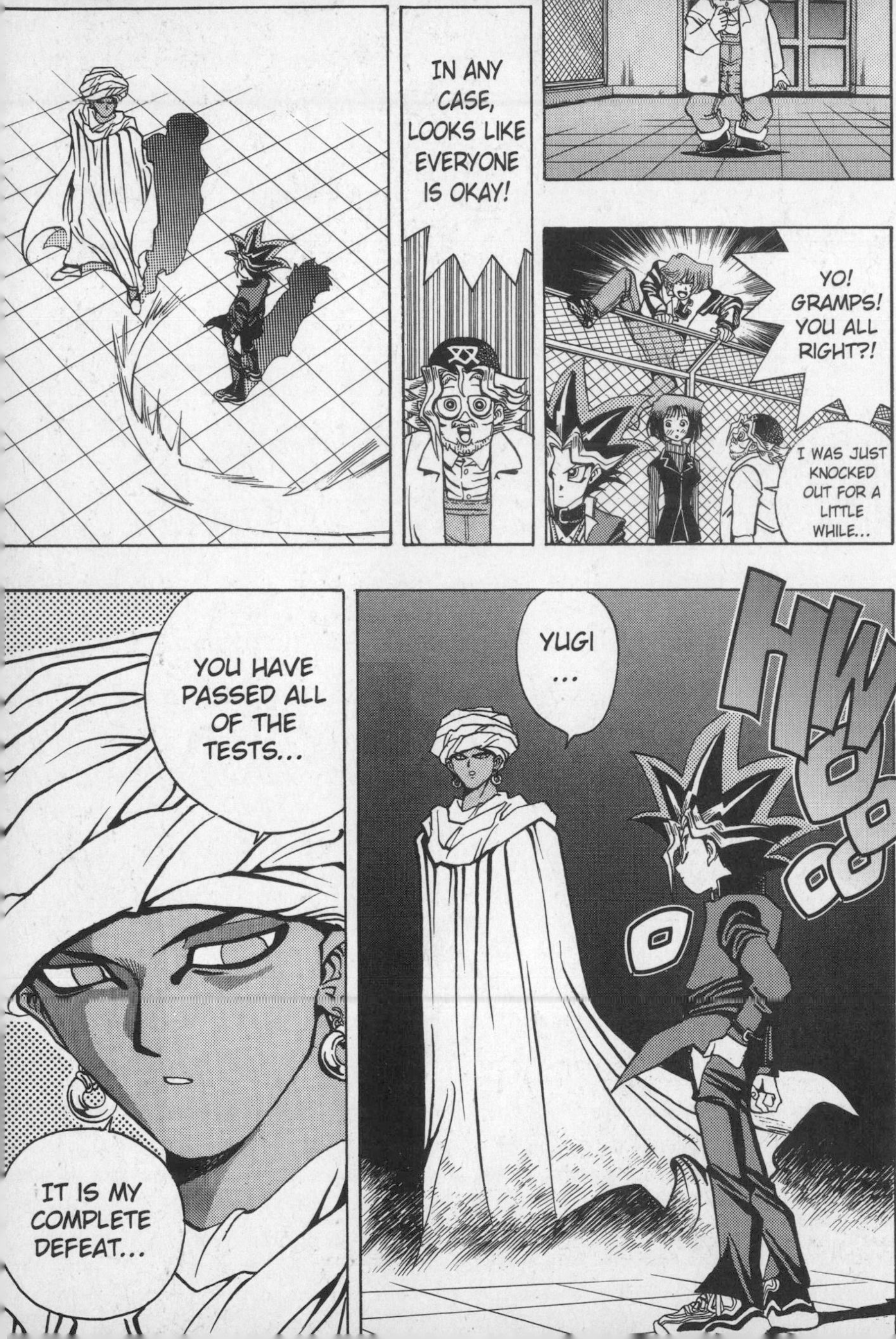
YO! GRAMPS! YOU ALL RIGHT?!
I WAS JUST KNOCKED OUT FOR A LITTLE WHILE...
IN ANY CASE, LOOKS LIKE EVERYONE IS OKAY!
YUGI ...
YOU HAVE PASSED ALL OF THE TESTS...
IT IS MY COMPLETE DEFEAT...

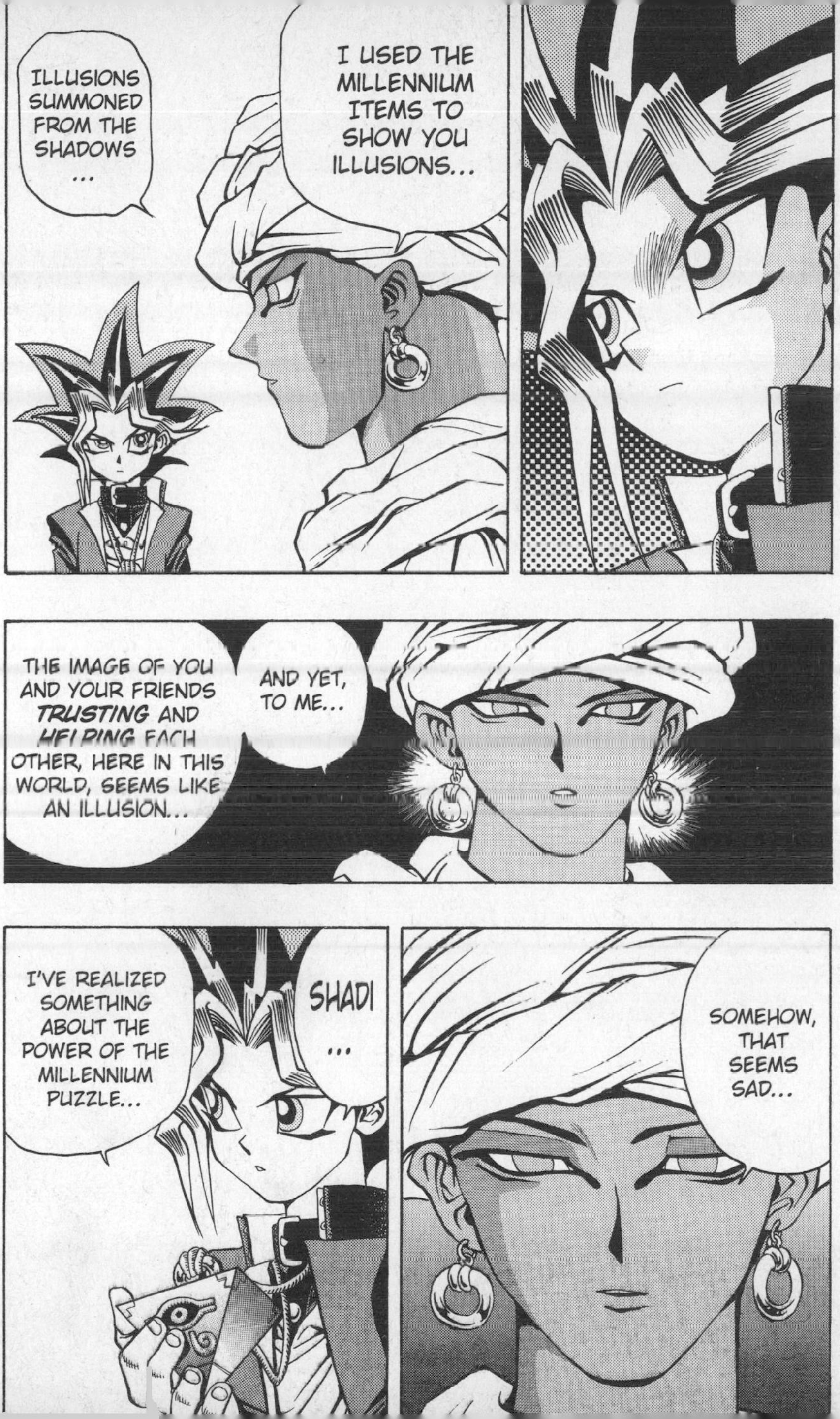
I USED THE MILLENNIUM ITEMS TO SHOW YOU ILLUSIONS...
ILLUSIONS SUMMONED FROM THE SHADOWS ...
AND YET, TO ME...
THE IMAGE OF YOU AND YOUR FRIENDS *TRUSTING* AND *HELPING* EACH OTHER, HERE IN THIS WORLD, SEEMS LIKE AN ILLUSION...
SOMEHOW, THAT SEEMS SAD...
SHADI ...
I'VE REALIZED SOMETHING ABOUT THE POWER OF THE MILLENNIUM PUZZLE...

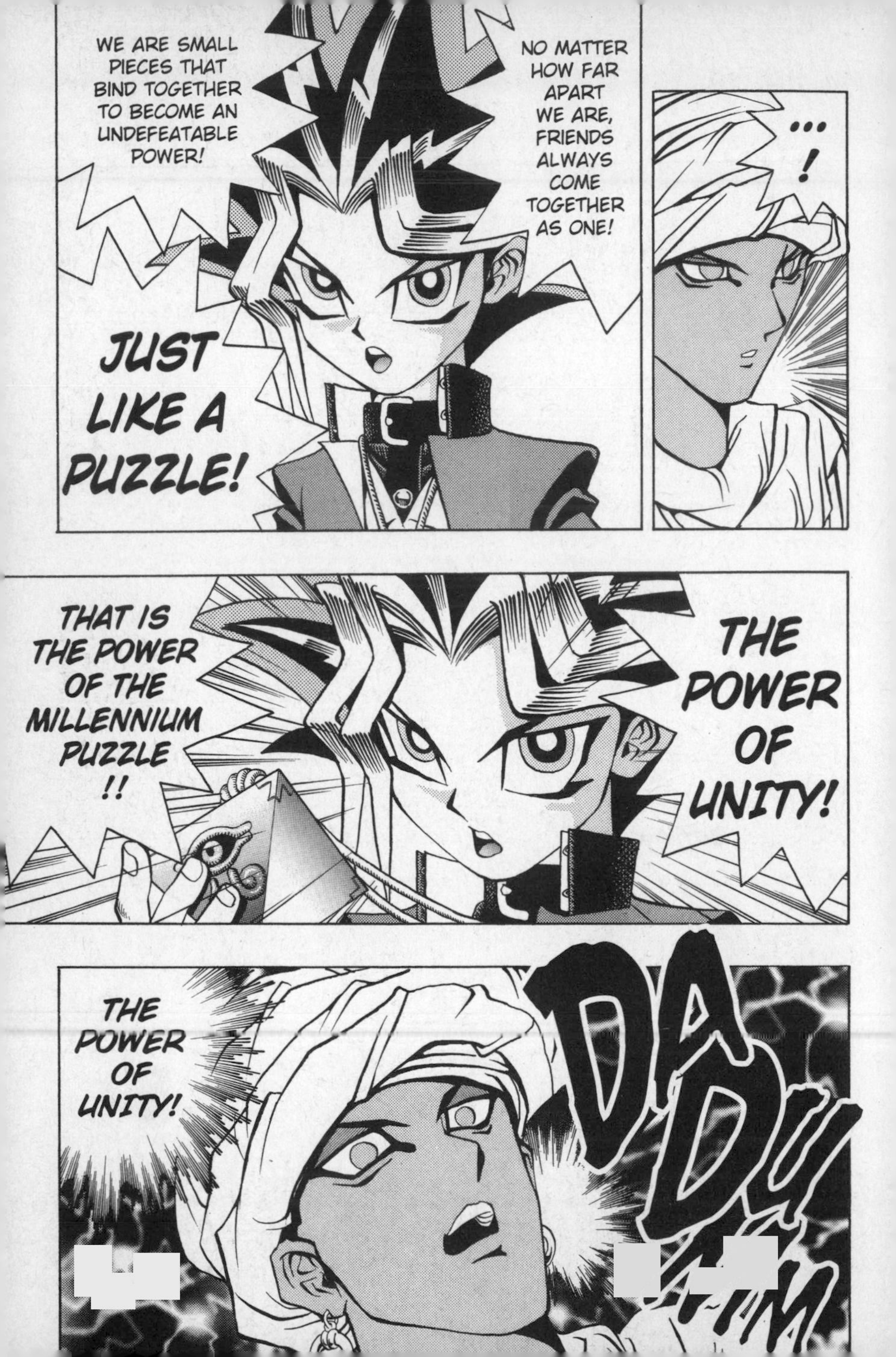
...!
NO MATTER HOW FAR APART WE ARE, FRIENDS ALWAYS COME TOGETHER AS ONE!
WE ARE SMALL PIECES THAT BIND TOGETHER TO BECOME AN UNDEFEATABLE POWER!
JUST LIKE A PUZZLE!
THE POWER OF UNITY!
THAT IS THE POWER OF THE MILLENNIUM PUZZLE!!
DA DU M
THE POWER OF UNITY!

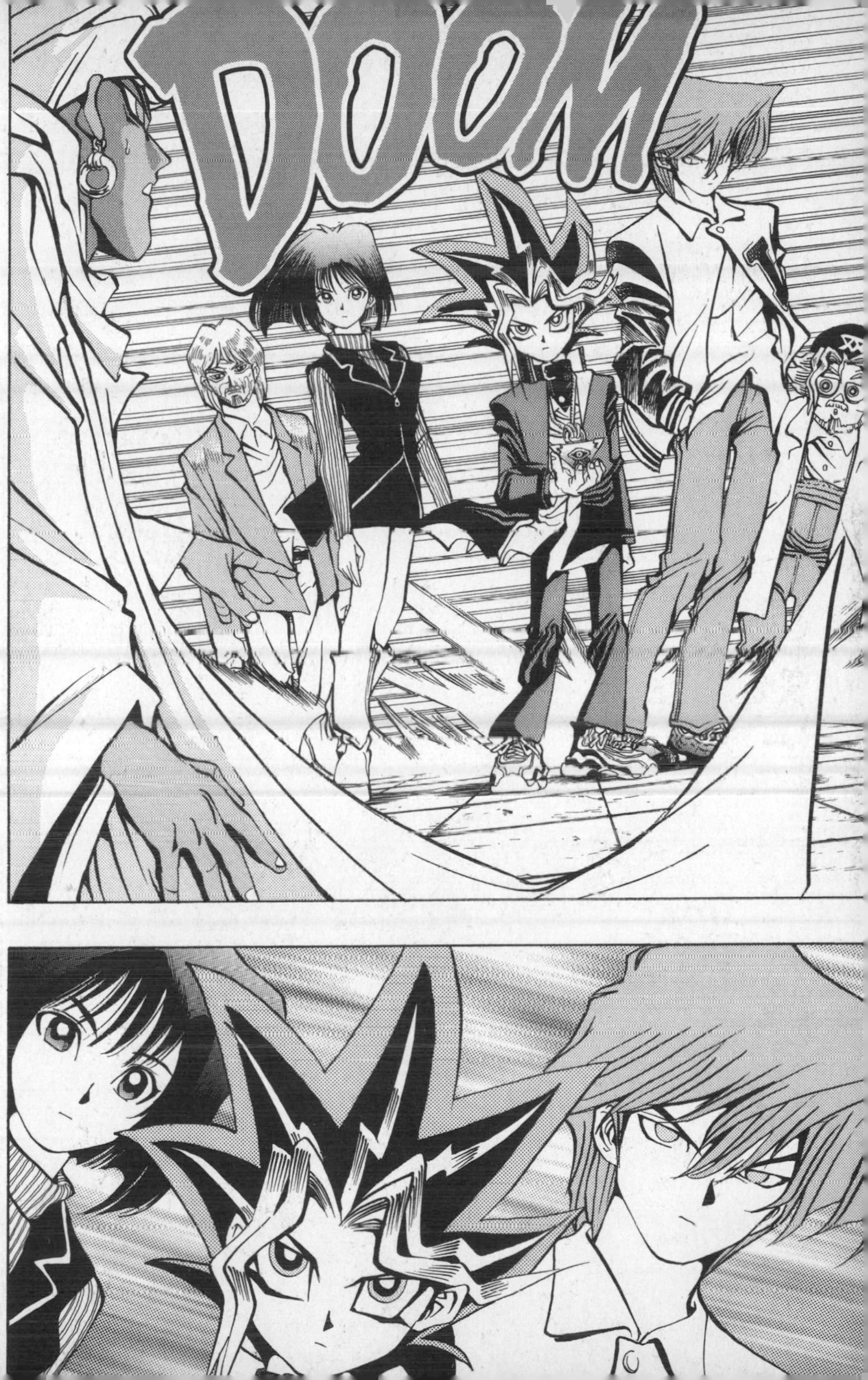
DOOM

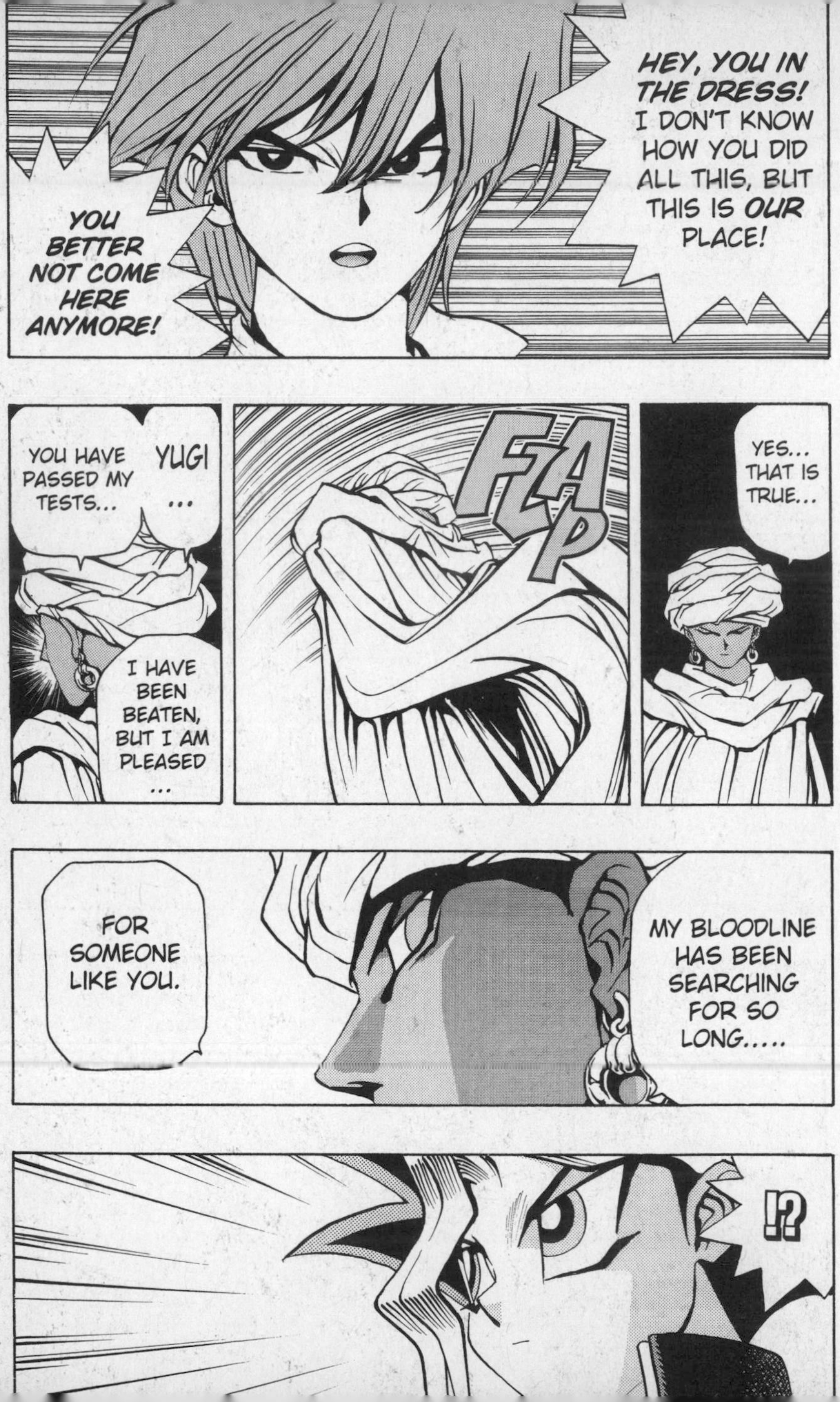
HEY, YOU IN THE DRESS! I DON'T KNOW HOW YOU DID ALL THIS, BUT THIS IS OUR PLACE!
YOU BETTER NOT COME HERE ANYMORE!
YES... THAT IS TRUE...
FLAP
YUGI ...
YOU HAVE PASSED MY TESTS...
I HAVE BEEN BEATEN, BUT I AM PLEASED ...
MY BLOODLINE HAS BEEN SEARCHING FOR SO LONG.....
FOR SOMEONE LIKE YOU.
!?

READ THIS WAY

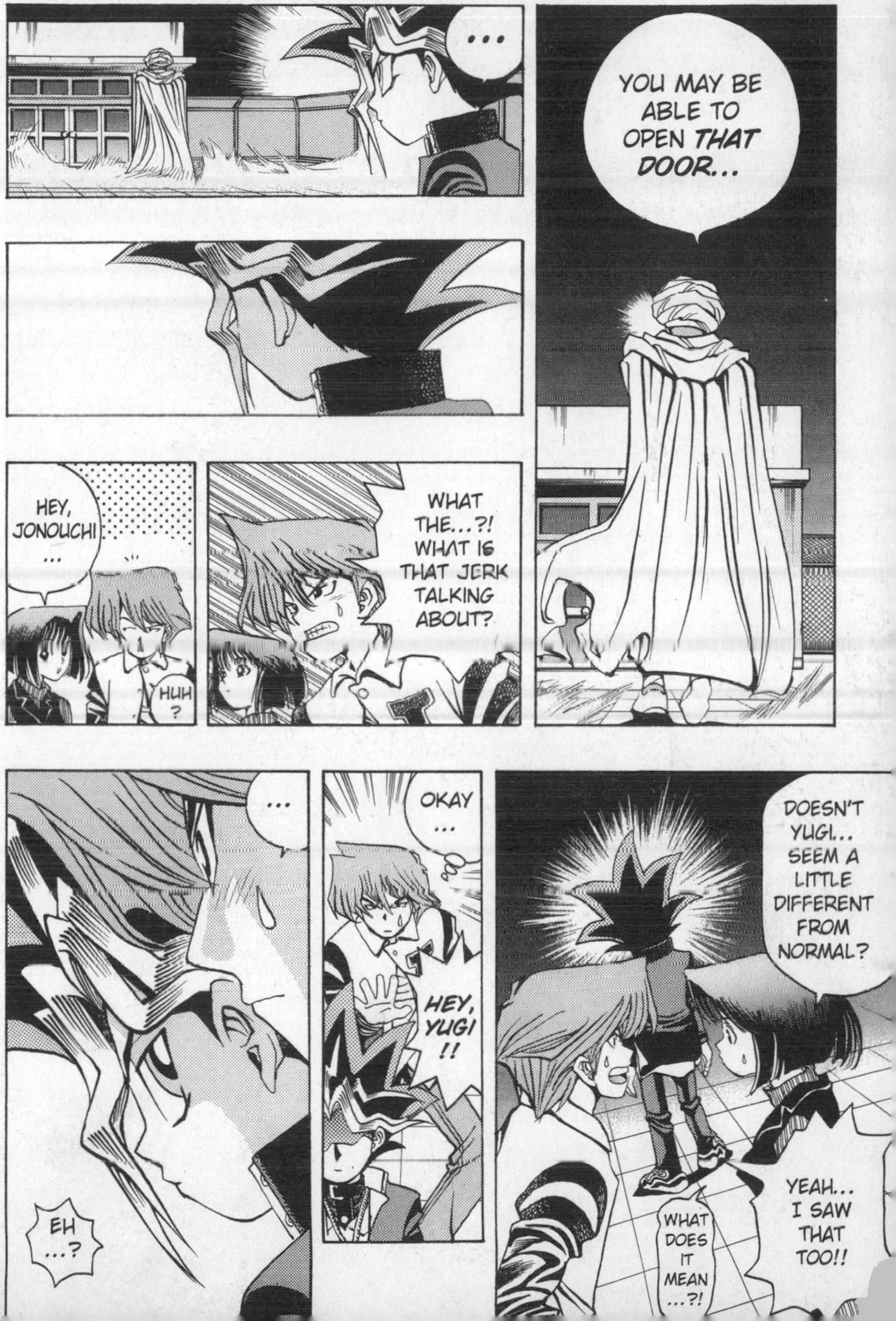
YOU MAY BE ABLE TO OPEN *THAT DOOR*...
...
WHAT THE...?! WHAT IS THAT JERK TALKING ABOUT?
HEY, JONOUCHI ...
HUH ?
DOESN'T YUGI... SEEM A LITTLE DIFFERENT FROM NORMAL?
YEAH... I SAW THAT TOO!!
WHAT DOES IT MEAN ...?!
OKAY ...
HEY, YUGI !!
...
EH ...?

READ THIS WAY

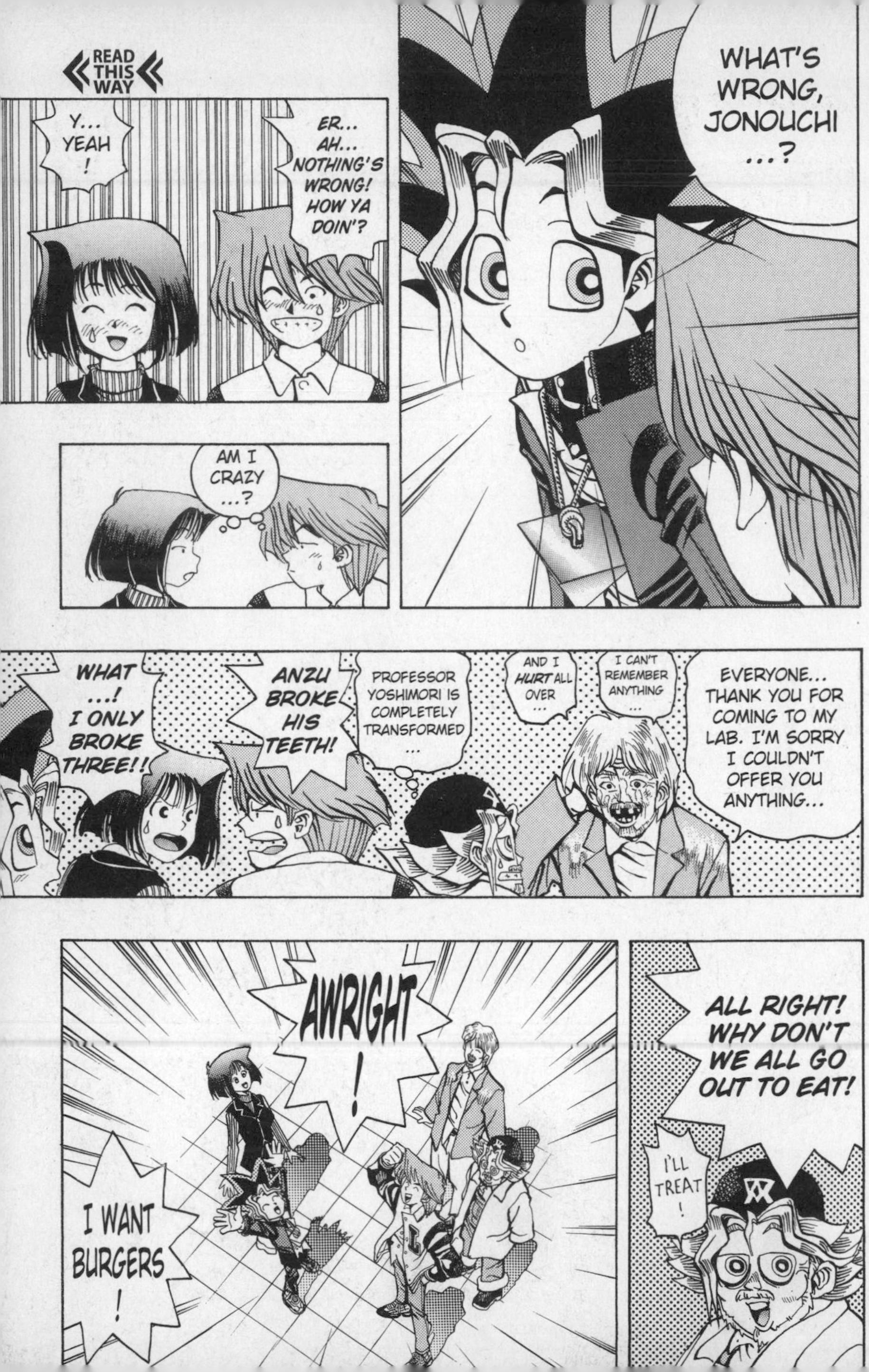
WHAT'S WRONG, JONOUCHI ...?
ER... AH... NOTHING'S WRONG! HOW YA DOIN'?
Y... YEAH!
AM I CRAZY ...?
EVERYONE... THANK YOU FOR COMING TO MY LAB. I'M SORRY I COULDN'T OFFER YOU ANYTHING...
I CAN'T REMEMBER ANYTHING ...
AND I HURT ALL OVER ...
PROFESSOR YOSHIMORI IS COMPLETELY TRANSFORMED ...
ANZU BROKE HIS TEETH!
WHAT ...! I ONLY BROKE THREE!!
ALL RIGHT! WHY DON'T WE ALL GO OUT TO EAT!
I'LL TREAT!
AWRIGHT!
I WANT BURGERS!

RUMB
SHU

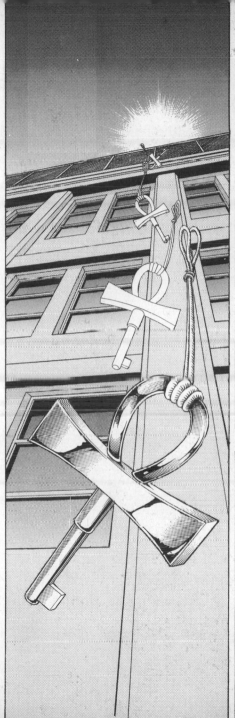

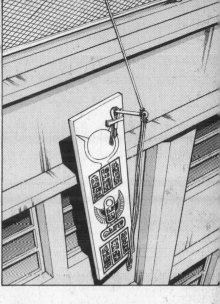

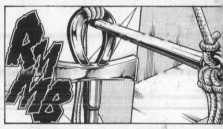

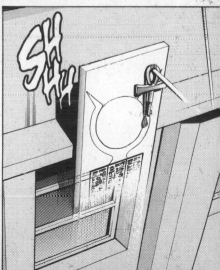

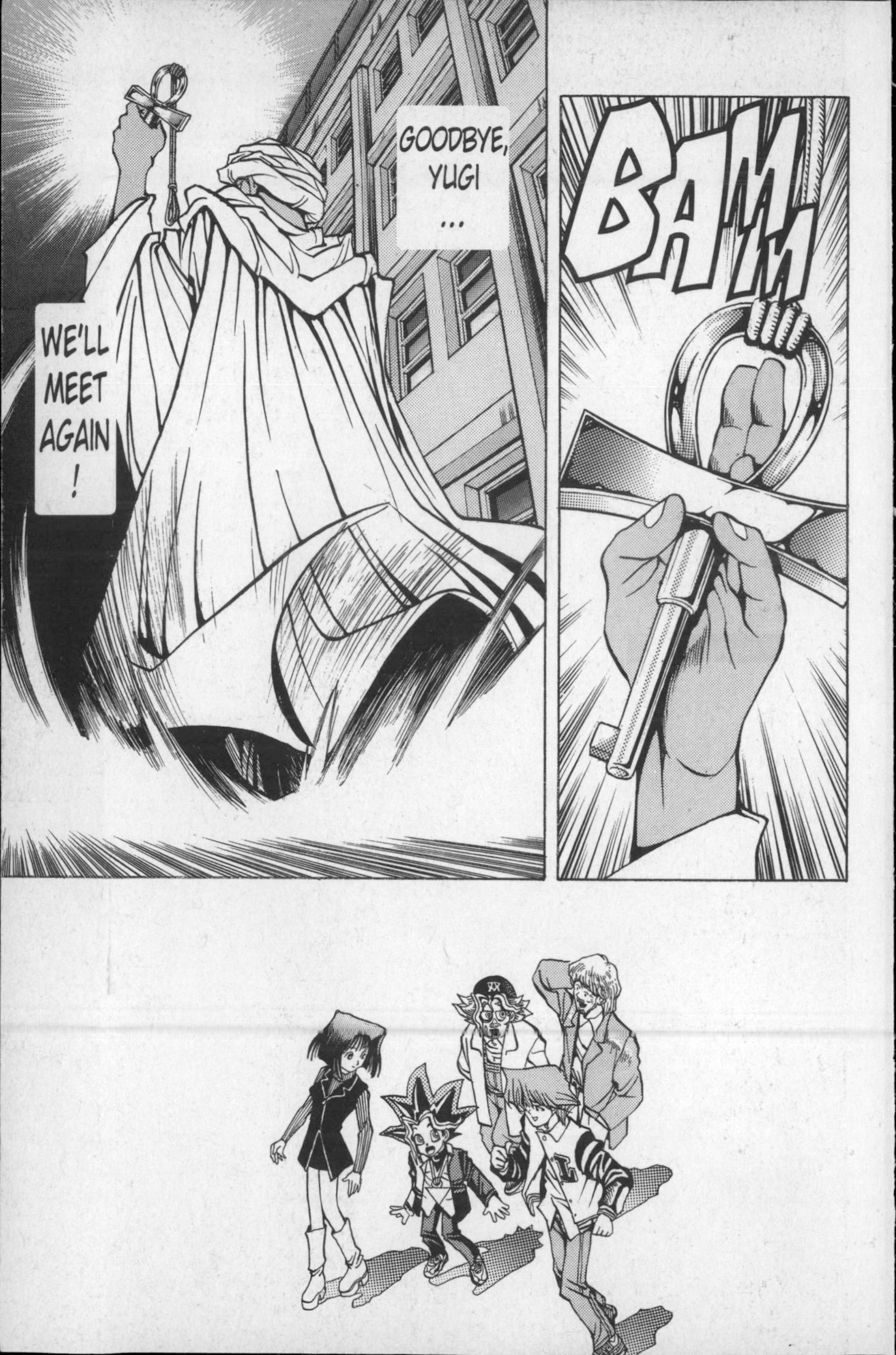
BAM
GOODBYE, YUGI ...
WE'LL MEET AGAIN !

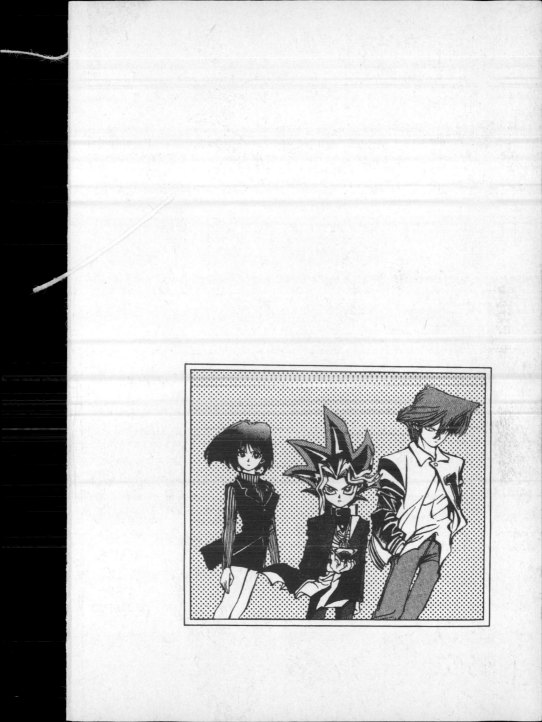

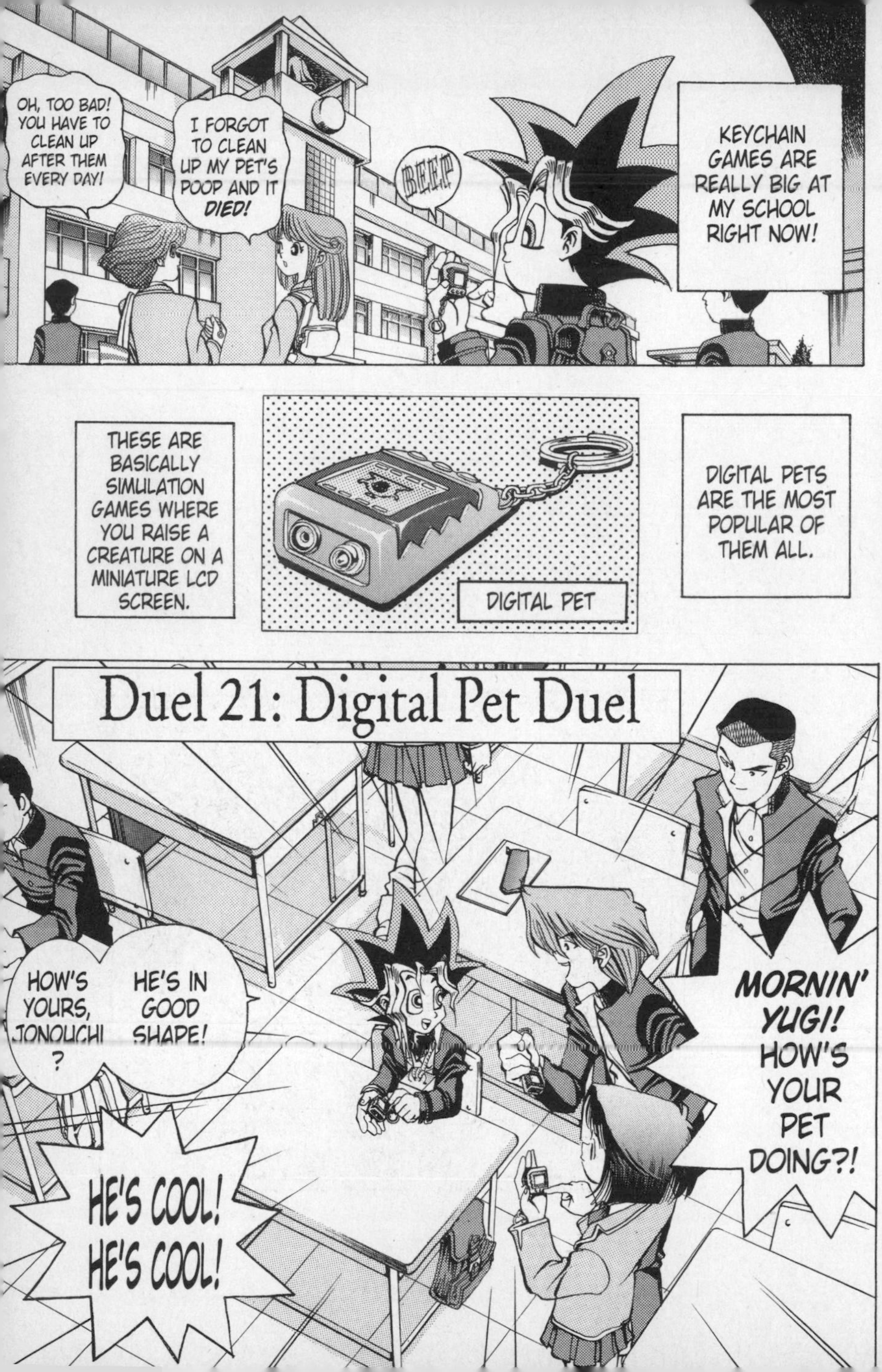
KEYCHAIN GAMES ARE REALLY BIG AT MY SCHOOL RIGHT NOW!
BEEP
I FORGOT TO CLEAN UP MY PET'S POOP AND IT *DIED!*
OH, TOO BAD! YOU HAVE TO CLEAN UP AFTER THEM EVERY DAY!
DIGITAL PETS ARE THE MOST POPULAR OF THEM ALL.
DIGITAL PET
THESE ARE BASICALLY SIMULATION GAMES WHERE YOU RAISE A CREATURE ON A MINIATURE LCD SCREEN.
Duel 21: Digital Pet Duel
*MORNIN' YUGI!* HOW'S YOUR PET DOING?!
HE'S IN GOOD SHAPE!
HOW'S YOURS, JONOUCHI?
HE'S COOL! HE'S COOL!

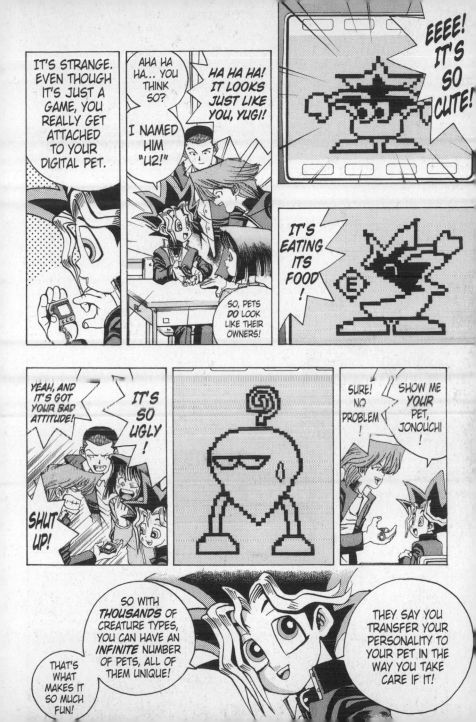

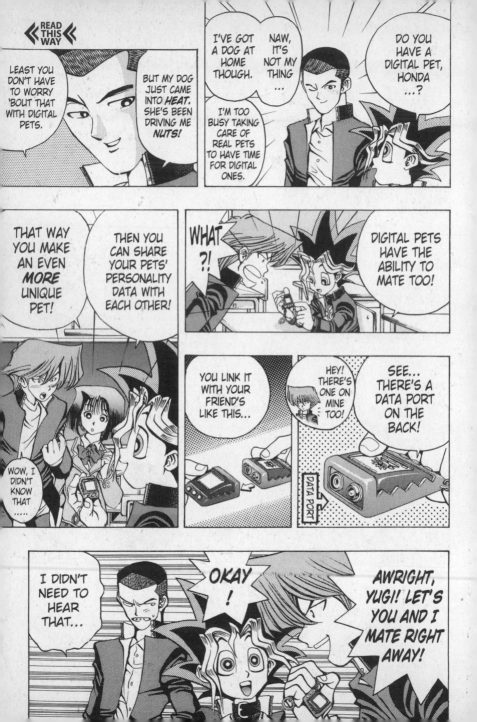

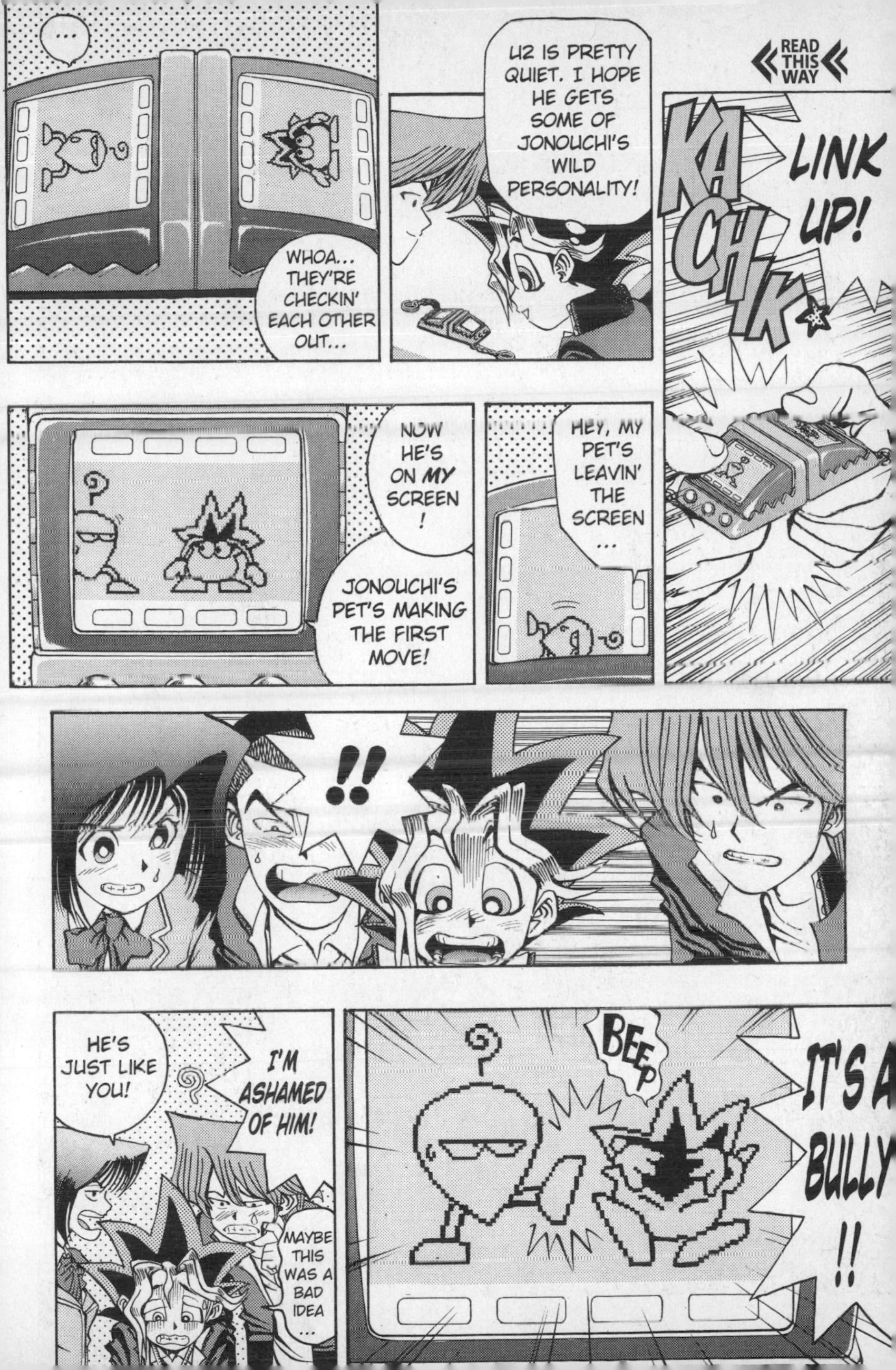
READ THIS WAY
LINK UP!
KA CHIK
U2 IS PRETTY QUIET. I HOPE HE GETS SOME OF JONOUCHI'S WILD PERSONALITY!
...
WHOA... THEY'RE CHECKIN' EACH OTHER OUT...
HEY, MY PET'S LEAVIN' THE SCREEN ...
NOW HE'S ON *MY* SCREEN !
JONOUCHI'S PET'S MAKING THE FIRST MOVE!
!!
IT'S A BULLY !!
BEEP
I'M ASHAMED OF HIM!
HE'S JUST LIKE YOU!
MAYBE THIS WAS A BAD IDEA ...

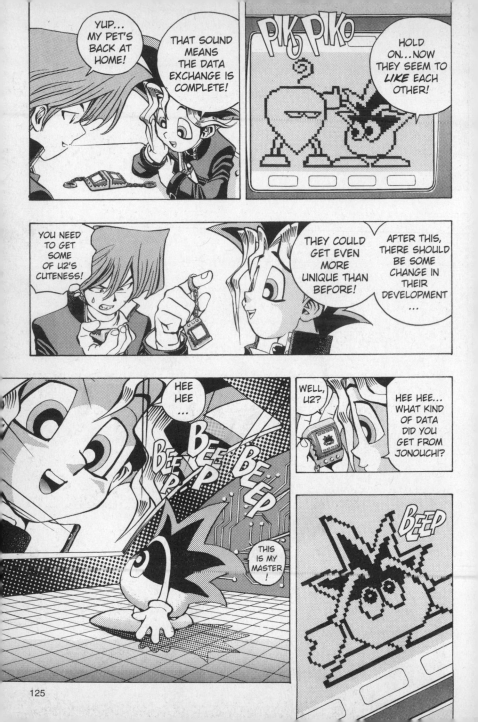

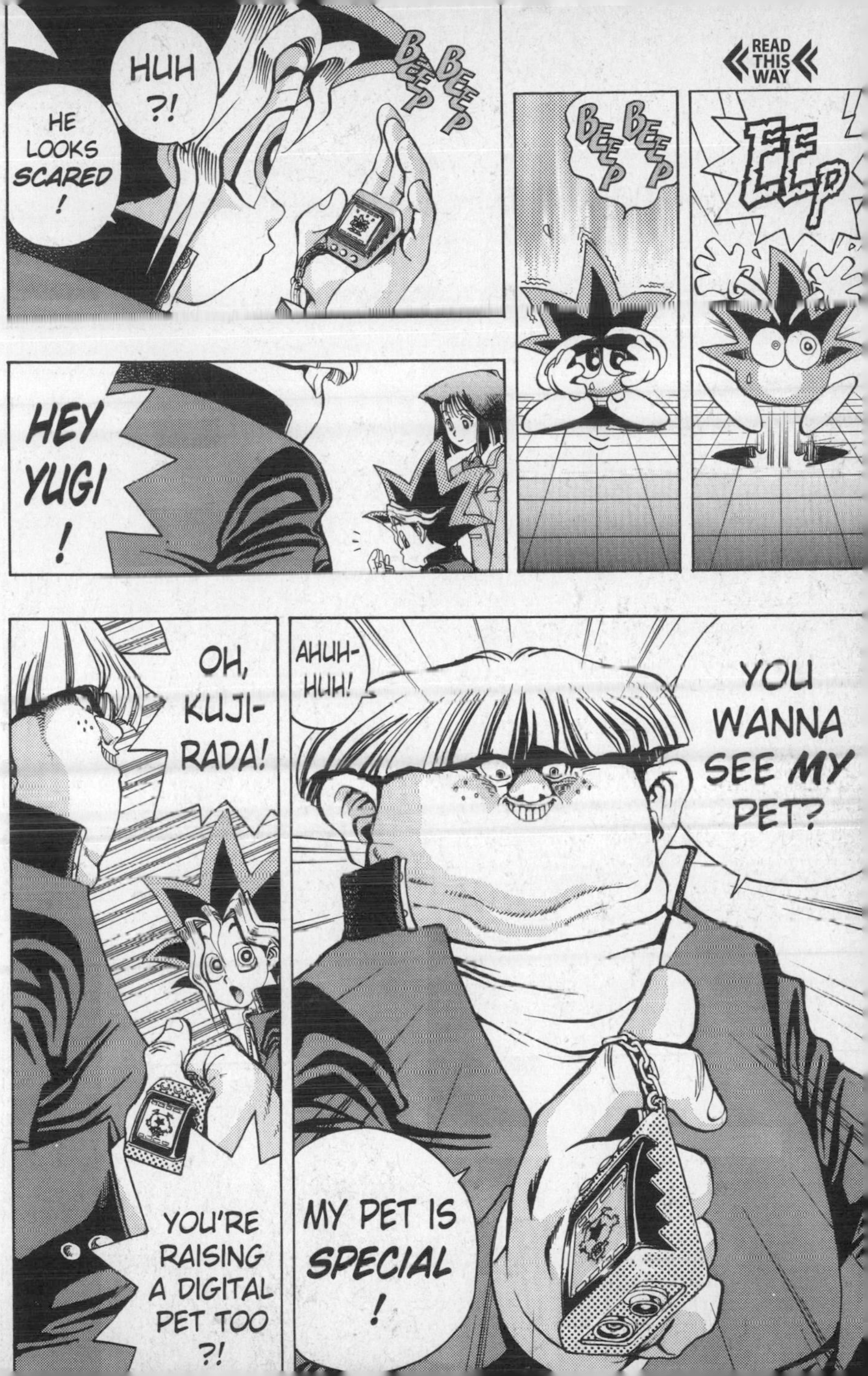
READ THIS WAY
EEP
BEEP BEEP
BEEP BEEP
HUH ?!
HE LOOKS SCARED !
HEY YUGI !
AHUH-HUH!
YOU WANNA SEE MY PET?
MY PET IS SPECIAL !
OH, KUJI-RADA!
YOU'RE RAISING A DIGITAL PET TOO ?!

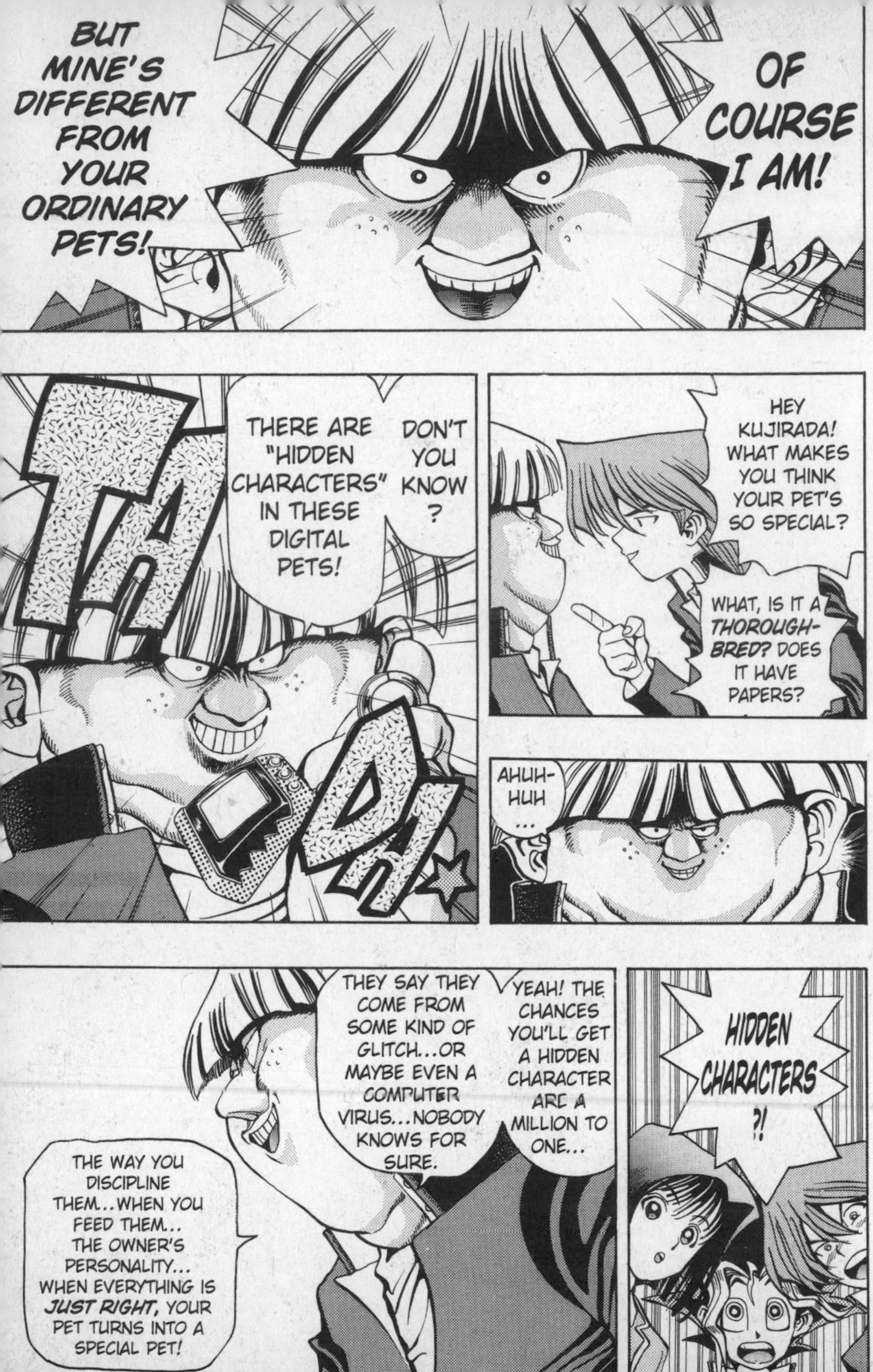
OF COURSE I AM!
BUT MINE'S DIFFERENT FROM YOUR ORDINARY PETS!
HEY KUJIRADA! WHAT MAKES YOU THINK YOUR PET'S SO SPECIAL?
WHAT, IS IT A *THOROUGHBRED?* DOES IT HAVE PAPERS?
AHUH-HUH ...
DON'T YOU KNOW ?
THERE ARE "HIDDEN CHARACTERS" IN THESE DIGITAL PETS!
TA DA
HIDDEN CHARACTERS ?!
YEAH! THE CHANCES YOU'LL GET A HIDDEN CHARACTER ARE A MILLION TO ONE...
THEY SAY THEY COME FROM SOME KIND OF GLITCH...OR MAYBE EVEN A COMPUTER VIRUS...NOBODY KNOWS FOR SURE.
THE WAY YOU DISCIPLINE THEM...WHEN YOU FEED THEM... THE OWNER'S PERSONALITY... WHEN EVERYTHING IS *JUST RIGHT*, YOUR PET TURNS INTO A SPECIAL PET!

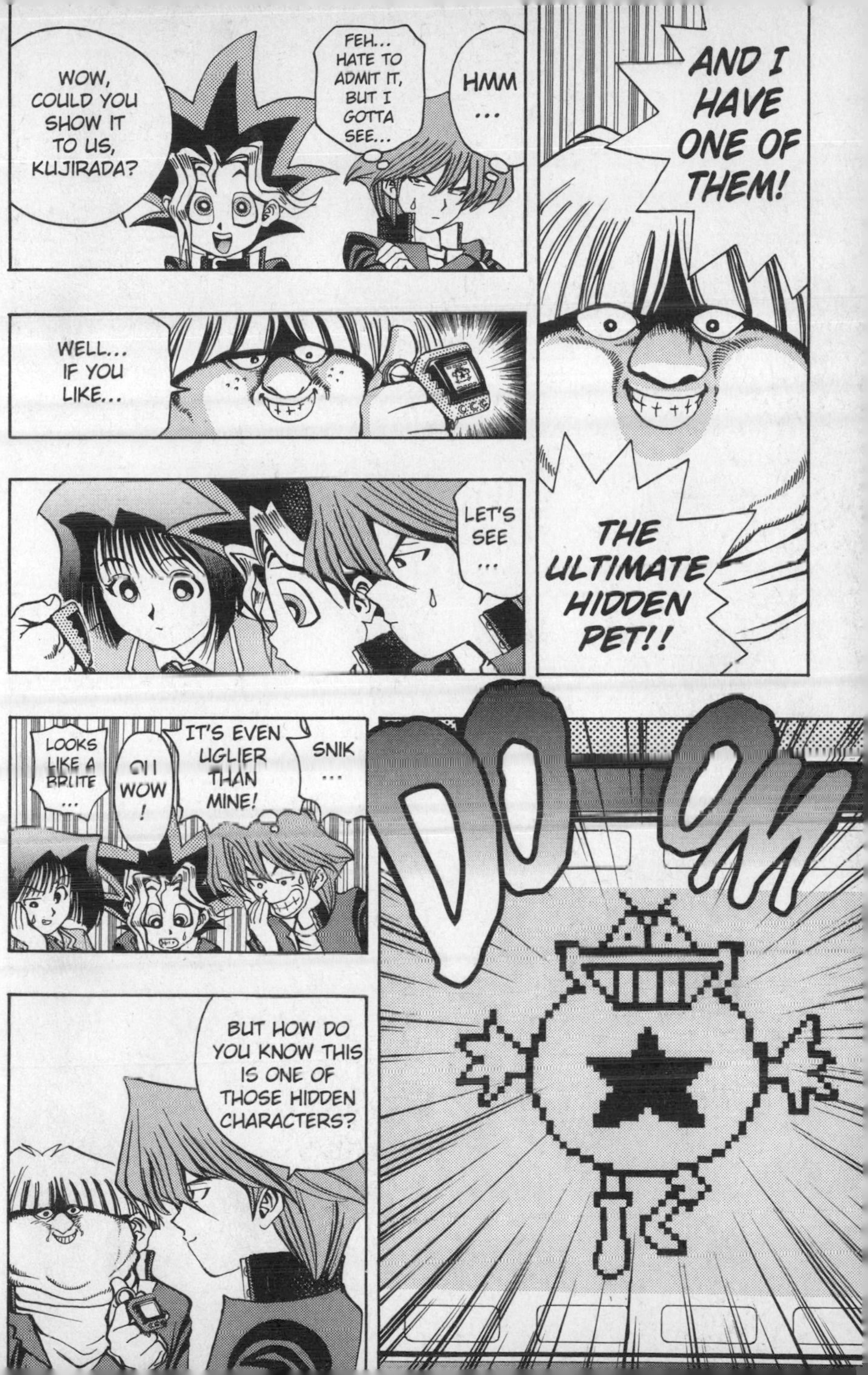

AND I HAVE ONE OF THEM!
THE ULTIMATE HIDDEN PET!!
HMM...
FEH... HATE TO ADMIT IT, BUT I GOTTA SEE...
WOW, COULD YOU SHOW IT TO US, KUJIRADA?
WELL... IF YOU LIKE...
LET'S SEE...
DOOM
SNIK...
IT'S EVEN UGLIER THAN MINE!
OH WOW!
LOOKS LIKE A BRUTE...
BUT HOW DO YOU KNOW THIS IS ONE OF THOSE HIDDEN CHARACTERS?

READ THIS WAY

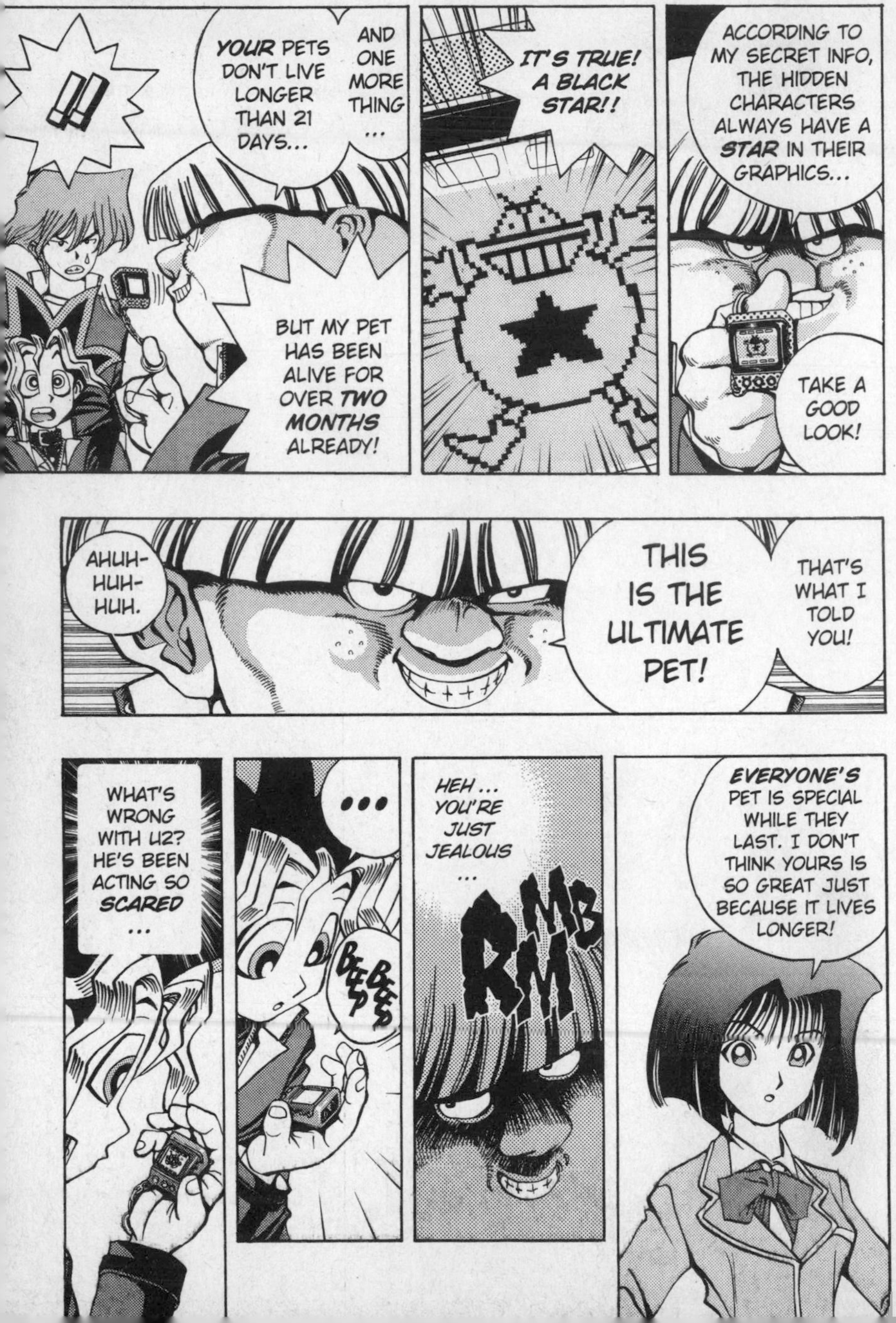
ACCORDING TO MY SECRET INFO, THE HIDDEN CHARACTERS ALWAYS HAVE A STAR IN THEIR GRAPHICS...
TAKE A GOOD LOOK!
IT'S TRUE! A BLACK STAR!!
AND ONE MORE THING...
YOUR PETS DON'T LIVE LONGER THAN 21 DAYS...
!!
BUT MY PET HAS BEEN ALIVE FOR OVER TWO MONTHS ALREADY!
THAT'S WHAT I TOLD YOU!
THIS IS THE ULTIMATE PET!
AHUH-HUH-HUH.
EVERYONE'S PET IS SPECIAL WHILE THEY LAST. I DON'T THINK YOURS IS SO GREAT JUST BECAUSE IT LIVES LONGER!
HEH... YOU'RE JUST JEALOUS...
RMB RMB
...
BEEP BEEP
WHAT'S WRONG WITH U2? HE'S BEEN ACTING SO SCARED...

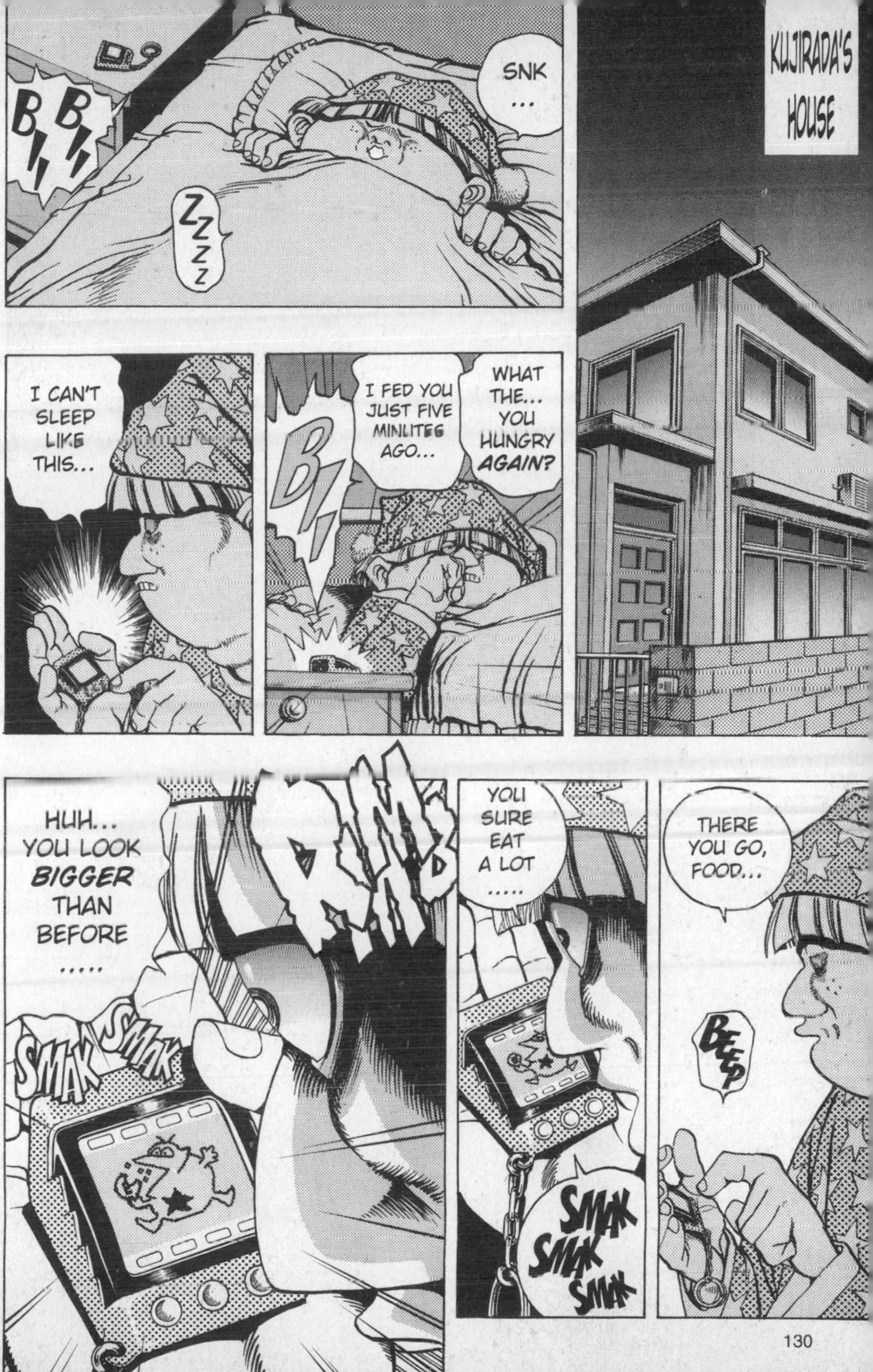
KUJIRADA'S HOUSE
SNK ...
BI BI
ZZZZ
WHAT THE... YOU HUNGRY *AGAIN?*
I FED YOU JUST FIVE MINUTES AGO...
BI
I CAN'T SLEEP LIKE THIS...
THERE YOU GO, FOOD...
BEEP
YOU SURE EAT A LOT .....
SMAK SMAK SMAK
HUH... YOU LOOK *BIGGER* THAN BEFORE .....
SMAK SMAK

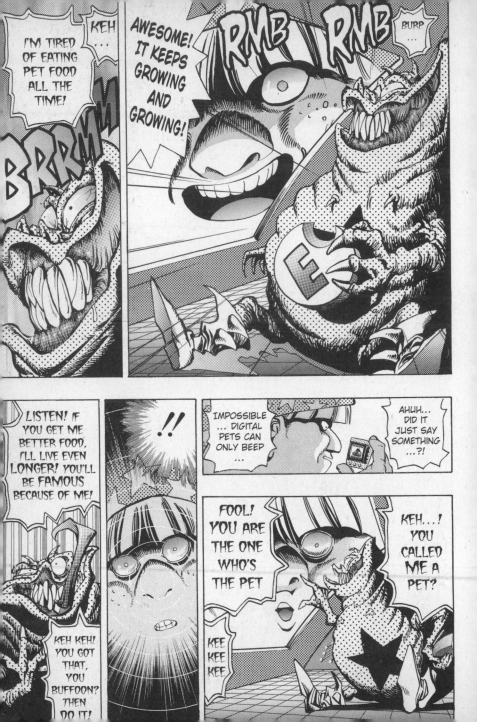

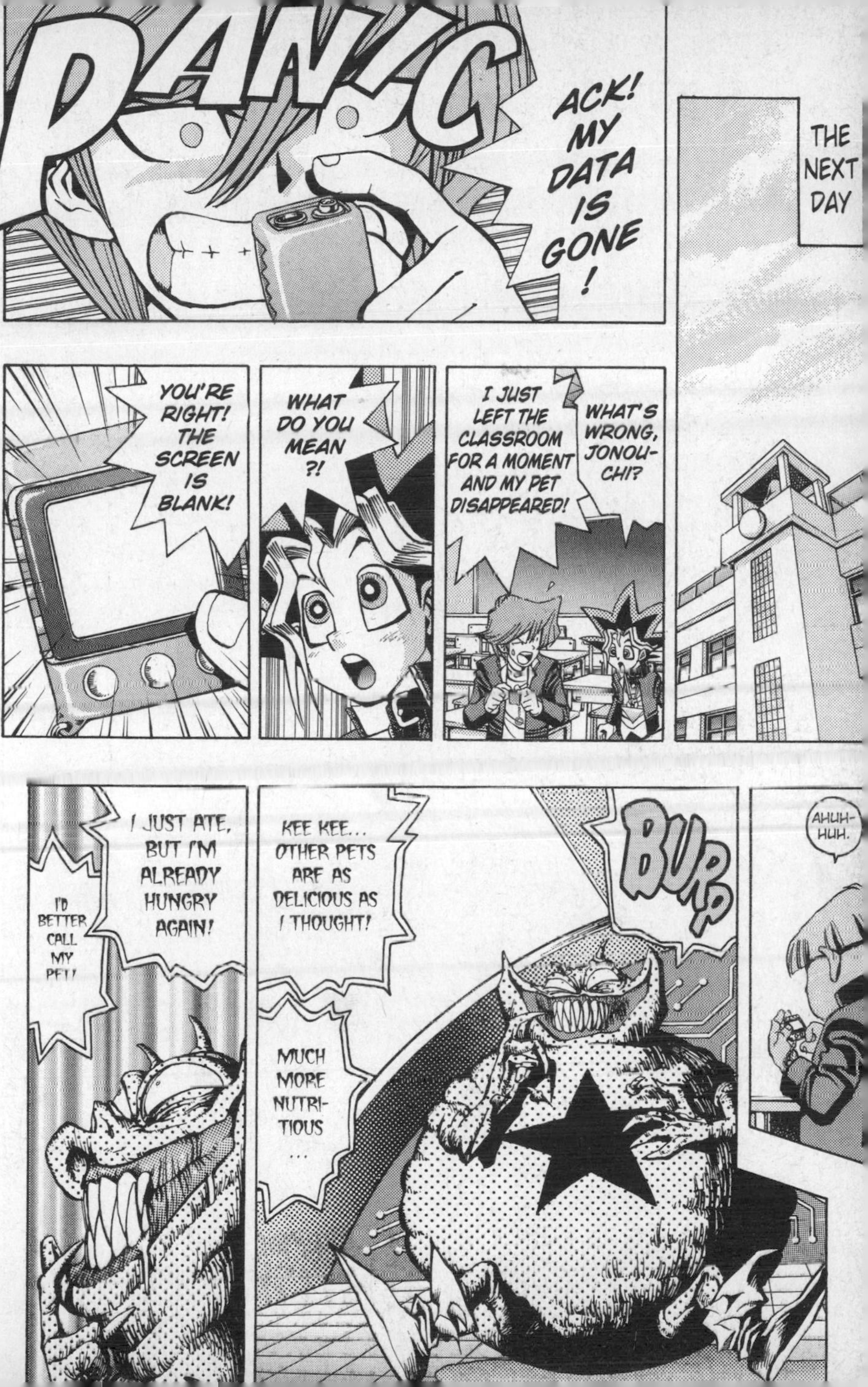
THE NEXT DAY
PANIC
ACK! MY DATA IS GONE!
WHAT'S WRONG, JONOUCHI?
I JUST LEFT THE CLASSROOM FOR A MOMENT AND MY PET DISAPPEARED!
WHAT DO YOU MEAN?!
YOU'RE RIGHT! THE SCREEN IS BLANK!
AHUH-HUH.
BURP
KEE KEE... OTHER PETS ARE AS DELICIOUS AS I THOUGHT!
MUCH MORE NUTRITIOUS...
I JUST ATE, BUT I'M ALREADY HUNGRY AGAIN!
I'D BETTER CALL MY PET!

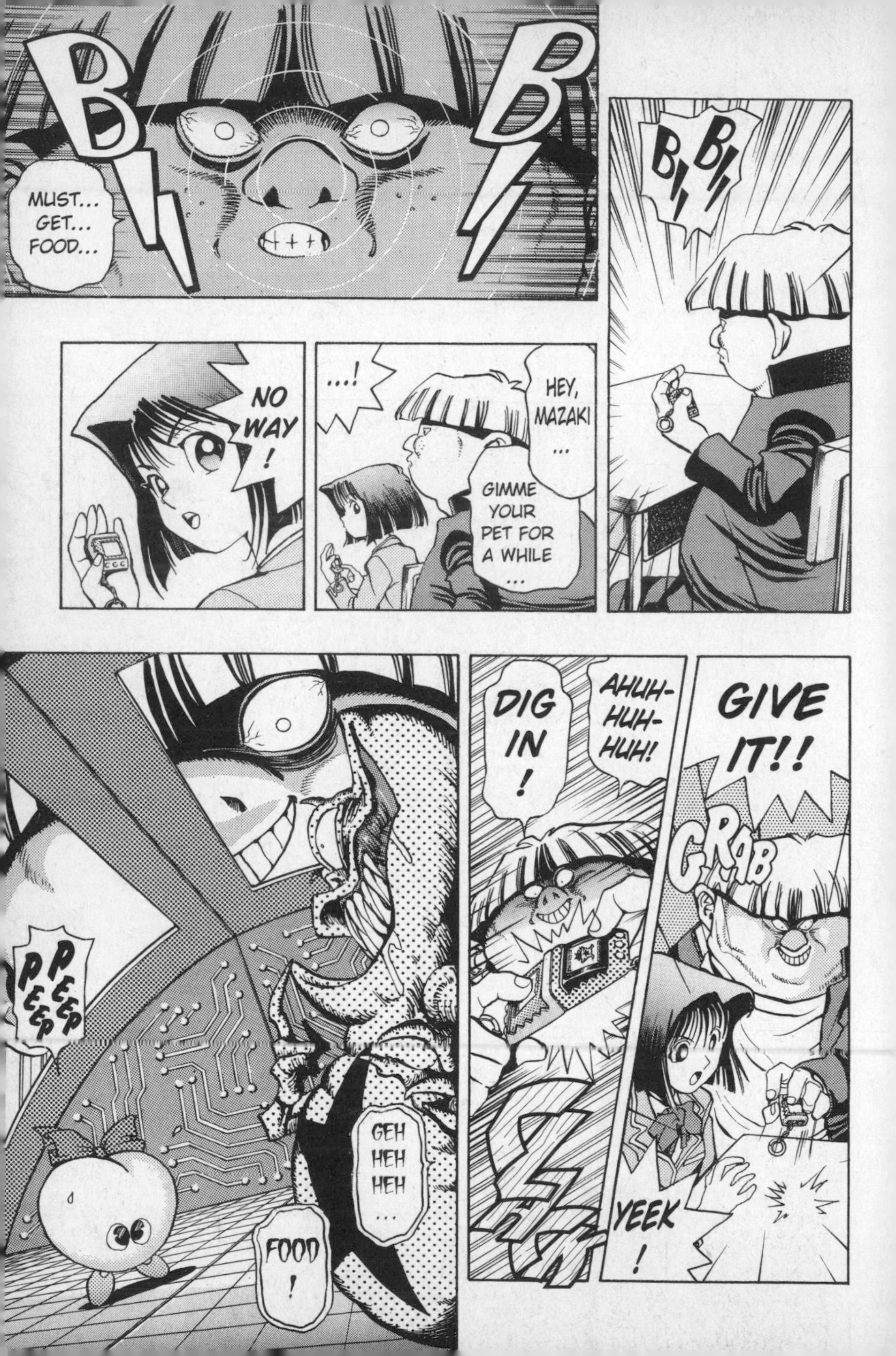
BI BI
B B
MUST... GET... FOOD...
HEY, MAZAKI ...
GIMME YOUR PET FOR A WHILE ...
...!
NO WAY !
GIVE IT!!
GRAB
YEEK !
AHUH-HUH-HUH!
DIG IN !
PEEP PEEP
GEH HEH HEH ...
FOOD !

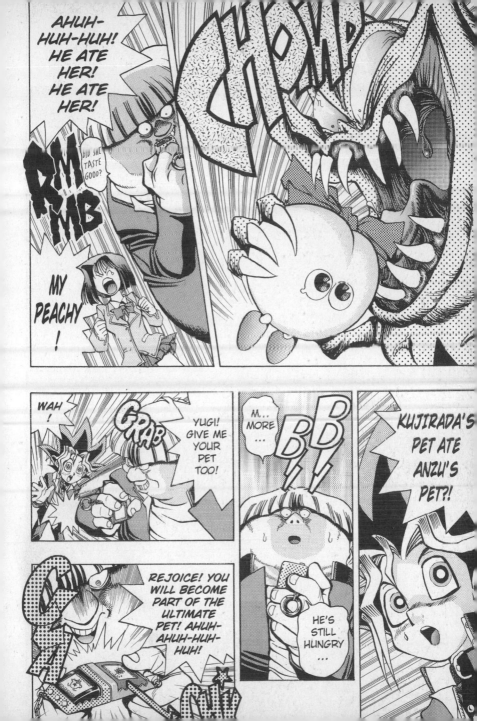

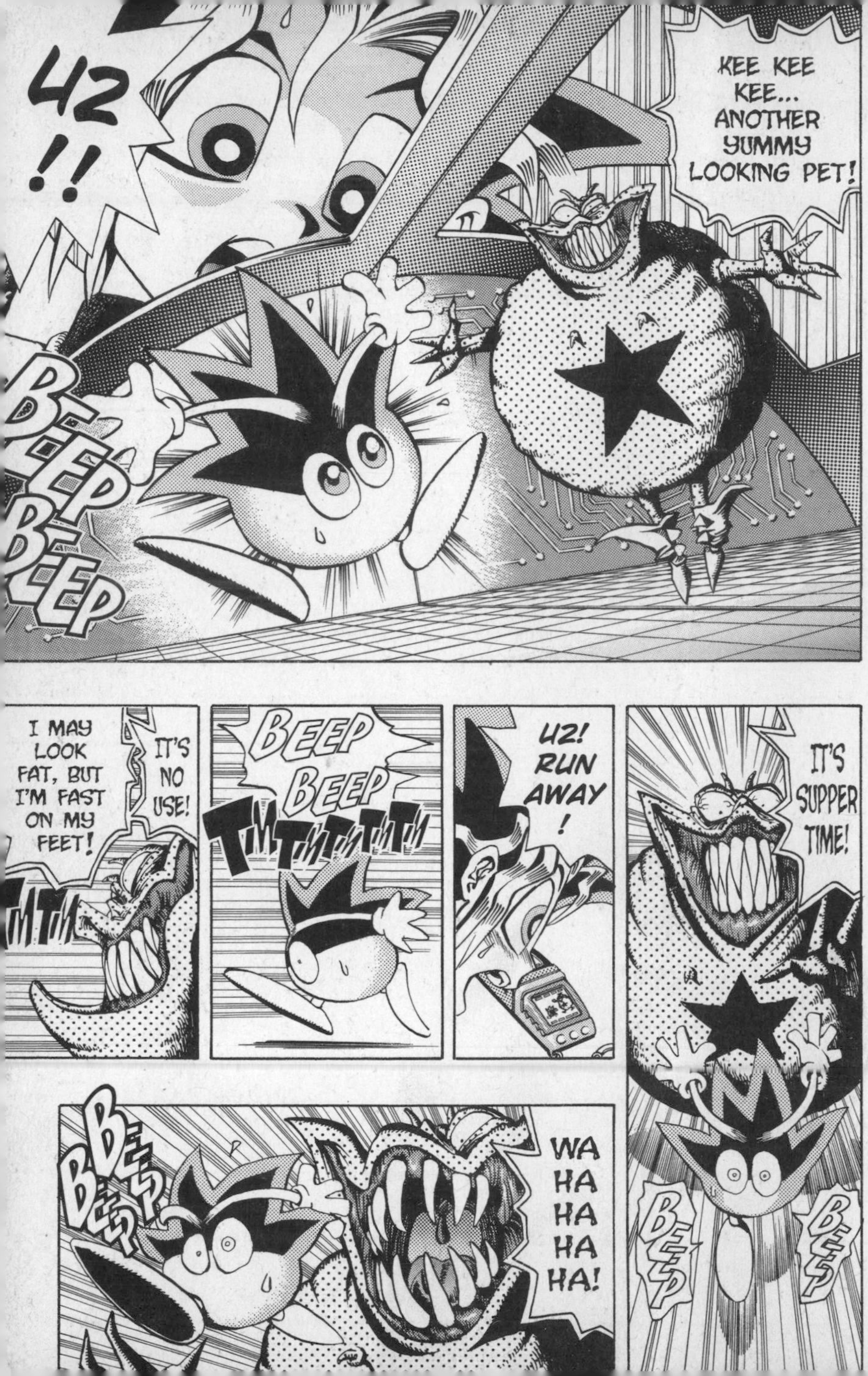
KEE KEE KEE... ANOTHER YUMMY LOOKING PET!
U2 !!
BEEP BEEP BEEP
IT'S SUPPER TIME!
BEEP
BEEP
U2! RUN AWAY!
BEEP BEEP
IT'S NO USE!
I MAY LOOK FAT, BUT I'M FAST ON MY FEET!
WA HA HA HA HA HA!
BEEP BEEP

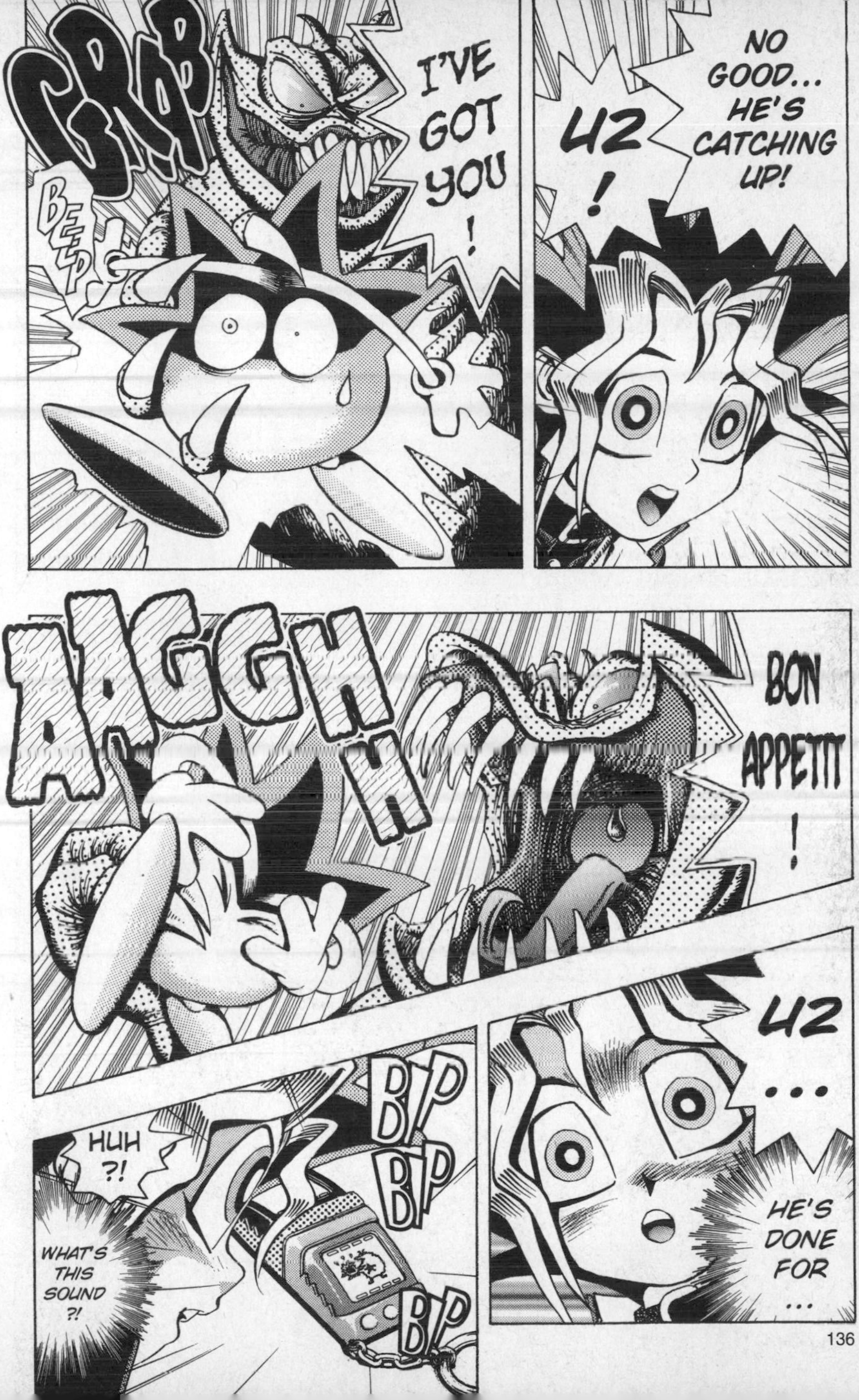

NO GOOD... HE'S CATCHING UP!
UZ!
I'VE GOT YOU!
GRAB
BEEP
BON APPETITT!
AAGGHH
UZ...
HE'S DONE FOR...
BIP
BIP
BIP
HUH?!
WHAT'S THIS SOUND?!

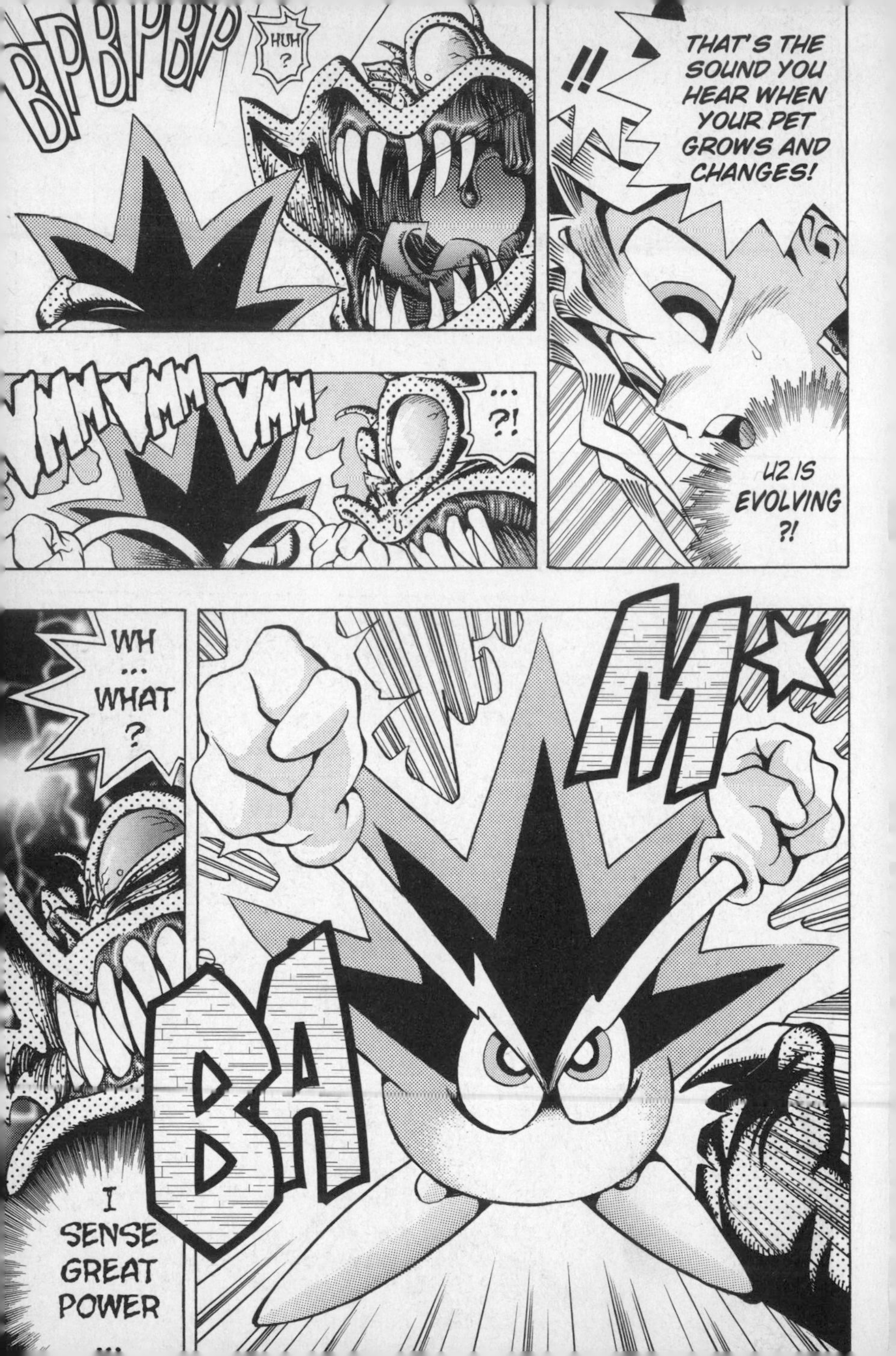
!!
THAT'S THE SOUND YOU HEAR WHEN YOUR PET GROWS AND CHANGES!
U2 IS EVOLVING ?!
BIPBIPBIP
HUH ?
VMMVMM VMM
... ?!
BAM
WH ... WHAT ?
I SENSE GREAT POWER ...

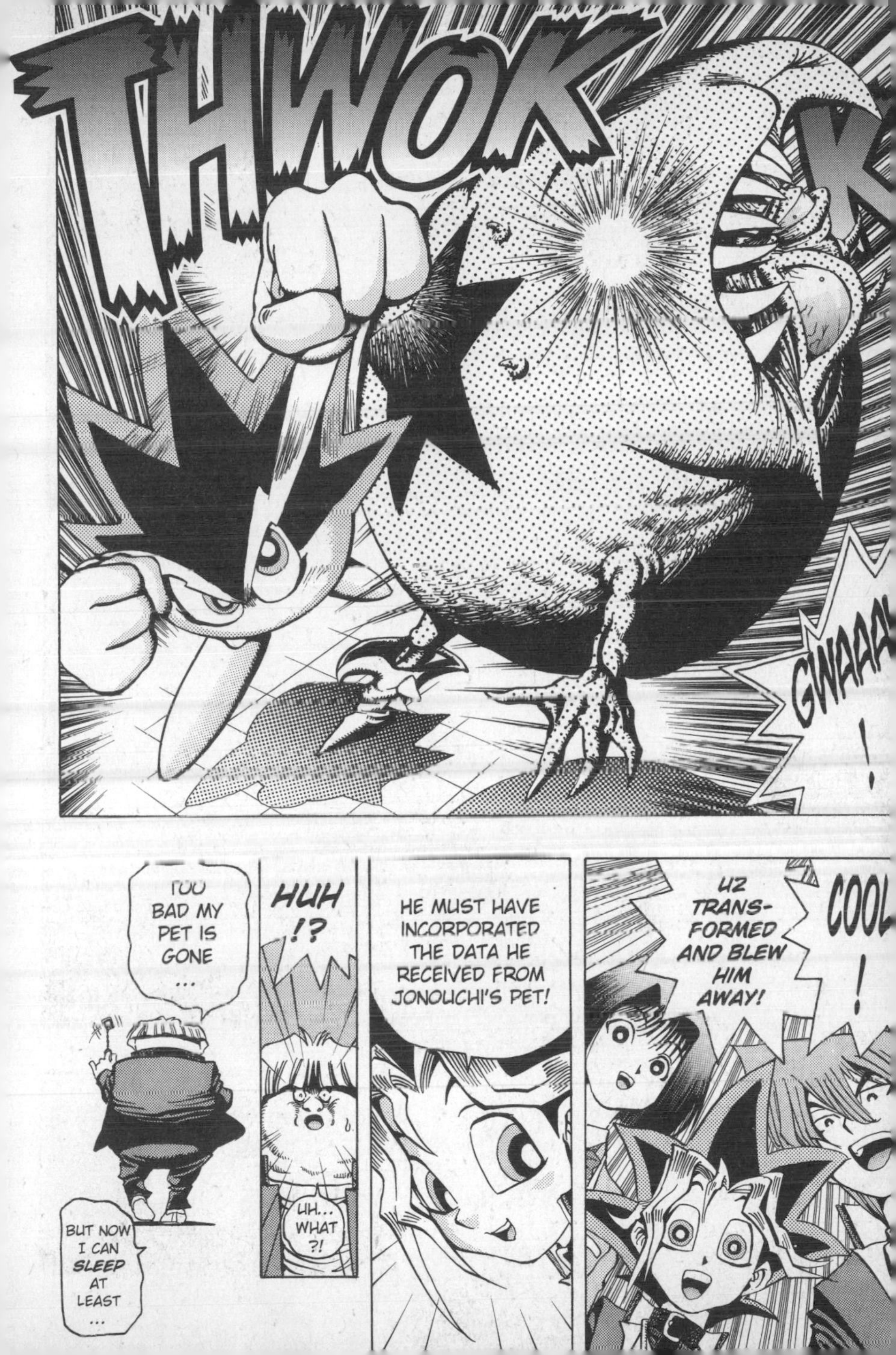
THWOK
GWAAA
!
COOL
!
UZ TRANSFORMED AND BLEW HIM AWAY!
HE MUST HAVE INCORPORATED THE DATA HE RECEIVED FROM JONOUCHI'S PET!
HUH !?
UH... WHAT ?!
TOO BAD MY PET IS GONE ...
BUT NOW I CAN SLEEP AT LEAST ...

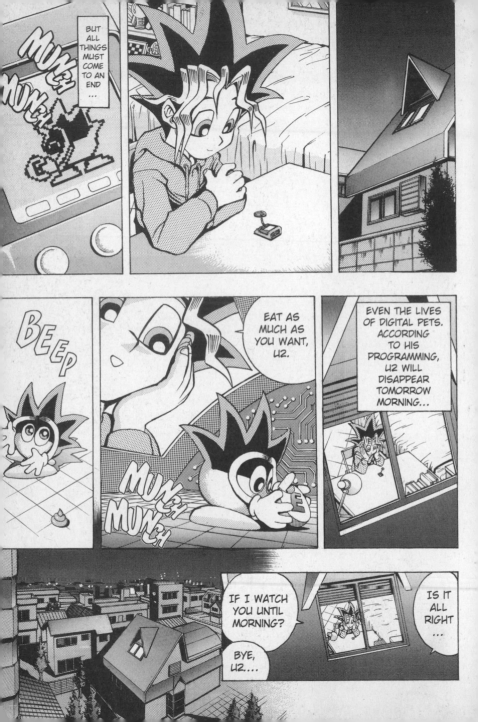

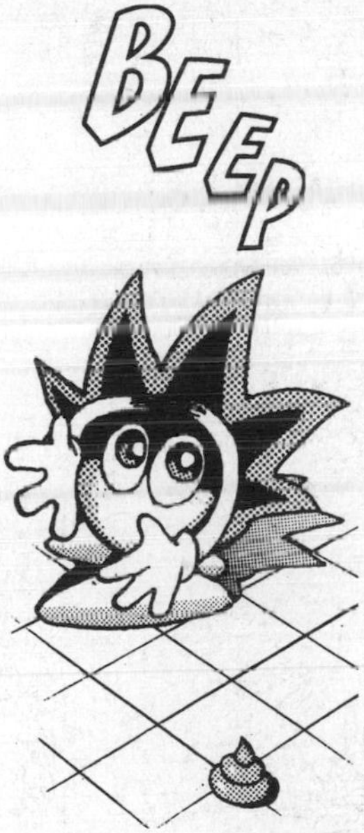
BEEP

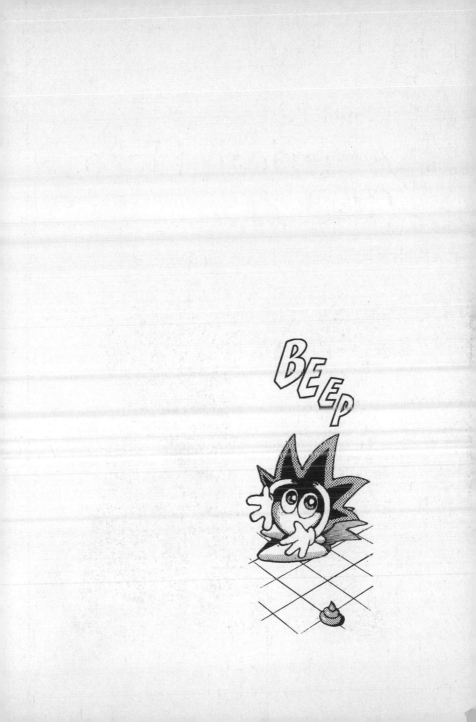

# Duel 22:
# American Hero
# (Part 1)

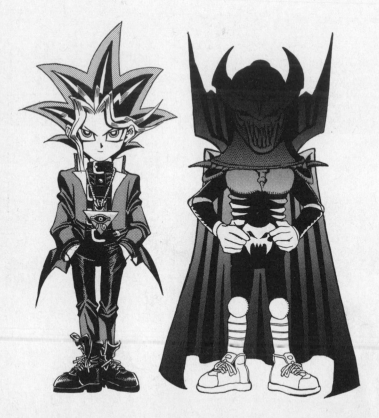

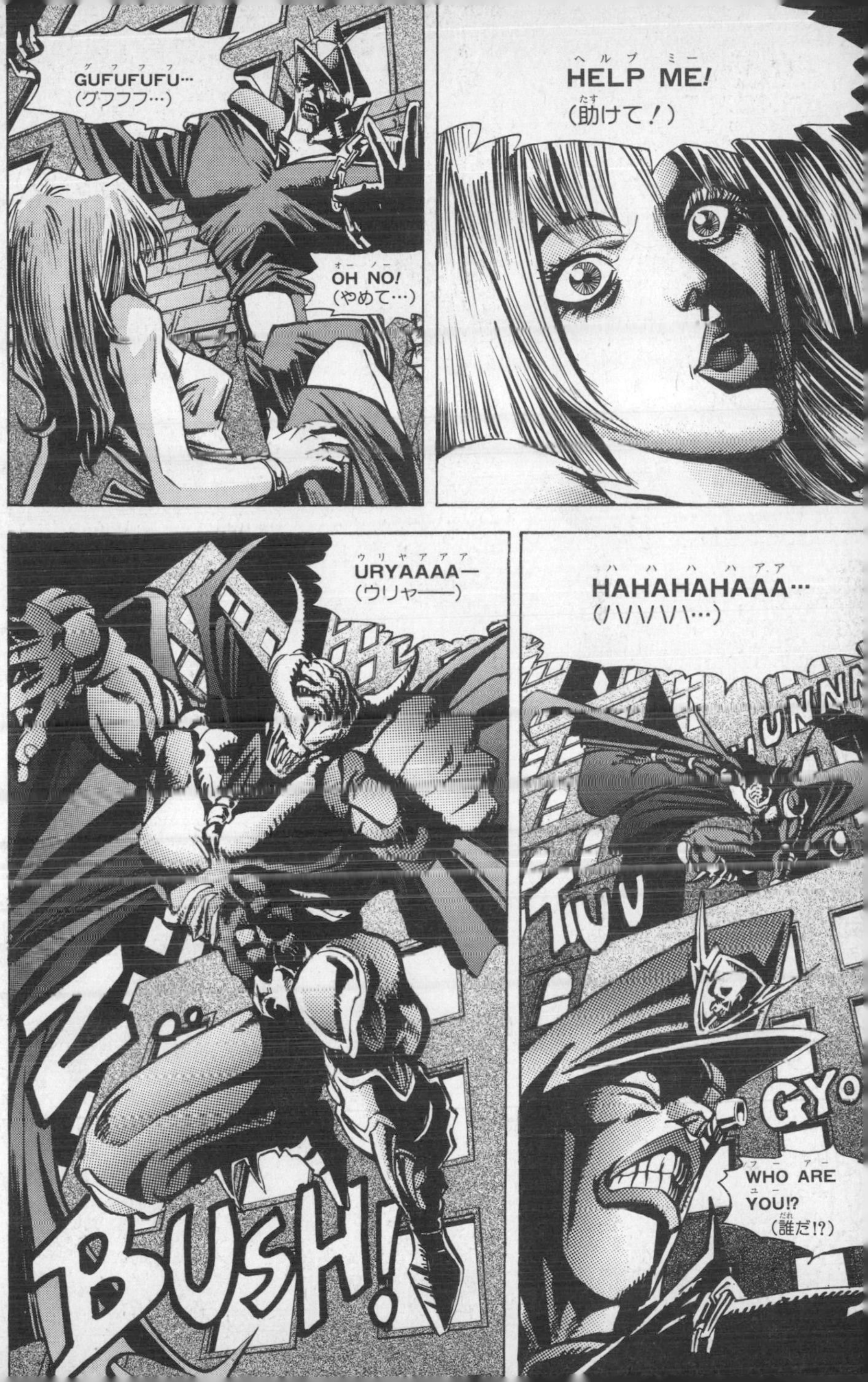
HELP ME!
(助けて!)
GUFUFUFU…
(グフフフ…)
OH NO!
(やめて…)
HAHAHAHAAA…
(ハハハハ…)
GYO
WHO ARE YOU!?
(誰だ!?)
URYAAAA—
(ウリャ——)
BUSH!

READ THIS WAY

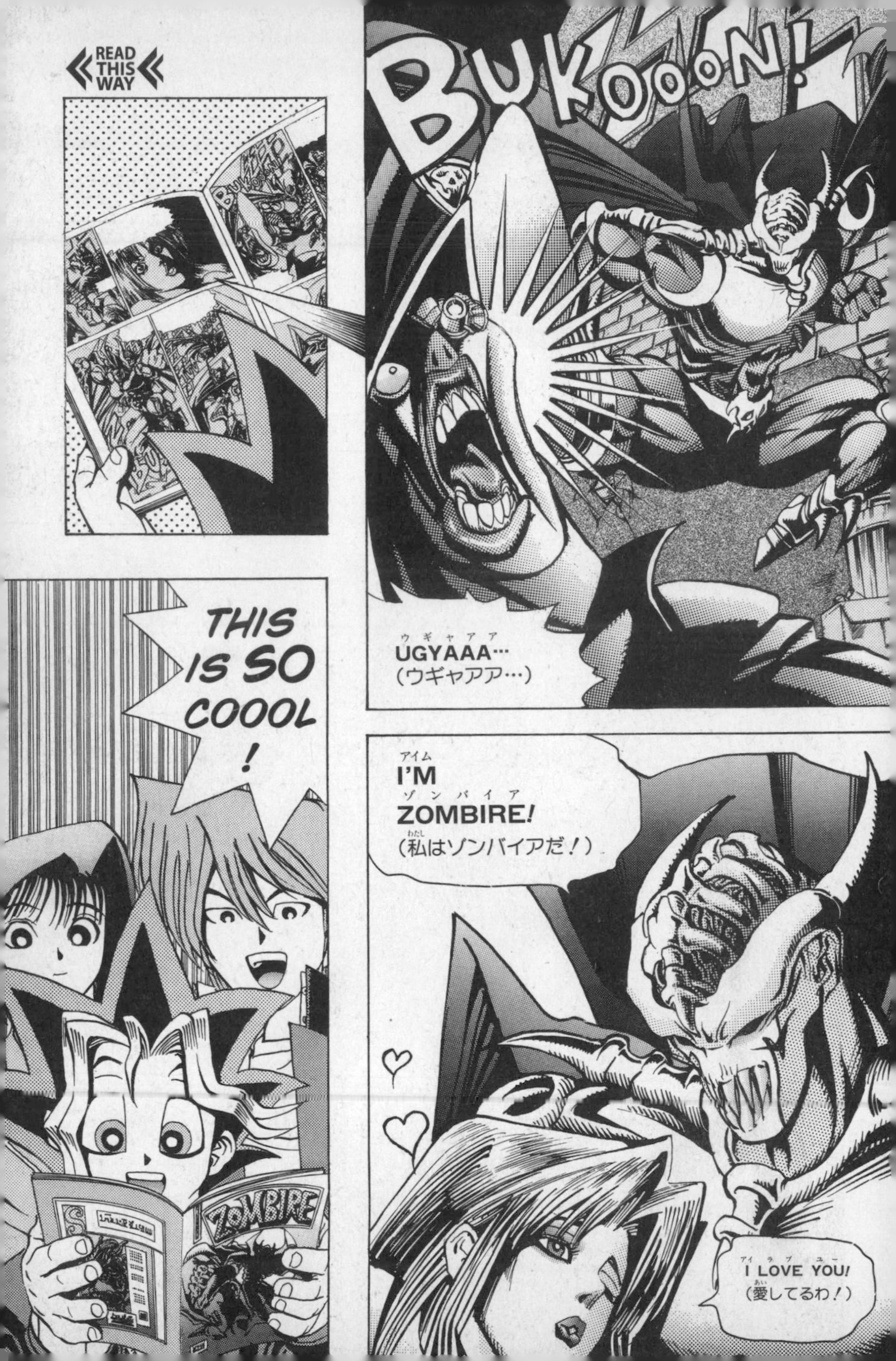
BUKOOON!
UGYAAA… (ウギャアア…)
I'M ZOMBIRE! (私はゾンバイアだ！)
I LOVE YOU! (愛してるわ！)
THIS IS SO COOOL!
ZOMBIRE

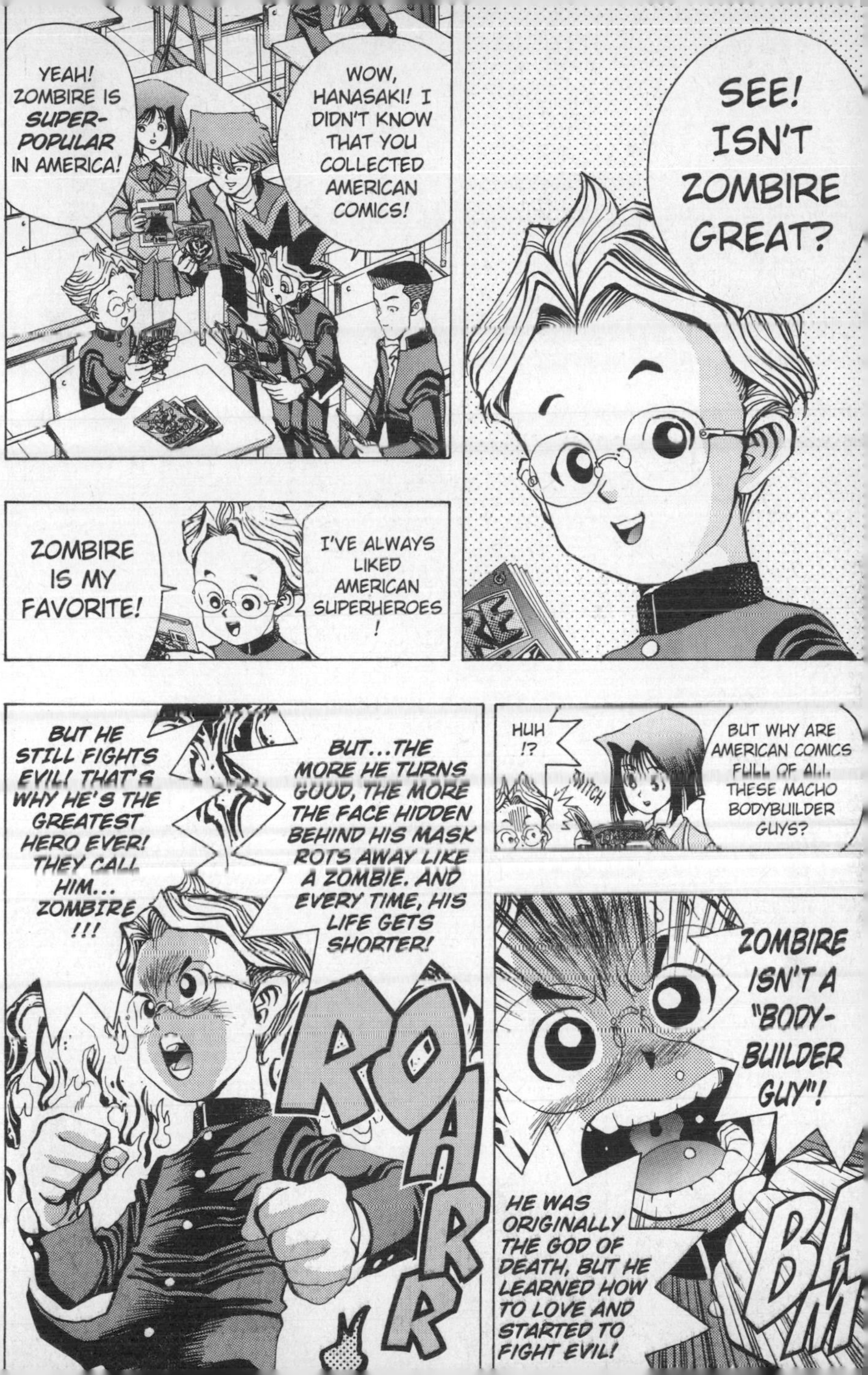
SEE! ISN'T ZOMBIRE GREAT?
WOW, HANASAKI! I DIDN'T KNOW THAT YOU COLLECTED AMERICAN COMICS!
YEAH! ZOMBIRE IS SUPER-POPULAR IN AMERICA!
I'VE ALWAYS LIKED AMERICAN SUPERHEROES!
ZOMBIRE IS MY FAVORITE!
BUT WHY ARE AMERICAN COMICS FULL OF ALL THESE MACHO BODYBUILDER GUYS?
HUH !?
TWITCH
ZOMBIRE ISN'T A "BODY-BUILDER GUY"!
BAM
HE WAS ORIGINALLY THE GOD OF DEATH, BUT HE LEARNED HOW TO LOVE AND STARTED TO FIGHT EVIL!
BUT...THE MORE HE TURNS GOOD, THE MORE THE FACE HIDDEN BEHIND HIS MASK ROTS AWAY LIKE A ZOMBIE. AND EVERY TIME, HIS LIFE GETS SHORTER!
BUT HE STILL FIGHTS EVIL! THAT'S WHY HE'S THE GREATEST HERO EVER! THEY CALL HIM... ZOMBIRE !!!
ROARR

READ THIS WAY

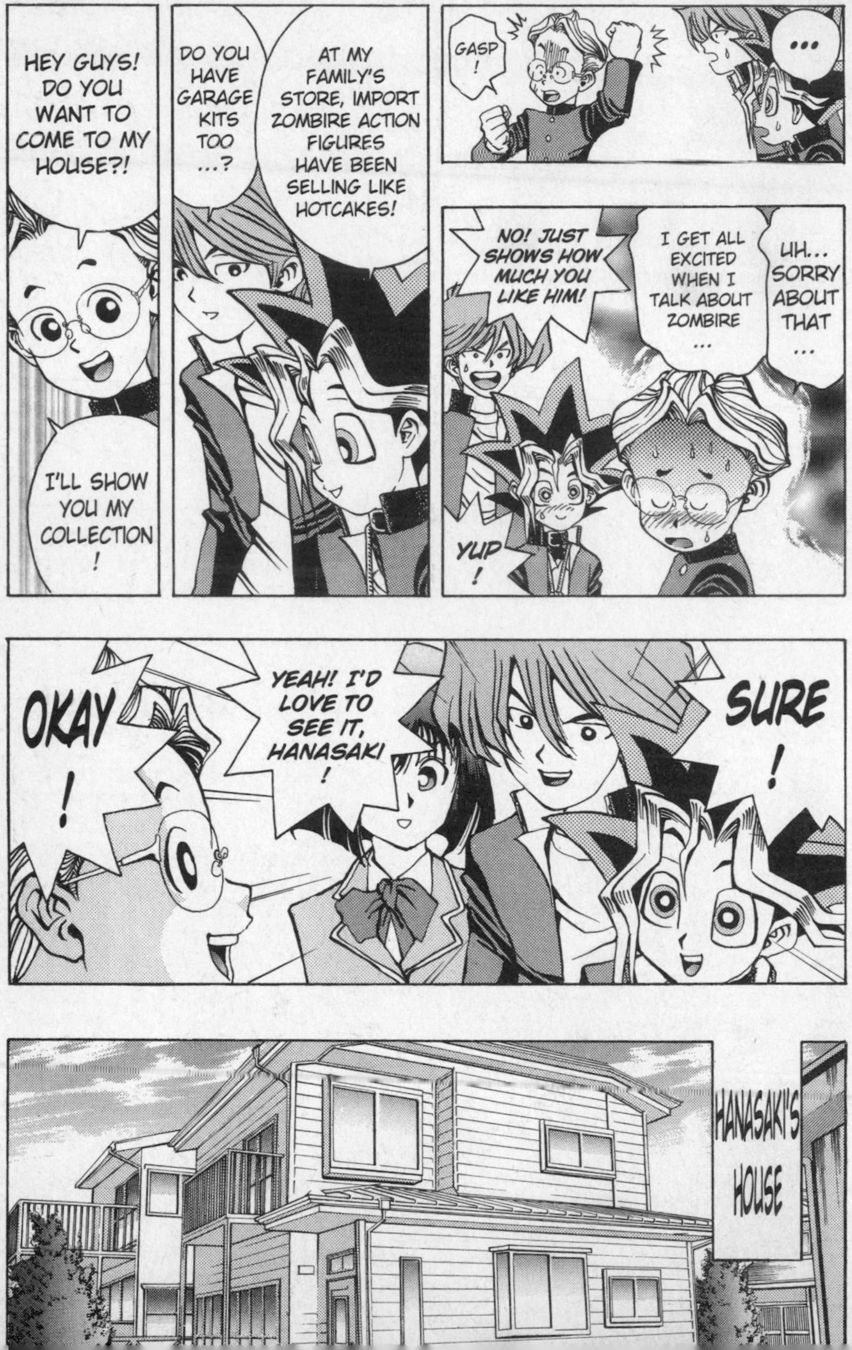

...
GASP!
UH... SORRY ABOUT THAT...
I GET ALL EXCITED WHEN I TALK ABOUT ZOMBIRE...
NO! JUST SHOWS HOW MUCH YOU LIKE HIM!
YUP!
AT MY FAMILY'S STORE, IMPORT ZOMBIRE ACTION FIGURES HAVE BEEN SELLING LIKE HOTCAKES!
DO YOU HAVE GARAGE KITS TOO...?
HEY GUYS! DO YOU WANT TO COME TO MY HOUSE?!
I'LL SHOW YOU MY COLLECTION!
SURE!
YEAH! I'D LOVE TO SEE IT, HANASAKI!
OKAY!
HANASAKI'S HOUSE

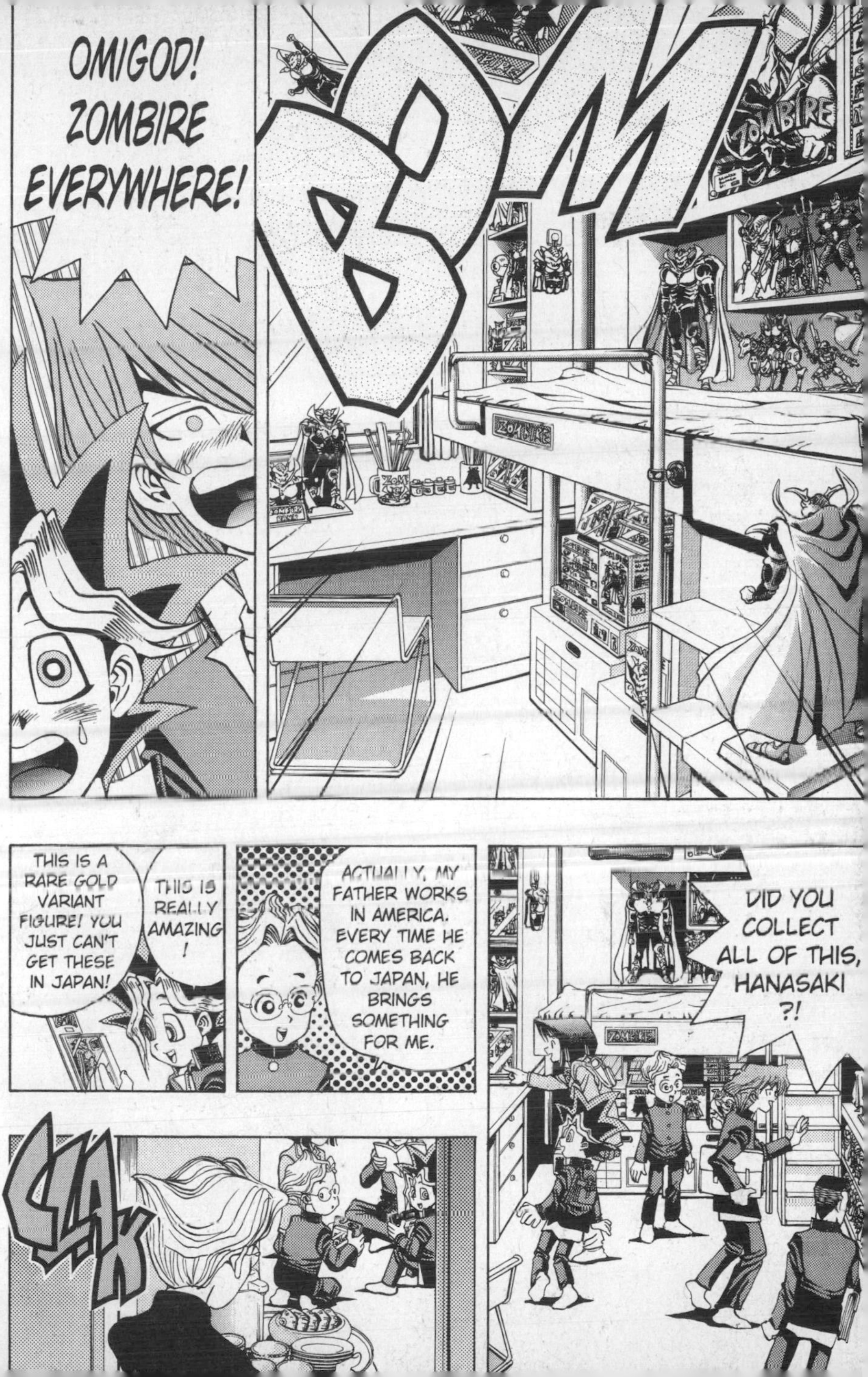
ZOMBIRE
OMIGOD! ZOMBIRE EVERYWHERE!
DID YOU COLLECT ALL OF THIS, HANASAKI ?!
ACTUALLY, MY FATHER WORKS IN AMERICA. EVERY TIME HE COMES BACK TO JAPAN, HE BRINGS SOMETHING FOR ME.
THIS IS REALLY AMAZING!
THIS IS A RARE GOLD VARIANT FIGURE! YOU JUST CAN'T GET THESE IN JAPAN!
CLAK

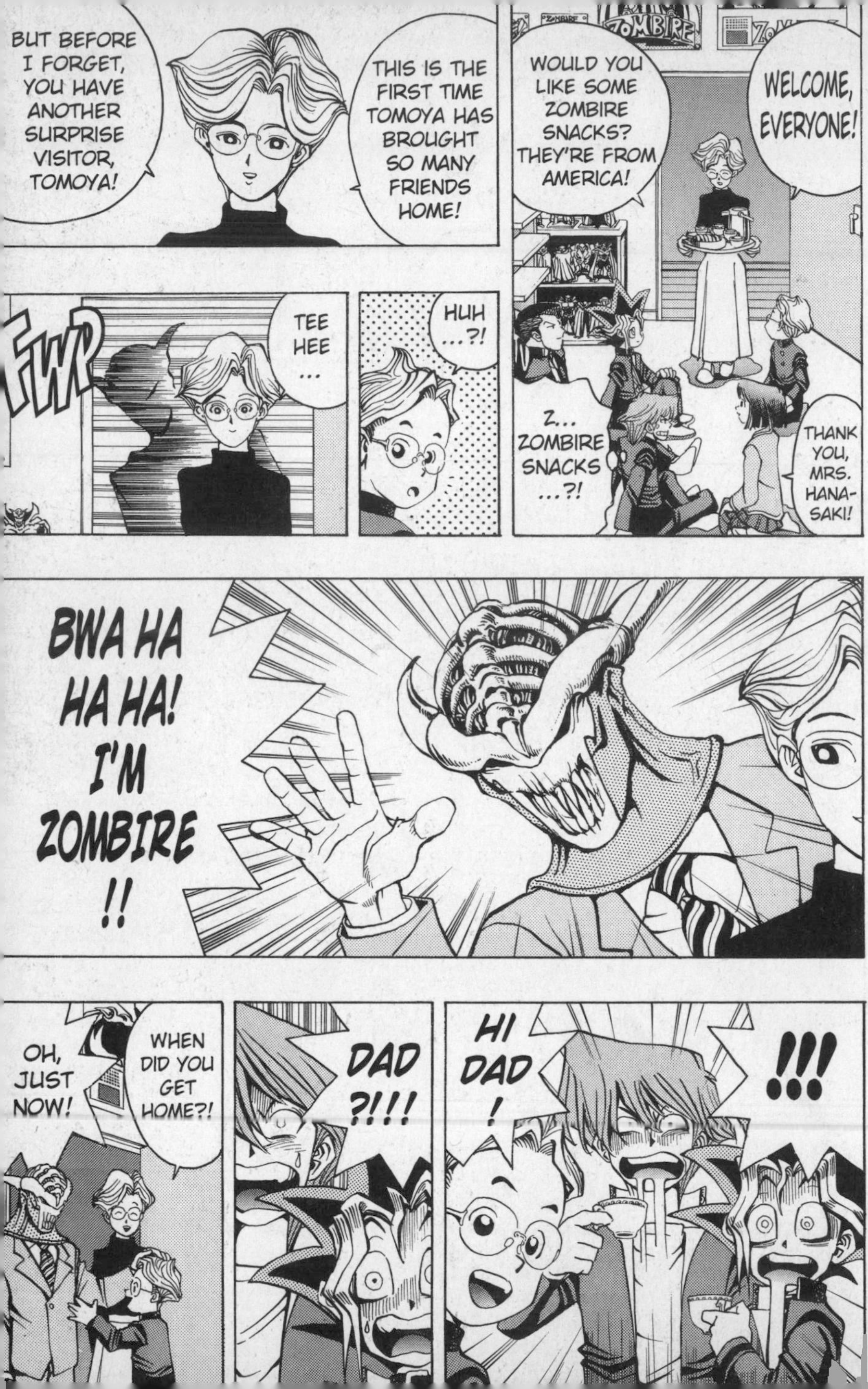
WELCOME, EVERYONE!
WOULD YOU LIKE SOME ZOMBIRE SNACKS? THEY'RE FROM AMERICA!
THANK YOU, MRS. HANA-SAKI!
Z... ZOMBIRE SNACKS ...?!
THIS IS THE FIRST TIME TOMOYA HAS BROUGHT SO MANY FRIENDS HOME!
BUT BEFORE I FORGET, YOU HAVE ANOTHER SURPRISE VISITOR, TOMOYA!
HUH ...?!
TEE HEE ...
FWP
BWA HA HA HA! I'M ZOMBIRE !!
!!!
HI DAD !
DAD ?!!!
WHEN DID YOU GET HOME?!
OH, JUST NOW!

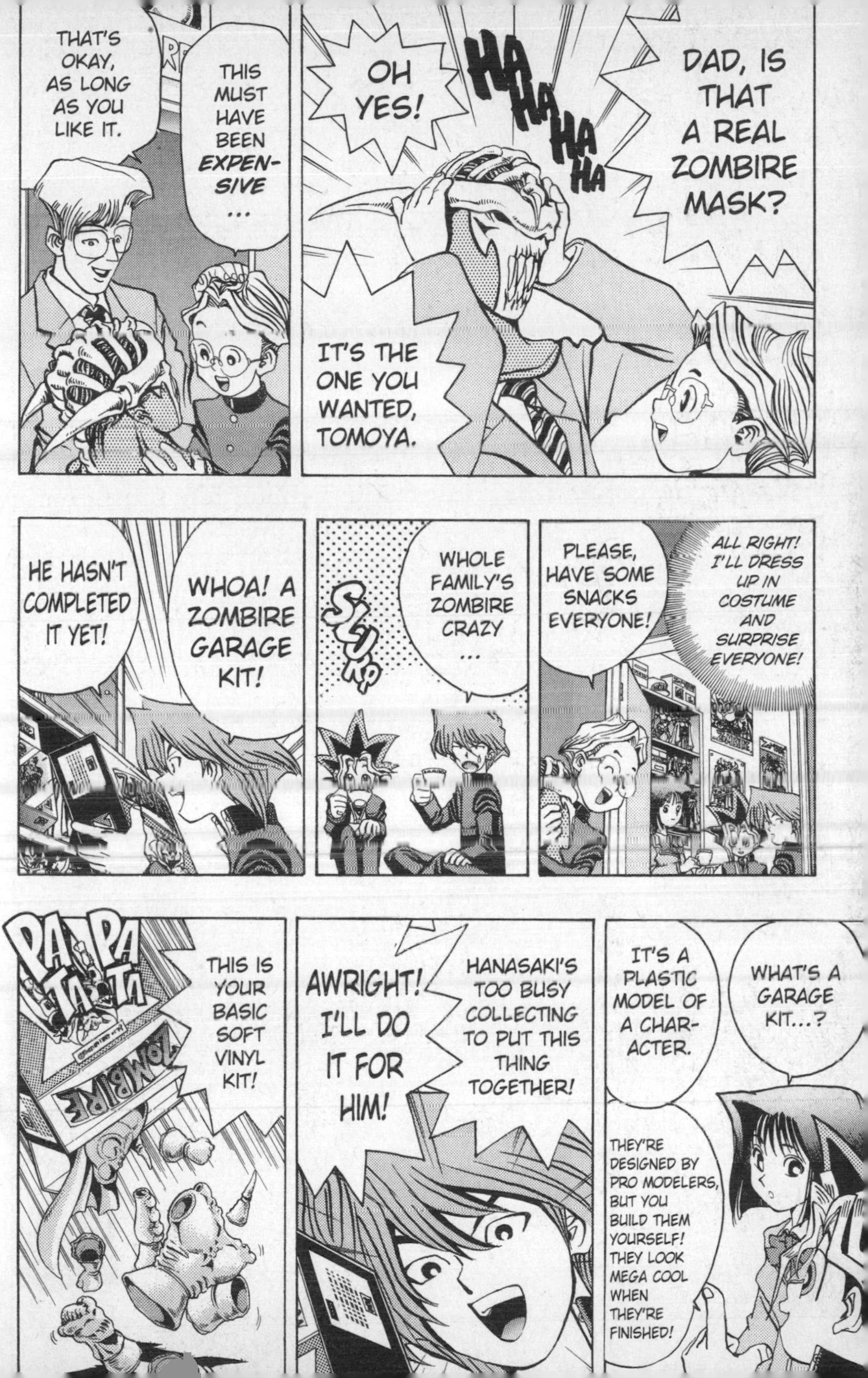
DAD, IS THAT A REAL ZOMBIRE MASK?
HA HA HA HA
OH YES!
IT'S THE ONE YOU WANTED, TOMOYA.
THIS MUST HAVE BEEN *EXPENSIVE* ...
THAT'S OKAY, AS LONG AS YOU LIKE IT.
*ALL RIGHT! I'LL DRESS UP IN COSTUME AND SURPRISE EVERYONE!*
PLEASE, HAVE SOME SNACKS EVERYONE!
WHOLE FAMILY'S ZOMBIRE CRAZY ...
SLURP
WHOA! A ZOMBIRE GARAGE KIT!
HE HASN'T COMPLETED IT YET!
WHAT'S A GARAGE KIT...?
IT'S A PLASTIC MODEL OF A CHARACTER.
THEY'RE DESIGNED BY PRO MODELERS, BUT YOU BUILD THEM YOURSELF! THEY LOOK MEGA COOL WHEN THEY'RE FINISHED!
HANASAKI'S TOO BUSY COLLECTING TO PUT THIS THING TOGETHER!
AWRIGHT! I'LL DO IT FOR HIM!
THIS IS YOUR BASIC SOFT VINYL KIT!
PA TA PA TA
ZOMBIRE

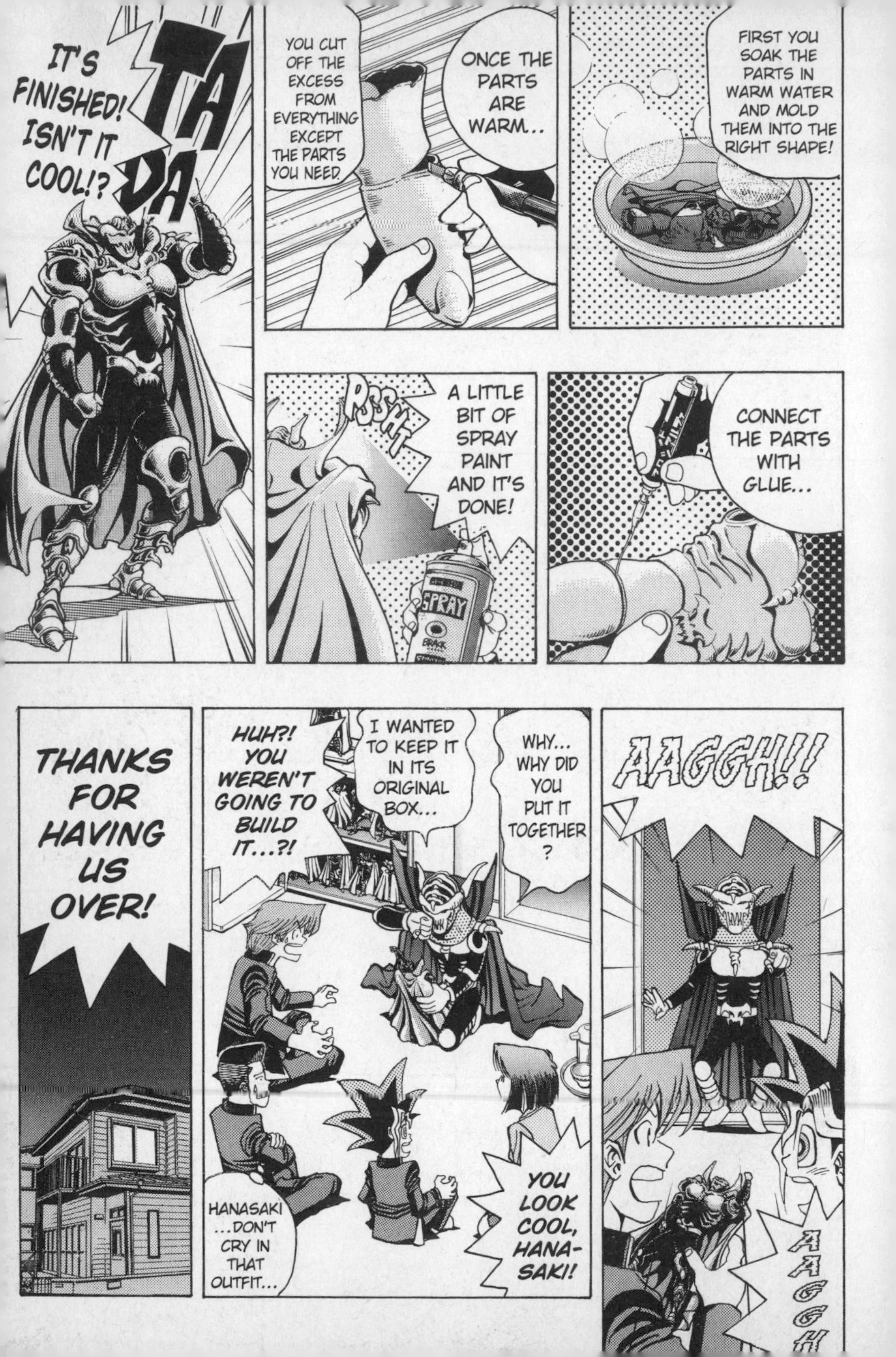
FIRST YOU SOAK THE PARTS IN WARM WATER AND MOLD THEM INTO THE RIGHT SHAPE!
ONCE THE PARTS ARE WARM...
YOU CUT OFF THE EXCESS FROM EVERYTHING EXCEPT THE PARTS YOU NEED.
CONNECT THE PARTS WITH GLUE...
PSSHT
A LITTLE BIT OF SPRAY PAINT AND IT'S DONE!
SPRAY
TA DA
IT'S FINISHED! ISN'T IT COOL!?
AAGGH!!
AAGGH
WHY... WHY DID YOU PUT IT TOGETHER?
I WANTED TO KEEP IT IN ITS ORIGINAL BOX...
HUH?! YOU WEREN'T GOING TO BUILD IT...?!
YOU LOOK COOL, HANASAKI!
HANASAKI ...DON'T CRY IN THAT OUTFIT...
THANKS FOR HAVING US OVER!

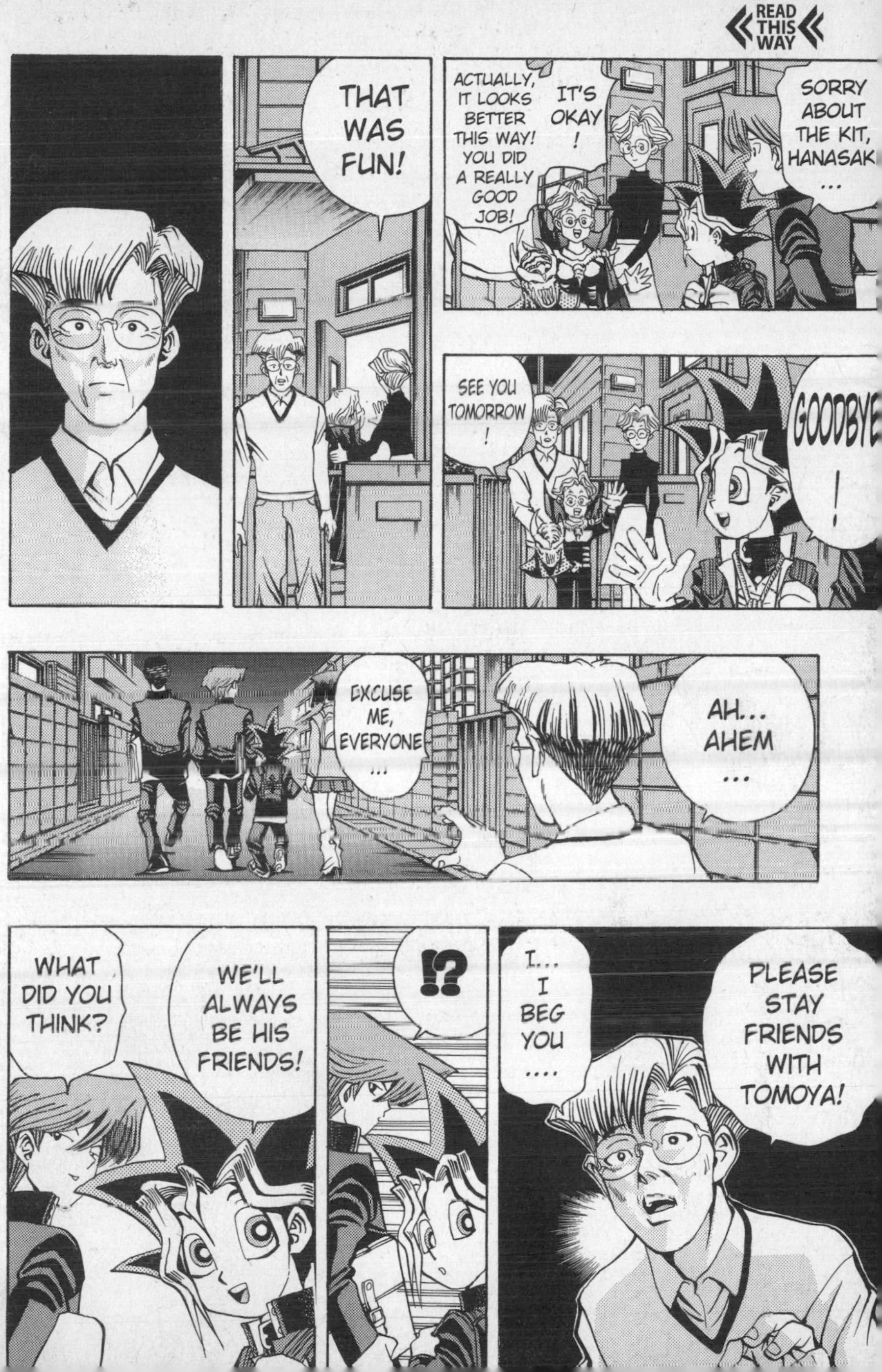
READ THIS WAY
SORRY ABOUT THE KIT, HANASAK...
IT'S OKAY!
ACTUALLY, IT LOOKS BETTER THIS WAY! YOU DID A REALLY GOOD JOB!
GOODBYE!
SEE YOU TOMORROW!
THAT WAS FUN!
AH... AHEM...
EXCUSE ME, EVERYONE...
PLEASE STAY FRIENDS WITH TOMOYA!
I... I BEG YOU....
!?
WE'LL ALWAYS BE HIS FRIENDS!
WHAT DID YOU THINK?

READ THIS WAY

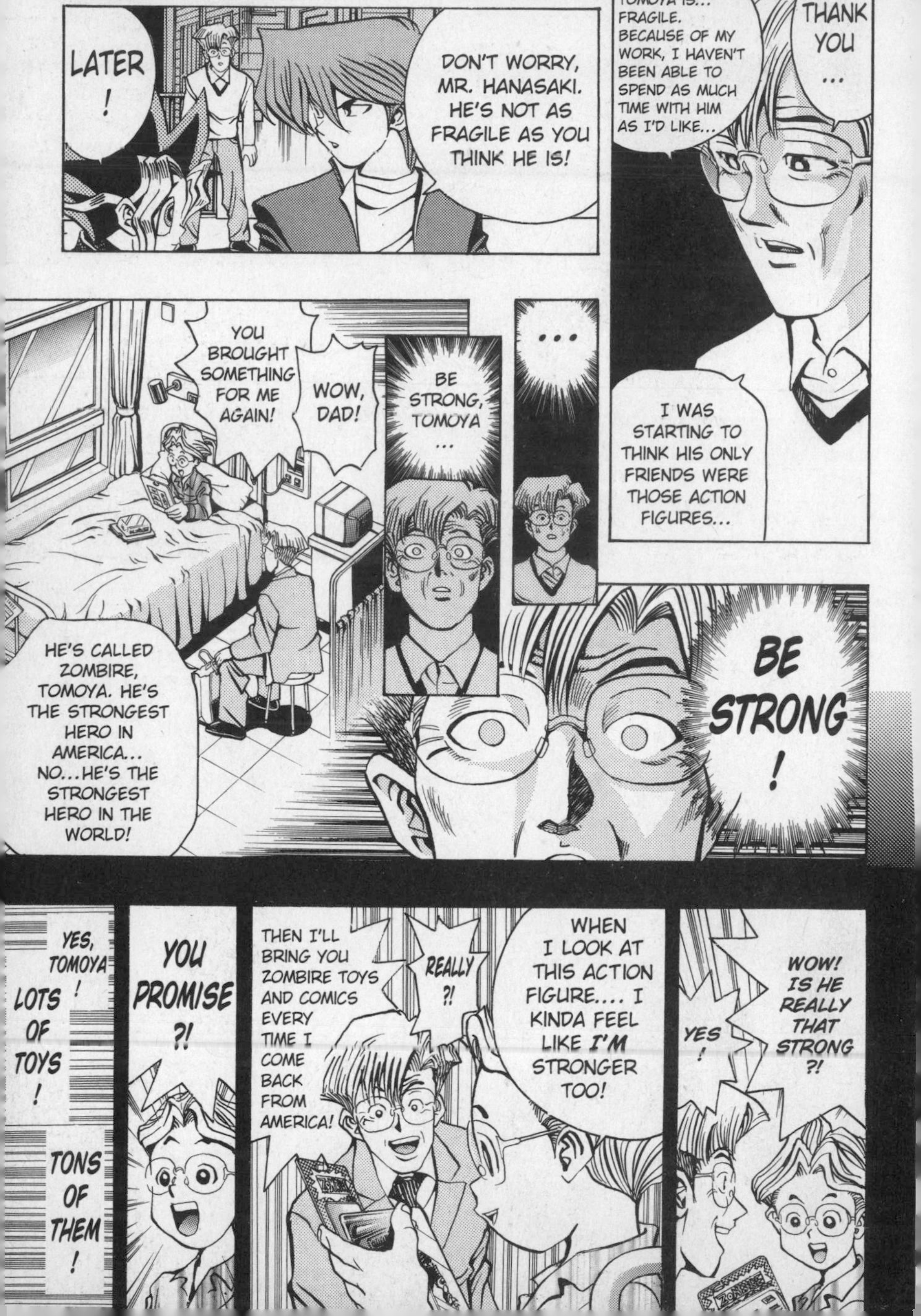
THANK YOU ...
TO BE HONEST, TOMOYA IS... FRAGILE. BECAUSE OF MY WORK, I HAVEN'T BEEN ABLE TO SPEND AS MUCH TIME WITH HIM AS I'D LIKE...
I WAS STARTING TO THINK HIS ONLY FRIENDS WERE THOSE ACTION FIGURES...
DON'T WORRY, MR. HANASAKI. HE'S NOT AS FRAGILE AS YOU THINK HE IS!
LATER!
BE STRONG!
...
BE STRONG, TOMOYA ...
WOW, DAD!
YOU BROUGHT SOMETHING FOR ME AGAIN!
HE'S CALLED ZOMBIRE, TOMOYA. HE'S THE STRONGEST HERO IN AMERICA... NO...HE'S THE STRONGEST HERO IN THE WORLD!
WOW! IS HE REALLY THAT STRONG?!
YES!
WHEN I LOOK AT THIS ACTION FIGURE.... I KINDA FEEL LIKE *I'M* STRONGER TOO!
REALLY?!
THEN I'LL BRING YOU ZOMBIRE TOYS AND COMICS EVERY TIME I COME BACK FROM AMERICA!
YOU PROMISE?!
YES, TOMOYA!
LOTS OF TOYS!
TONS OF THEM!

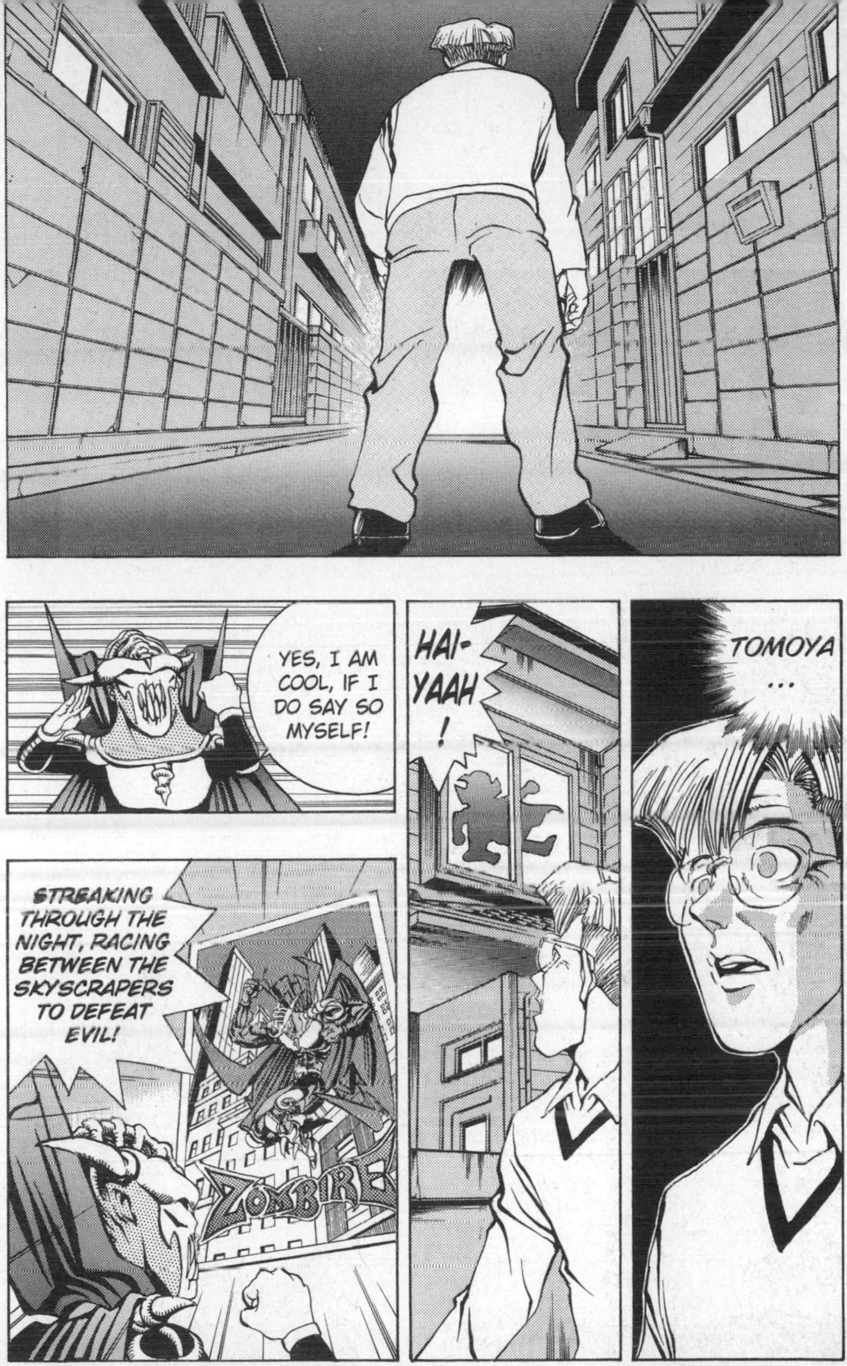
TOMOYA ...
HAI-YAAH!
YES, I AM COOL, IF I DO SAY SO MYSELF!
STREAKING THROUGH THE NIGHT, RACING BETWEEN THE SKYSCRAPERS TO DEFEAT EVIL!
ZOMBIRE

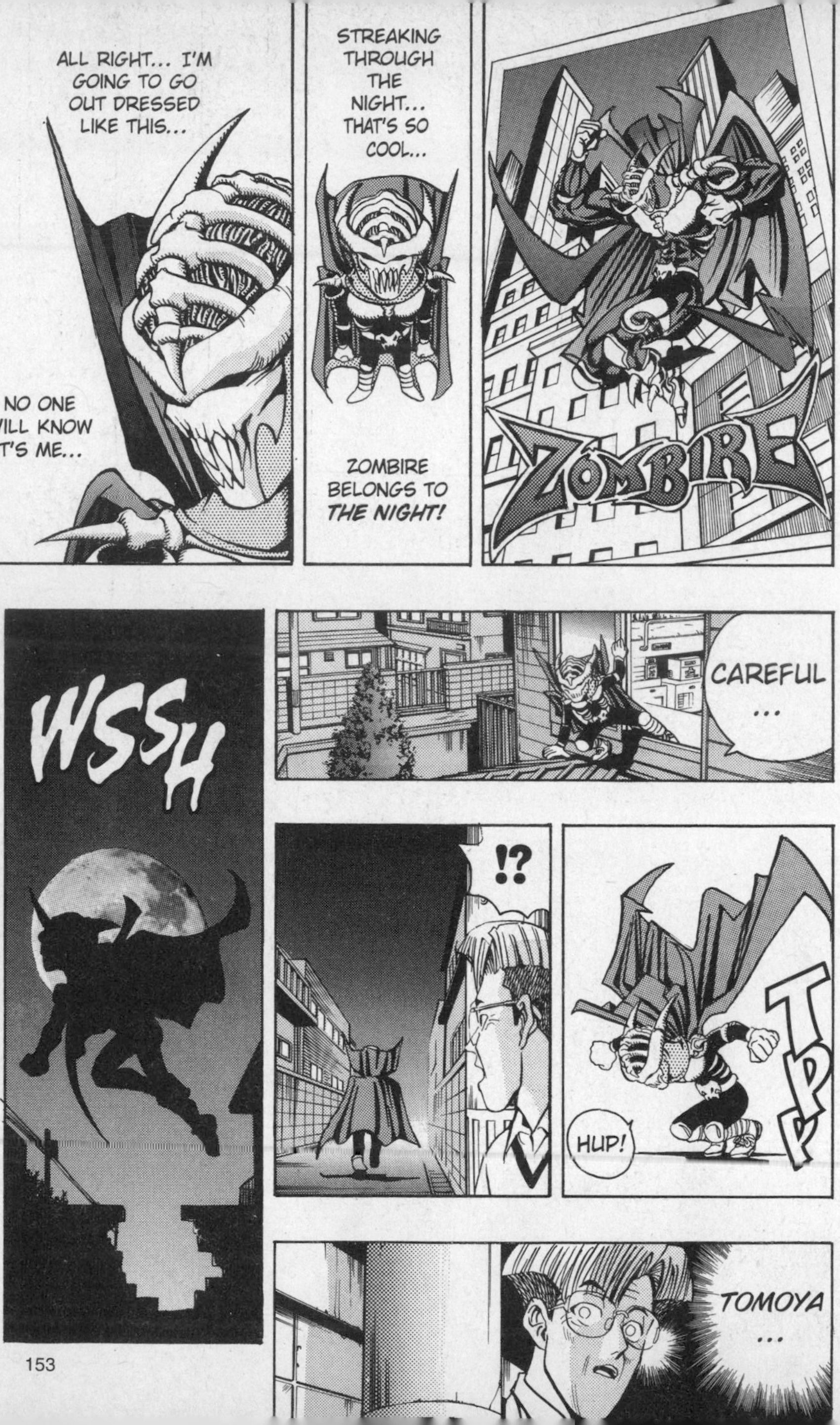
ZOMBIRE
STREAKING THROUGH THE NIGHT... THAT'S SO COOL...
ZOMBIRE BELONGS TO *THE NIGHT!*
ALL RIGHT... I'M GOING TO GO OUT DRESSED LIKE THIS...
NO ONE WILL KNOW IT'S ME...
CAREFUL ...
TP
HUP!
!?
TOMOYA ...
WSSH

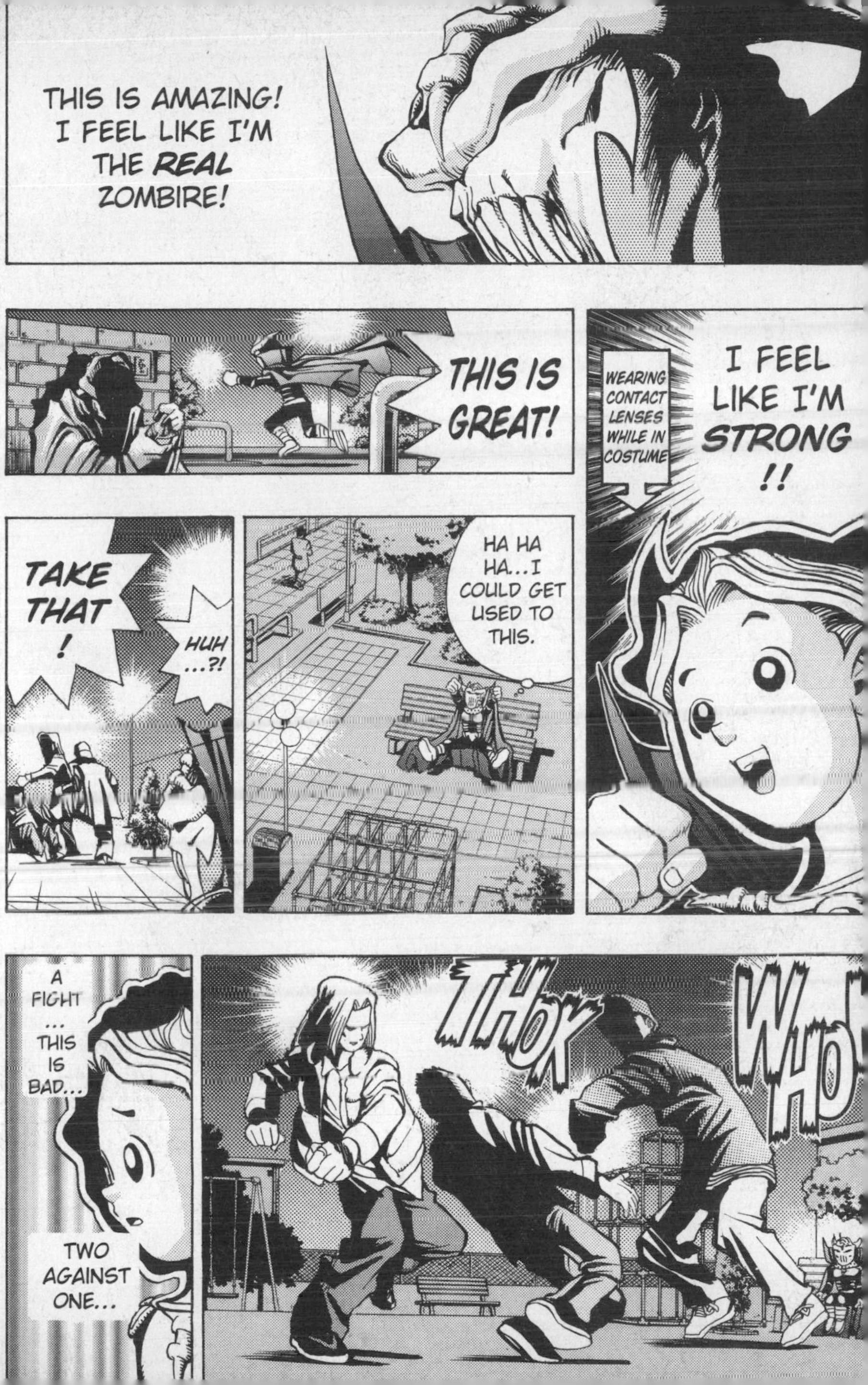
THIS IS AMAZING! I FEEL LIKE I'M THE REAL ZOMBIRE!
WEARING CONTACT LENSES WHILE IN COSTUME
I FEEL LIKE I'M STRONG !!
THIS IS GREAT!
HA HA HA...I COULD GET USED TO THIS.
TAKE THAT !
HUH ...?!
THOK
A FIGHT ... THIS IS BAD...
TWO AGAINST ONE...

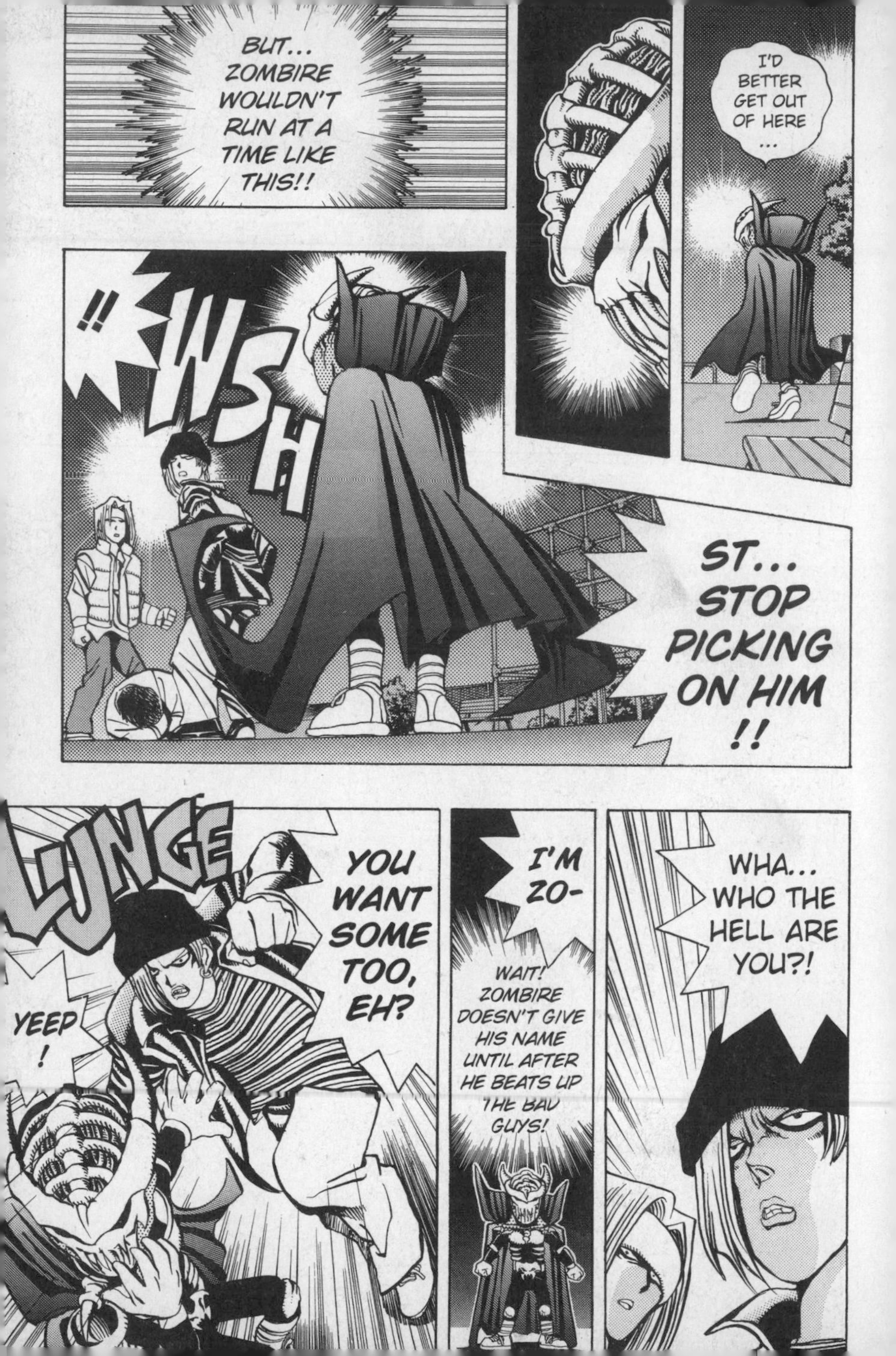
I'D BETTER GET OUT OF HERE ...
BUT... ZOMBIRE WOULDN'T RUN AT A TIME LIKE THIS!!
ST... STOP PICKING ON HIM!!
WSH
!!
WHA... WHO THE HELL ARE YOU?!
I'M ZO-
WAIT! ZOMBIRE DOESN'T GIVE HIS NAME UNTIL AFTER HE BEATS UP THE BAD GUYS!
YOU WANT SOME TOO, EH?
LUNGE
YEEP!

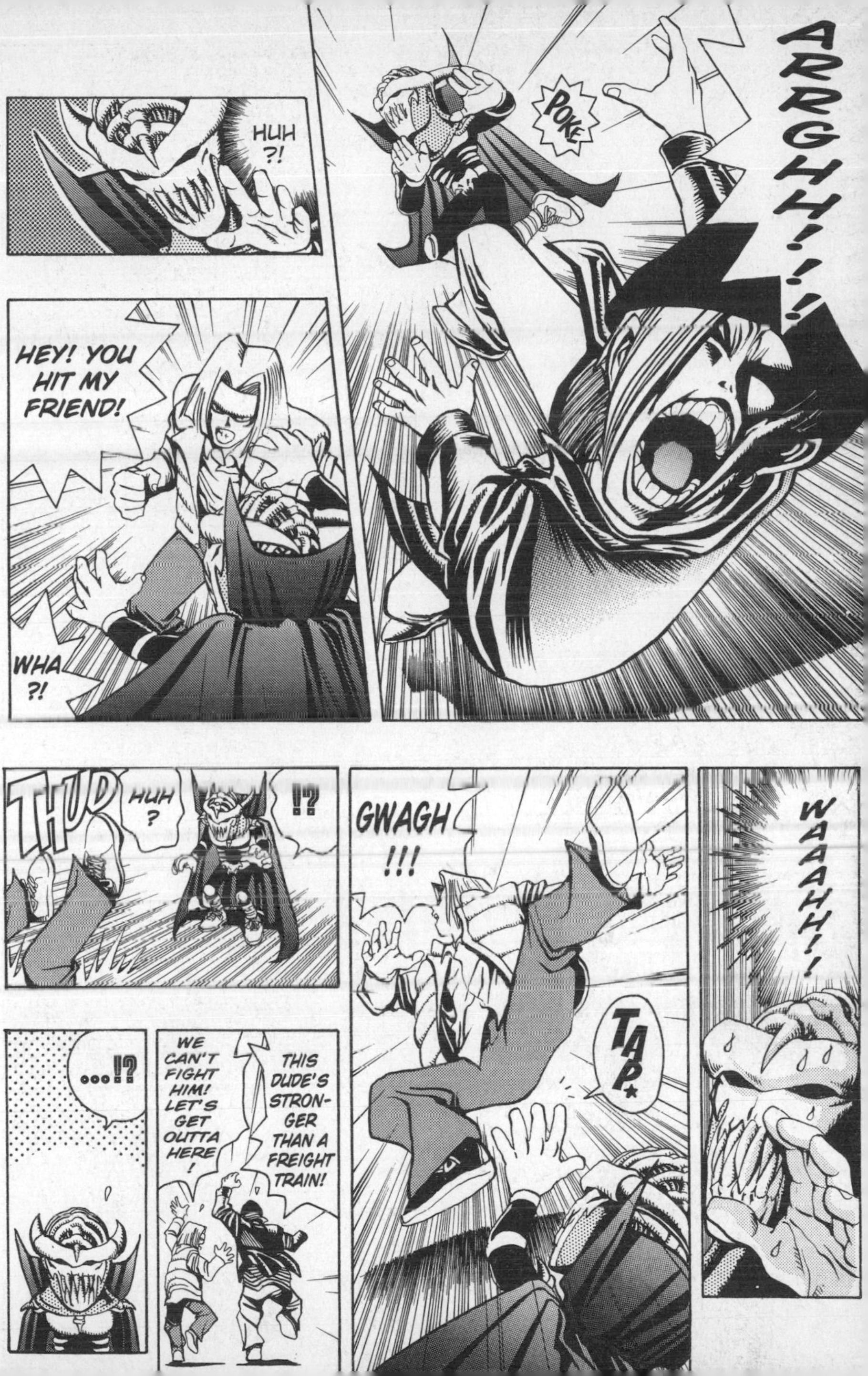
ARRGHH!!!
POKE
HUH ?!
HEY! YOU HIT MY FRIEND!
WHA ?!
WAAAHH!!
GWAGH !!!
TAP
!?
HUH ?
THUD
THIS DUDE'S STRONGER THAN A FREIGHT TRAIN!
WE CAN'T FIGHT HIM! LET'S GET OUTTA HERE!
...!?

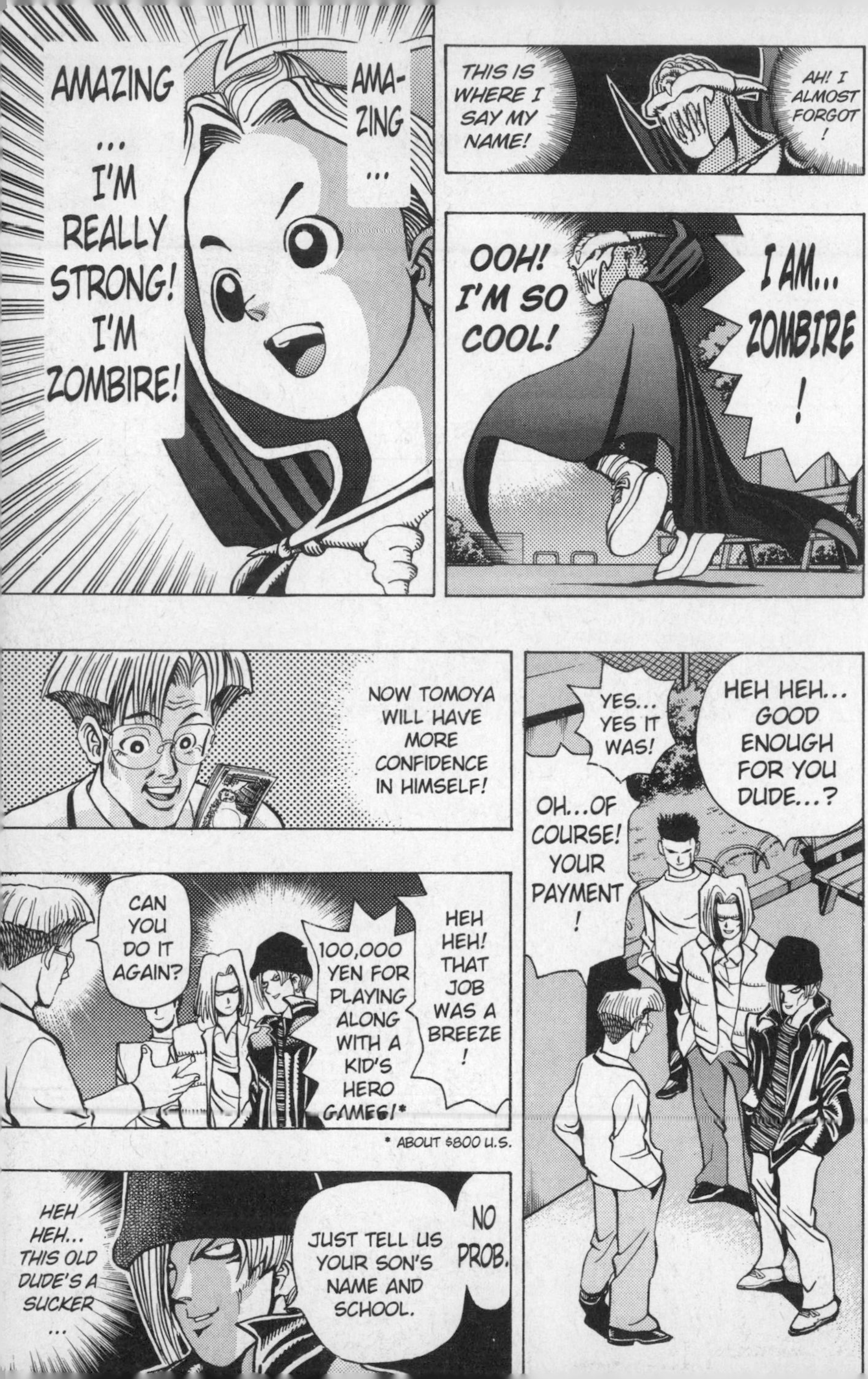
AH! I ALMOST FORGOT!
THIS IS WHERE I SAY MY NAME!
I AM... ZOMBIRE!
OOH! I'M SO COOL!
AMA-ZING...
AMAZING... I'M REALLY STRONG! I'M ZOMBIRE!
HEH HEH... GOOD ENOUGH FOR YOU DUDE...?
YES... YES IT WAS!
OH...OF COURSE! YOUR PAYMENT!
NOW TOMOYA WILL HAVE MORE CONFIDENCE IN HIMSELF!
HEH HEH! THAT JOB WAS A BREEZE!
100,000 YEN FOR PLAYING ALONG WITH A KID'S HERO GAMES!*
CAN YOU DO IT AGAIN?
NO PROB.
JUST TELL US YOUR SON'S NAME AND SCHOOL.
HEH HEH... THIS OLD DUDE'S A SUCKER...

* ABOUT $800 U.S.

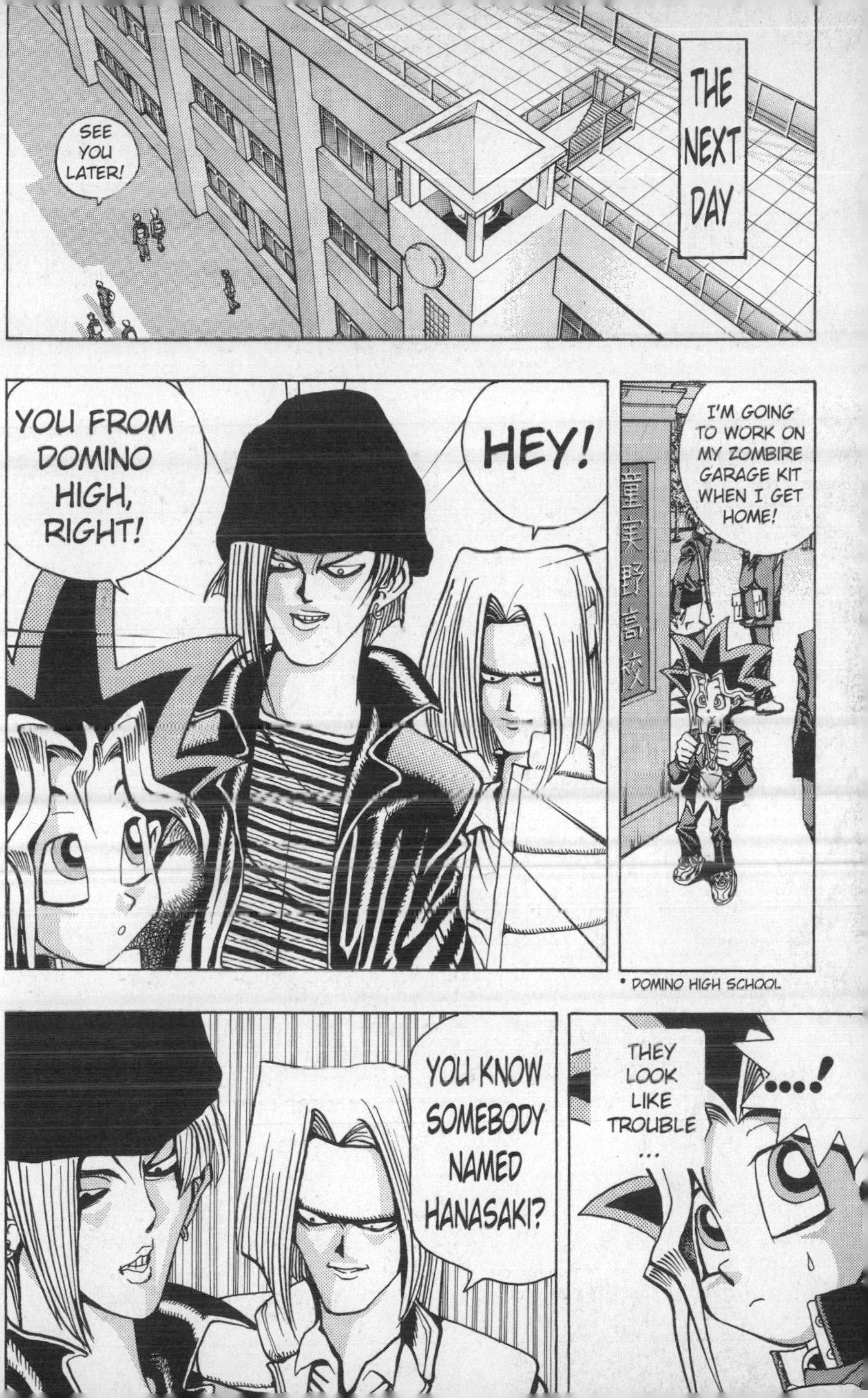
THE NEXT DAY
SEE YOU LATER!
I'M GOING TO WORK ON MY ZOMBIRE GARAGE KIT WHEN I GET HOME!
* DOMINO HIGH SCHOOL
HEY!
YOU FROM DOMINO HIGH, RIGHT!
...!
THEY LOOK LIKE TROUBLE ...
YOU KNOW SOMEBODY NAMED HANASAKI?

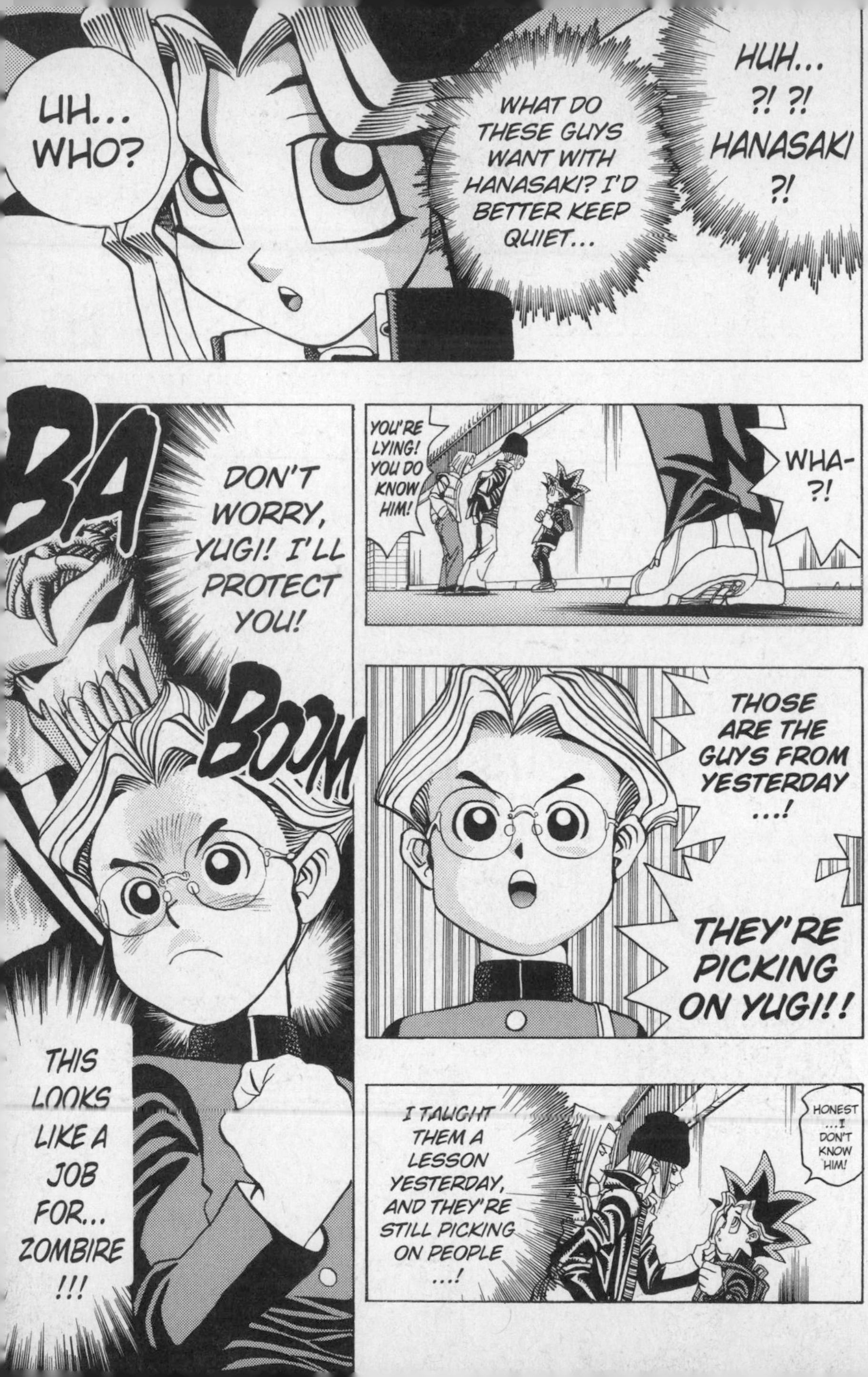
HUH... ?! ?! HANASAKI ?!
WHAT DO THESE GUYS WANT WITH HANASAKI? I'D BETTER KEEP QUIET...
UH... WHO?
WHA- ?!
YOU'RE LYING! YOU DO KNOW HIM!
THOSE ARE THE GUYS FROM YESTERDAY ...!
THEY'RE PICKING ON YUGI!!
HONEST ...I DON'T KNOW HIM!
I TAUGHT THEM A LESSON YESTERDAY, AND THEY'RE STILL PICKING ON PEOPLE ...!
BA
DON'T WORRY, YUGI! I'LL PROTECT YOU!
BOOM
THIS LOOKS LIKE A JOB FOR... ZOMBIRE !!!

ZOMBIRE

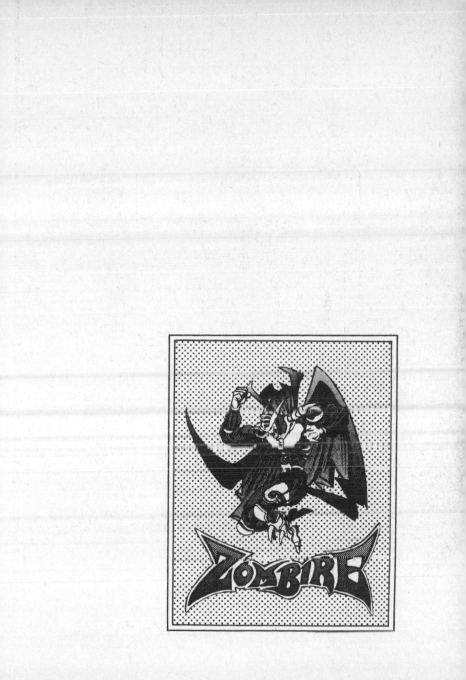

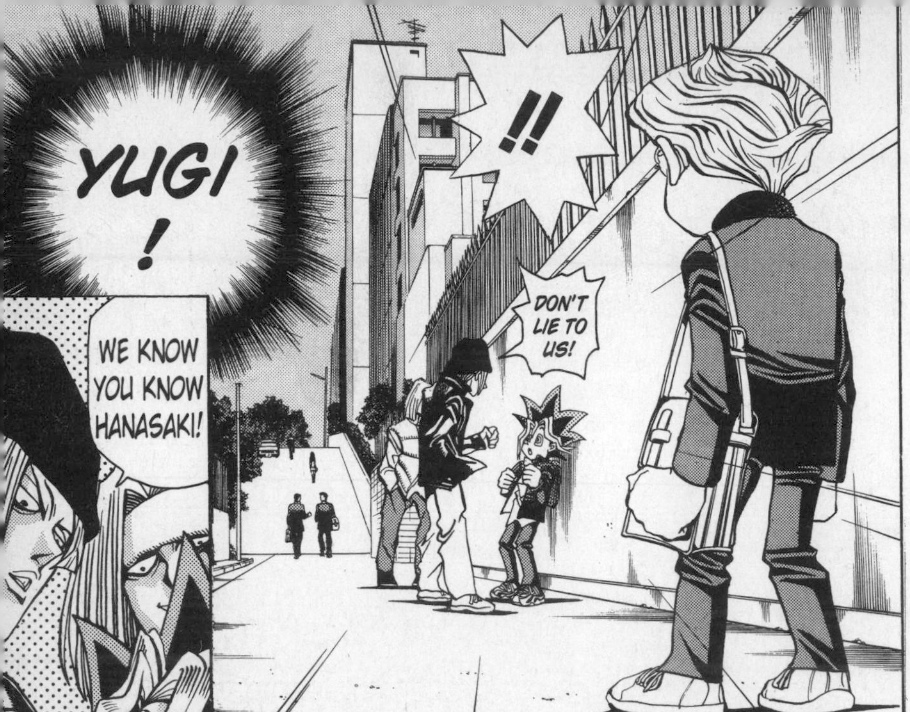
!!
DON'T LIE TO US!
THOSE PUNKS ARE PICKING ON PEOPLE AGAIN!
TMP
TMP
YUGI!
WE KNOW YOU KNOW HANASAKI!
REALLY! I DON'T!

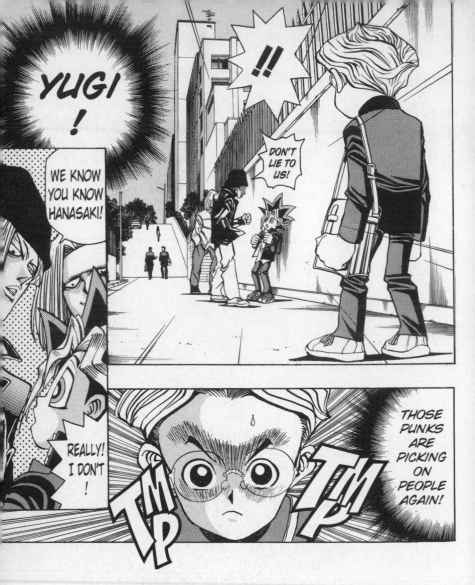

# Duel 23:
# American Hero (Part 2)

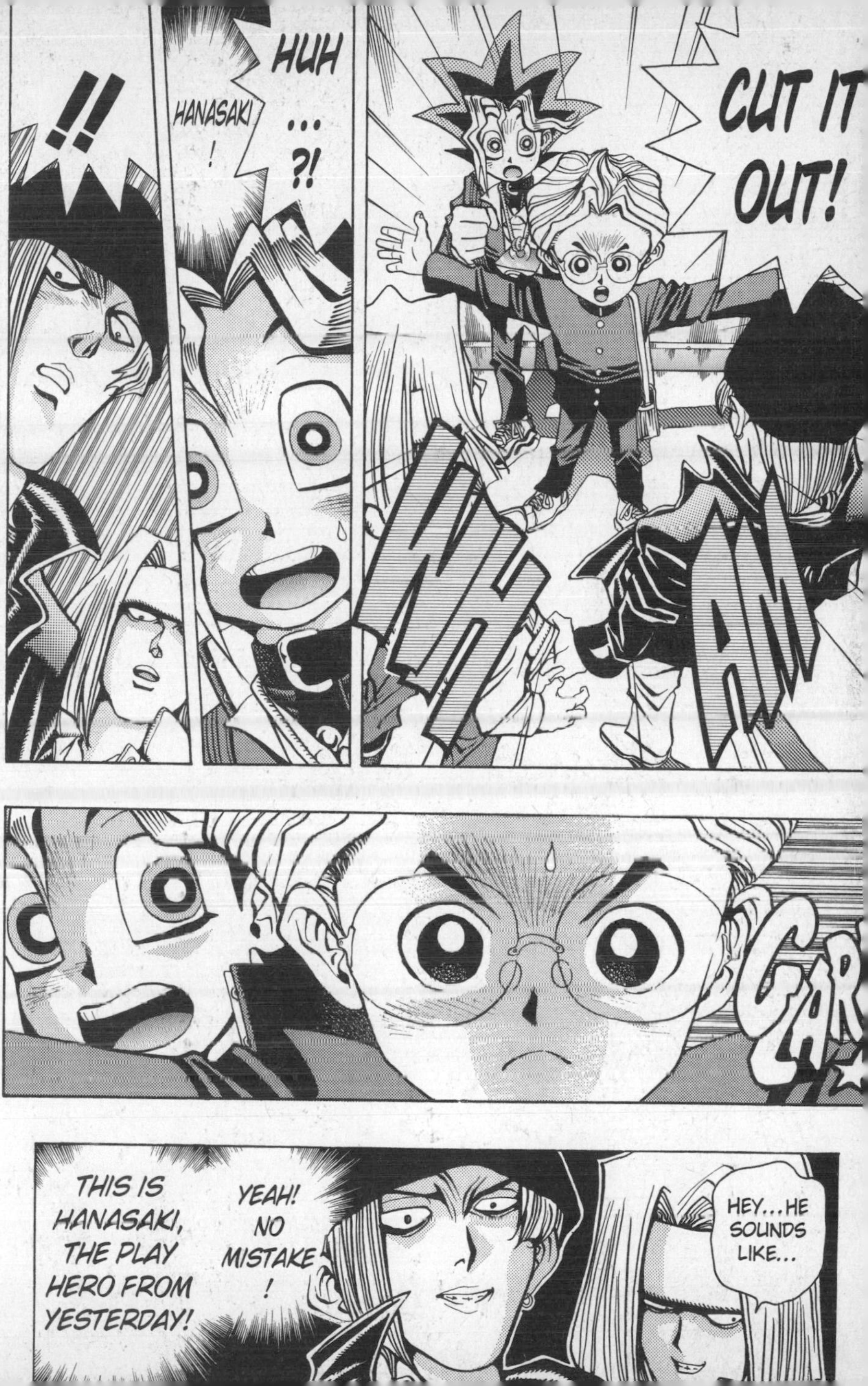
CUT IT OUT!
WHAM
HUH ... ?!
HANASAKI!
!!
GAR
HEY...HE SOUNDS LIKE...
YEAH! NO MISTAKE!
THIS IS HANASAKI, THE PLAY HERO FROM YESTERDAY!

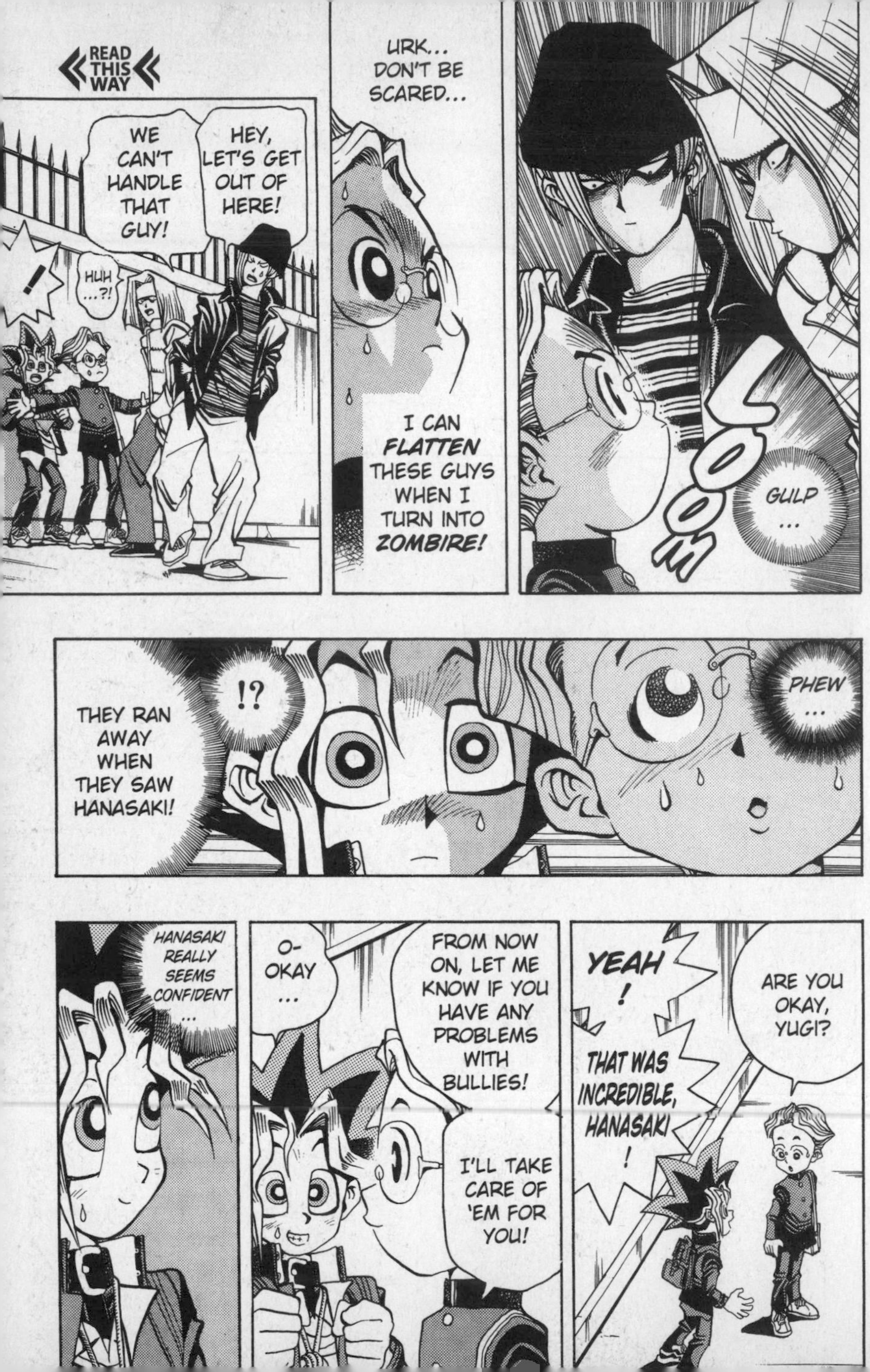
READ THIS WAY
GULP ...
LOOOOM
URK... DON'T BE SCARED...
I CAN FLATTEN THESE GUYS WHEN I TURN INTO ZOMBIRE!
HEY, LET'S GET OUT OF HERE!
WE CAN'T HANDLE THAT GUY!
HUH ...?!
!
PHEW ...
!?
THEY RAN AWAY WHEN THEY SAW HANASAKI!
ARE YOU OKAY, YUGI?
YEAH!
THAT WAS INCREDIBLE, HANASAKI!
FROM NOW ON, LET ME KNOW IF YOU HAVE ANY PROBLEMS WITH BULLIES!
I'LL TAKE CARE OF 'EM FOR YOU!
O-OKAY ...
HANASAKI REALLY SEEMS CONFIDENT ...

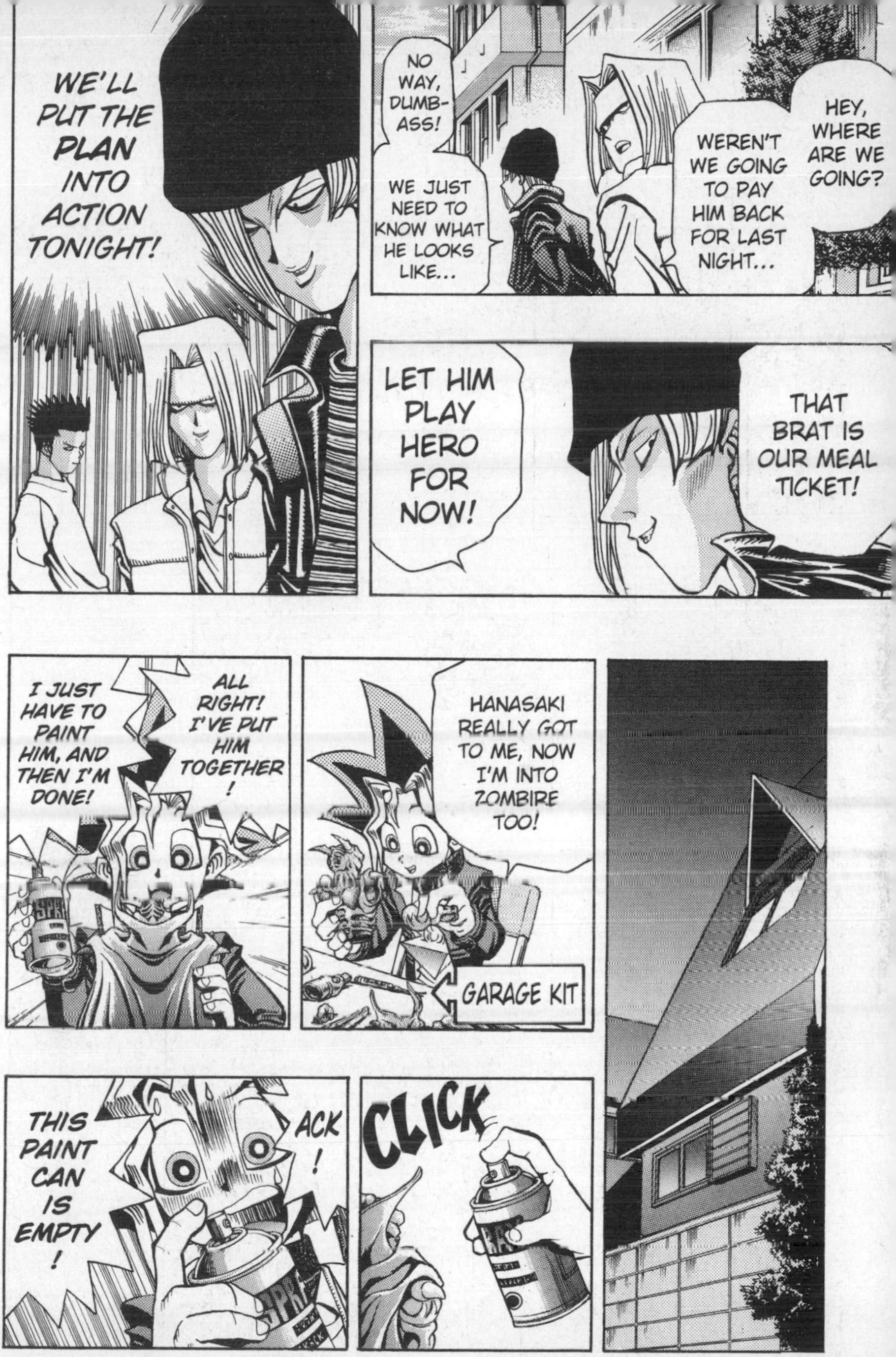

HEY, WHERE ARE WE GOING?
WEREN'T WE GOING TO PAY HIM BACK FOR LAST NIGHT...
NO WAY, DUMB-ASS!
WE JUST NEED TO KNOW WHAT HE LOOKS LIKE...
THAT BRAT IS OUR MEAL TICKET!
LET HIM PLAY HERO FOR NOW!
WE'LL PUT THE PLAN INTO ACTION TONIGHT!
HANASAKI REALLY GOT TO ME, NOW I'M INTO ZOMBIRE TOO!
GARAGE KIT
ALL RIGHT! I'VE PUT HIM TOGETHER!
I JUST HAVE TO PAINT HIM, AND THEN I'M DONE!
CLICK
ACK!
THIS PAINT CAN IS EMPTY!

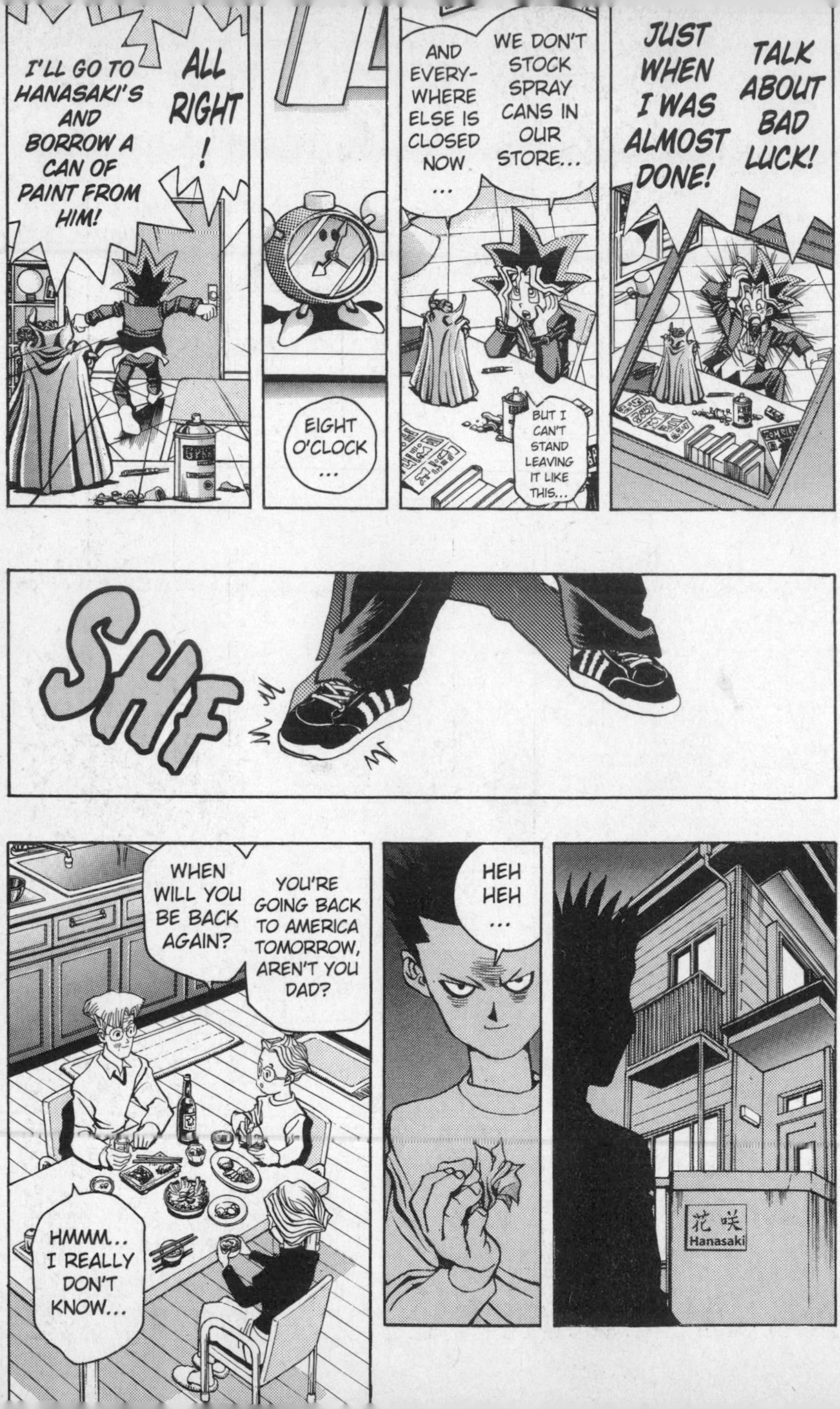
TALK ABOUT BAD LUCK!
JUST WHEN I WAS ALMOST DONE!
WE DON'T STOCK SPRAY CANS IN OUR STORE...
AND EVERY-WHERE ELSE IS CLOSED NOW ...
BUT I CAN'T STAND LEAVING IT LIKE THIS...
EIGHT O'CLOCK ...
ALL RIGHT!
I'LL GO TO HANASAKI'S AND BORROW A CAN OF PAINT FROM HIM!
SHF
花咲
Hanasaki
HEH HEH ...
YOU'RE GOING BACK TO AMERICA TOMORROW, AREN'T YOU DAD?
WHEN WILL YOU BE BACK AGAIN?
HMMM.. I REALLY DON'T KNOW...

READ THIS WAY

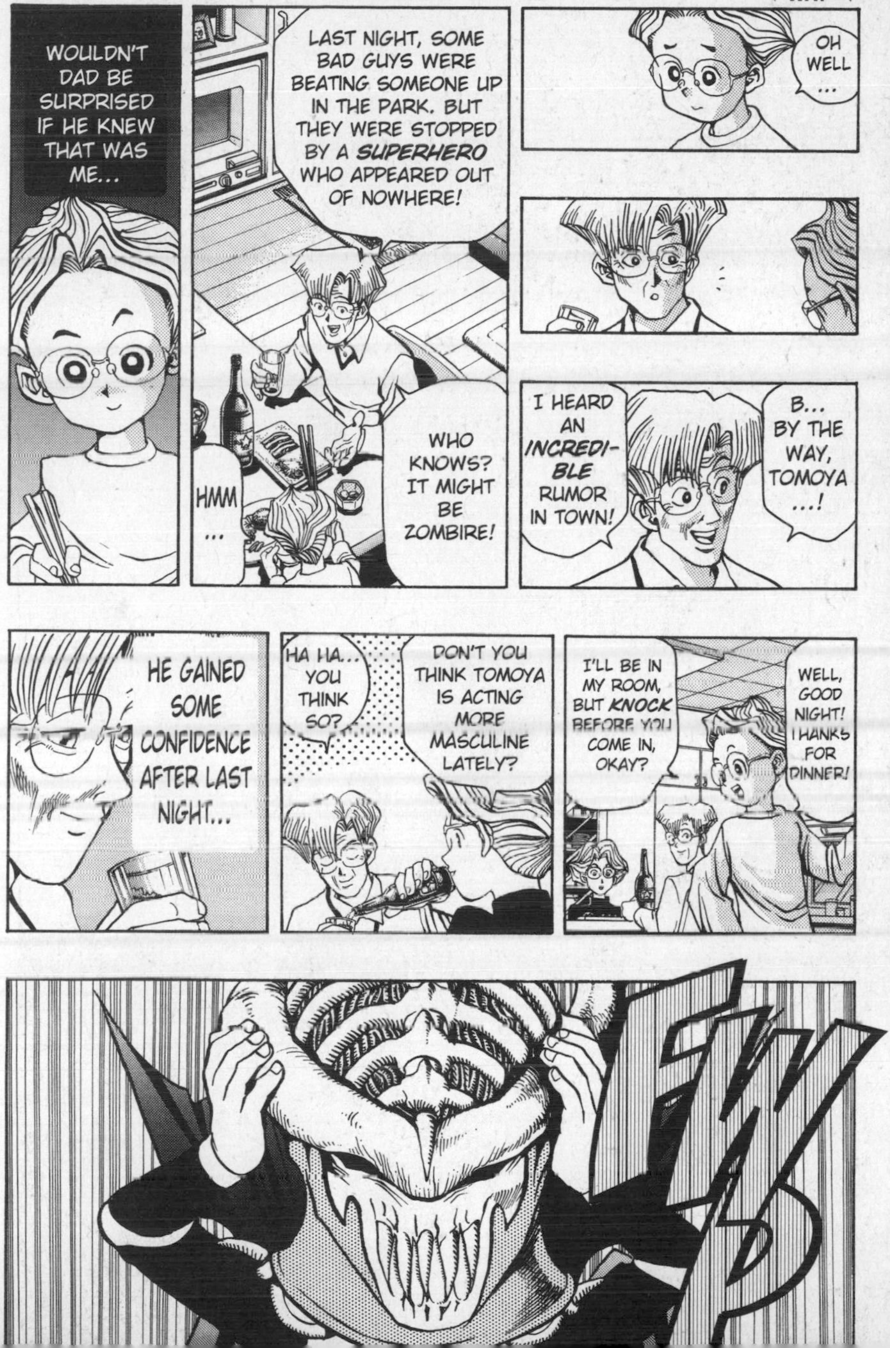
OH WELL ...
B... BY THE WAY, TOMOYA ...!
I HEARD AN INCREDIBLE RUMOR IN TOWN!
LAST NIGHT, SOME BAD GUYS WERE BEATING SOMEONE UP IN THE PARK. BUT THEY WERE STOPPED BY A SUPERHERO WHO APPEARED OUT OF NOWHERE!
WHO KNOWS? IT MIGHT BE ZOMBIRE!
HMM ...
WOULDN'T DAD BE SURPRISED IF HE KNEW THAT WAS ME...
WELL, GOOD NIGHT! THANKS FOR DINNER!
I'LL BE IN MY ROOM, BUT KNOCK BEFORE YOU COME IN, OKAY?
DON'T YOU THINK TOMOYA IS ACTING MORE MASCULINE LATELY?
HA HA... YOU THINK SO?
HE GAINED SOME CONFIDENCE AFTER LAST NIGHT...

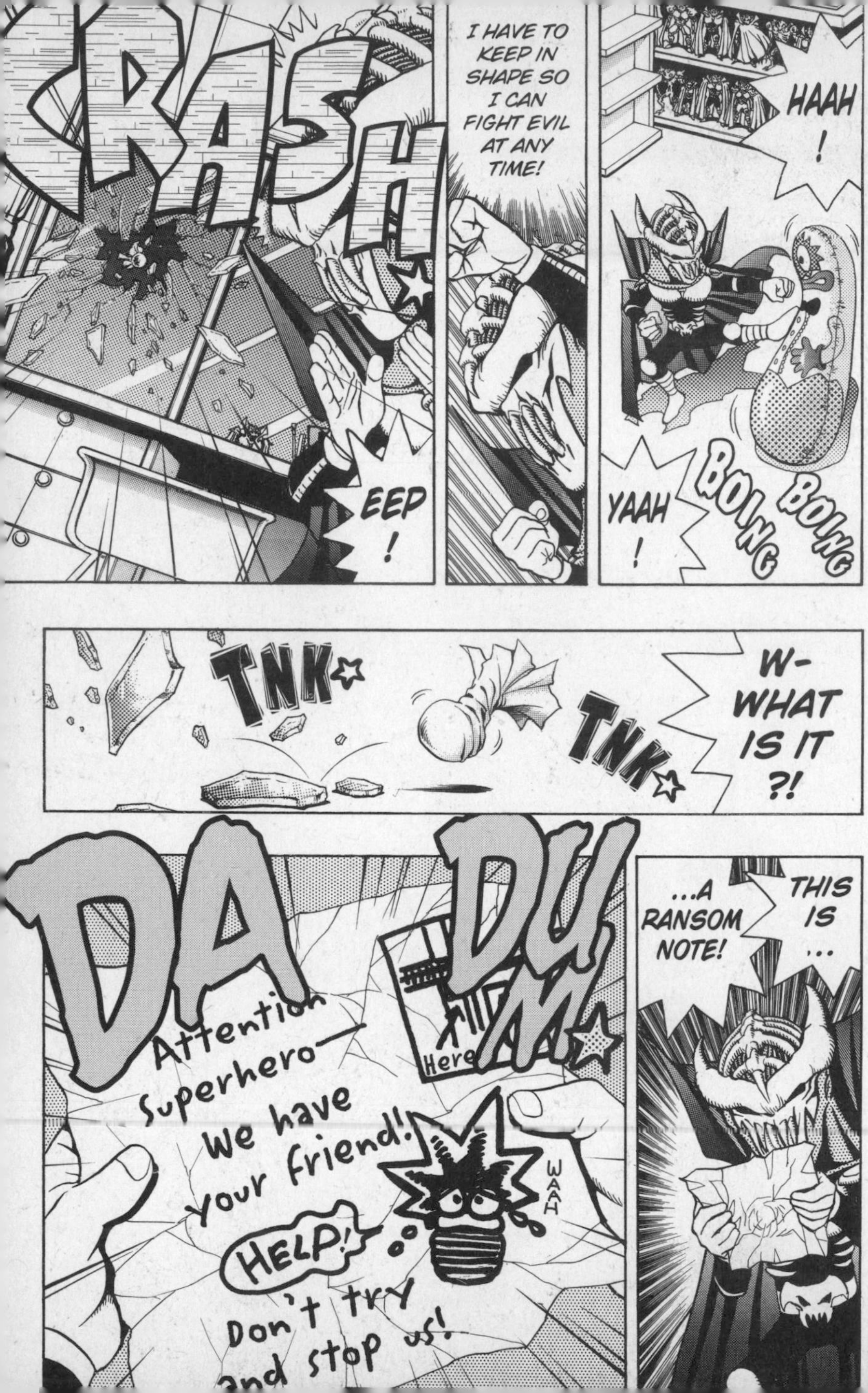
HAAH!
YAAH!
BOING
BOING
I HAVE TO KEEP IN SHAPE SO I CAN FIGHT EVIL AT ANY TIME!
CRASH
EEP!
W-WHAT IS IT ?!
TNK
TNK
THIS IS ...
...A RANSOM NOTE!
DA DUM
Here
Attention Superhero— We have your friend!
HELP!
WAAH
Don't try and stop us!

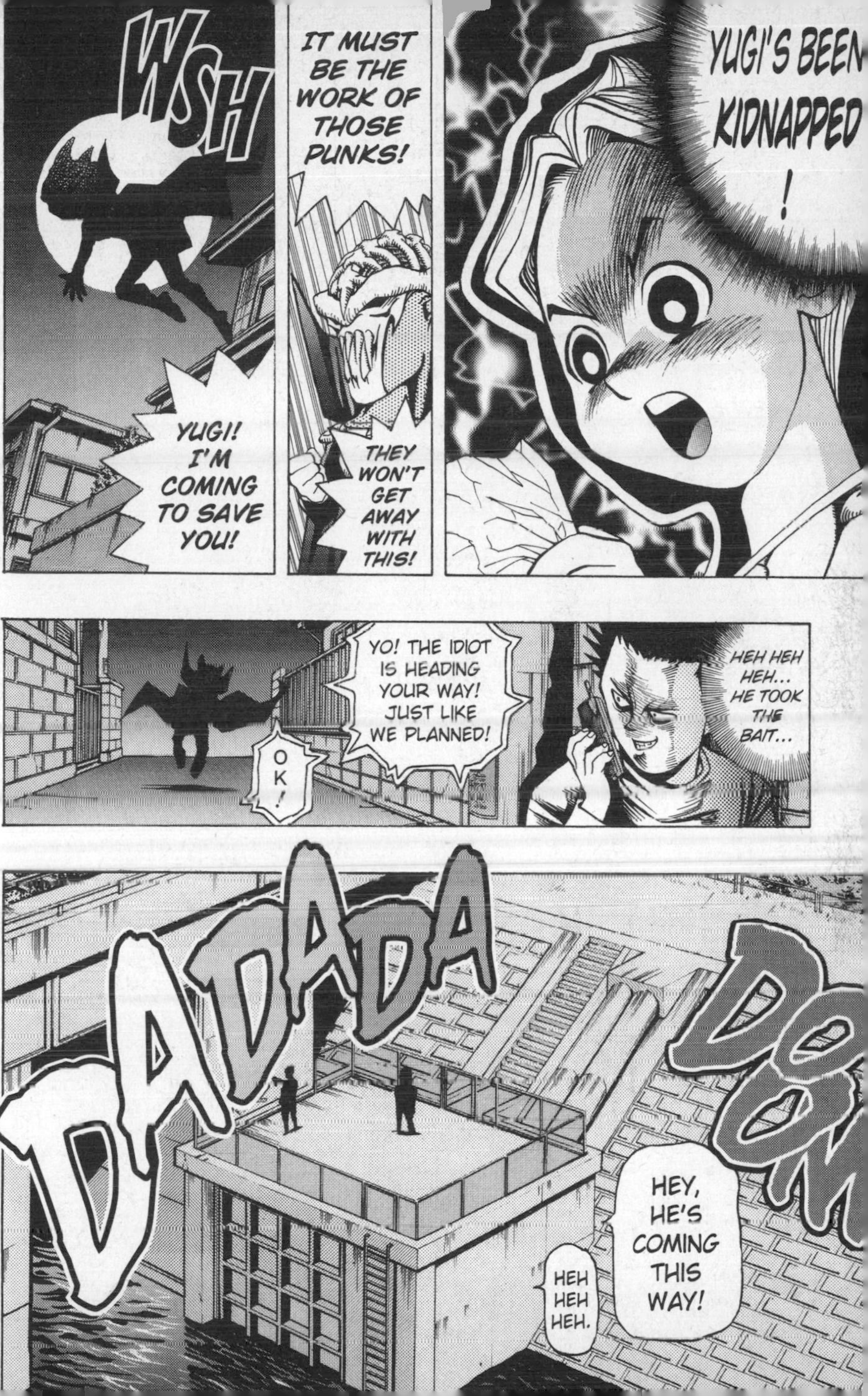
YUGI'S BEEN KIDNAPPED !
IT MUST BE THE WORK OF THOSE PUNKS!
THEY WON'T GET AWAY WITH THIS!
WSH
YUGI! I'M COMING TO SAVE YOU!
HEH HEH HEH... HE TOOK THE BAIT...
YO! THE IDIOT IS HEADING YOUR WAY! JUST LIKE WE PLANNED!
OK!
DADADA
HEY, HE'S COMING THIS WAY!
HEH HEH HEH.

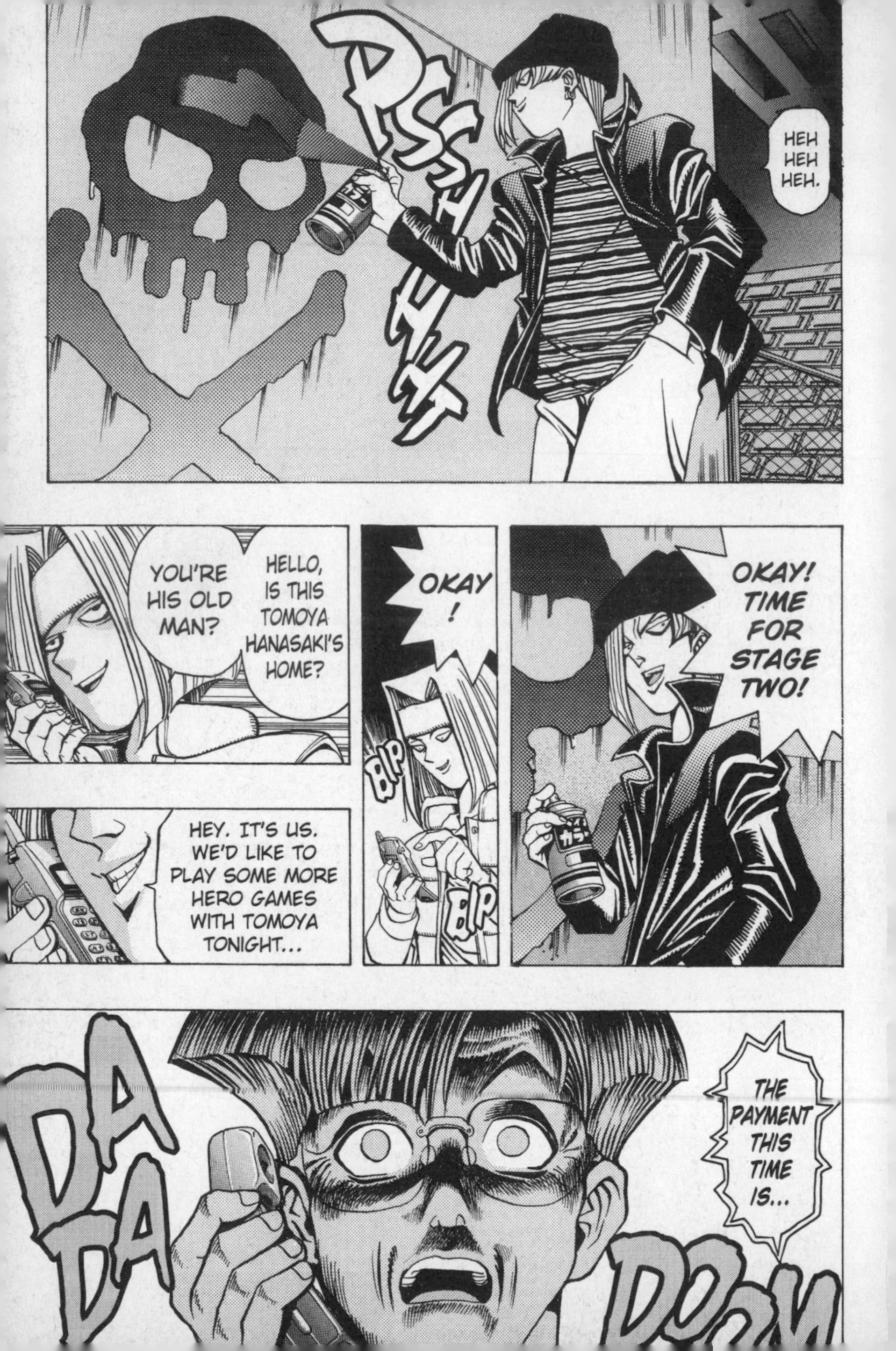
HEH HEH HEH.
PSSHHHHH
OKAY! TIME FOR STAGE TWO!
OKAY!
BIP
BIP
HELLO, IS THIS TOMOYA HANASAKI'S HOME?
YOU'RE HIS OLD MAN?
HEY. IT'S US. WE'D LIKE TO PLAY SOME MORE HERO GAMES WITH TOMOYA TONIGHT...
THE PAYMENT THIS TIME IS...
DA DA
DOOM

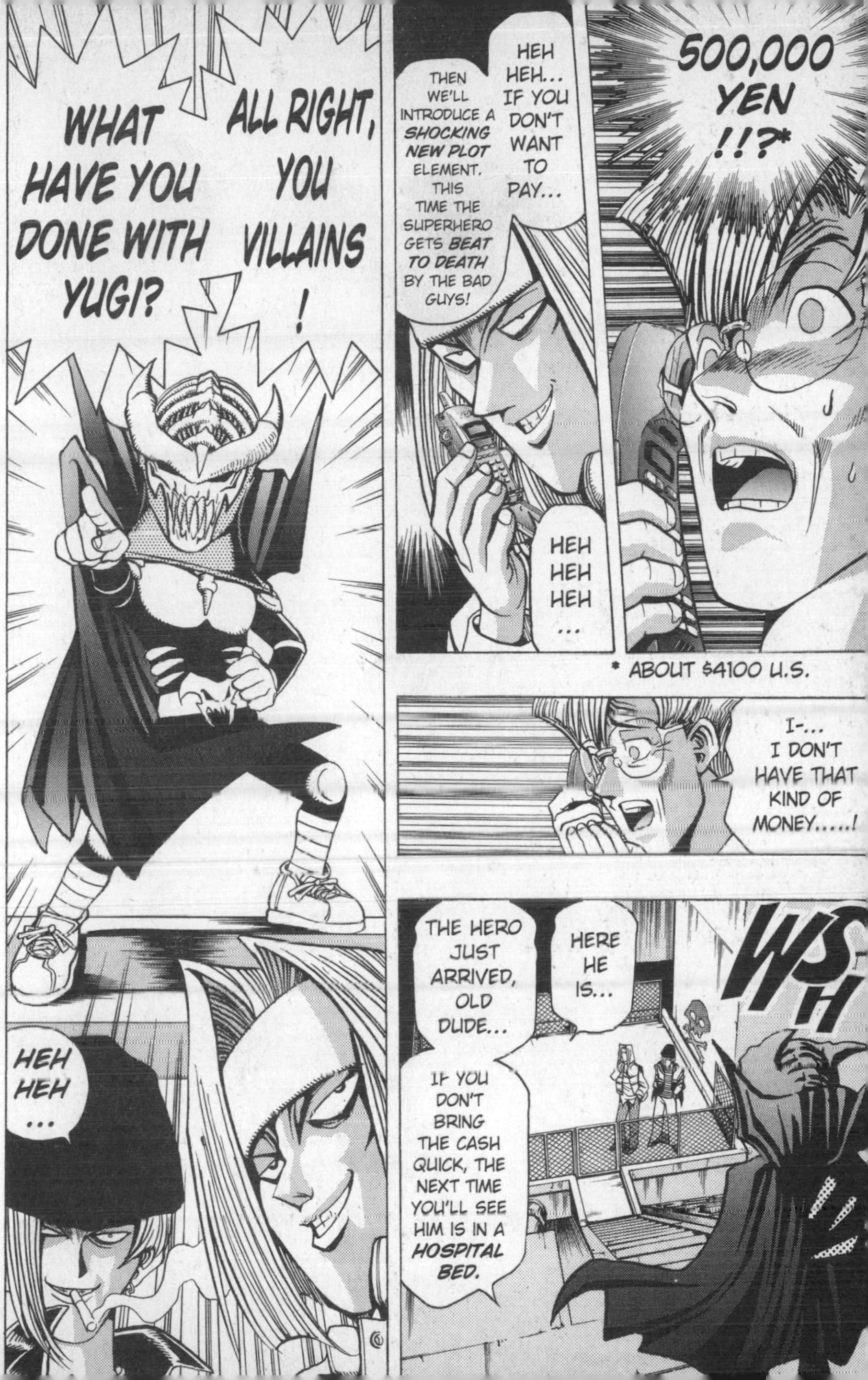
500,000 YEN !!?*
HEH HEH... IF YOU DON'T WANT TO PAY...
THEN WE'LL INTRODUCE A SHOCKING NEW PLOT ELEMENT. THIS TIME THE SUPERHERO GETS BEAT TO DEATH BY THE BAD GUYS!
HEH HEH HEH ...
* ABOUT $4100 U.S.
I-... I DON'T HAVE THAT KIND OF MONEY.....!
WSH
HERE HE IS...
THE HERO JUST ARRIVED, OLD DUDE...
IF YOU DON'T BRING THE CASH QUICK, THE NEXT TIME YOU'LL SEE HIM IS IN A HOSPITAL BED.
ALL RIGHT, YOU VILLAINS !
WHAT HAVE YOU DONE WITH YUGI?
HEH HEH ...

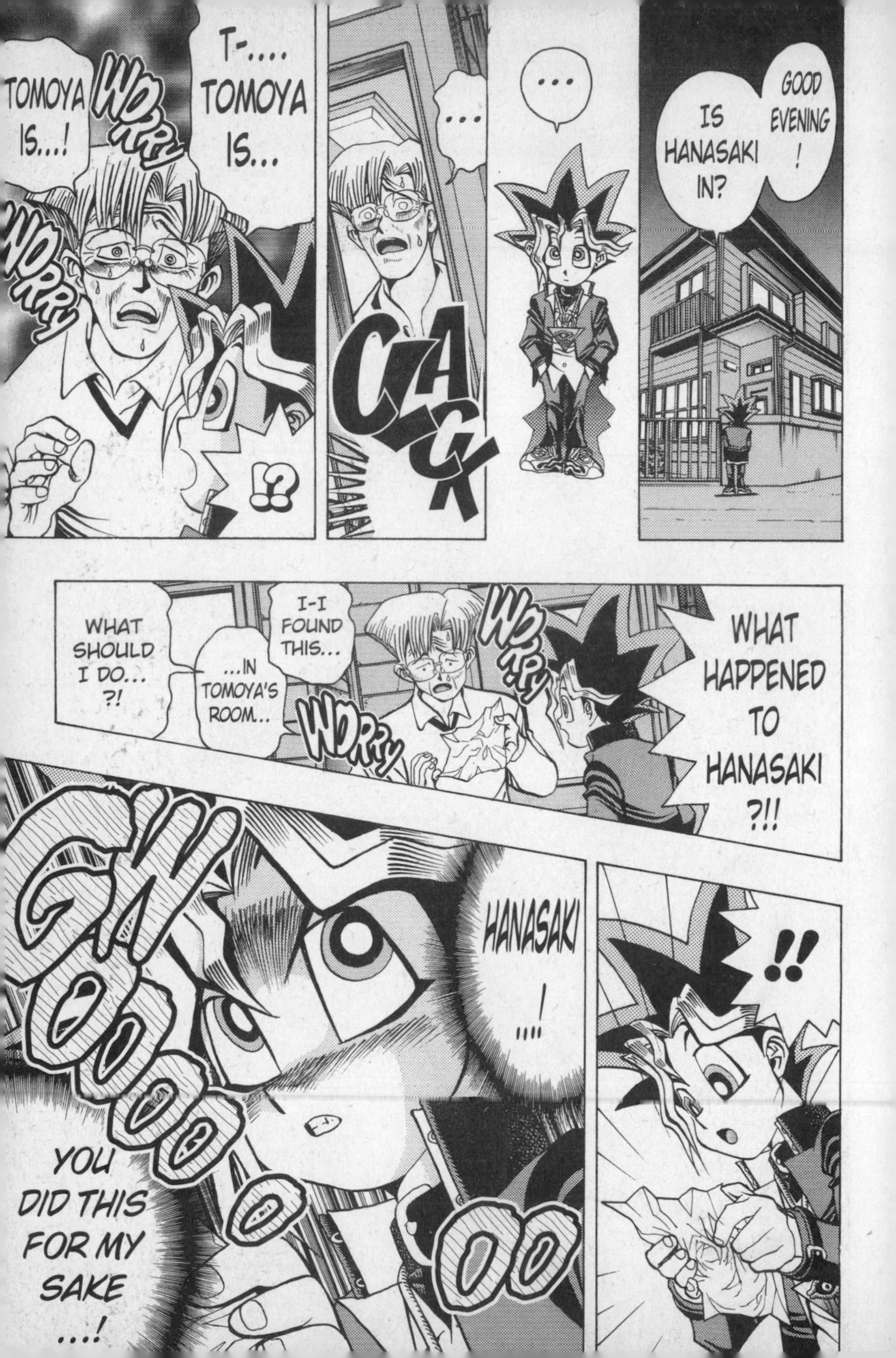
GOOD EVENING !
IS HANASAKI IN?
...
...
CLACK
T-.... TOMOYA IS...
WORRY
TOMOYA IS...!
WORRY
!?
WHAT HAPPENED TO HANASAKI ?!!
WORRY
I-I FOUND THIS...
...IN TOMOYA'S ROOM...
WHAT SHOULD I DO... ?!
WORRY
!!
HANASAKI ....!
GWOOOOOOOOOO
YOU DID THIS FOR MY SAKE ...!

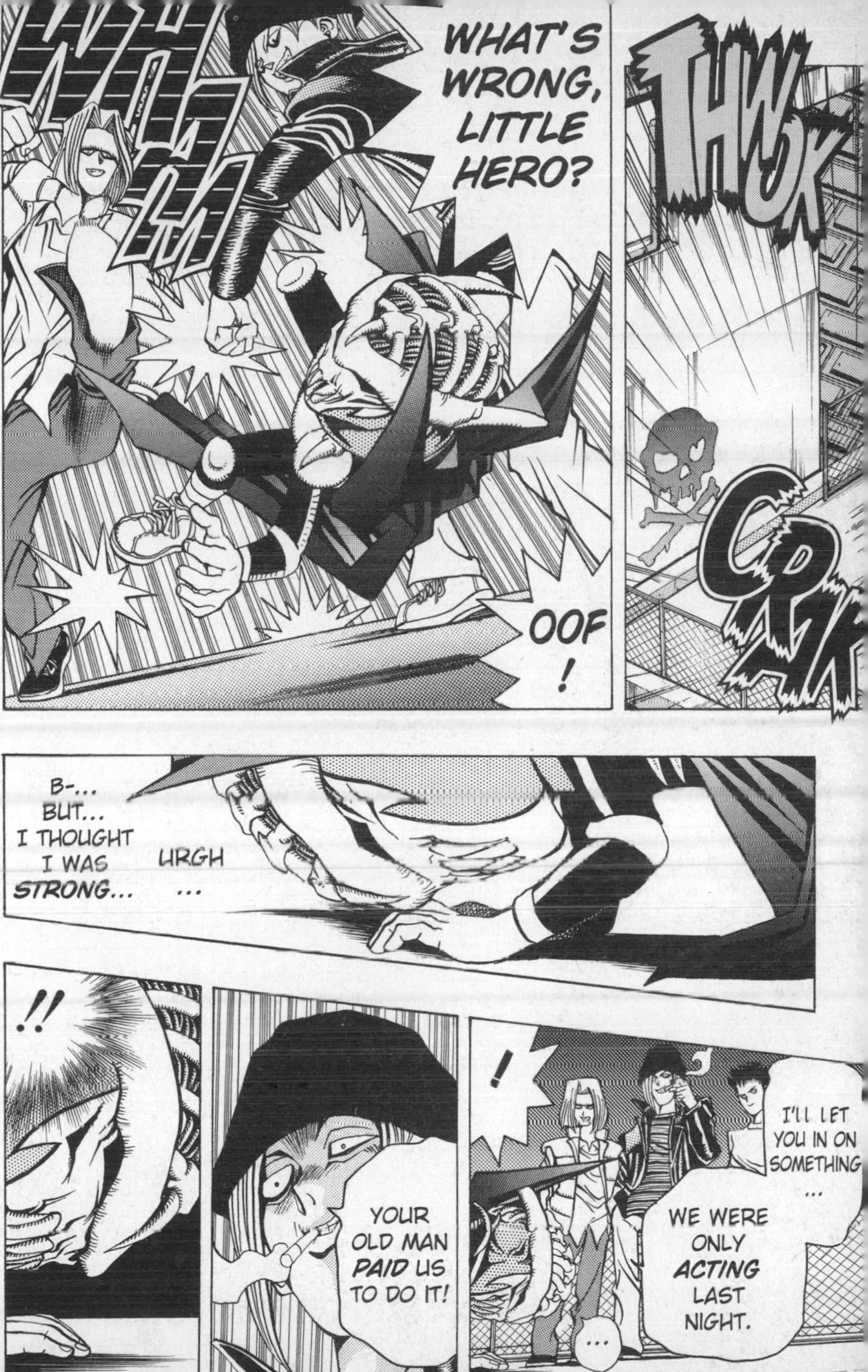
THWOK
CRAK
WHAT'S WRONG, LITTLE HERO?
OOF!
URGH...
B-... BUT... I THOUGHT I WAS STRONG...
!
I'LL LET YOU IN ON SOMETHING...
WE WERE ONLY ACTING LAST NIGHT.
...
YOUR OLD MAN PAID US TO DO IT!
!!

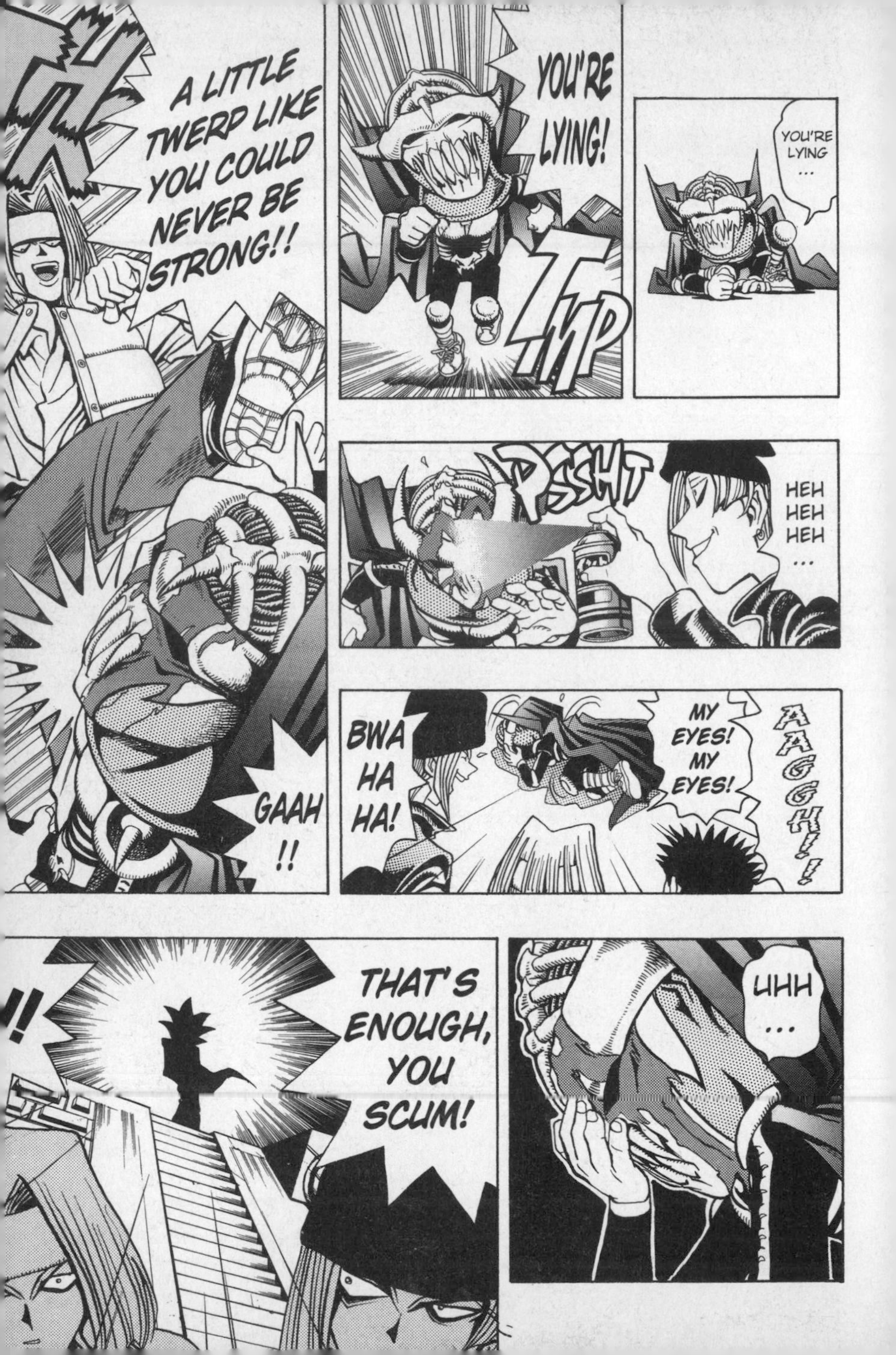
YOU'RE LYING ...
YOU'RE LYING!
TMP
PSSHT
HEH HEH HEH ...
AAGGH!!
MY EYES! MY EYES!
BWA HA HA!
A LITTLE TWERP LIKE YOU COULD NEVER BE STRONG!!
GAAH !!
UHH ...
THAT'S ENOUGH, YOU SCUM!
!!

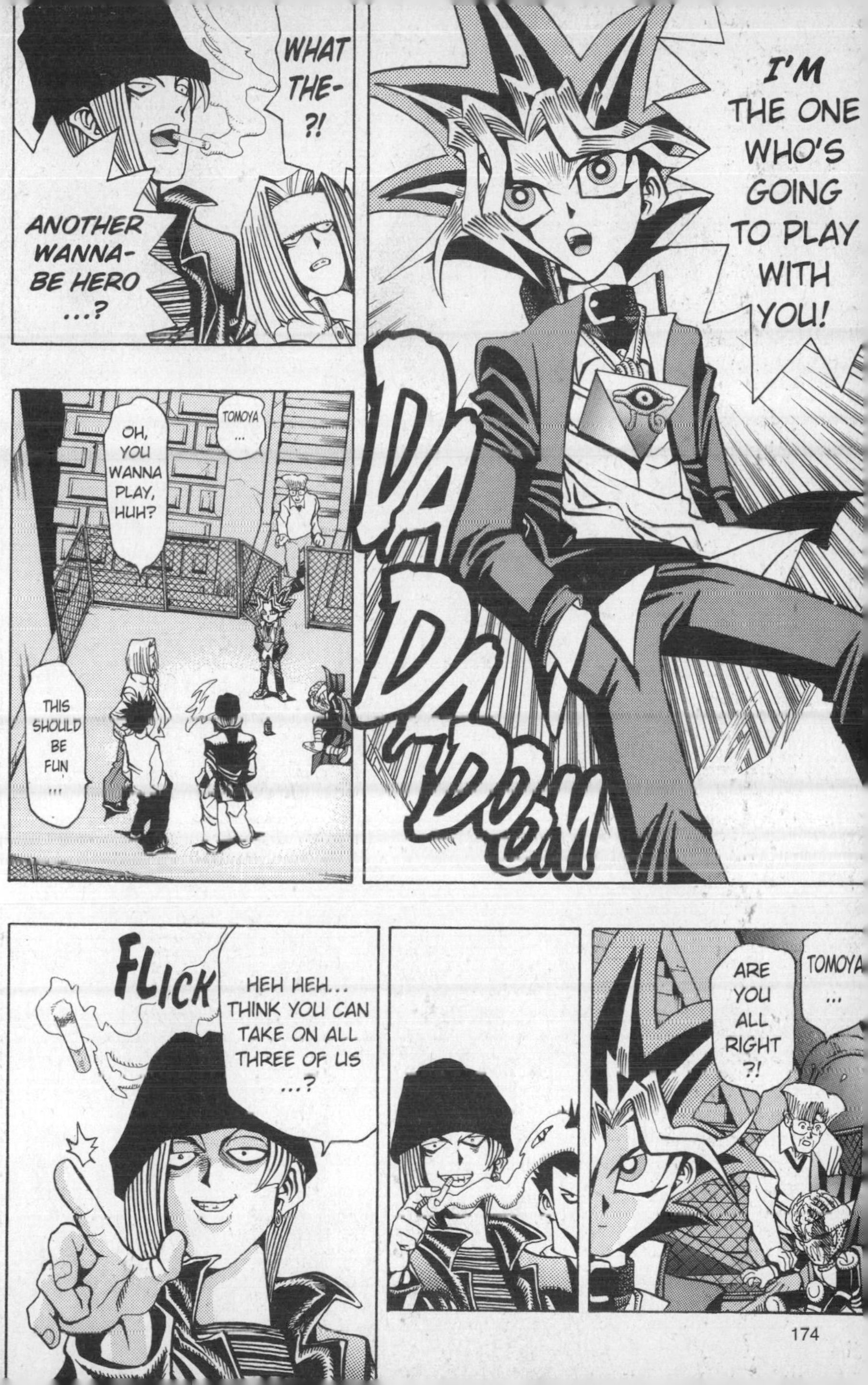
I'M THE ONE WHO'S GOING TO PLAY WITH YOU!
DA DA DOM
WHAT THE-?!
ANOTHER WANNA-BE HERO ...?
TOMOYA ...
OH, YOU WANNA PLAY, HUH?
THIS SHOULD BE FUN ...
TOMOYA ...
ARE YOU ALL RIGHT ?!
FLICK
HEH HEH... THINK YOU CAN TAKE ON ALL THREE OF US ...?

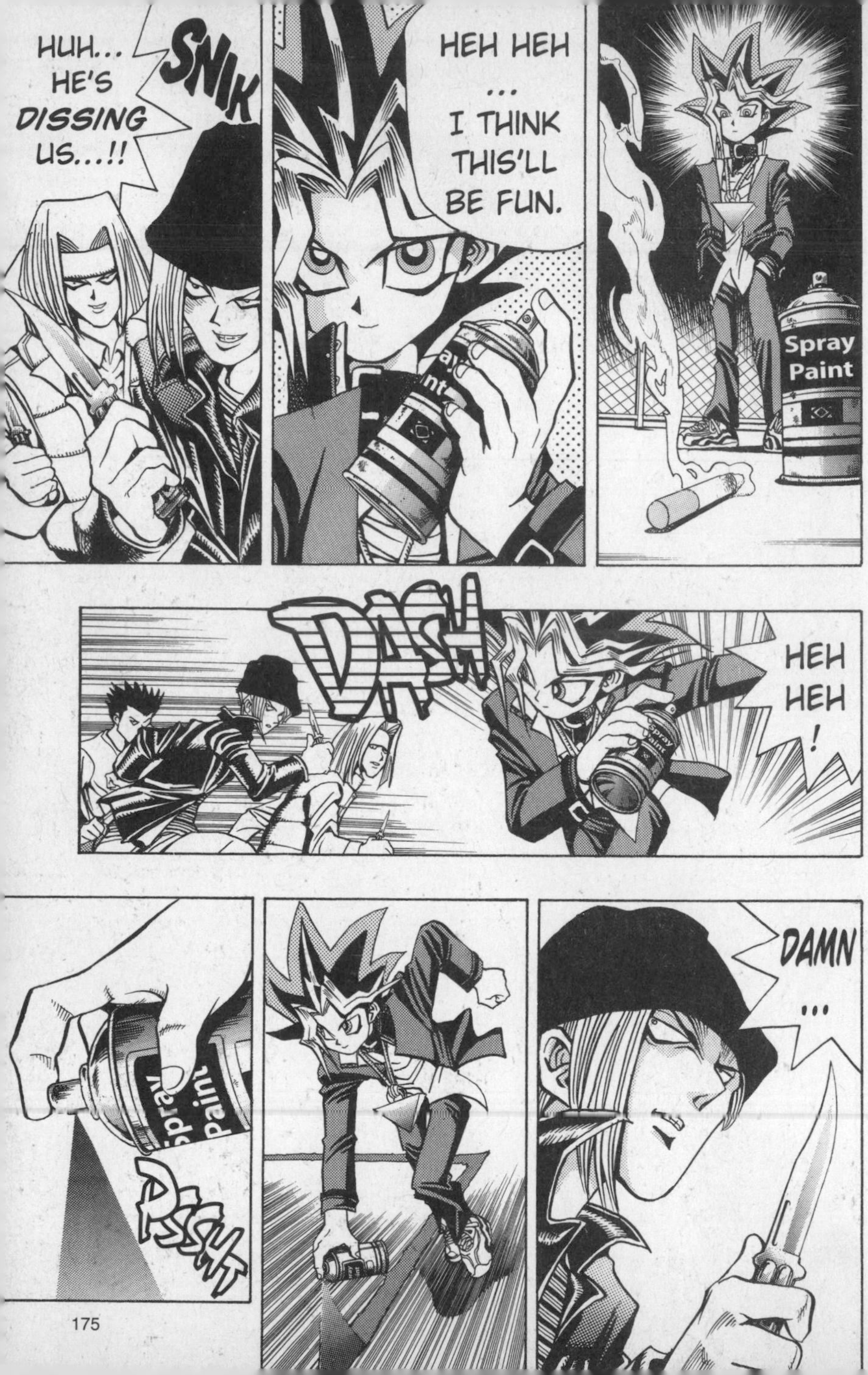
Spray Paint
HEH HEH ... I THINK THIS'LL BE FUN.
SNIK
HUH... HE'S DISSING US...!!
HEH HEH!
DASH
DAMN ...
Spray paint
PSSHT

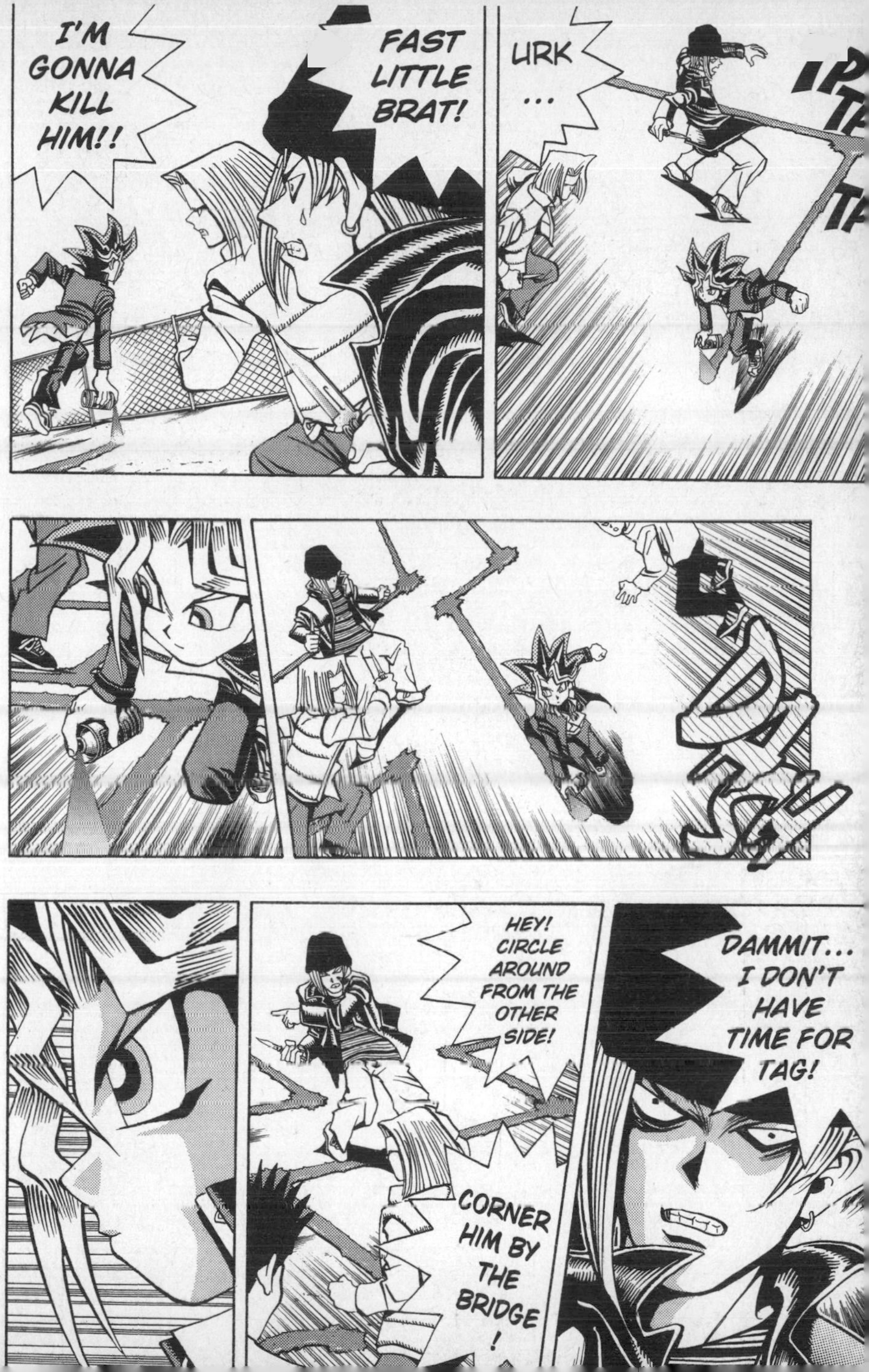
URK ...
FAST LITTLE BRAT!
I'M GONNA KILL HIM!!
DASH
DAMMIT... I DON'T HAVE TIME FOR TAG!
HEY! CIRCLE AROUND FROM THE OTHER SIDE!
CORNER HIM BY THE BRIDGE!

READ THIS WAY

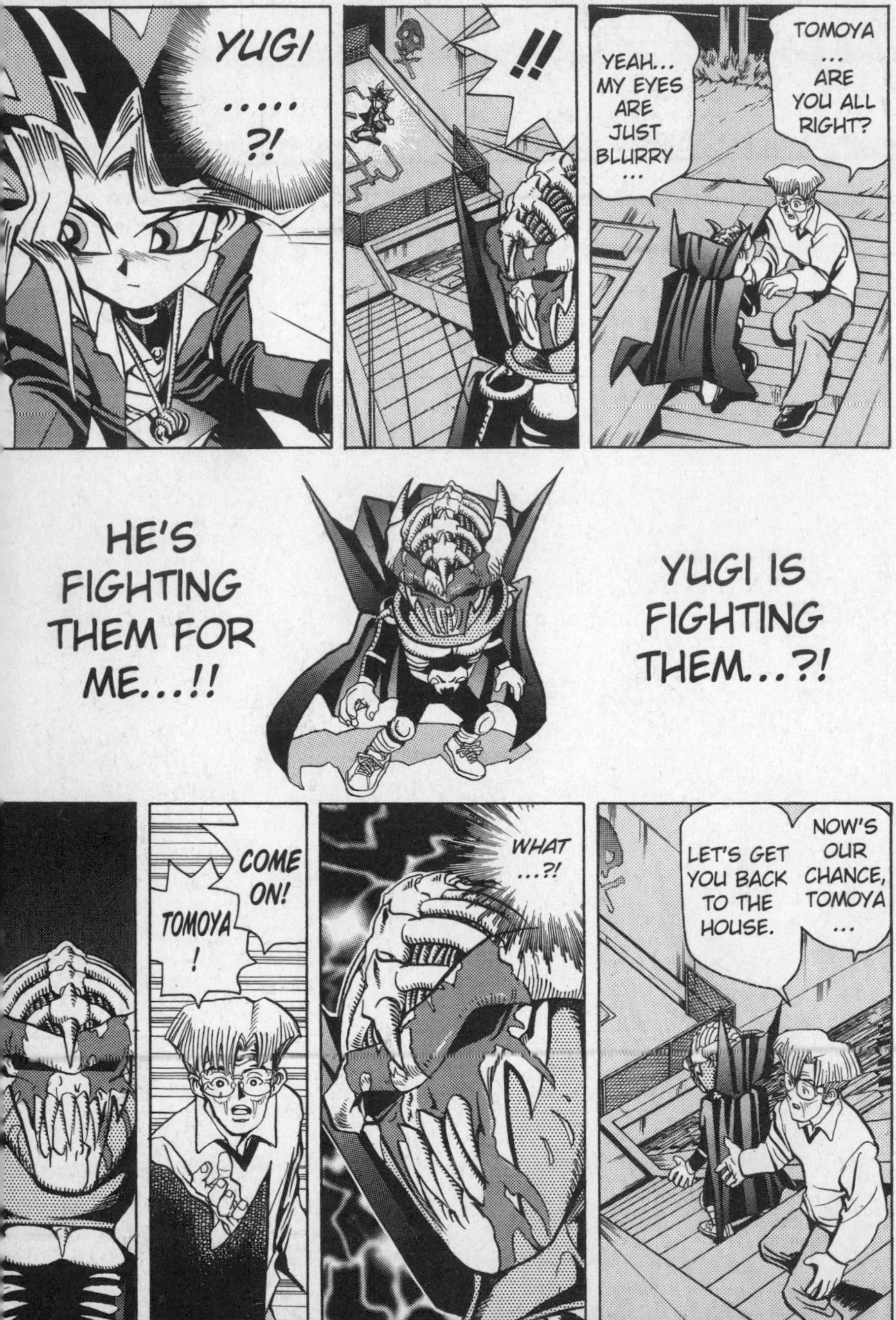

TOMOYA ... ARE YOU ALL RIGHT?
YEAH... MY EYES ARE JUST BLURRY ...
!!
YUGI .....?!
YUGI IS FIGHTING THEM...?!
HE'S FIGHTING THEM FOR ME...!!
NOW'S OUR CHANCE, TOMOYA ...
LET'S GET YOU BACK TO THE HOUSE.
WHAT ...?!
COME ON!
TOMOYA!

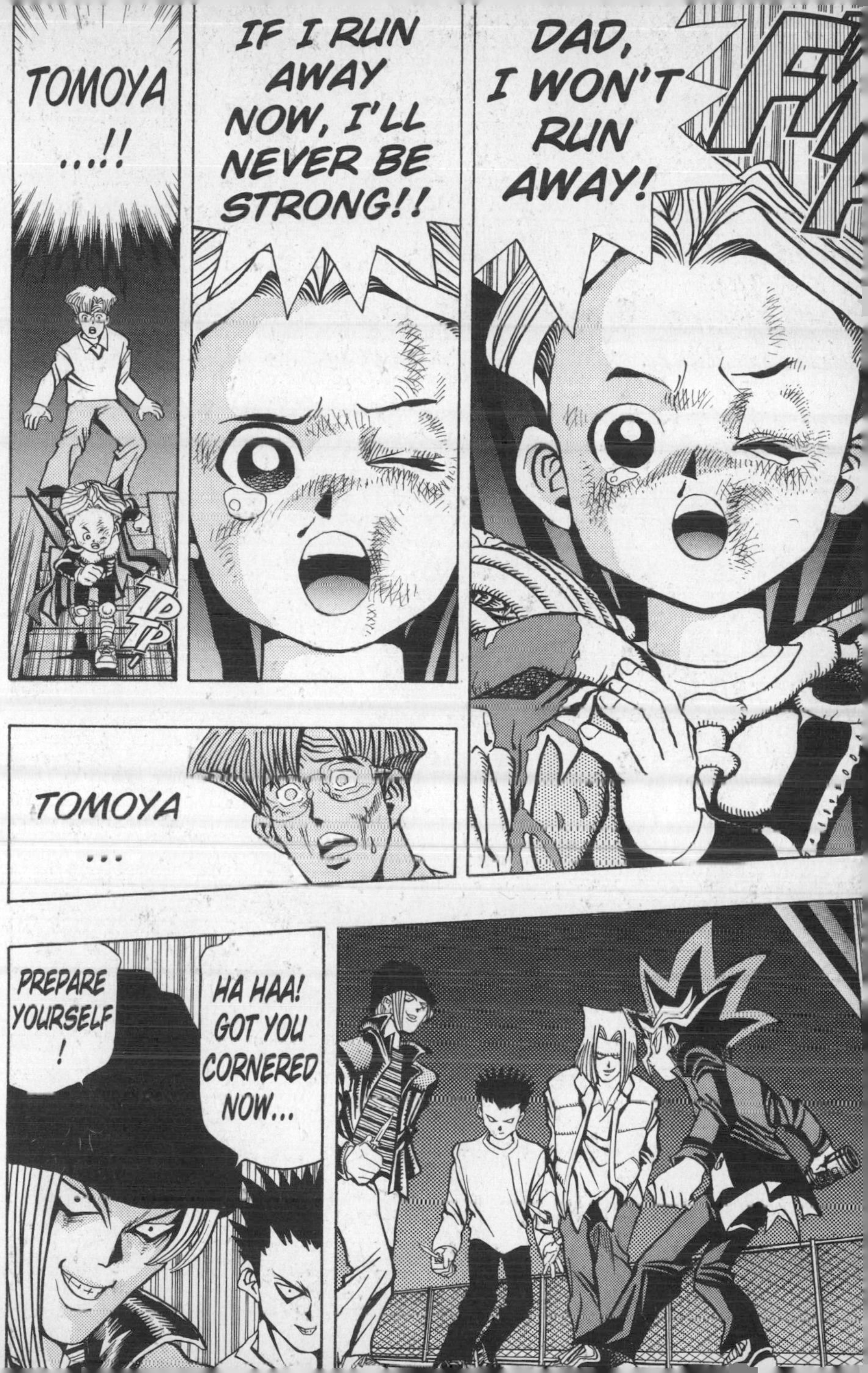
DAD, I WON'T RUN AWAY!
IF I RUN AWAY NOW, I'LL NEVER BE STRONG!!
TOMOYA ...!!
TP TP
TOMOYA ...
HA HAA! GOT YOU CORNERED NOW...
PREPARE YOURSELF !

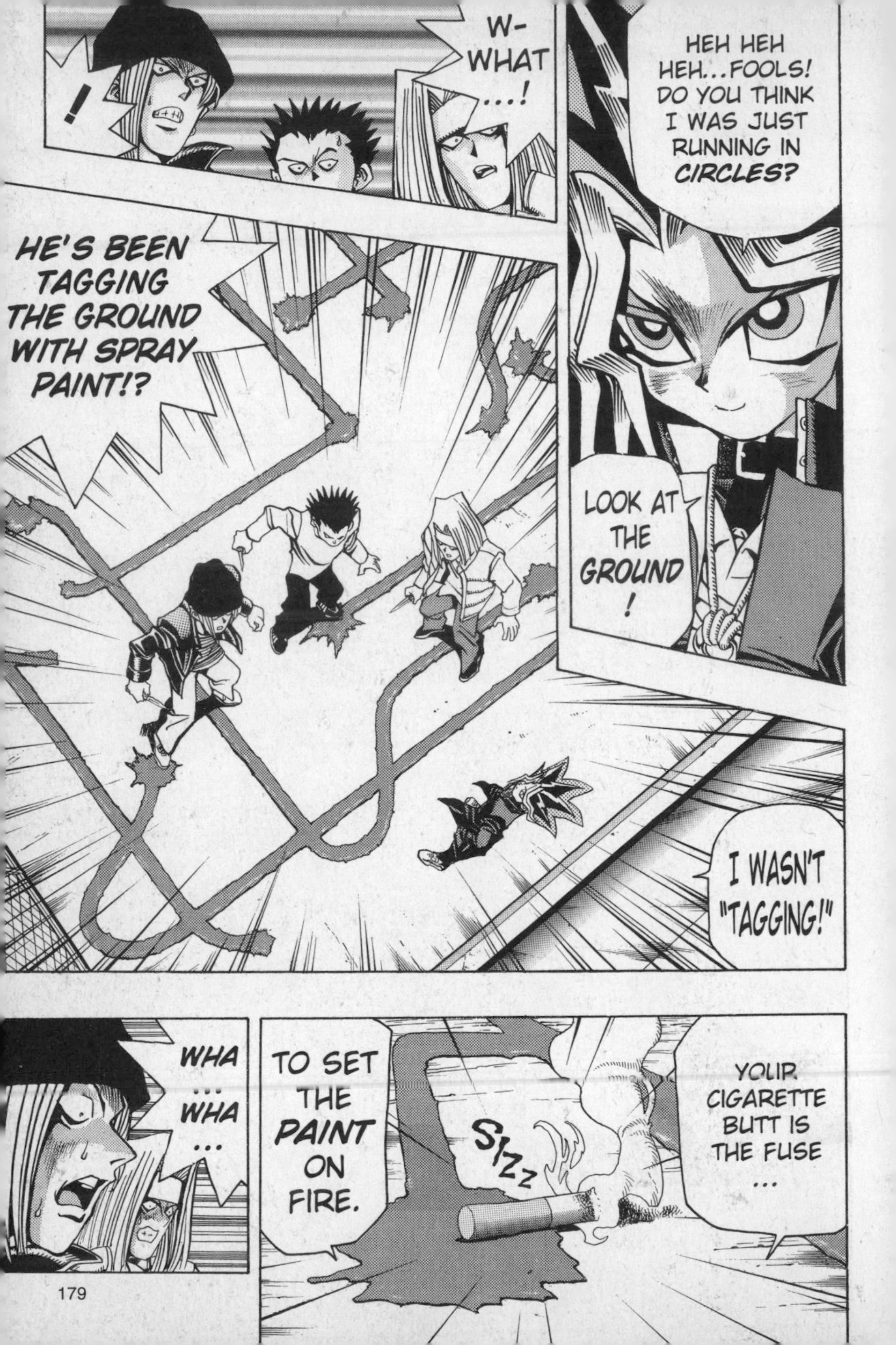
HEH HEH HEH...FOOLS! DO YOU THINK I WAS JUST RUNNING IN CIRCLES?
LOOK AT THE GROUND!
W-WHAT...!
!
HE'S BEEN TAGGING THE GROUND WITH SPRAY PAINT!?
I WASN'T "TAGGING!"
YOUR CIGARETTE BUTT IS THE FUSE...
TO SET THE PAINT ON FIRE.
SIZZ
WHA... WHA...

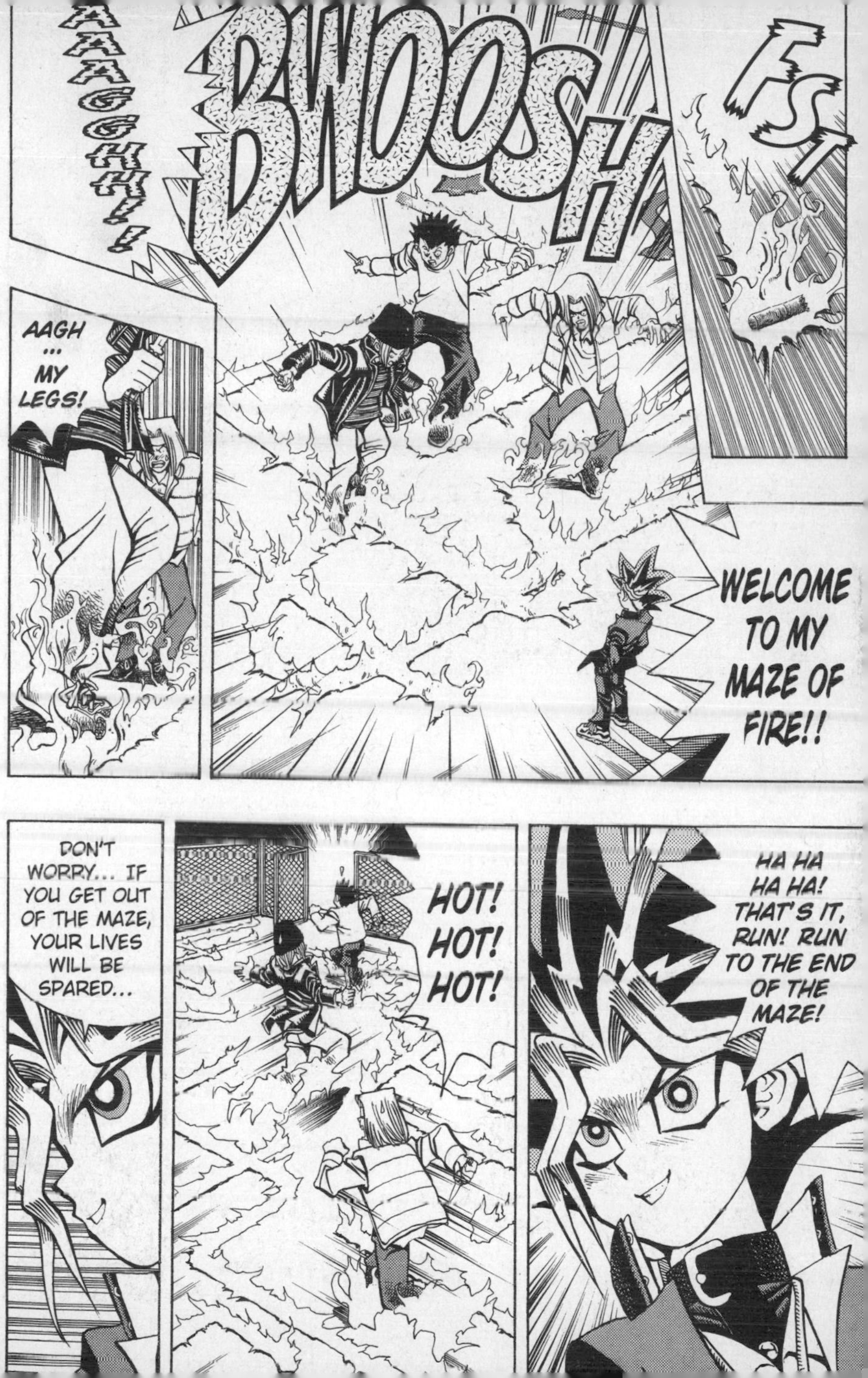
FST
BWOOSH
AAAGHH!!
WELCOME TO MY MAZE OF FIRE!!
AAGH ... MY LEGS!
HA HA HA HA! THAT'S IT, RUN! RUN TO THE END OF THE MAZE!
HOT! HOT! HOT!
DON'T WORRY... IF YOU GET OUT OF THE MAZE, YOUR LIVES WILL BE SPARED...

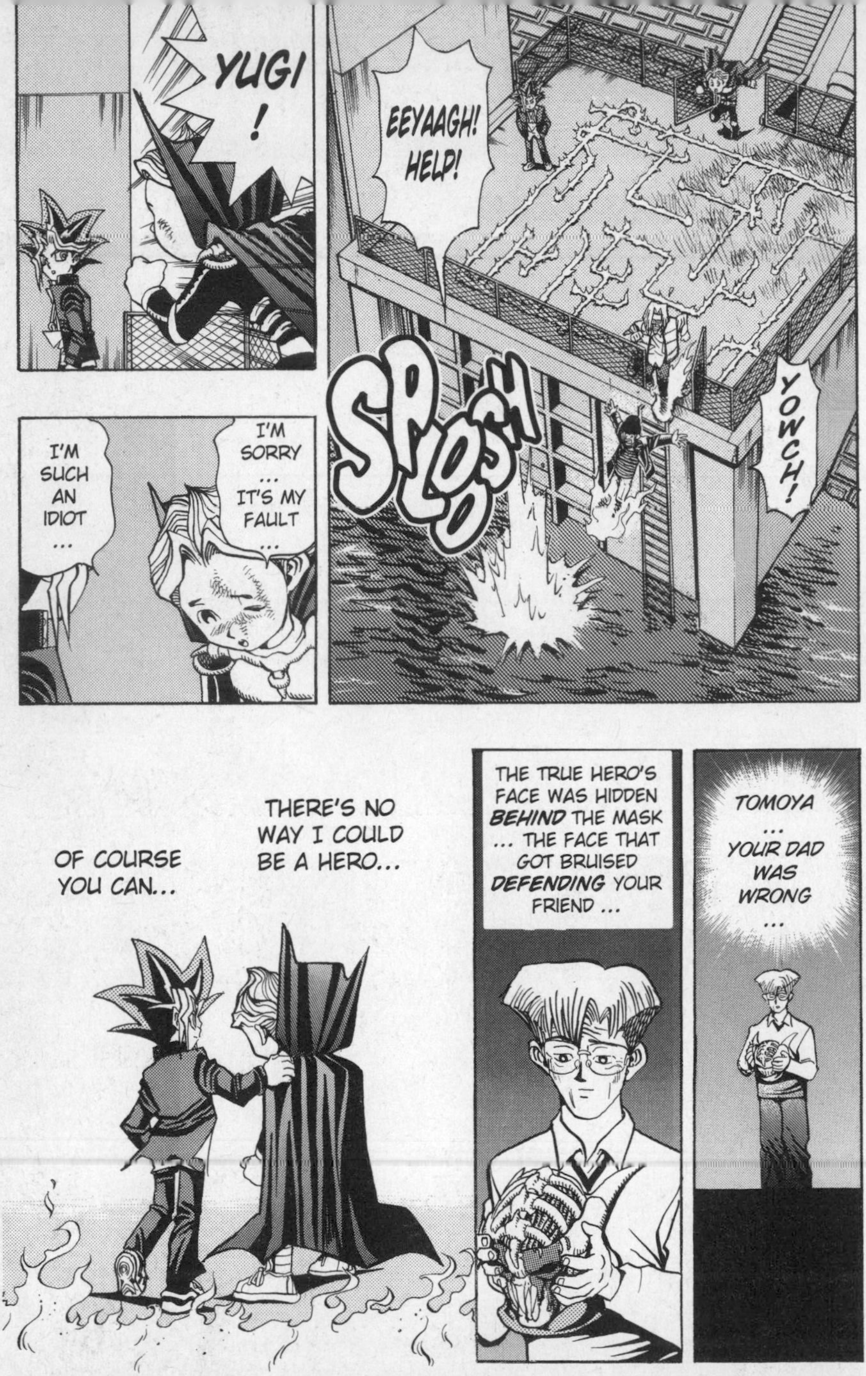
EEYAAGH! HELP!
YOWCH!
SPLOOSH
YUGI!
I'M SORRY ... IT'S MY FAULT ...
I'M SUCH AN IDIOT ...
TOMOYA ... YOUR DAD WAS WRONG ...
THE TRUE HERO'S FACE WAS HIDDEN BEHIND THE MASK ... THE FACE THAT GOT BRUISED DEFENDING YOUR FRIEND ...
THERE'S NO WAY I COULD BE A HERO...
OF COURSE YOU CAN...

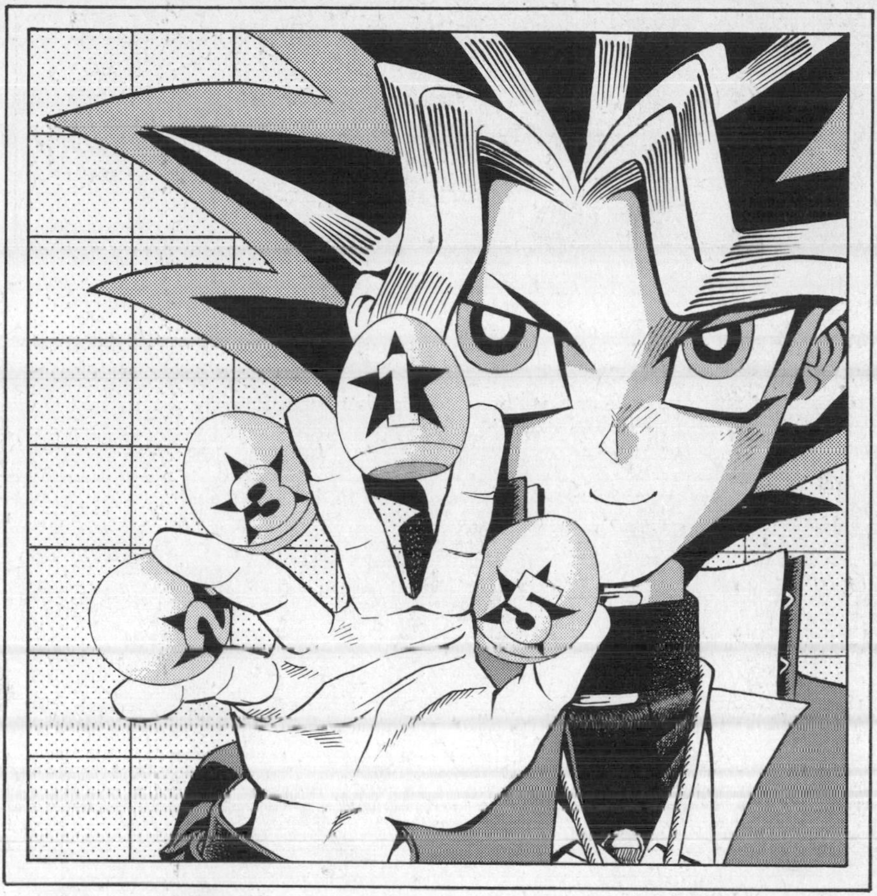

# Duel 24:
# Capsule Monster Chess

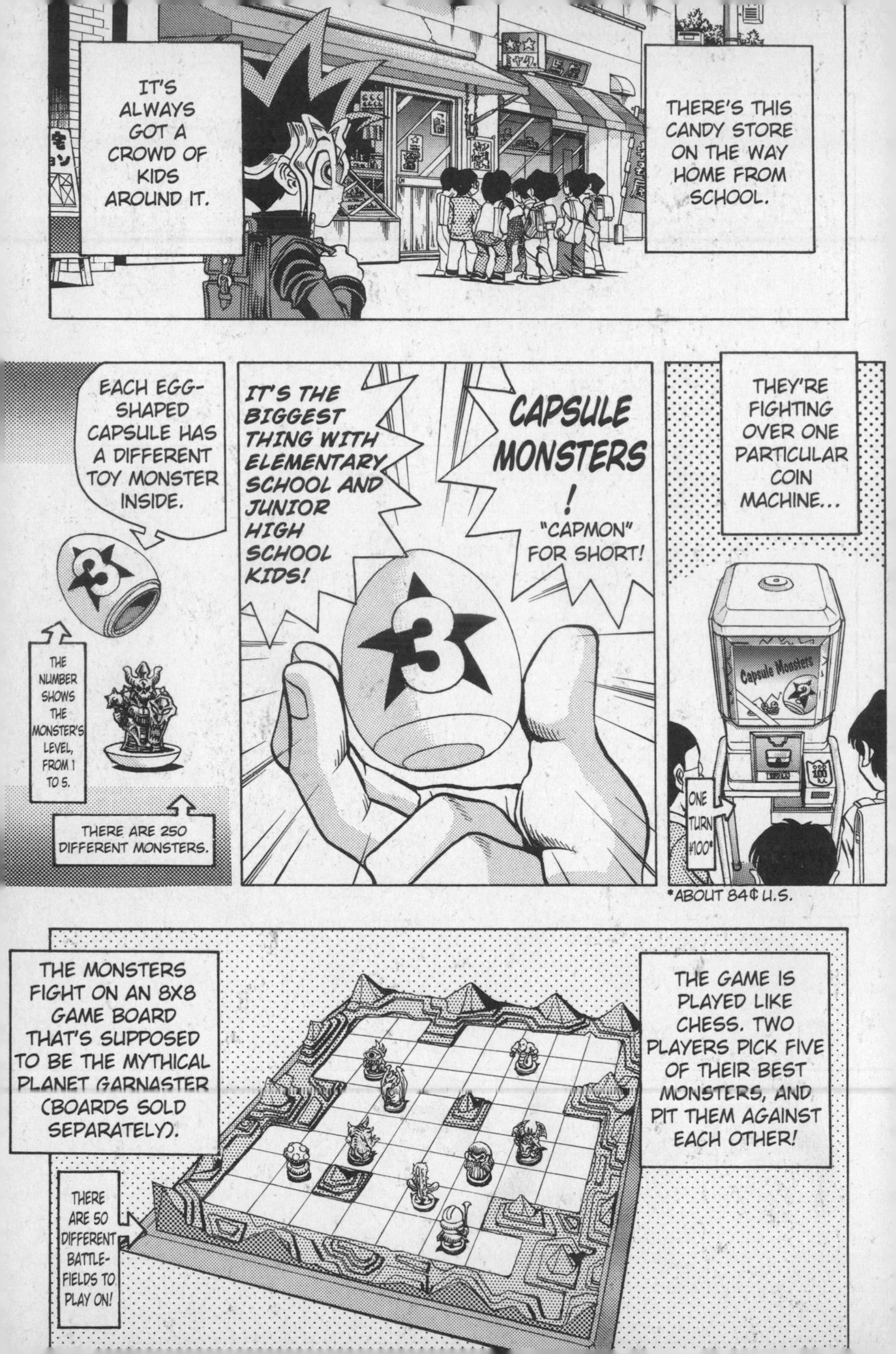
THERE'S THIS CANDY STORE ON THE WAY HOME FROM SCHOOL.
IT'S ALWAYS GOT A CROWD OF KIDS AROUND IT.
THEY'RE FIGHTING OVER ONE PARTICULAR COIN MACHINE...
Capsule Monsters
ONE TURN ¥100*
*ABOUT 84¢ U.S.
CAPSULE MONSTERS!
"CAPMON" FOR SHORT!
IT'S THE BIGGEST THING WITH ELEMENTARY SCHOOL AND JUNIOR HIGH SCHOOL KIDS!
EACH EGG-SHAPED CAPSULE HAS A DIFFERENT TOY MONSTER INSIDE.
THE NUMBER SHOWS THE MONSTER'S LEVEL, FROM 1 TO 5.
THERE ARE 250 DIFFERENT MONSTERS.
THE GAME IS PLAYED LIKE CHESS. TWO PLAYERS PICK FIVE OF THEIR BEST MONSTERS, AND PIT THEM AGAINST EACH OTHER!
THE MONSTERS FIGHT ON AN 8X8 GAME BOARD THAT'S SUPPOSED TO BE THE MYTHICAL PLANET GARNASTER (BOARDS SOLD SEPARATELY).
THERE ARE 50 DIFFERENT BATTLEFIELDS TO PLAY ON!

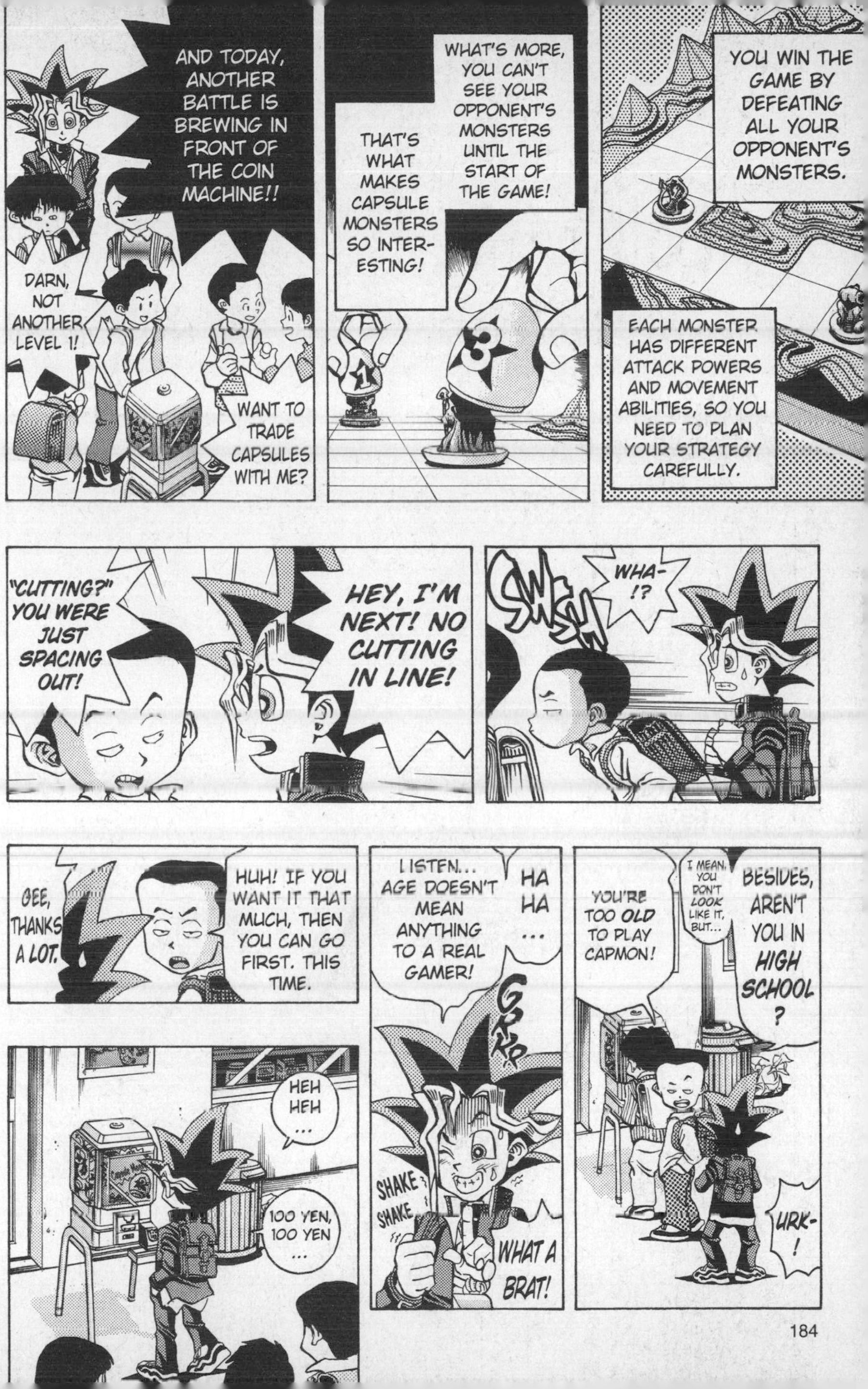
YOU WIN THE GAME BY DEFEATING ALL YOUR OPPONENT'S MONSTERS.
EACH MONSTER HAS DIFFERENT ATTACK POWERS AND MOVEMENT ABILITIES, SO YOU NEED TO PLAN YOUR STRATEGY CAREFULLY.
WHAT'S MORE, YOU CAN'T SEE YOUR OPPONENT'S MONSTERS UNTIL THE START OF THE GAME!
THAT'S WHAT MAKES CAPSULE MONSTERS SO INTER-ESTING!
AND TODAY, ANOTHER BATTLE IS BREWING IN FRONT OF THE COIN MACHINE!!
DARN, NOT ANOTHER LEVEL 1!
WANT TO TRADE CAPSULES WITH ME?
WHA-!?
HEY, I'M NEXT! NO CUTTING IN LINE!
"CUTTING?" YOU WERE JUST SPACING OUT!
BESIDES, AREN'T YOU IN HIGH SCHOOL?
I MEAN, YOU DON'T LOOK LIKE IT, BUT...
YOU'RE TOO OLD TO PLAY CAPMON!
URK-!
HA HA ...
LISTEN... AGE DOESN'T MEAN ANYTHING TO A REAL GAMER!
SHAKE SHAKE
WHAT A BRAT!
HUH! IF YOU WANT IT THAT MUCH, THEN YOU CAN GO FIRST. THIS TIME.
GEE, THANKS A LOT.
HEH HEH ...
100 YEN, 100 YEN ...

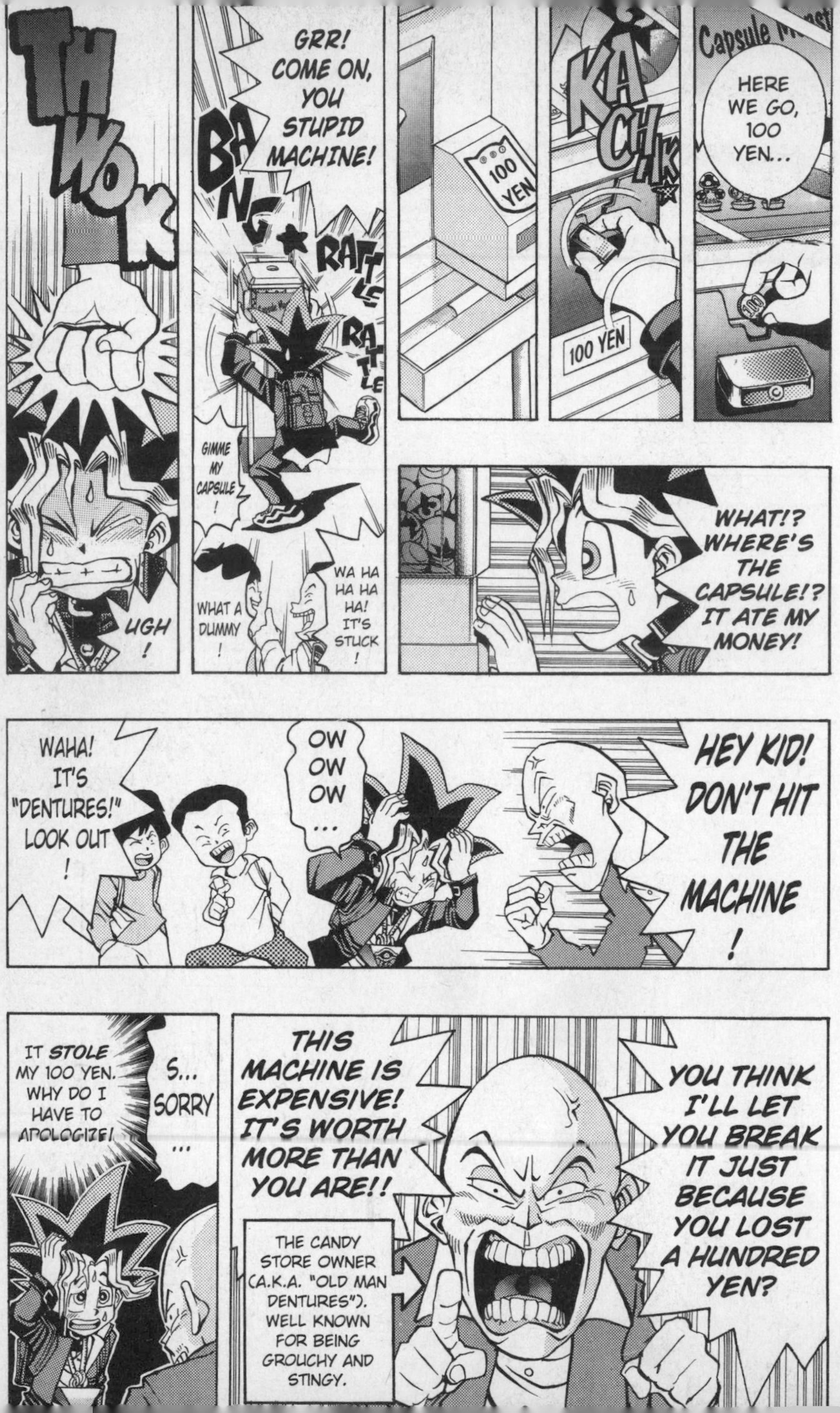
Capsule M
HERE WE GO, 100 YEN...
100
KA CHIK
100 YEN
100 YEN
WHAT!? WHERE'S THE CAPSULE!? IT ATE MY MONEY!
GRR! COME ON, YOU STUPID MACHINE!
BANG
RATTLE RATTLE
GIMME MY CAPSULE!
WA HA HA HA HA! IT'S STUCK!
WHAT A DUMMY!
THWOK
UGH!
HEY KID! DON'T HIT THE MACHINE!
OW OW OW...
WAHA! IT'S "DENTURES!" LOOK OUT!
YOU THINK I'LL LET YOU BREAK IT JUST BECAUSE YOU LOST A HUNDRED YEN?
THIS MACHINE IS EXPENSIVE! IT'S WORTH MORE THAN YOU ARE!!
THE CANDY STORE OWNER (A.K.A. "OLD MAN DENTURES"). WELL KNOWN FOR BEING GROUCHY AND STINGY.
S... SORRY...
IT *STOLE* MY 100 YEN. WHY DO I HAVE TO APOLOGIZE!

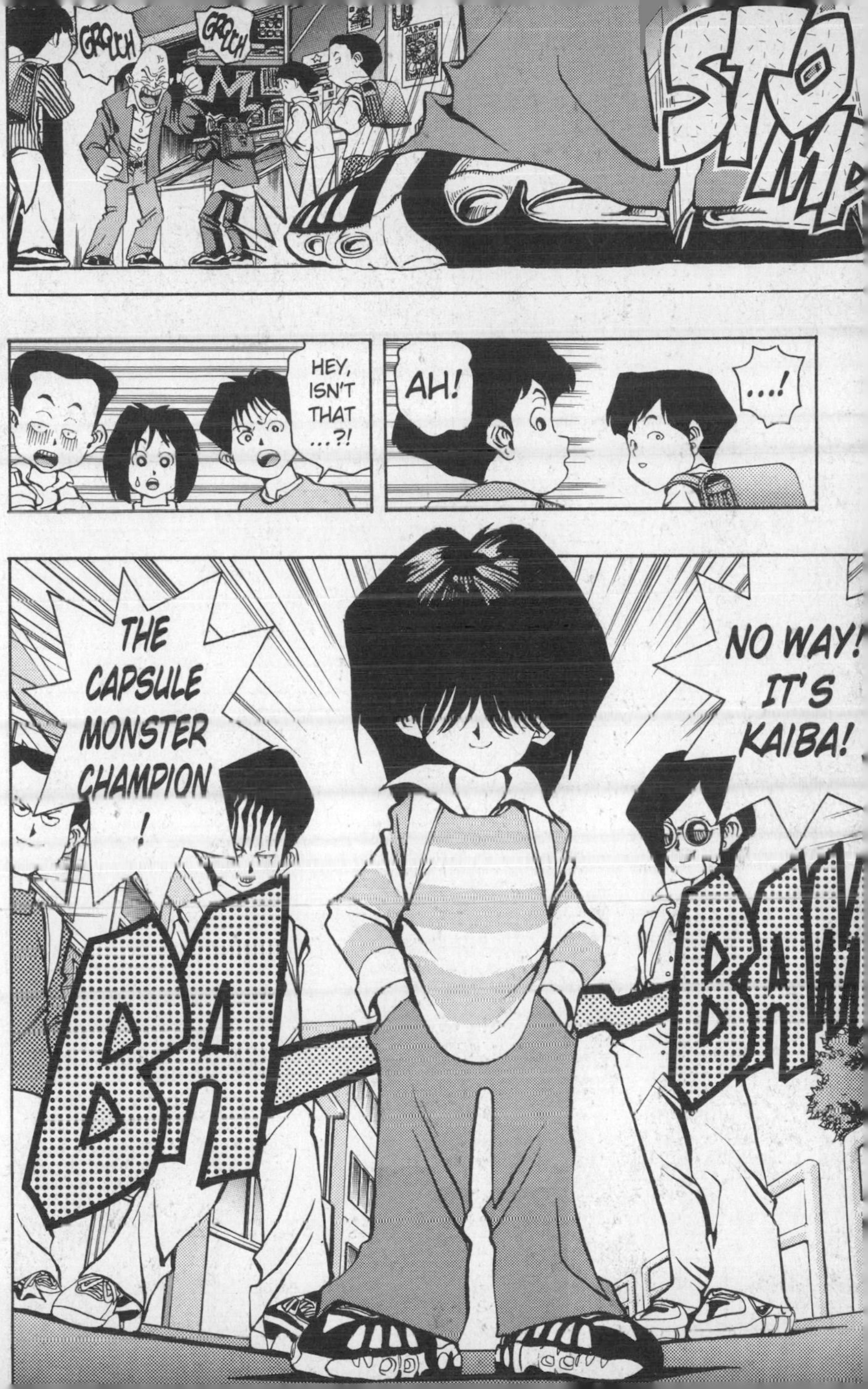
STOMP
GROUCH
GROUCH
...!
AH!
HEY, ISN'T THAT ...?!
NO WAY! IT'S KAIBA!
THE CAPSULE MONSTER CHAMPION!
BAM
BA

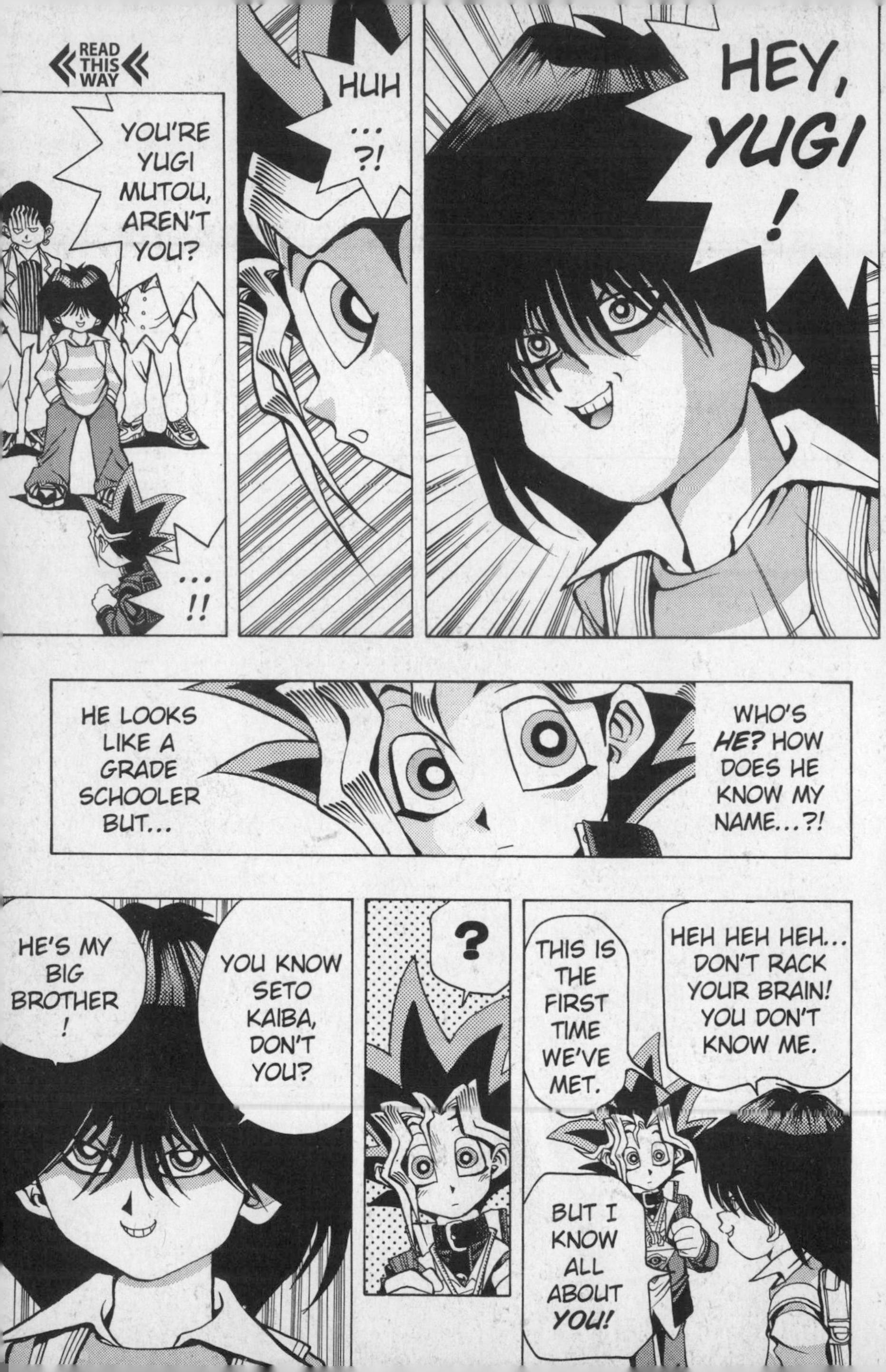
READ THIS WAY
HEY, YUGI!
HUH...?!
YOU'RE YUGI MUTOU, AREN'T YOU?
...!!
WHO'S HE? HOW DOES HE KNOW MY NAME...?!
HE LOOKS LIKE A GRADE SCHOOLER BUT...
HEH HEH HEH... DON'T RACK YOUR BRAIN! YOU DON'T KNOW ME.
THIS IS THE FIRST TIME WE'VE MET.
BUT I KNOW ALL ABOUT YOU!
?
YOU KNOW SETO KAIBA, DON'T YOU?
HE'S MY BIG BROTHER!

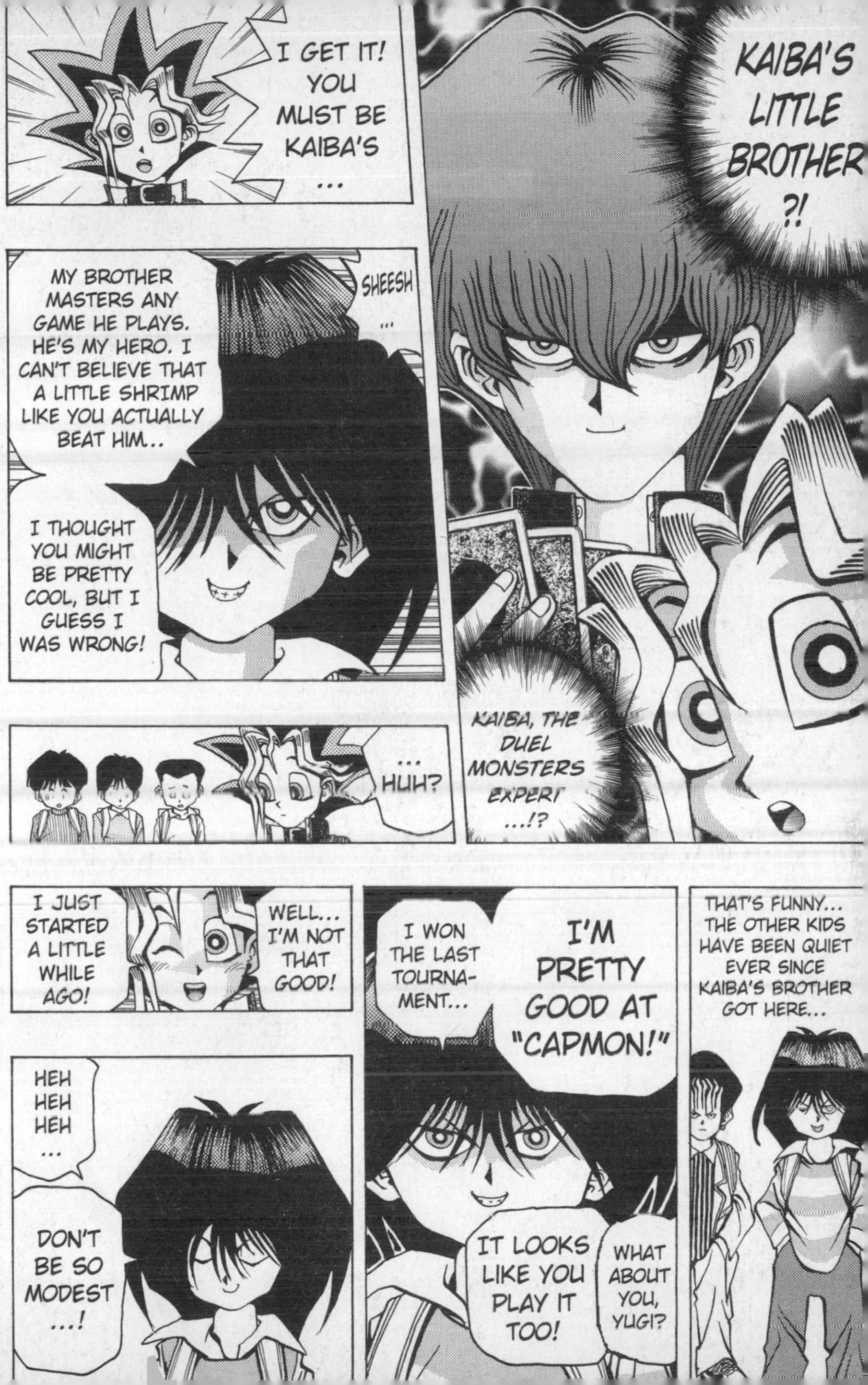
I GET IT! YOU MUST BE KAIBA'S ...
KAIBA'S LITTLE BROTHER ?!
MY BROTHER MASTERS ANY GAME HE PLAYS. HE'S MY HERO. I CAN'T BELIEVE THAT A LITTLE SHRIMP LIKE YOU ACTUALLY BEAT HIM...
SHEESH ...
I THOUGHT YOU MIGHT BE PRETTY COOL, BUT I GUESS I WAS WRONG!
... HUH?
KAIBA, THE DUEL MONSTERS EXPERT ...!?
I WON THE LAST TOURNA-MENT...
I'M PRETTY GOOD AT "CAPMON!"
IT LOOKS LIKE YOU PLAY IT TOO!
WHAT ABOUT YOU, YUGI?
WELL... I'M NOT THAT GOOD!
I JUST STARTED A LITTLE WHILE AGO!
HEH HEH HEH ...
DON'T BE SO MODEST ...!
THAT'S FUNNY... THE OTHER KIDS HAVE BEEN QUIET EVER SINCE KAIBA'S BROTHER GOT HERE...

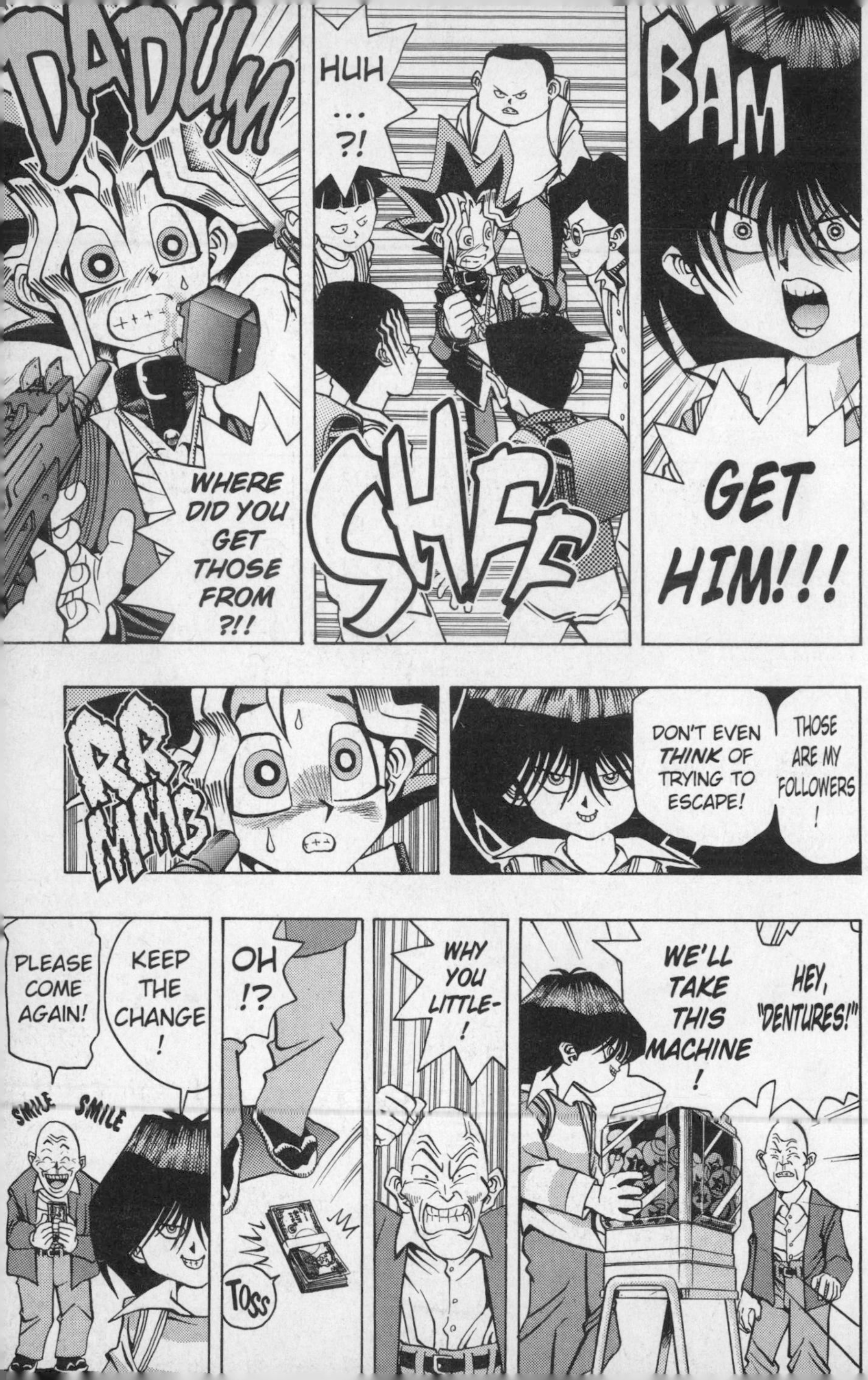
BAM
GET HIM!!!
HUH ...?!
SHF
DADUM
WHERE DID YOU GET THOSE FROM ?!!
THOSE ARE MY FOLLOWERS!
DON'T EVEN THINK OF TRYING TO ESCAPE!
RRMMB
HEY, "DENTURES!"
WE'LL TAKE THIS MACHINE!
WHY YOU LITTLE-!
OH !?
TOSS
KEEP THE CHANGE!
PLEASE COME AGAIN!
SMILE
SMILE

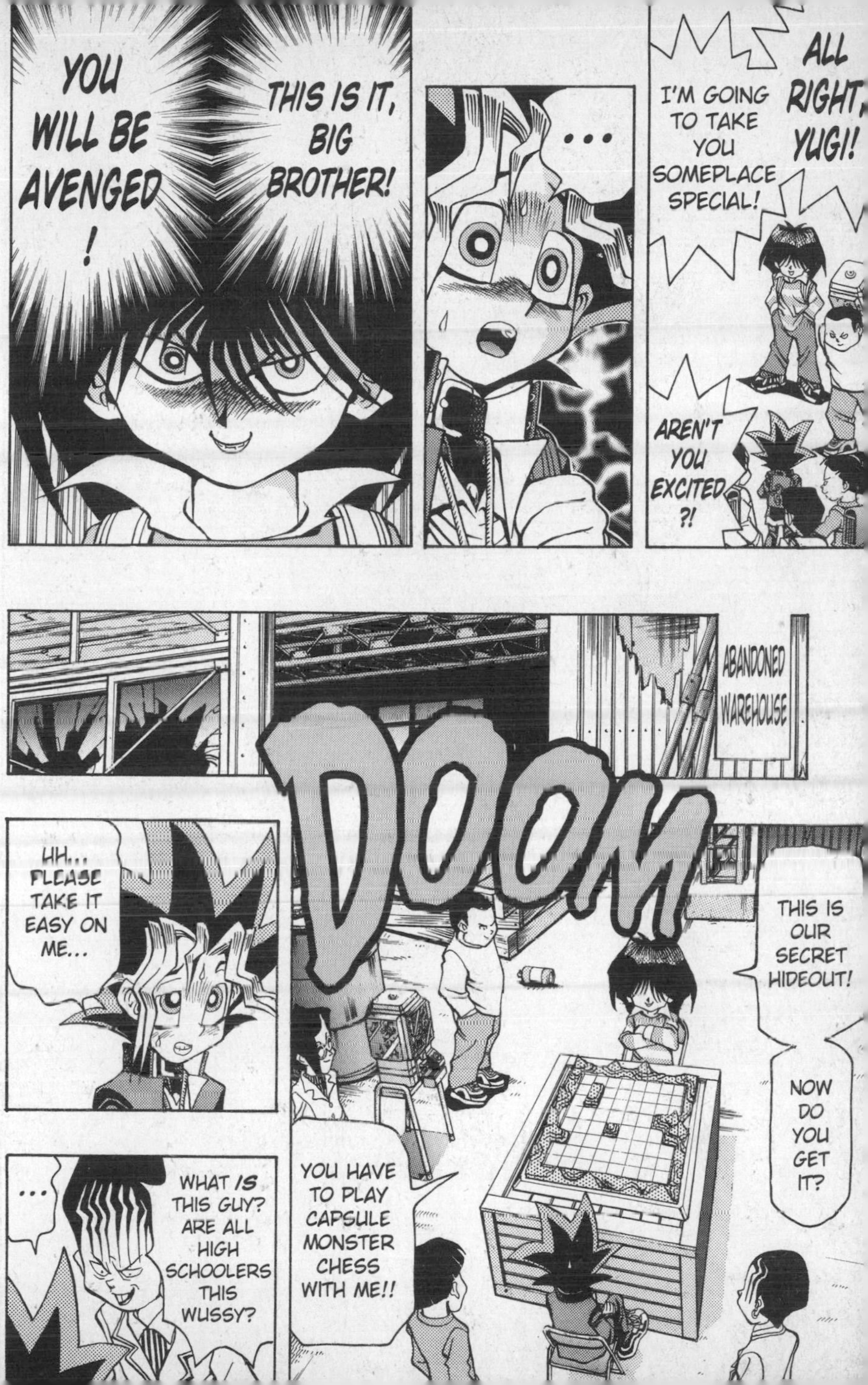
ALL RIGHT, YUGI!
I'M GOING TO TAKE YOU SOMEPLACE SPECIAL!
AREN'T YOU EXCITED ?!
...
THIS IS IT, BIG BROTHER!
YOU WILL BE AVENGED !
ABANDONED WAREHOUSE
DOOM
THIS IS OUR SECRET HIDEOUT!
NOW DO YOU GET IT?
YOU HAVE TO PLAY CAPSULE MONSTER CHESS WITH ME!!
UH... PLEASE TAKE IT EASY ON ME...
...
WHAT IS THIS GUY? ARE ALL HIGH SCHOOLERS THIS WUSSY?

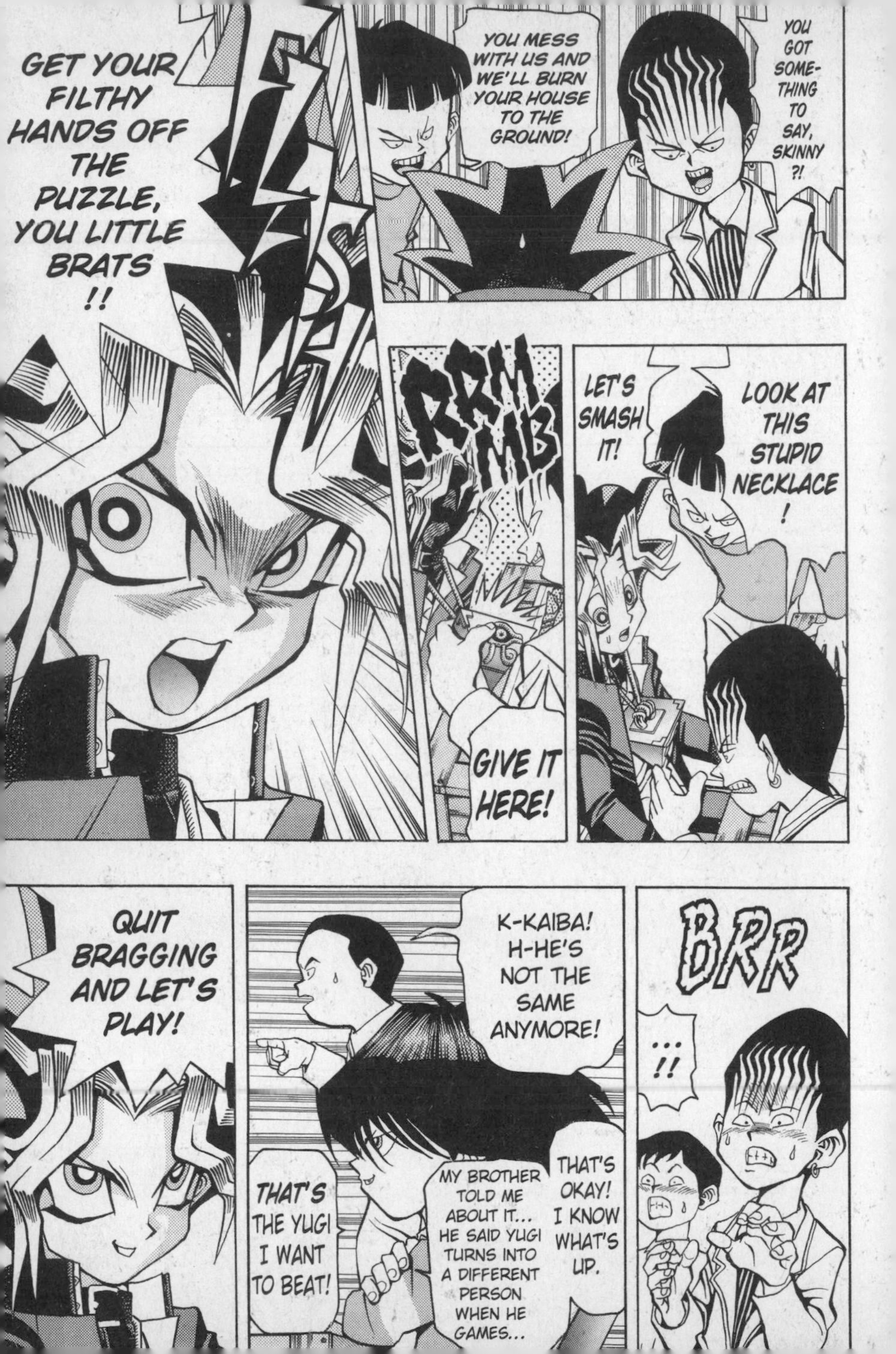
YOU GOT SOMETHING TO SAY, SKINNY?!
YOU MESS WITH US AND WE'LL BURN YOUR HOUSE TO THE GROUND!
LOOK AT THIS STUPID NECKLACE!
LET'S SMASH IT!
RRMMB
GIVE IT HERE!
GET YOUR FILTHY HANDS OFF THE PUZZLE, YOU LITTLE BRATS!!
BRR
...!!
K-KAIBA! H-HE'S NOT THE SAME ANYMORE!
THAT'S OKAY! I KNOW WHAT'S UP.
MY BROTHER TOLD ME ABOUT IT... HE SAID YUGI TURNS INTO A DIFFERENT PERSON WHEN HE GAMES...
THAT'S THE YUGI I WANT TO BEAT!
QUIT BRAGGING AND LET'S PLAY!

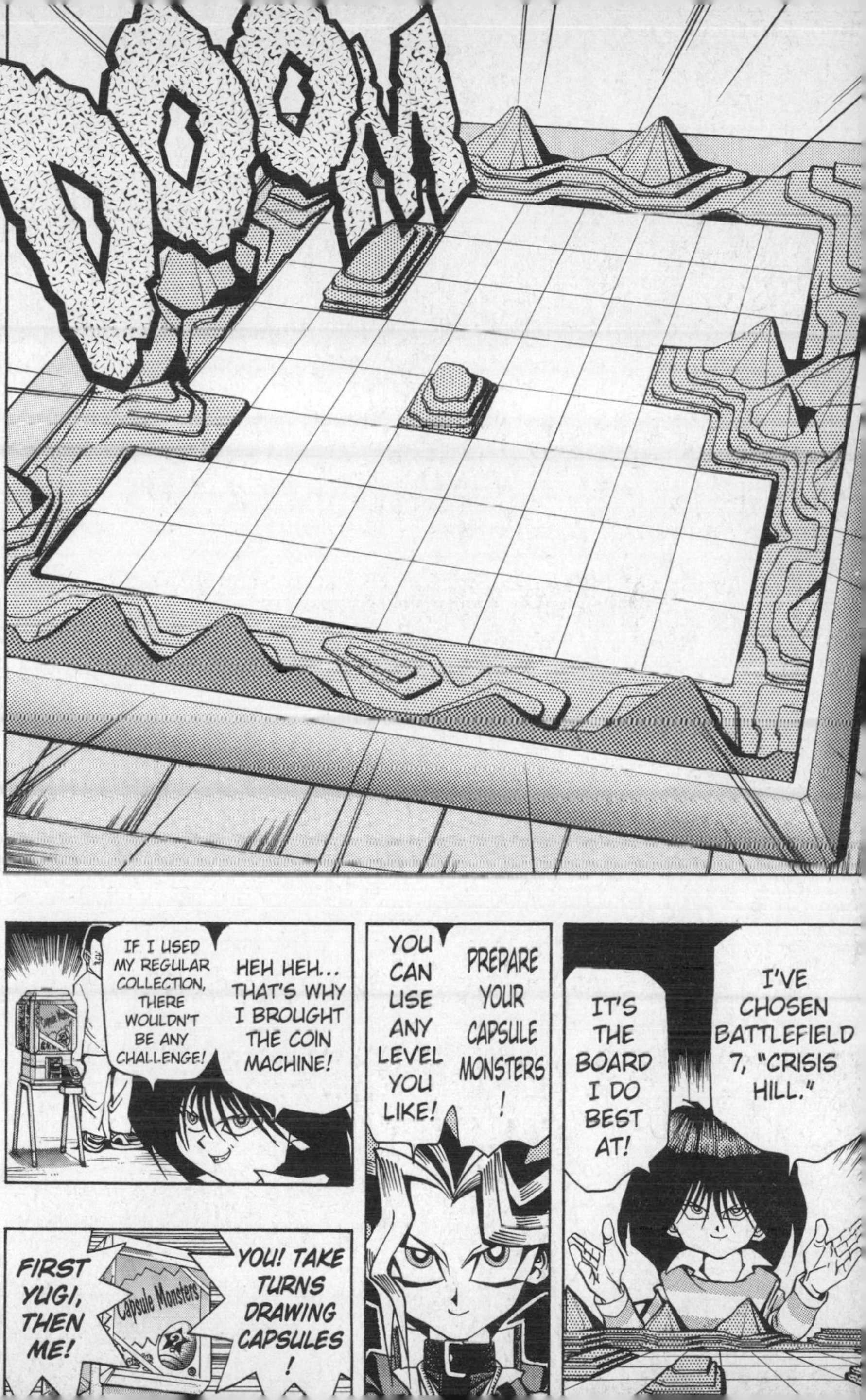
DOOM
I'VE CHOSEN BATTLEFIELD 7, "CRISIS HILL."
IT'S THE BOARD I DO BEST AT!
PREPARE YOUR CAPSULE MONSTERS!
YOU CAN USE ANY LEVEL YOU LIKE!
HEH HEH... THAT'S WHY I BROUGHT THE COIN MACHINE!
IF I USED MY REGULAR COLLECTION, THERE WOULDN'T BE ANY CHALLENGE!
YOU! TAKE TURNS DRAWING CAPSULES!
FIRST YUGI, THEN ME!
Capsule Monsters

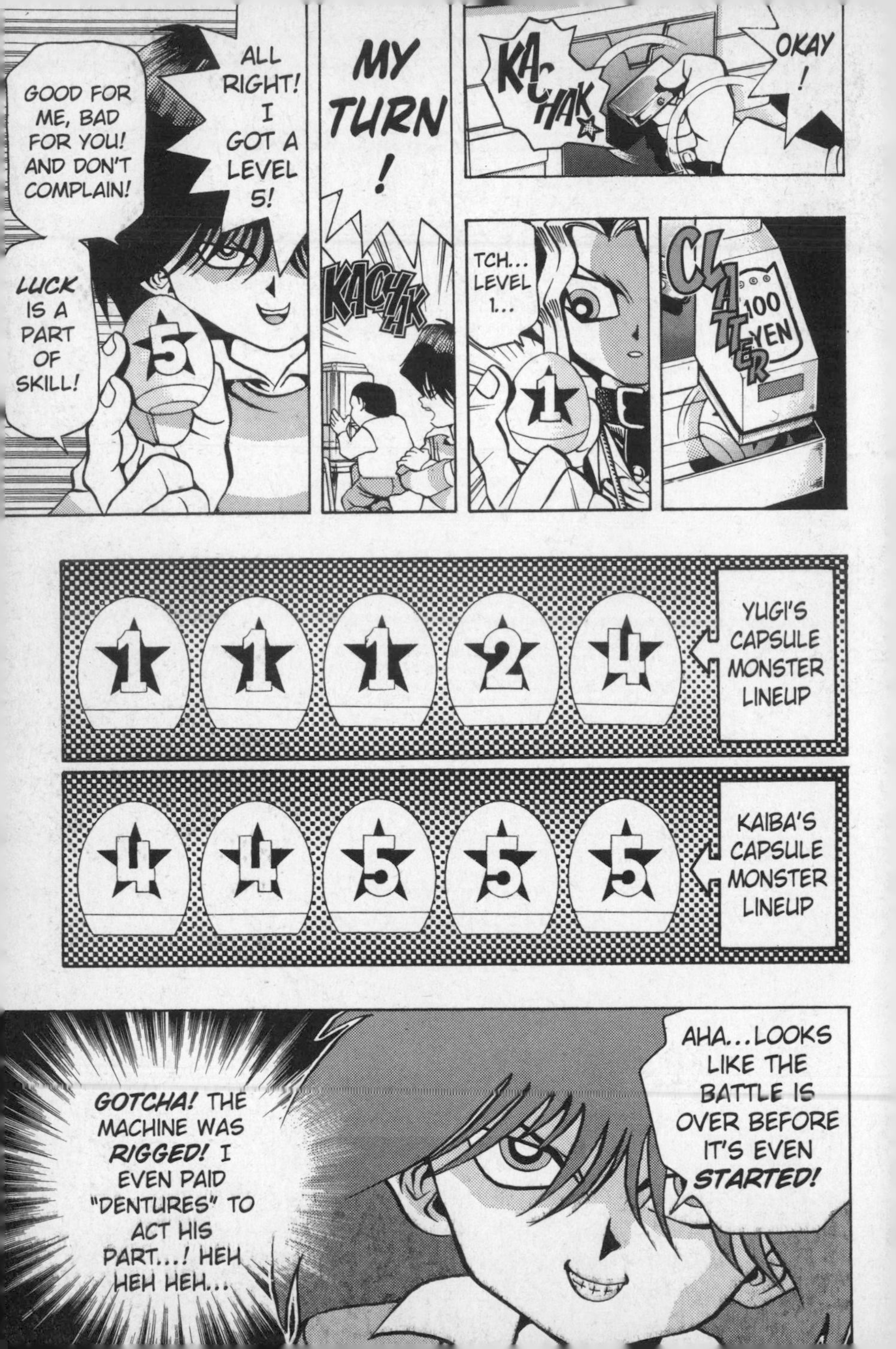
OKAY!
KACHAK
CLATTER
100 YEN
TCH... LEVEL 1...
MY TURN!
KACHAK
ALL RIGHT! I GOT A LEVEL 5!
GOOD FOR ME, BAD FOR YOU! AND DON'T COMPLAIN!
LUCK IS A PART OF SKILL!
YUGI'S CAPSULE MONSTER LINEUP
1 1 1 2 4
KAIBA'S CAPSULE MONSTER LINEUP
4 4 5 5 5
AHA...LOOKS LIKE THE BATTLE IS OVER BEFORE IT'S EVEN STARTED!
GOTCHA! THE MACHINE WAS RIGGED! I EVEN PAID "DENTURES" TO ACT HIS PART...! HEH HEH HEH...

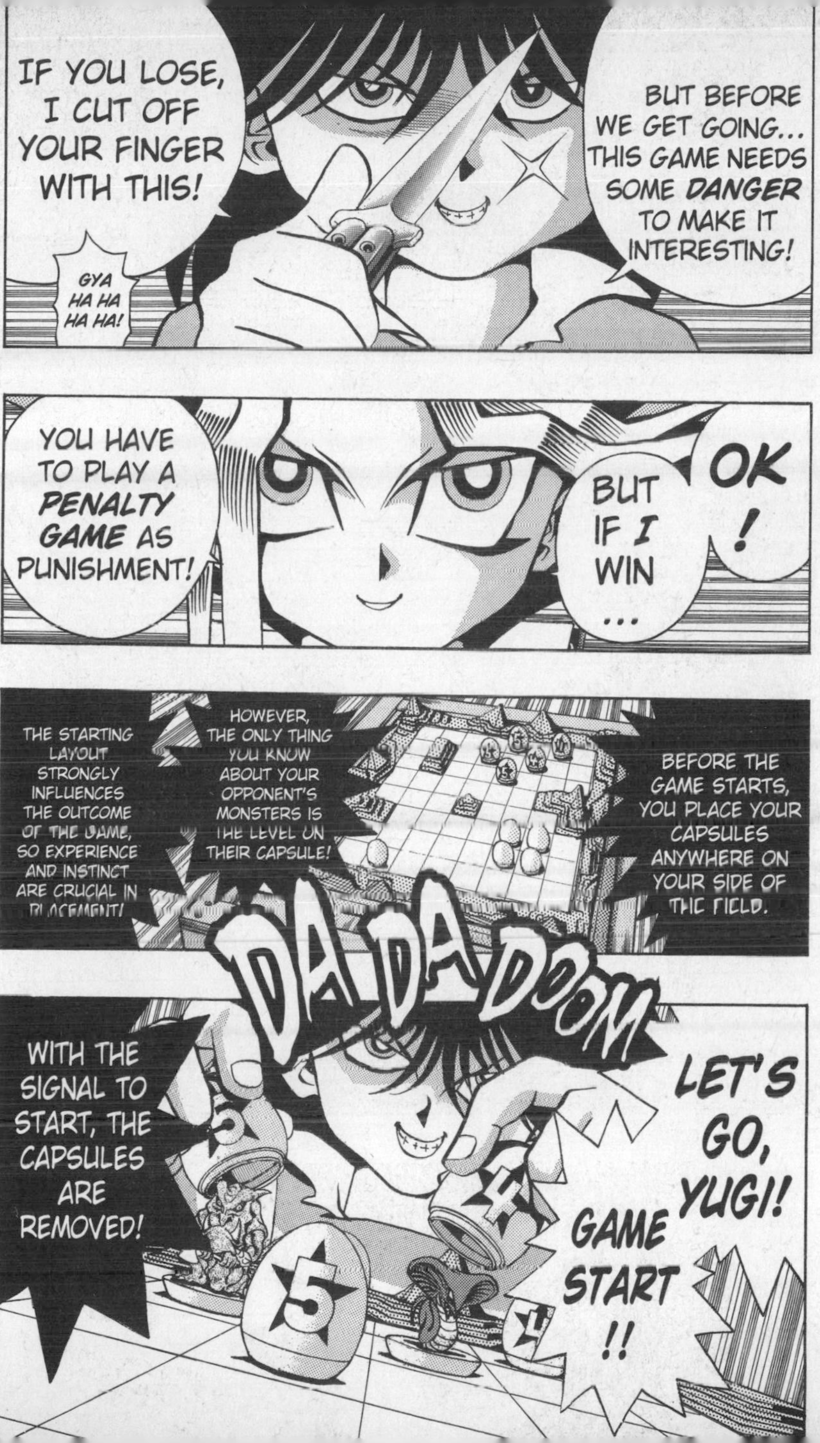
BUT BEFORE WE GET GOING... THIS GAME NEEDS SOME DANGER TO MAKE IT INTERESTING!
IF YOU LOSE, I CUT OFF YOUR FINGER WITH THIS!
GYA HA HA HA HA!
OK!
BUT IF I WIN...
YOU HAVE TO PLAY A PENALTY GAME AS PUNISHMENT!
BEFORE THE GAME STARTS, YOU PLACE YOUR CAPSULES ANYWHERE ON YOUR SIDE OF THE FIELD.
HOWEVER, THE ONLY THING YOU KNOW ABOUT YOUR OPPONENT'S MONSTERS IS THE LEVEL ON THEIR CAPSULE!
THE STARTING LAYOUT STRONGLY INFLUENCES THE OUTCOME OF THE GAME, SO EXPERIENCE AND INSTINCT ARE CRUCIAL IN PLACEMENT!
DA DA DOOM
LET'S GO, YUGI!
GAME START!!
WITH THE SIGNAL TO START, THE CAPSULES ARE REMOVED!

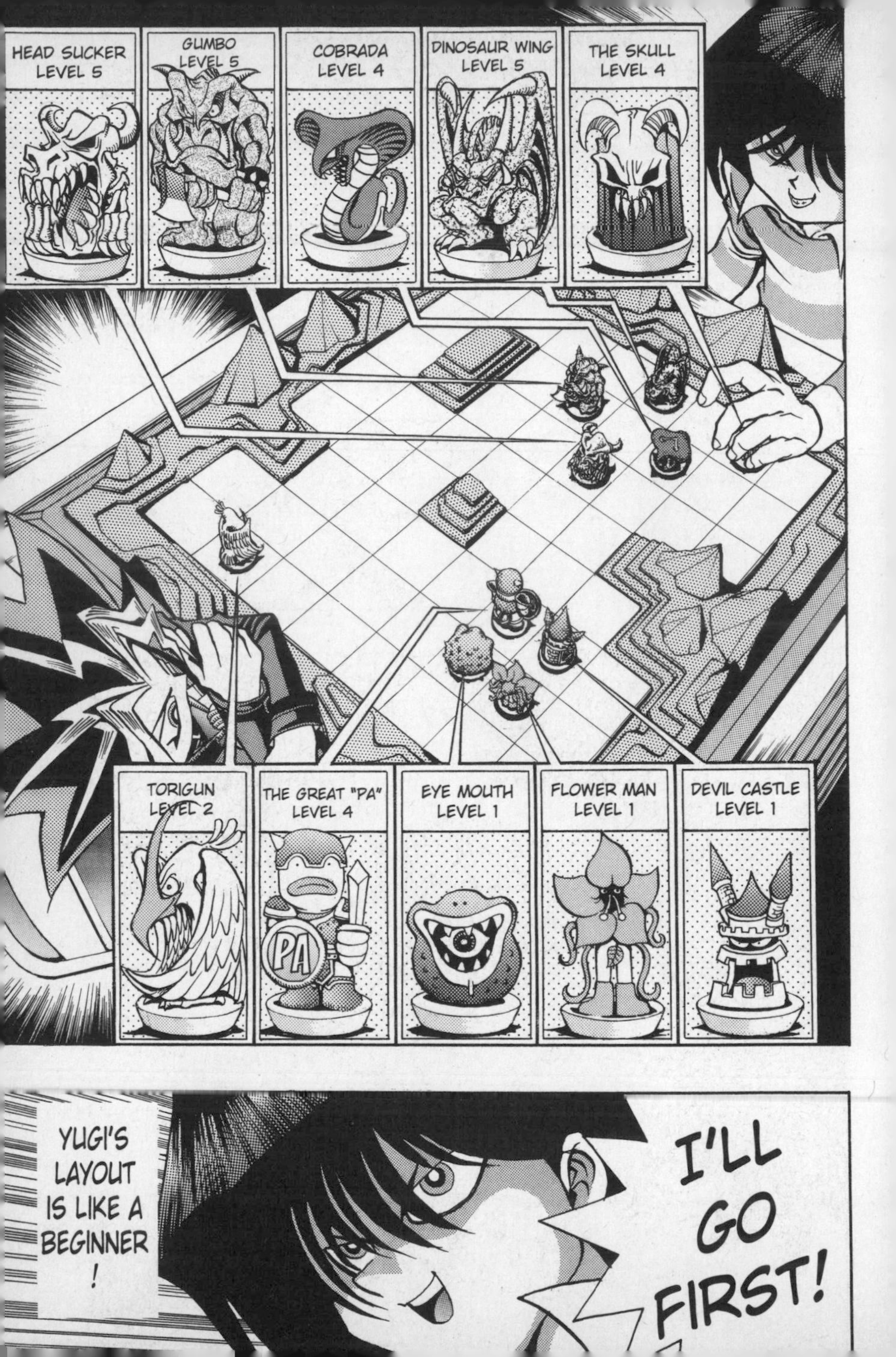
THE SKULL LEVEL 4
DINOSAUR WING LEVEL 5
COBRADA LEVEL 4
GUMBO LEVEL 5
HEAD SUCKER LEVEL 5
DEVIL CASTLE LEVEL 1
FLOWER MAN LEVEL 1
EYE MOUTH LEVEL 1
THE GREAT "PA" LEVEL 4
TORIGUN LEVEL 2
I'LL GO FIRST!
YUGI'S LAYOUT IS LIKE A BEGINNER !

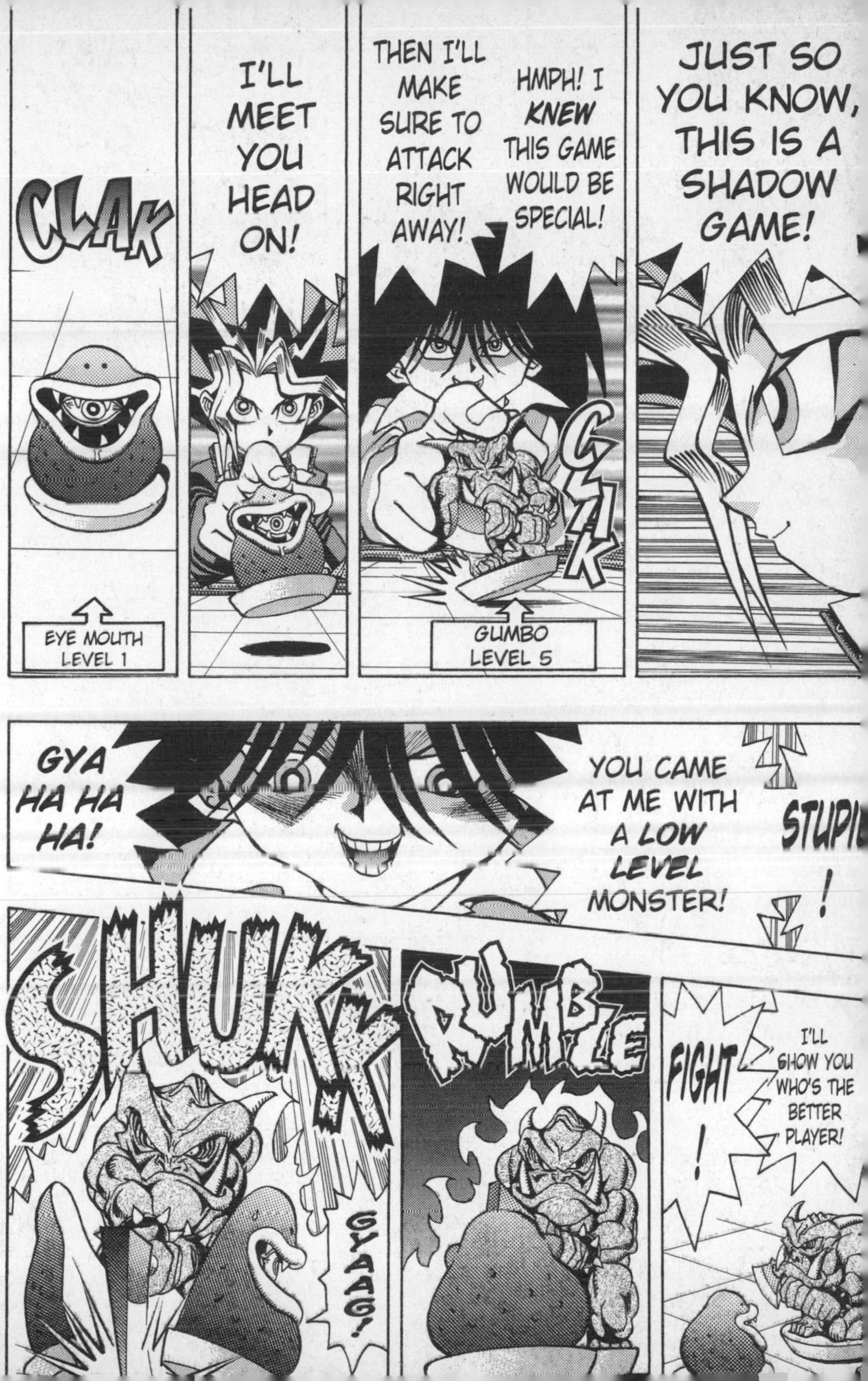

JUST SO YOU KNOW, THIS IS A SHADOW GAME!
HMPH! I KNEW THIS GAME WOULD BE SPECIAL!
THEN I'LL MAKE SURE TO ATTACK RIGHT AWAY!
CLAK
GUMBO LEVEL 5
I'LL MEET YOU HEAD ON!
CLAK
EYE MOUTH LEVEL 1
STUPI
!
YOU CAME AT ME WITH A LOW LEVEL MONSTER!
GYA HA HA HA!
I'LL SHOW YOU WHO'S THE BETTER PLAYER!
FIGHT!
RUMBLE
SHUK
GYAAG!

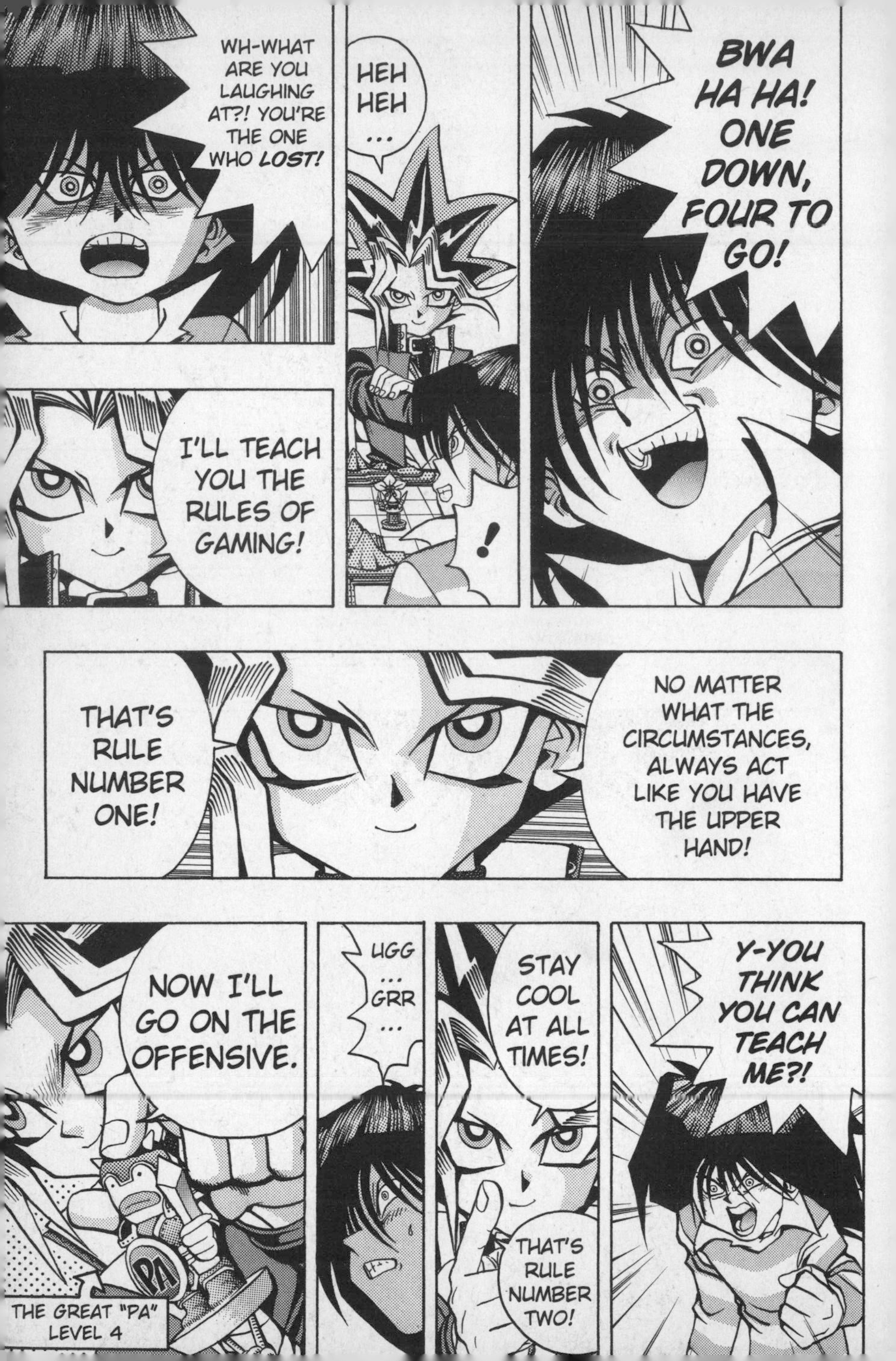
BWA HA HA! ONE DOWN, FOUR TO GO!
HEH HEH ...
!
WH-WHAT ARE YOU LAUGHING AT?! YOU'RE THE ONE WHO LOST!
I'LL TEACH YOU THE RULES OF GAMING!
NO MATTER WHAT THE CIRCUMSTANCES, ALWAYS ACT LIKE YOU HAVE THE UPPER HAND!
THAT'S RULE NUMBER ONE!
Y-YOU THINK YOU CAN TEACH ME?!
STAY COOL AT ALL TIMES!
THAT'S RULE NUMBER TWO!
UGG ... GRR ...
NOW I'LL GO ON THE OFFENSIVE.
THE GREAT "PA" LEVEL 4

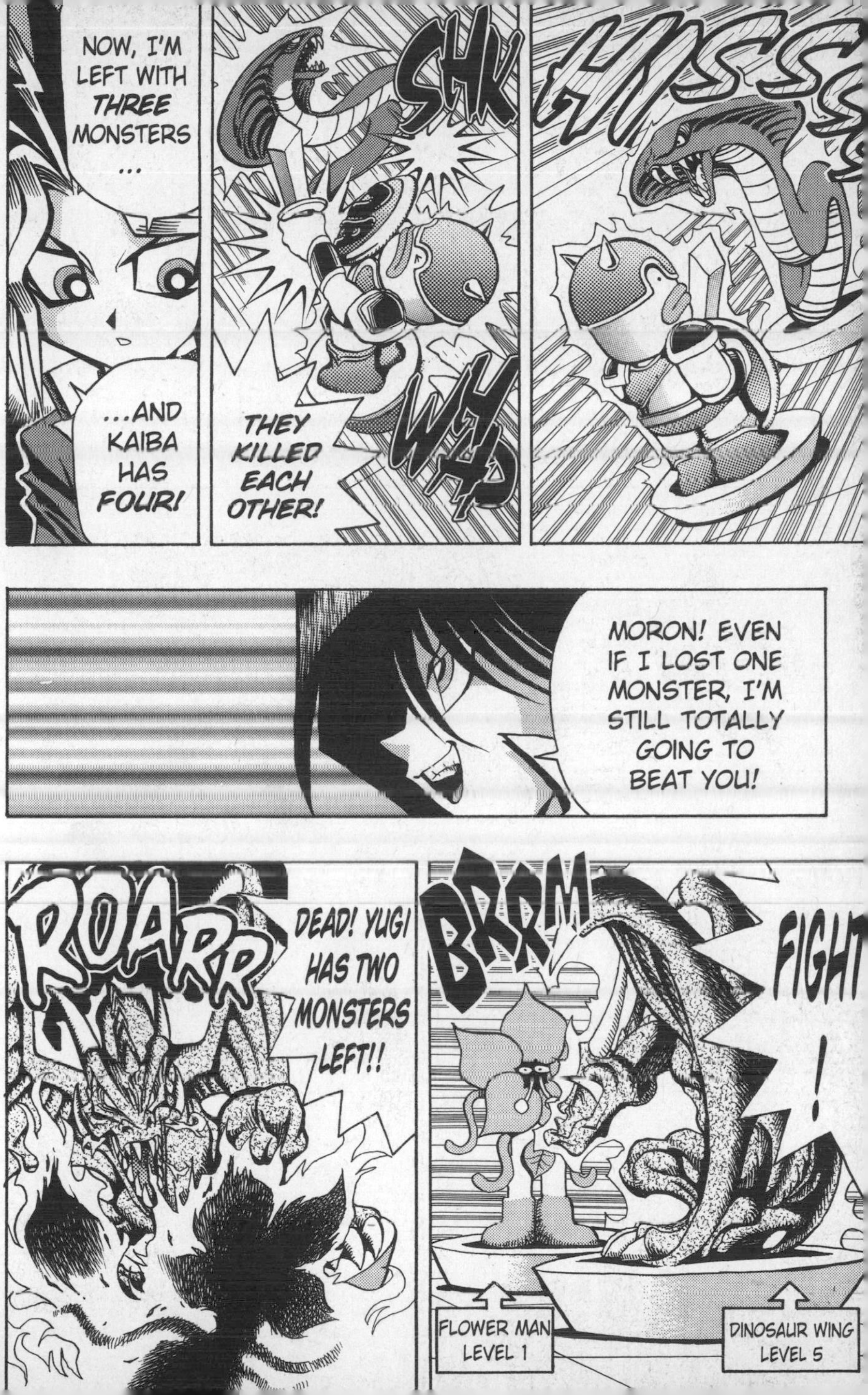
HISSS
SHK
THEY KILLED EACH OTHER!
NOW, I'M LEFT WITH THREE MONSTERS ...
...AND KAIBA HAS FOUR!
MORON! EVEN IF I LOST ONE MONSTER, I'M STILL TOTALLY GOING TO BEAT YOU!
FIGHT !
BRRM
DINOSAUR WING LEVEL 5
FLOWER MAN LEVEL 1
DEAD! YUGI HAS TWO MONSTERS LEFT!!
ROARR

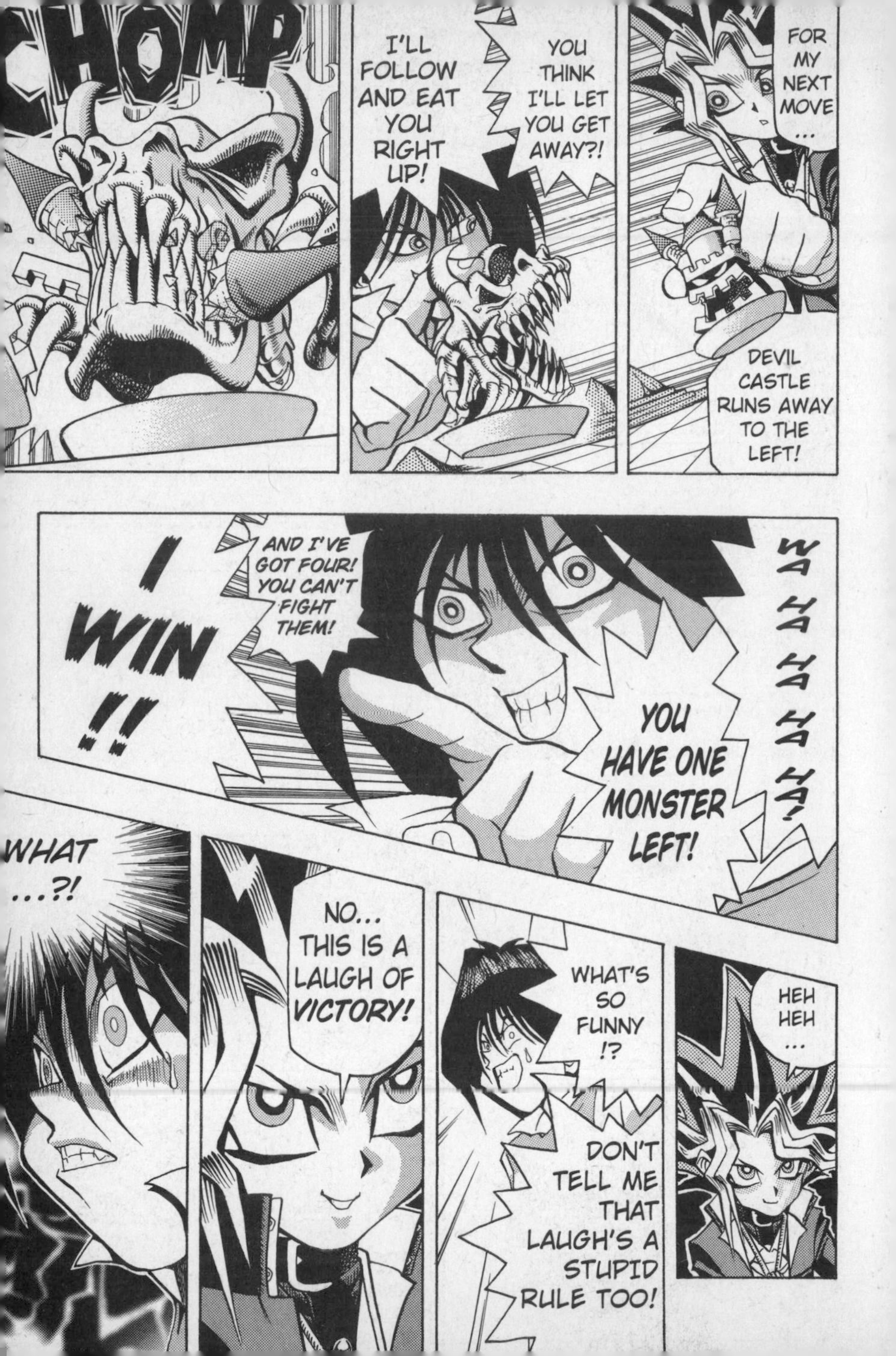
FOR MY NEXT MOVE ...
DEVIL CASTLE RUNS AWAY TO THE LEFT!
YOU THINK I'LL LET YOU GET AWAY?!
I'LL FOLLOW AND EAT YOU RIGHT UP!
CHOMP
WA HA HA HA HA HA!
YOU HAVE ONE MONSTER LEFT!
AND I'VE GOT FOUR! YOU CAN'T FIGHT THEM!
I WIN!!
HEH HEH ...
WHAT'S SO FUNNY !?
DON'T TELL ME THAT LAUGH'S A STUPID RULE TOO!
NO... THIS IS A LAUGH OF VICTORY!
WHAT ...?!

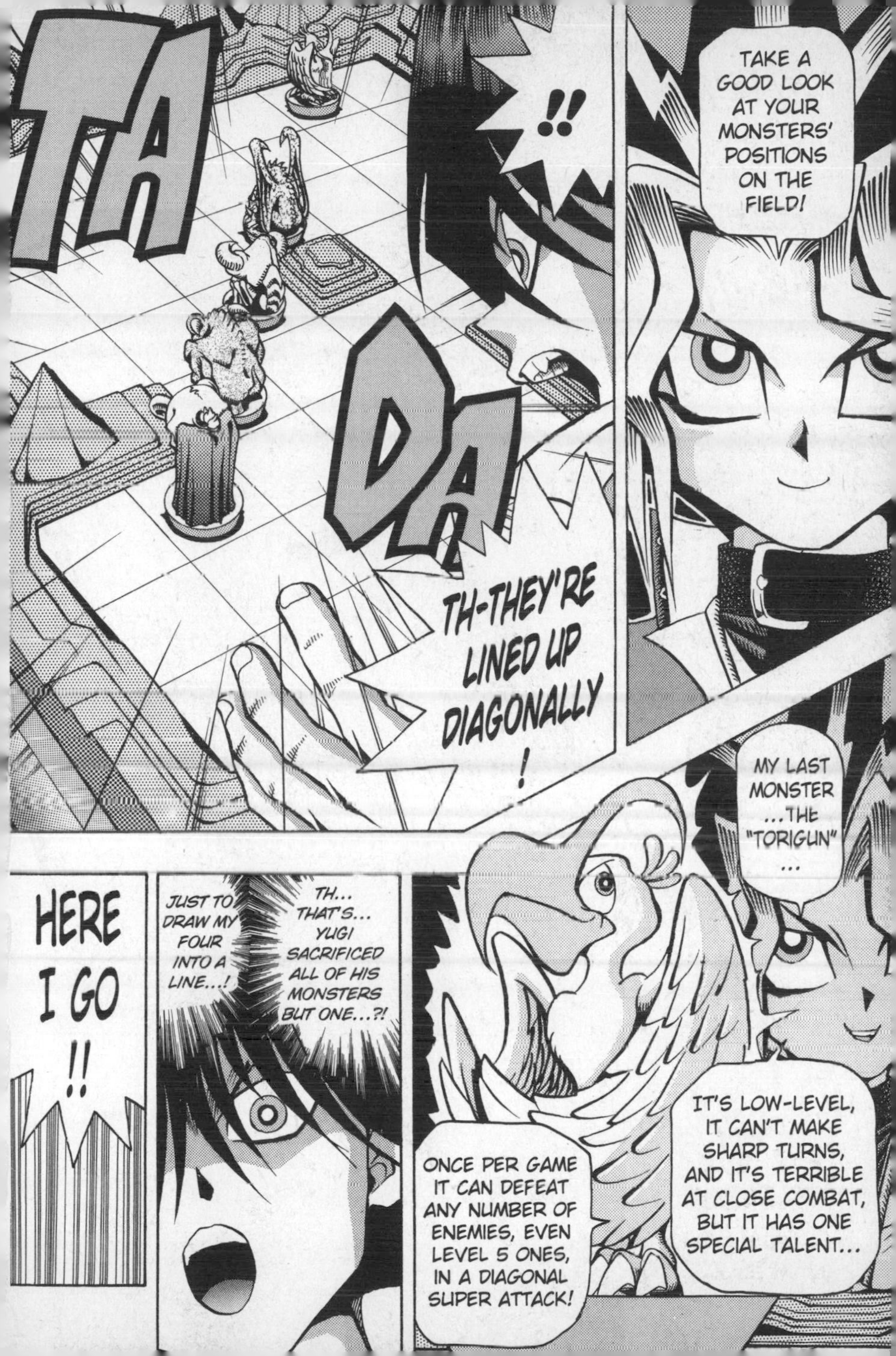

TAKE A GOOD LOOK AT YOUR MONSTERS' POSITIONS ON THE FIELD!
!!
TA
DA
TH-THEY'RE LINED UP DIAGONALLY!
MY LAST MONSTER ...THE "TORIGUN" ...
IT'S LOW-LEVEL, IT CAN'T MAKE SHARP TURNS, AND IT'S TERRIBLE AT CLOSE COMBAT, BUT IT HAS ONE SPECIAL TALENT...
ONCE PER GAME IT CAN DEFEAT ANY NUMBER OF ENEMIES, EVEN LEVEL 5 ONES, IN A DIAGONAL SUPER ATTACK!
TH... THAT'S... YUGI SACRIFICED ALL OF HIS MONSTERS BUT ONE...?!
JUST TO DRAW MY FOUR INTO A LINE...!
HERE I GO!!

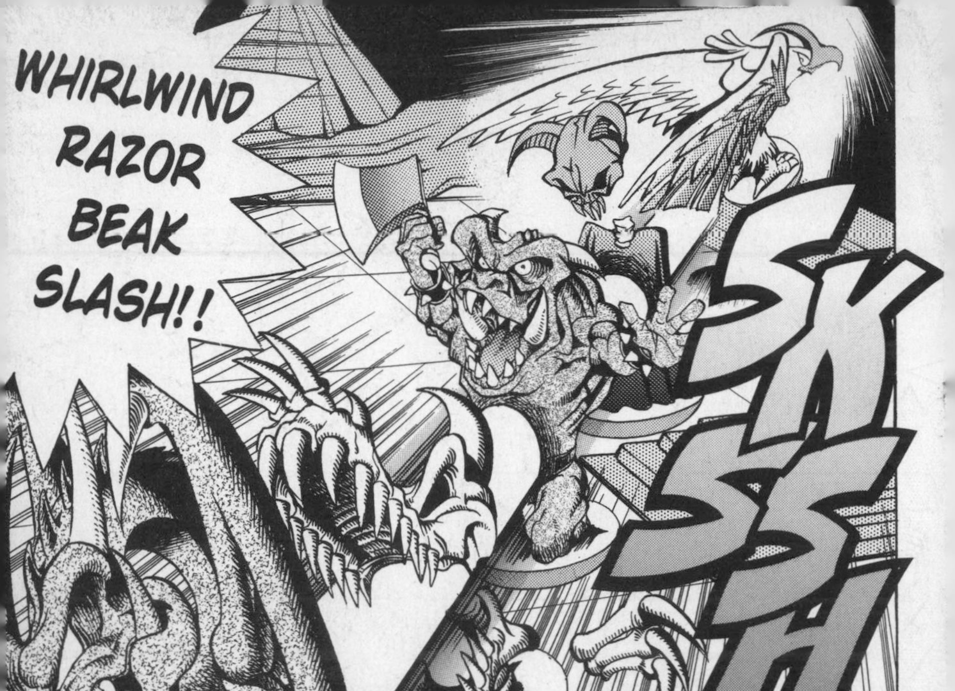
WHIRLWIND RAZOR BEAK SLASH!!
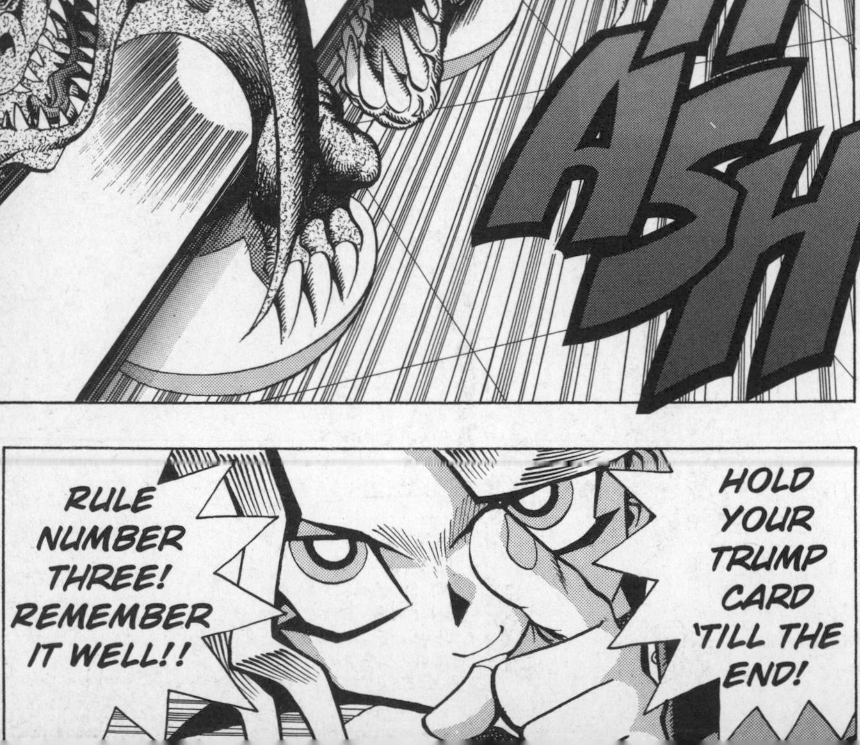
HOLD YOUR TRUMP CARD 'TILL THE END!
RULE NUMBER THREE! REMEMBER IT WELL!!

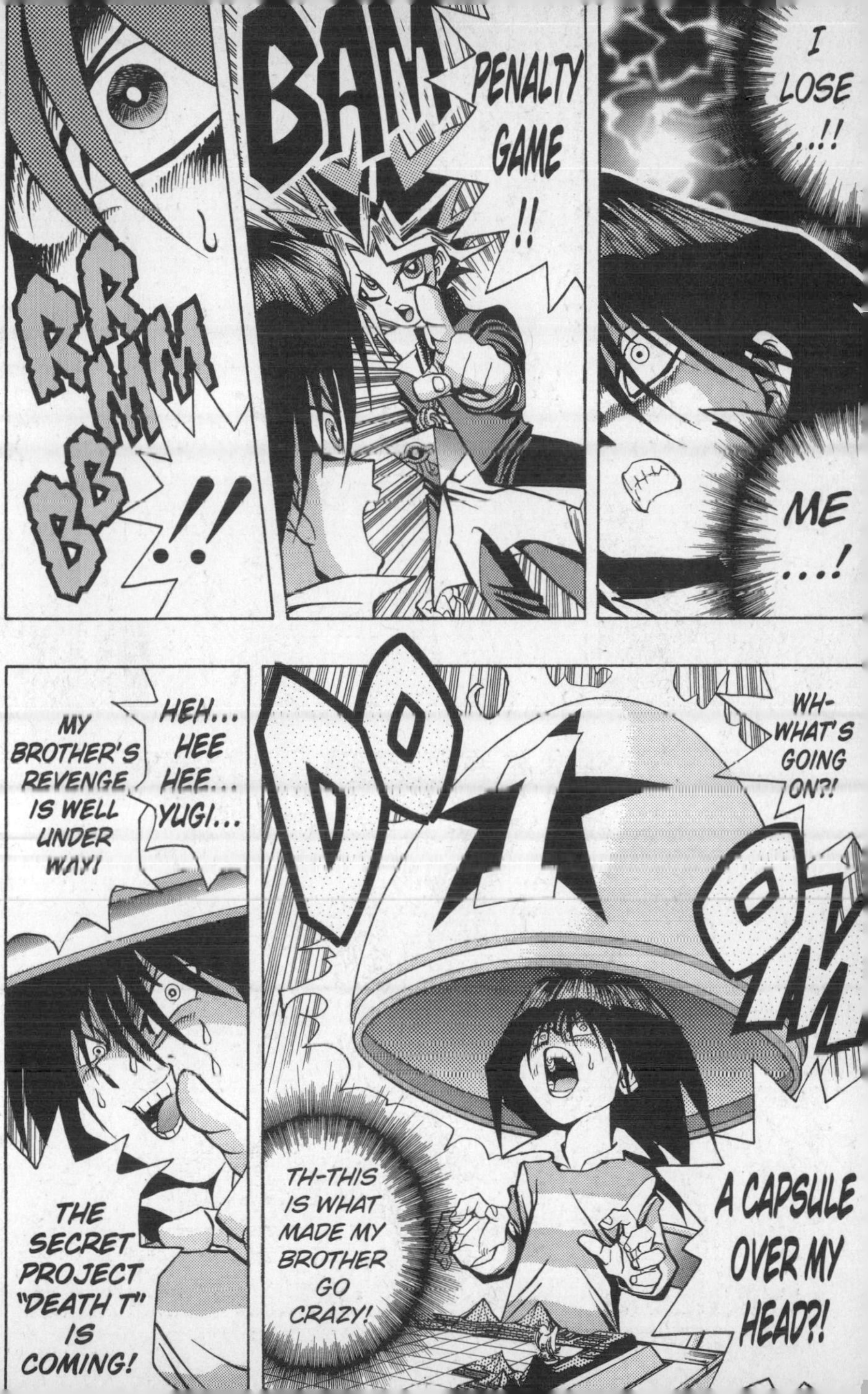

I LOSE ..!!
ME ...!
BAM
PENALTY GAME !!
RRMMBB!!
WH- WHAT'S GOING ON?!
DOOM
A CAPSULE OVER MY HEAD?!
TH-THIS IS WHAT MADE MY BROTHER GO CRAZY!
HEH... HEE HEE... YUGI...
MY BROTHER'S REVENGE IS WELL UNDER WAY!
THE SECRET PROJECT "DEATH T" IS COMING!

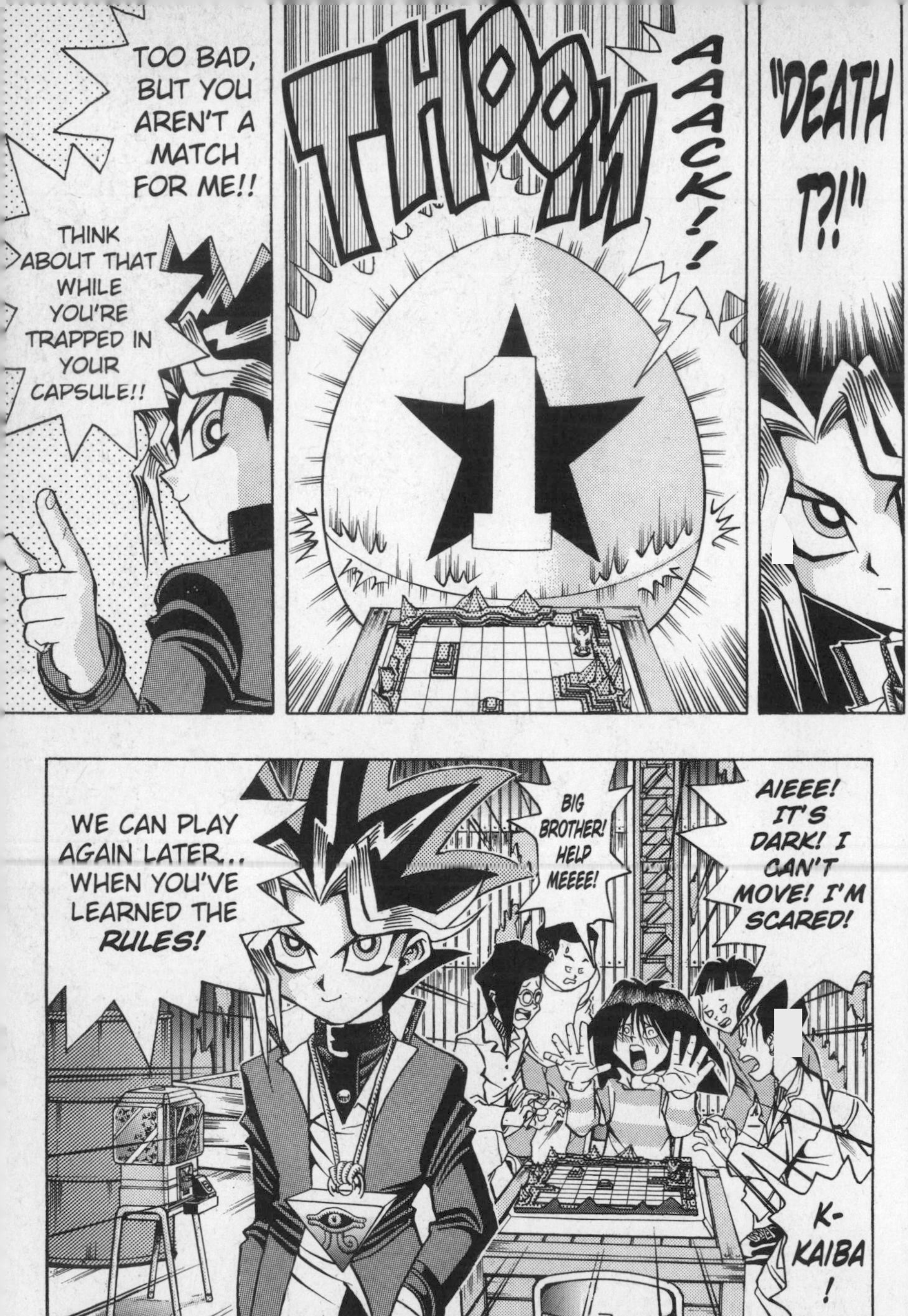
"DEATH T?!"
THOOM
AAACK!!
TOO BAD, BUT YOU AREN'T A MATCH FOR ME!!
THINK ABOUT THAT WHILE YOU'RE TRAPPED IN YOUR CAPSULE!!
AIEEE! IT'S DARK! I CAN'T MOVE! I'M SCARED!
BIG BROTHER! HELP MEEEE!
WE CAN PLAY AGAIN LATER.. WHEN YOU'VE LEARNED THE *RULES!*
K-KAIBA!

TO BE CONTINUED IN YU-GI-OH! VOL. 4!

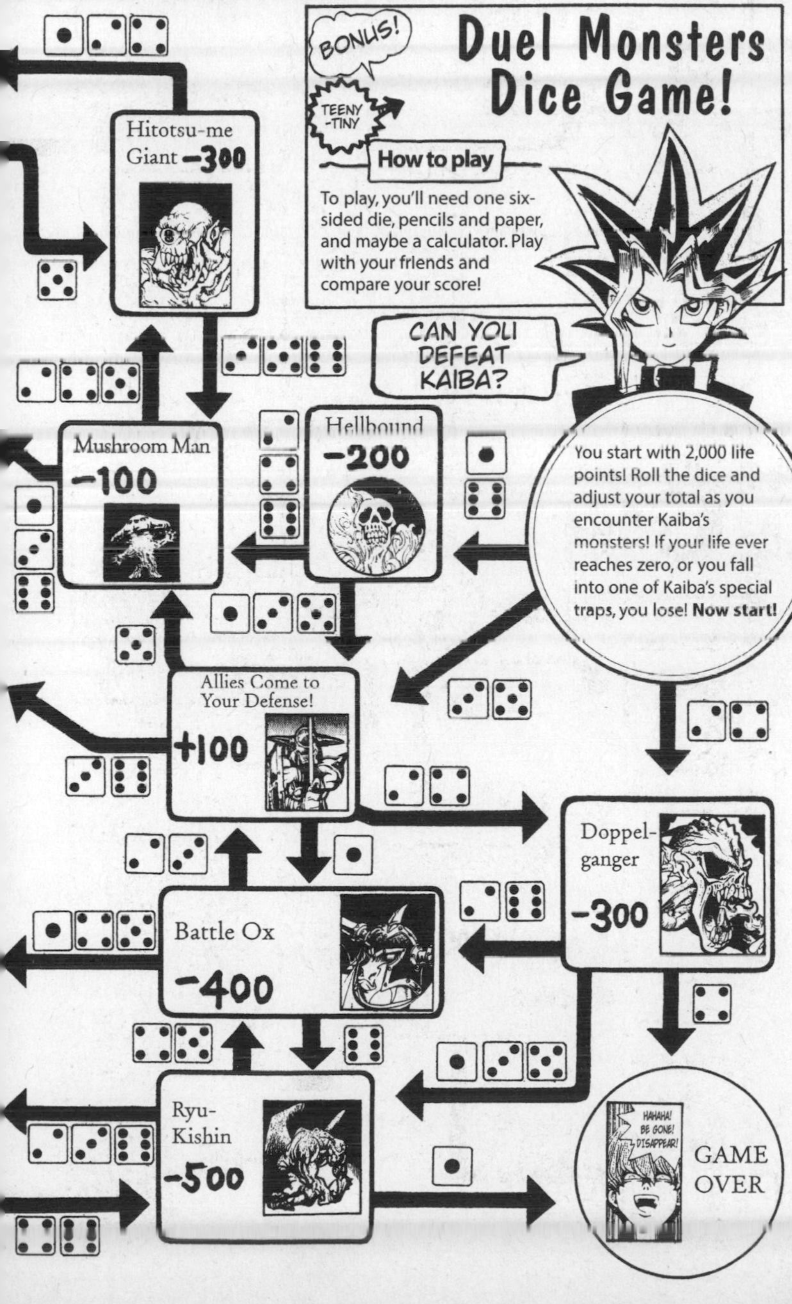
BONUS!
TEENY-TINY
Duel Monsters Dice Game!
How to play
To play, you'll need one six-sided die, pencils and paper, and maybe a calculator. Play with your friends and compare your score!
CAN YOU DEFEAT KAIBA?
You start with 2,000 life points! Roll the dice and adjust your total as you encounter Kaiba's monsters! If your life ever reaches zero, or you fall into one of Kaiba's special traps, you lose! Now start!
Hitotsu-me Giant -300
Hellbound -200
Mushroom Man -100
Allies Come to Your Defense! +100
Doppel-ganger -300
Battle Ox -400
Ryu-Kishin -500
HAHAHA! BE GONE! DISAPPEAR!
GAME OVER

# STAGE 1

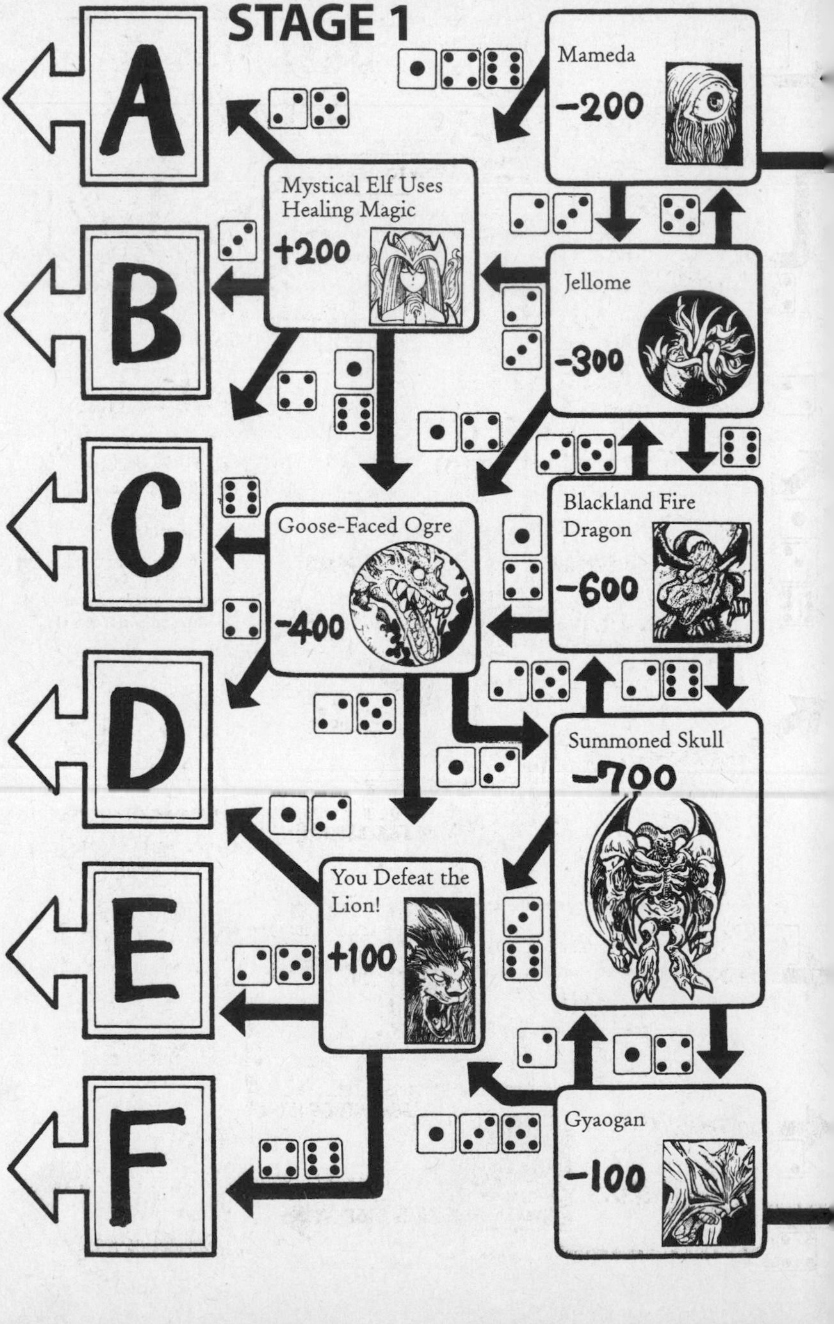
A
B
C
D
E
F
Mameda
-200
Mystical Elf Uses Healing Magic
+200
Jellome
-300
Goose-Faced Ogre
-400
Blackland Fire Dragon
-600
Summoned Skull
-700
You Defeat the Lion!
+100
Gyaogan
-100

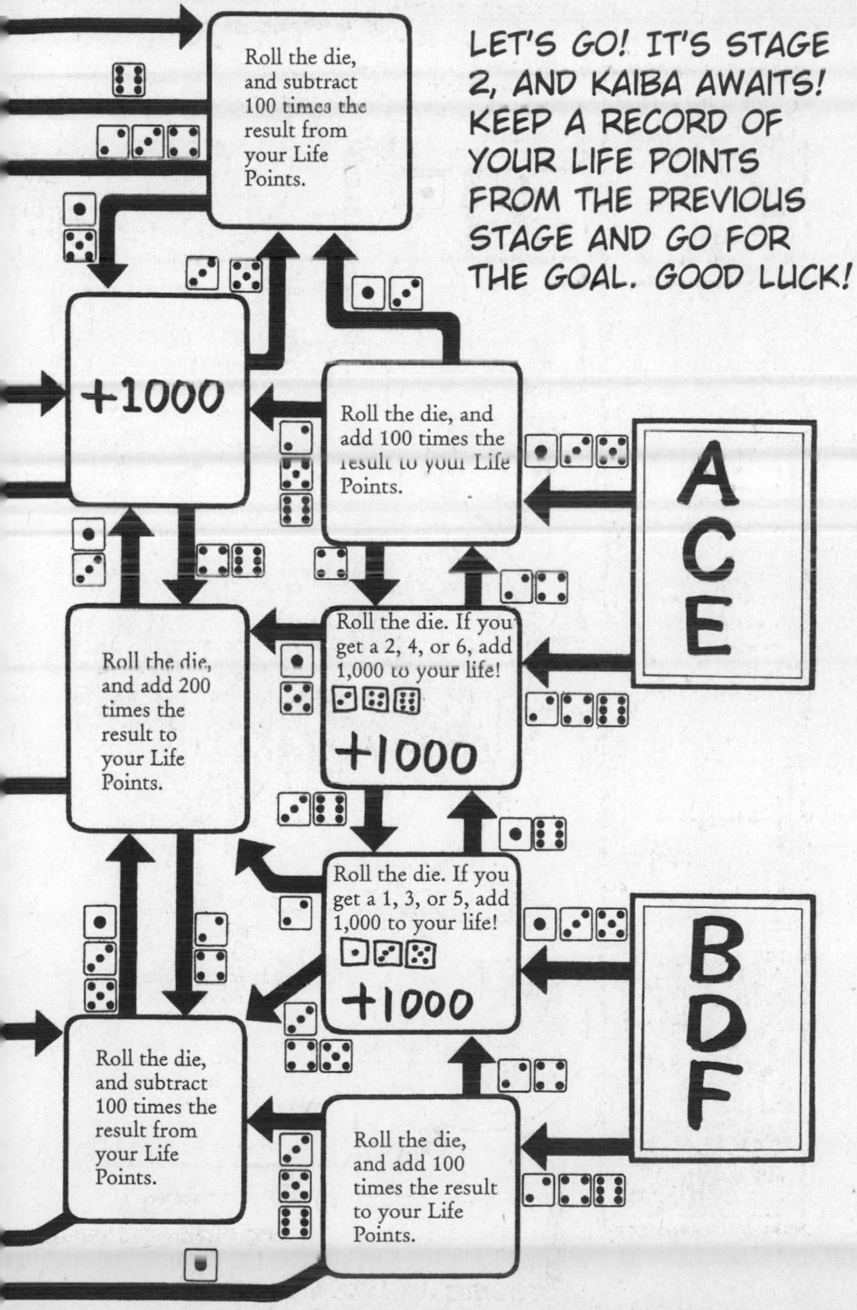
LET'S GO! IT'S STAGE 2, AND KAIBA AWAITS! KEEP A RECORD OF YOUR LIFE POINTS FROM THE PREVIOUS STAGE AND GO FOR THE GOAL. GOOD LUCK!
Roll the die, and subtract 100 times the result from your Life Points.
+1000
Roll the die, and add 100 times the result to your Life Points.
A
C
E
Roll the die, and add 200 times the result to your Life Points.
Roll the die. If you get a 2, 4, or 6, add 1,000 to your life!
+1000
Roll the die. If you get a 1, 3, or 5, add 1,000 to your life!
+1000
B
D
F
Roll the die, and subtract 100 times the result from your Life Points.
Roll the die, and add 100 times the result to your Life Points.

# GOAL

YOU WIN !!!

How did you measure up?

- Over 3,000 points = Game Expert
- Over 5,000 points = Game Master
- Over 10,000 points = Game God!

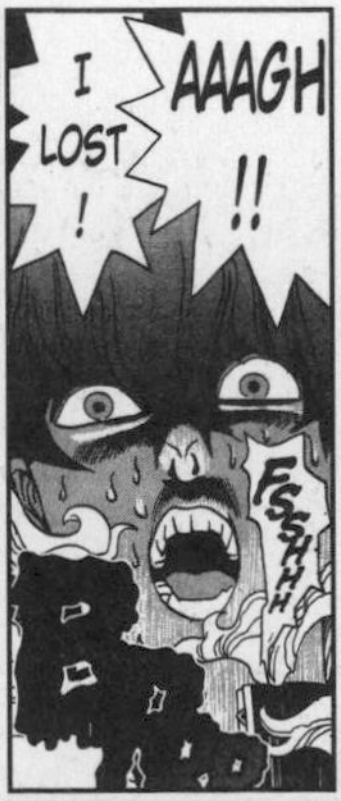

AAAGH !!
I LOST !
FSSHHH


Roll the die. If you get a 1, 3, or 5, multiply your life points by three.

GAME OVER

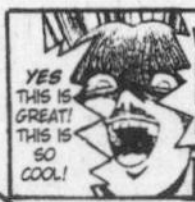

WA HA HA HA!!
YES THIS IS GREAT! THIS IS SO COOL!


Roll the die, and add 100 times the result to your Life Points.

Roll the die, and subtract 100 times the result from your Life Points.

KAIBA STAGE
Blue-Eyes White Dragon
(3,000 Life Points)

3000

If your life points are higher, proceed to the goal!

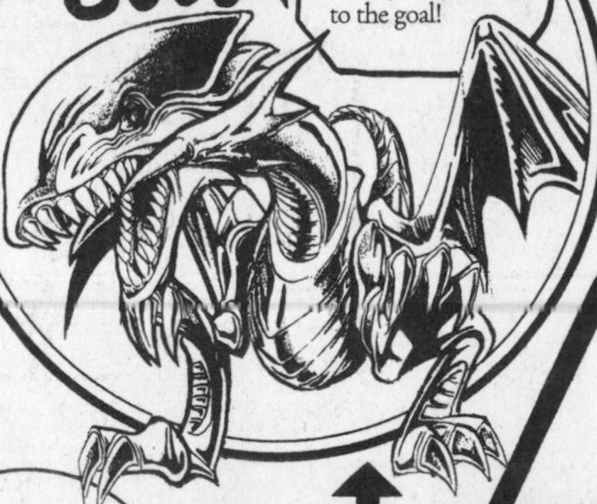

GAME OVER

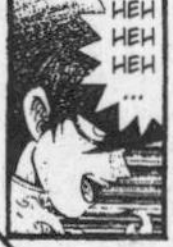

HEH HEH HEH ...


Roll the die, and add 100 times the result to your Life Points.

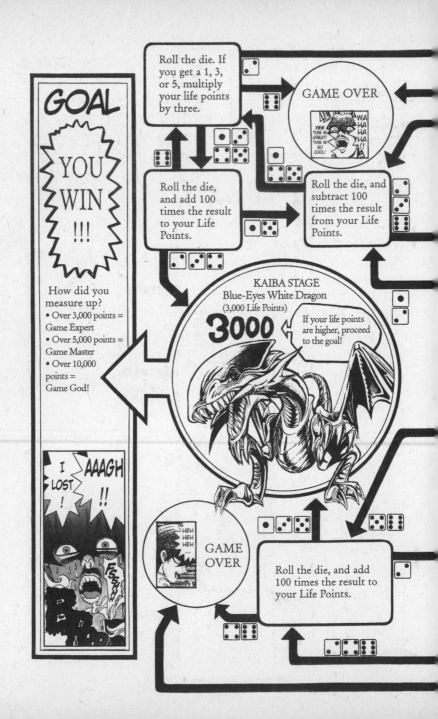

## IN THE NEXT VOLUME...

*Kaiba's back—and this time it's personal!* When Yugi beat his spoiled classmate at the collectible card game "Duel Monsters," he didn't realize that Kaiba was Japan's #1 gamer, the impossibly rich heir to the Kaiba Corporation, and a madman who would stop at nothing to get revenge! Now, a simple sleepover at Kaiba's house turns into a struggle for survival as Yugi and his friends must survive Kaiba's mysterious and deadly "Death-T"—with the life of Yugi's grandfather at stake! It's the most shocking **Yu-Gi-Oh!** volume yet!

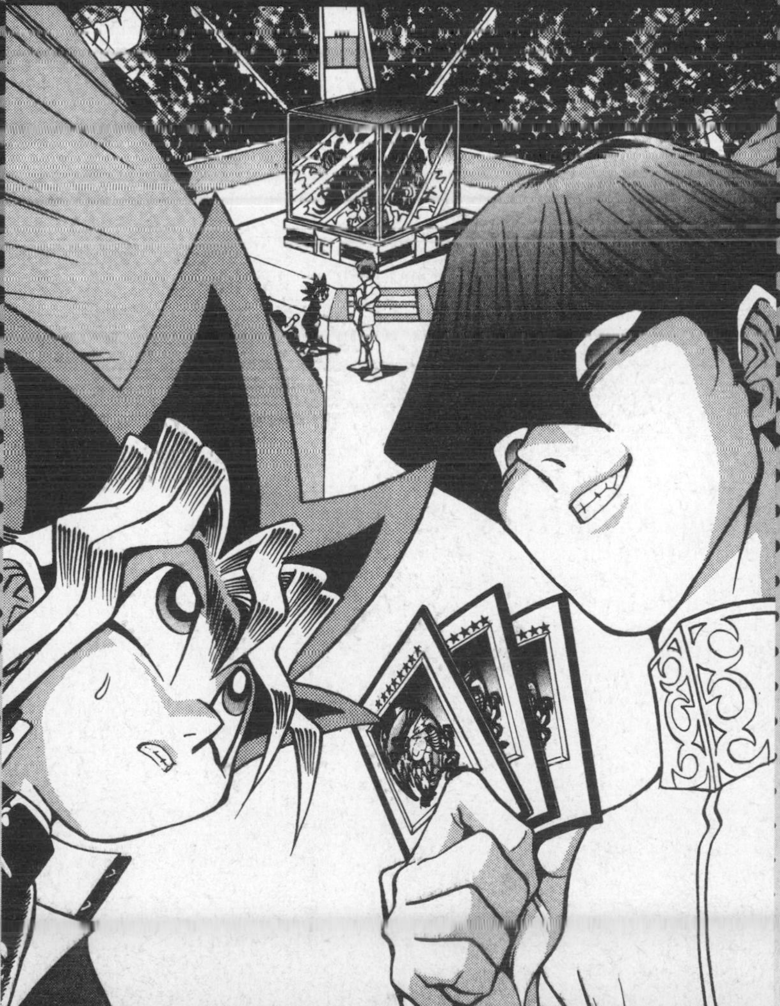

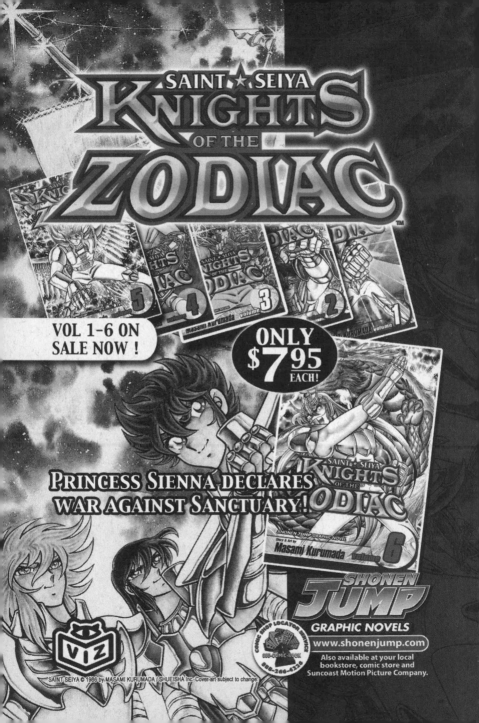

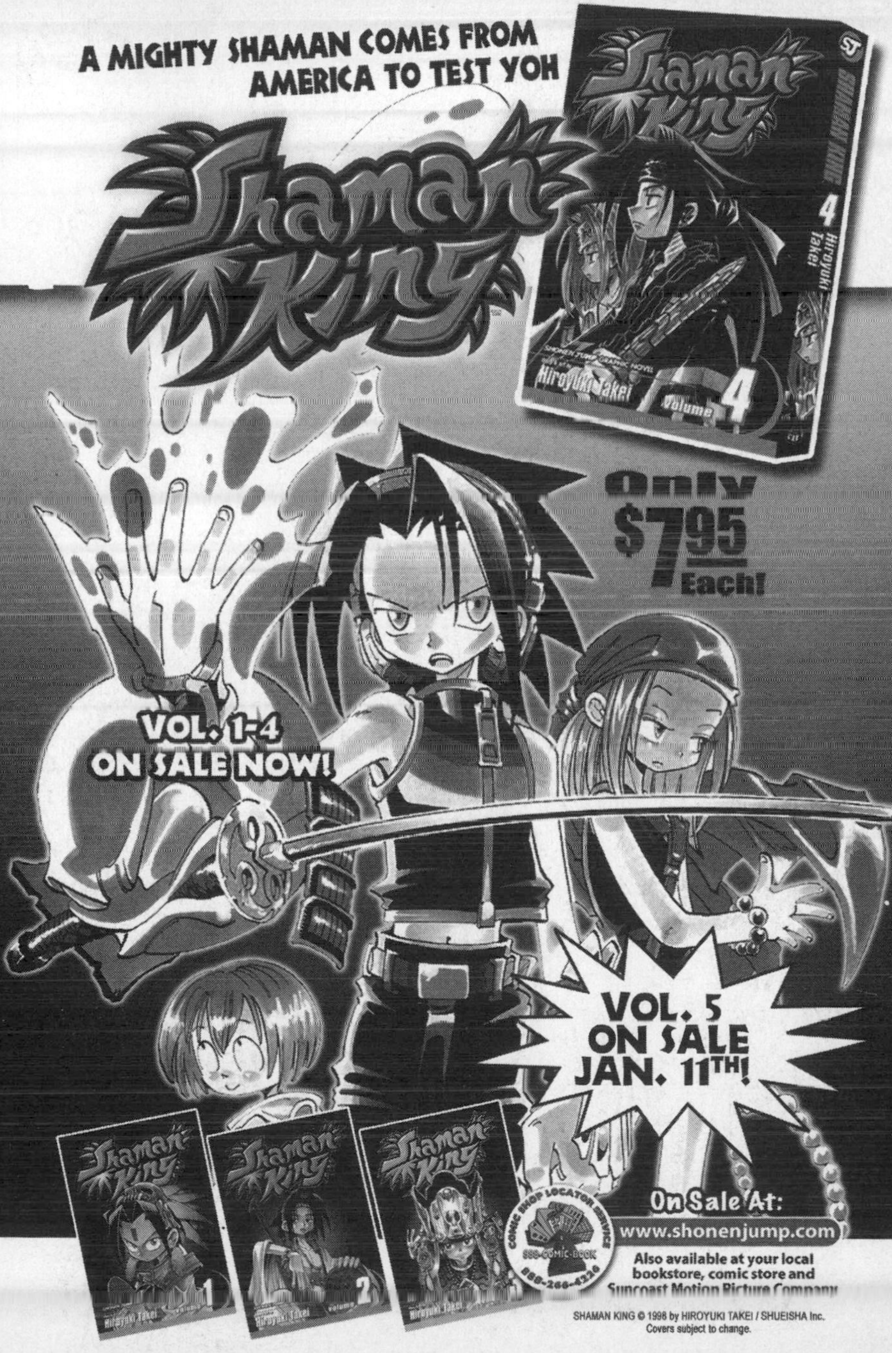

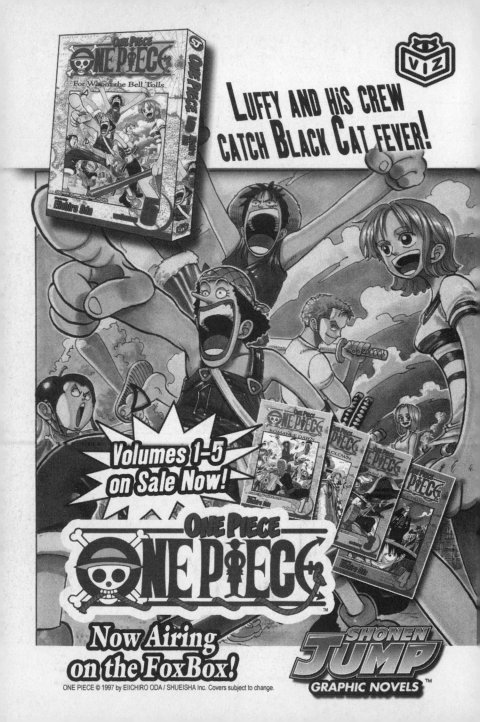

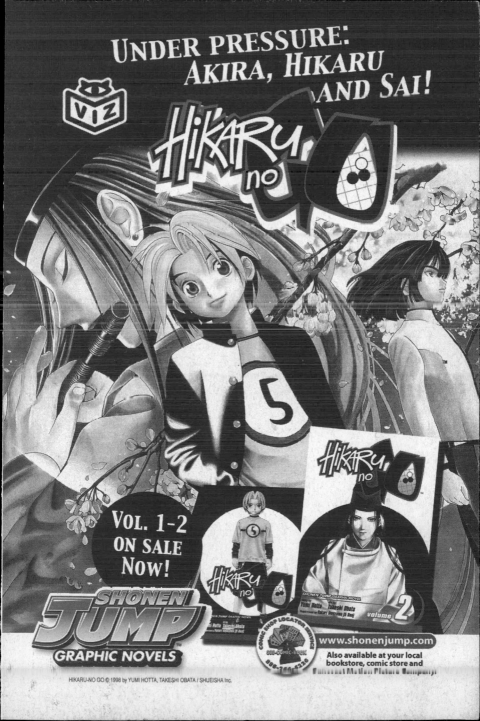

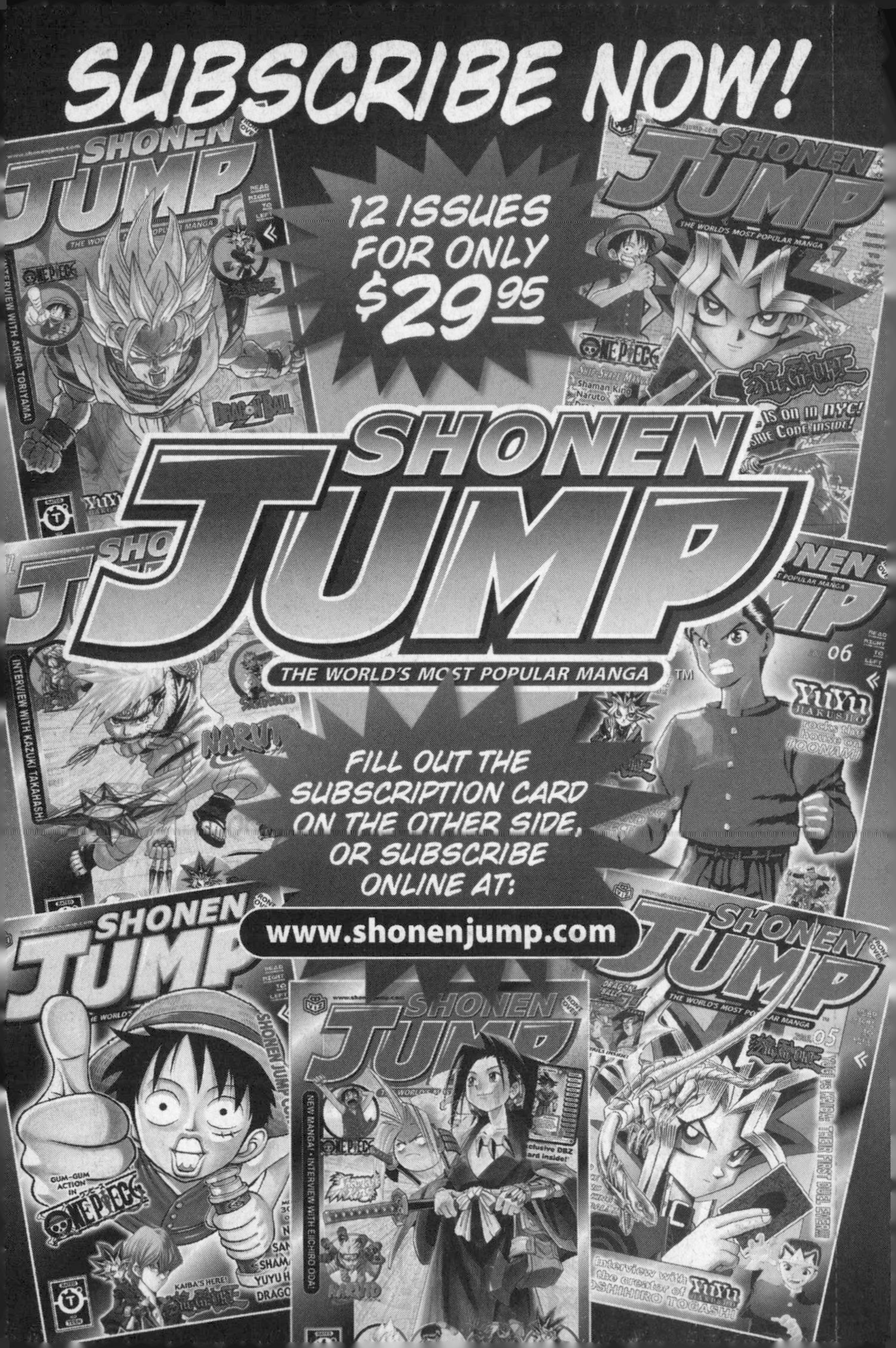

SUBSCRIBE NOW!
12 ISSUES FOR ONLY $29.95
SHONEN JUMP
THE WORLD'S MOST POPULAR MANGA ™
FILL OUT THE SUBSCRIPTION CARD ON THE OTHER SIDE, OR SUBSCRIBE ONLINE AT:
www.shonenjump.com

## COMPLETE OUR SURVEY AND LET US KNOW WHAT YOU THINK!

☐ Please do NOT send me information about VIZ and SHONEN JUMP products, news and events, special offers, or other information.

☐ Please do NOT send me information from VIZ's trusted business partners.

**Name:** ______________________________

**Address:** ______________________________

**City:** ____________ **State:** ______ **Zip:** ____________

**E-mail:** ______________________________

☐ **Male** ☐ **Female** **Date of Birth** (mm/dd/yyyy): ___/___/___ ( Under 13? Parental consent required )

**What race/ethnicity do you consider yourself?** (please check one)

☐ Asian/Pacific Islander ☐ Black/African American ☐ Hispanic/Latino

☐ Native American/Alaskan Native ☐ White/Caucasian ☐ Other: ____________

**What SHONEN JUMP Graphic Novel did you purchase?** (indicate title purchased)

______________________________

**What other SHONEN JUMP Graphic Novels, if any, do you own?** (indicate title(s) owned)

______________________________

______________________________

**Reason for purchase:** (check all that apply)

☐ Special offer ☐ Favorite title ☐ Gift

☐ Recommendation ☐ Read in SHONEN JUMP Magazine

☐ Read excerpt in the SHONEN JUMP Compilation Edition

☐ Other ____________

**Where did you make your purchase?** (please check one)

☐ Comic store ☐ Bookstore ☐ Mass/Grocery Store

☐ Newsstand ☐ Video/Video Game Store ☐ Other: ____________

☐ Online (site: ______________________________)

**Do you read SHONEN JUMP Magazine?**

- ☐ Yes
- ☐ No **(if no, skip the next two questions)**

Do you subscribe?

- ☐ Yes
- ☐ No

If you do not subscribe, how often do you purchase SHONEN JUMP Magazine?

- ☐ 1-3 issues a year
- ☐ 4-6 issues a year
- ☐ more than 7 issues a year

**What genre of manga would you like to read as a SHONEN JUMP Graphic Novel?**
**(please check two)**

- ☐ Adventure
- ☐ Comic Strip
- ☐ Science Fiction
- ☐ Fighting
- ☐ Horror
- ☐ Romance
- ☐ Fantasy
- ☐ Sports

**Which do you prefer? (please check one)**

- ☐ Reading right-to-left
- ☐ Reading left-to-right

**Which do you prefer? (please check one)**

- ☐ Sound effects in English
- ☐ Sound effects in Japanese with English captions
- ☐ Sound effects in Japanese only with a glossary at the back

**THANK YOU! Please send the completed form to:**

VIZ Survey
42 Catharine St.
Poughkeepsie, NY 12601

**All information provided will be used for internal purposes only. We promise not to sell or otherwise divulge your information.**